Contents (this volume)

Contents (volume two)

Academic Libraries and the Academy:

Strategies and Approaches to Demonstrate Your Value, Impact, and Return on Investment

VOLUME ONE

Marwin Britto and Kirsten Kinsley

Association of College and Research Libraries
A division of the American Library Association
Chicago, Illinois 2018

The paper used in this publication meets the minimum requirements of American National Standard for Information Sciences–Permanence of Paper for Printed Library Materials, ANSI Z39.48-1992. ∞

Cataloging-in-Publication data is on file with the Library of Congress.

Copyright ©2018 by the Association of College and Research Libraries.
All rights reserved except those which may be granted by Sections 107 and 108 of the Copyright Revision Act of 1976.

Printed in the United States of America.

22 21 20 19 18   5 4 3 2 1

Foreword

Megan Oakleaf

Reflection is the hallmark of an effective practitioner. At the core of reflection is a spirit of introspection, a willingness to consider and question one's own thoughts and actions. In professional roles, practitioners engage in reflection by considering the implications of their actions and leveraging a sense of doubt. Practitioners who allow themselves to doubt whether (or to what degree) their efforts lead to desired outcomes open a mental space through which awareness and learning may enter.

In educational spheres, assessment is a key tool for reflective practice. It is hard to overstate the importance of assessment; it is the lifeblood of teaching and learning. Without assessment, educators sever their relationships with learners, resulting in instructional efforts that succeed only by chance and may often fail to reach, support, or empower learners. In contrast, educational practitioners who conduct assessments 1) gain insights into the needs, goals, and values of their learners; 2) design learning experiences that meet students where they are, engage them in meaningful ways, and enable them to attain greater agency in their own lives; and 3) reflect and improve throughout each iterative teaching cycle, ultimately increasing the value of education for their present and future learners.

As active contributors to the educational mission of their institutions, academic librarians can expand student access to learning, ensure students are able to persist and attain their goals, and scaffold student experiences to aid attainment of independent learning capacity. They can support students as they develop productive self-awareness, metacognition, and self-actualization in a variety of contexts, including their immediate learning environments, the broader community, and the world around them. They *can* fulfill these educational roles; however, to *ensure* that they do, librarians must engage in reflection and assessment. Academic librarians who practice reflective assessment participate in "triple-loop" learning, thereby exploring whether they're providing library services, resources, and spaces in the "right" ways, for the "right" reasons, and whether those "right" reasons align with professional convictions about information, education, and the role of libraries in higher education. The act of engaging in deep assessment as a reflective practice can be both revelatory and energizing for librarians, and the results of such assessments have a number of uses: a guide for daily library decision-making, a map for long-term library strategy decisions, and/or a communication tool for outreach to other members of the institutional community. For these reasons, all librarians should engage in reflective assessment; both the process and product of assessment enables librarians to articulate, own, and enact their role within academic libraries and the academy, writ large. Indeed, it is insufficient to deploy library services, resources, and spaces in hopes that they will contribute to student learning; rather, libraries must develop assessments to determine the degree to which their efforts contribute to student learning, use the results of their assessments to expand in areas that appear to make an impact on student learning, and re-imagine areas that do not. This is the most important purpose of assessment of academic library contributions to student learning: to improve and expand the ways in which libraries and librarians help students learn. Thus, the impact of the academic library on student learning is a vital component of library efforts to capture, convey, and communicate value. Librarians who seek to establish, grow, acknowledge, support, and reward the ways in which libraries support student learning often need to demonstrate the value of their existing efforts as part of an ongoing cycle to ensure that library services, resources, and spaces can continue and expand their contributions to student learning.

Likewise, librarians must demonstrate their value in other contexts. Academic libraries contribute to the success of their institutions in myriad areas: 1) faculty concerns such as teaching, research, grant seeking, and support for promotion and tenure; 2) institutional priorities including prestige or image, affordability, efficiency, accreditation, and preparation for changing student demographics; 3) community issues like development, inclusion, economic growth, and the education of an engaged citizenry; and 4) larger values including information literacy, critical thinking, and innovation. Reflective assessment of the library's contribution to these institutional missions may include projects that assess library collections, space, systems, and personal connections, such as faculty-librarian collaborations. Related library assessment efforts may explore library user experiences, the role of libraries in institutional program review or accreditation, return-on-investment analysis, or more inward-looking assessments of organizational change or strategic planning processes.

To this end, this book, *Academic Libraries and the Academy: Strategies and Approaches to Demonstrate Your Value*, supports librarians as reflective practitioners in search of pathways to get started, gain traction, and galvanize existing efforts to convey the value of the library. Based on a case study approach, this resource collects and presents the lived experience of librarians across the globe as they seek to define, demonstrate, and articulate the value of their libraries. Presented in four sections, *Academic Libraries and the Academy* provides guidance for librarians at any stage of the assessment and value demonstration process. Helpfully, the authors have followed an established format in each chapter. Each case begins with the context of an assessment, describes the library's communication of the assessment results and impact, continues with explanations of the ways librarians leveraged their findings, and closes with librarian reflections on each assessment project. The authors also provided useful information at the outset of each case, such as project foci, implicated data, selected methodology, timeframes, costs, and results. Structured presentation makes this text unique among library assessment publications and an invaluable tool for libraries and librarians committed to reflection and the pursuit of demonstrated value. Indeed, the range of projects, the deep treatment of each, and the organizational structures asserted by the authors combine to make this publication an assessment handbook of sorts, one that makes library assessment practice accessible to newcomers, provides sufficient detail to guide established practitioners, and offers a scan of the library assessment environment sure to educate and excite assessment researchers and students alike.

Introduction and Context

Demonstrating Value through Library Assessment

The concept of using assessment to demonstrate value in academic libraries is not new. Assessment models have been evident in various aspects of work in academic libraries for decades. Orr's Evaluation Model (see figure I.1), looking at academic libraries more holistically in terms of inputs and outputs, in relation to quality and value, was one of the first systemic models and considered a seminal work in the field.[1] Since that time, many variants and elaborations of this model and other approaches (e.g., contingent valuation method, library cube model, etc.) have appeared in the library assessment literature, all with the goal of providing a framework for academic and public libraries to evaluate and assess the qualitative and economic value of their various library resources, including services, programs, collections, and facilities.

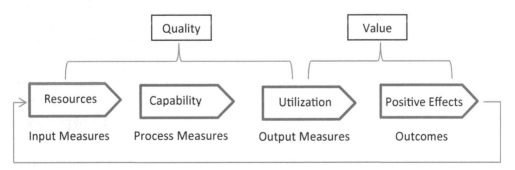

Figure I.1
Orr's evaluation model.

Library assessment in academic libraries typically involves a wide range of activities. Some examples are the required reporting of benchmarking data to various agencies, such as ARL (the Association of Research Libraries) as well as state and regional accrediting bodies, assessing library instruction and teaching, and determining the efficacy of library collections, programming, services, and facilities. Most of these activities focus on input/output measures or what many call "counting." However, more recently there has been a renewed interest in assessment activities in academic libraries that can demonstrate impact, value, and the return on investment. One of the primary drivers of this interest, particularly in the United States, has been a steady decrease in public funding coupled with a dramatic shift in funding formulas for public institutions of higher education.

Funding in Public Higher Education Institutions in the United States

In 2012, Thomas Mortenson, a senior scholar at the Pell Institute for the Study of Opportunity in Higher Education, projected that the average state fiscal support for higher education will effectively reach zero by 2059 (based on state appropriations trends for public higher education in the United States since 1980).[2] Mortenson reported that state fiscal support in 2011 had decreased by an average of 40.2 percent compared to 1980, with some states reducing their funding for higher education by as much as 69.4 percent. Comparing the 2015–2016 academic year to the 2007–2008 academic year when the recession hit, state spending nationwide in the US was still down more than 18 percent on average, with nine states having cut funding by more than 30 percent, and two states over 50 percent.[3] Over the last few decades, there has been a trend for increasing numbers of state public higher education institutions to transition from state-funded institutions (more than 50 percent of their operating budget is funded by the state appropriations) to state-assisted (less than 50 percent funded). This has been in sharp contrast to how other countries have invested in public higher education. In 2012, the Organization for Economic Co-operation and Development (OECD), a consortium of thirty-five member countries, found that across all thirty-five countries, 70 percent of the funding in higher education comes from public coffers, while in the United States, a mere 38 percent does.[4]

Historically, in the United States, state public institutions of higher education have been publically funded by state governments based on full-time student enrollments. In 1995, the US was first among OECD member countries in college graduation rates.[5] Unfortunately, over the past two decades, US college graduation rates have steadily declined.[6] In 2014, the US ranked nineteenth in graduation rates out of the twenty-eight countries OECD studied. These and other low outcome measures, such as poor job placement rates and time to complete a degree, have disappointed legislators and policy-makers across the United States and prompted them to demand greater levels of transparency and accountability for state funding of public education. This has meant a shift toward outcome-based measures such as performance-based funding. Miao defines performance-based funding as "a system based on allocating a portion of a state's higher education budget according to specific performance measures,"[7] such as graduate rates, transfer rates, time to degree, and the number of low-income and minority graduates. As of January 2015, approximately thirty-five states had adopted a performance-based funding formula or were in the process of transitioning to one.[8] The percentage of state funding allocated based on performance measures varies widely by state, ranging from less than 1 percent of base funding in Illinois to 100 percent of state funding in Tennessee (i.e., after a base amount is provided for operational support). Figure I.2 from the National Conference of State Legislatures shows the commitment by state in 2015 to performance-based funding for higher education. This trend toward performance or outcome-based metrics to award public funding is also evident in Canada's higher education environment.[9]

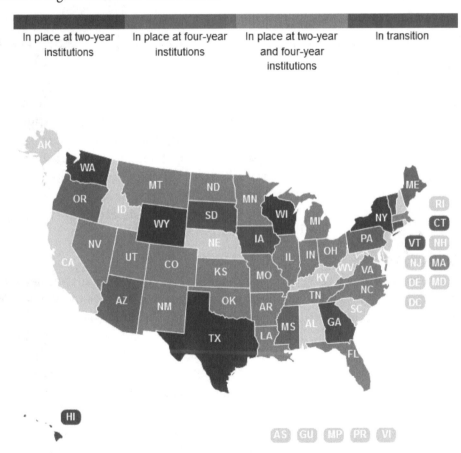

Figure I.2
Performance-Based Funding for Higher Education by U.S. State.

Decreased student enrollments, diminished budgets, and the fiscal reality of declining state appropriations are forcing administrators to more closely examine the allocation of funds and resources across the institution. The expression "doing more with less" has become an all too common mantra in higher education. In the past, most academic libraries have benefitted from the assumption that since people perceived them as a public good, there was little expectation for them to have to justify their existence nor account for the spending of their budget. But now, with increased expectations of accountability and transparency for budget expenditures, institutions scrambling to "do more with less," and the emergence of new budgeting models that view units as either cost centers or profit centers, academic libraries are under new pressures and scrutiny. Academic libraries, viewed in budgetary terms as a cost center as they bring in little to no direct revenue, are realizing the incredible importance and necessity of clearly articulating to their institutional administrators their contributions to institutional outcomes, their short-term and long-term value, and in essence, their return-on-investment. This type of evidence-based advocacy tends to be new ground for many academic libraries in North America and around the world.

Library Organizations Supporting the "Value of Academic Libraries" Initiative

Fortunately, academic libraries are not alone in learning how to build knowledge and capacity to advocate for and provide evidence of their value and worth to institutional administrators. For more than a decade, a number of library nonprofit organizations have developed and launched robust resources and customizable materials to provide ongoing support and assistance to academic libraries in this effort. These include the Association of College and Research Libraries (ACRL), the largest division within the American Library Association (ALA), and the Association of Research Libraries (ARL).

Association of College and Research Libraries

ACRL, the largest division of the ALA with more than 10,500 members, is a professional association of academic librarians "dedicated to enhancing the ability of academic library and information professionals to serve the information needs of the higher education community and to improve learning, teaching, and research."[10] Every few years, the ACRL Research Planning and Review Committee authors a document on top trends in academic libraries. In 2012 and then again in 2014, the committee identified the value and contributions of libraries to student success and communicated this value as a top trend and priority for academic libraries.[11]

ACRL has played an instrumental role in advancing the conversation on the value of academic libraries. ACRL's five-year Plan for Excellence, implemented in 2011, focused on three areas, the first of which was Value of Academic Libraries. The goal of this focus area was described as "Academic libraries demonstrate alignment with and impact on institutional outcomes."[12]

In 2010, the ACRL Assessment Committee developed a Value of Academic Libraries Toolkit website to help academic librarians demonstrate the value of libraries to their users, institutions, and communities.[13] The toolkit provided open access to related bibliographies; studies, grants and reports; white papers and in-depth treatments; marketing tools and presentations; academic library ROI/value calculators; blogs; best practices; and assessment tools. The committee was subsequently eliminated when ACRL decided to make the Value of Academic Libraries movement a priority in its focus (J. Stein, personal communication, March 13, 2015). The website and toolkit, although still containing valuable research and documentation from 2010 and prior, has been superseded by an updated website: the ACRL Value of Academic Libraries website.[14]

The Assessment in Action: Academic Libraries and Student Success project, an IMLS-funded initiative, has been an important and systemic project that ACRL first launched in 2012. This initiative was designed to develop and sustain a professional development program for librarians to prepare them to lead collaborative campus efforts to assess and demonstrate the library's impact on student learning and academic success on each of their campuses. Over the span of the three-year project (beginning in April 2014 and ending in June 2016), more than 200 institutions of all types participated in the project. Several publications have been released documenting the success of this project and highlighting a number of case studies.[15] In 2017, ACRL launched a one-day workshop to build on the Assessment in Action curriculum and to focus on strategic and sustainable assessment. The Assessment in Action website offers more details about this workshop, as well as the history of this initiative, including a list of interim and final reports from various participating institutions.[16]

Association of Research Libraries

The ARL is a nonprofit organization of 125 research libraries at comprehensive research institutions in North America that share similar research missions, aspirations, and achievements.[17] ARL has been actively involved in promoting and supporting various Value of Academic Libraries initiatives. The "Statistics & Assessment" section on ARL's website states that its purpose is to "focus on articulating the value of research libraries by describing and measuring their performance and contributions to research, scholarship, and community college."[18] The section houses a number of ARL's services and products directly addressing this topic, including the association's ARL Statistics, ClimateQUAL, LibQUAL+, MINES for Libraries, StatsQUAL, and LibValue.

Some Success, but More Work to Be Done

Despite these concerted efforts by ACRL and ARL and documented success for many academic libraries, challenges still persist for others. In 2017, an ACRL research team reviewed 357 articles on library assessment and drew the conclusion that "librarians experience difficulty articulating their value to higher education administrators and other stakeholders… and use a small variety of methods, which may not match the methods relevant to senior leadership."[19] Furthermore, the team recommended that "librarians and library administrators must continue to develop best practices and effective documentation to demonstrate value and be willing to share these practices and documentation cross-institutionally."[20]

Our set is a shining example of just this—best practices, lessons learned, approaches and strategies of how librarians, library professionals, and others in academic libraries around the world are successfully providing evidence of their contributions to student academic success and effectively demonstrating their library's value and worth to institutional administrators and stakeholders. There is no "one-size-fits-all" approach to demonstrating a library's worth and value, and accordingly our set shares a range of successful approaches and strategies utilized in different types of academic libraries around the world. Our set is also an opportunity to provide guidance and support to many of you—librarians, library professionals, and others involved in library assessment—who struggle to find the best approach and strategy at the right time in your assessment journey. Our set will help you build your knowledge in this area and teach you how to successfully articulate your academic library's value by following and selectively applying the many replicable and practical strategies and approaches shared in the forty-two case studies contained herein.

The Uniqueness of Our Set

This is not the first book (or set of books) to be published on library assessment, nor will it be the last, but we wanted ours to have a unique place in this pool. We carefully sought unique characteristics or features that we believe set ours apart from others in this space. These distinctive features include our international representation; our selection of case studies illuminating thought-provoking, insightful, practical, and replicable approaches and strategies to library assessment; the accessible structure and convenient organization of each book; and our summary profiles. We believe these make this set unique, more accessible, pragmatic, and a must-have for anyone involved in assessment in academic libraries worldwide. You will ultimately be the judge in determining whether we have achieved this goal. We elaborate on each of these four features in the remainder of this introduction.

International Representation

Because of the global significance of academic libraries needing to demonstrate their worth and value through thoughtful library assessment around the world, we wanted this set to be truly international in scope. To do this, we actively sought library assessment case studies from the far reaches of our planet. We are delighted to include case studies from authors and academic libraries in Africa, Asia, Europe, and the Middle East, as well as from North America. With the ubiquity of the Internet, it becomes easier for all of us to build upon each other's work and to explore, innovate, and share our experiences and lessons learned in library assessment. As a result of the range of replicable library assessment strategies and countries represented in this set, we believe this set will and should have an international appeal.

Our Selection of Cases

We received an overwhelming response of interest from authors who submitted proposals for consideration for inclusion in this set. Our intake comprised a wide range of high-quality case studies employing a variety of methodologies and aspects of librarianship, such as collections, services, facilities, information literacy, and program reviews. We carefully selected those cases that we thought were creative and innovative but also replicable and practical and would appeal to a host of individuals involved in different types of academic libraries across the globe. Selecting the final chapters to include in this set was no easy task, but we believe the assortment, innovation, and quality are the right combination. We believe you will agree!

Organization and Structure of This Set

How is this set organized and structured? We have organized the forty-two chapters of case studies into four distinct sections.

Each chapter begins with a chapter summary profile (which is described in the next section). For consistency, ease of reading, and comparative purposes, each chapter follows a similar structure that includes four foundational elements: context, communicating results and impact, leveraging the findings, and reflections. In addition, authors have added other appropriate content and elements depending on their particular topic.

Each of the four sections captures case studies that reflect a different stage of an academic library's assessment journey in terms of time, resources, and expertise. Collectively, the titles of the four sections employ a metaphor indicative of these stages, namely Seeding the Initiative; Low-Hanging Fruit; Reachable Fruit; and Hard-to-Reach Fruit. Our intent was to make it easier for you to connect and relate to case studies depending on your particular point in your assessment path and the extent of your access to resources, funding and expertise.

Volume One

- **Section 1: Seeding the Initiative.** The eight case studies in this first section explore the planning stages or "works-in-progress" in assessment that relate to the academic library's impact and value. The results of these efforts may not be imminent. Nevertheless, these case studies demonstrate the potential value and the importance of the initial design and planning stage.
- **Section 2: Low-Hanging Fruit.** These eleven case studies offer stories of assessments that are easy to measure, short-term (less than one year), low-cost, require few resources (staff or tools), and are easily replicable at similar academic libraries.

Volume Two

- **Section 3: Reachable Fruit** (with some effort). This section provides sixteen case studies that require more external and internal resources to measure, typically take more than six months to one year to collect and analyze, feature medium costs and resources (i.e., incentives, equipment, tools), and are replicable at other academic libraries that are similar in size or scope.

- **Section 4: Hard-to-Reach Fruit.** The seven case studies in this section include a range of assessment activities that are more difficult to measure and time- and resource-intensive, that require long-term data collection (e.g., longitudinal studies that require more than a year to collect a dataset or have measures that require more time, such as measuring a cohort's graduation rates), and that feature greater external partnerships, internal infrastructure, or additional resources to measure and analyze.

Summary Profiles

A unique and pragmatic feature of this set is the inclusion of chapter summary profiles. Each case study is preceded by a one-page summary presenting fourteen descriptors of the chapter's content that will allow you to quickly ascertain if the case study is of immediate interest based on your individual needs, interests, and goals. Our objective with these summary profiles is to help prioritize your reading choices. We hope you find the each chapter's summary profile a convenient and useful aid.

Enjoy the read!

Marwin and Kirsten (Co-Editors)

Notes

1. R. H. Orr, "Measuring the Goodness of Library Services: A General Framework for Considering Quantitative Measures." *Journal of Documentation* 29, no. 3 (1973): 318.
2. Thomas G. Mortenson, "State Funding: A Race to the Bottom," *Presidency*, 15, no. 1 (Winter 2012): 26.
3. Michael Mitchell, Michael Leachman, and Kathleen Masterson, "Funding Down, Tuition Up: State Cuts to Higher Education Threaten Quality and Affordability at Public Colleges," Center on Budget and Policy Priorities, Washington, DC, last updated August 15, 2016, https://www.cbpp.org/research/state-budget-and-tax/funding-down-tuition-up.
4. OECD, "United States—Country Note," Education at a Glance 2012: OECD Indicators, OECD Publishing, 2012, https://www.oecd.org/unitedstates/CN%20-%20United%20States.pdf.
5. Liz Weston, "OECD: The US Has Fallen Behind Other Countries in College Completion," *Business Insider*, September 9, 2014, http://www.businessinsider.com/r-us-falls-behind-in-college-competition-oecd-2014-9.
6. John Bound, Michael Lovenheim, and Sarah Turner, "Why Have College Completion Rates Declined? An Analysis of Changing Student Preparation and Collegiate Resources," NBER Working Paper No. 15566, National Bureau of Economic Research, Cambridge, MA, December 2009, http://www.nber.org/papers/w15566; Mortenson, "State Funding"; D. Shapiro, A. Dundar, P. Wakhungu, X. Yuan, and A. Harrel, *Completing College,* Signature Report No. 8a (Herndon, VA: National Student Clearinghouse Research Center, February 2015).
7. Kysie Miao, "Performance-Based Funding of Higher Education: A Detailed Look at Best Practices in 6 States," Center for American Progress, Washington, DC, August 2012, 1, https://cdn.americanprogress.org/wp-content/uploads/issues/2012/08/pdf/performance_funding.pdf..
8. National Conference of State Legislatures, "Performance-Based Funding for Higher Education,"

National Conference of State Legislatures, Denver, CO, July 31, 2015, http://www.ncsl.org/re-search/education/performance-funding.aspx.

9. Mary B. Ziskin, Don Hossler, Karyn Rabourn, Osman Cekic, and Youngsik Hwang, *Outcomes-Based Funding* (Toronto: Higher Education Quality Council of Ontario, 2014), http://www.heqco.ca/SiteCollectionDocuments/Outcomes-Based%20Funding%20ENG.pdf.

10. "About ACRL," Association of College and Research Libraries, accessed February 7, 2018, http://www.ala.org/acrl/aboutacrl.

11. ACRL Research Planning and Review Committee, "2012 Top Ten Trends in Academic Libraries: A Review of the Trends and Issues Affecting Academic Libraries in Higher Education," *College and Research Libraries News* 73, no. 6 (June 1, 2012): 311–20; ACRL Research Planning and Review Committee, "2014 Top Trends in Academic Libraries: A Review of the Trends and Issues Affecting Academic Libraries in Higher Education," *College and Research Libraries News* 75, no. 6 (June 1, 2014): 294–302.

12. Association of College and Research Libraries, *ACRL Plan for Excellence* (Chicago: Association of College and Research Libraries, 2011, revised 2017), 1, http://www.ala.org/acrl/aboutacrl/strategicplan/stratplan.

13. Association of College and Research Libraries, *Value of Academic Libraries Toolkit* (Chicago: Association of College and Research Libraries, October 2010), http://www.ala.org/acrl/issues/value/valueofacademiclibrariestoolkit.

14. Association of Colllege and Research Libraries, ACRL Value of Academic Libraries website, accessed February 12, 2018, http://www.acrl.ala.org/value/.

15. See Kara J. Malenfant, Lisa Janicke Hinchliffe, and Debra Gilchrist, "Assessment as Action Research: Bridging Academic Scholarship and Everyday Practice," *College and Research Libraries* 77, no. 2 (March 2016): 140–43, https://doi.org/10.5860/crl.77.2.140; Kara J. Malenfant and Karen Brown, *Creating Sustainable Assessment through Collaboration,* Occasional Paper No. 31 (Urbana, IL: University of Illinois and Indiana University, National Institute for Learning Outcomes Assessment [NILOA], November 2017), http://learningoutcomesassessment.org/documents/Occasional_Paper31.pdf.

16. Association of College and Research Libraries, Assessment in Action: Libraries and Student Success website, accessed February 12, 2018, http://www.ala.org/acrl/AiA.

17. "About," Association of Research Libraries, accessed February 7, 2018, http://www.arl.org/about#.VQHAco5v8g4.

18. "Statistics & Assessment," Association of Research Libraries, accessed February 7, 2018, http://www.arl.org/focus-areas/statistics-assessment#.VRBaBo7F98E.

19. ACRL Research Planning and Review Committee, *Environmental Scan 2017* (Chicago: Association of College and Research Libraries, March 2017), 38, http://www.ala.org/acrl/sites/ala.org.acrl/files/content/publications/whitepapers/EnvironmentalScan2017.pdf.

20. ACRL Research Planning and Review Committee, *Environmental Scan,* 39.

Bibliography

ACRL Research Planning and Review Committee. *Environmental Scan 2017.* Chicago: Association of College and Research Libraries, March 2017. http://www.ala.org/acrl/sites/ala.org.acrl/files/content/publications/whitepapers/EnvironmentalScan2017.pdf.

———. "2012 Top Ten Trends in Academic Libraries: A Review of the Trends and Issues Affecting Academic Libraries in Higher Education." *College and Research Libraries News* 73, no. 6 (June 1, 2012): 311–20.

———. "2014 Top Trends in Academic Libraries: A Review of the Trends and Issues Affecting Academic Libraries in Higher Education." *College and Research Libraries News* 75, no. 6 (June 1, 2014): 294–302.

Association of College and Research Libraries. "About ACRL." Association of College and Research Libraries. Accessed February 7, 2018. http://www.ala.org/acrl/aboutacrl.

———. ACRL Value of Academic Libraries website. Accessed February 12, 2018. http://www.acrl.ala.org/value/.

———. *ACRL Plan for Excellence*. Chicago: Association of College and Research Libraries, 2011, revised 2017. http://www.ala.org/acrl/aboutacrl/strategicplan/stratplan.

———. Assessment in Action: Libraries and Student Success website. Accessed February 12, 2018. http://www.ala.org/acrl/AiA.

———. *Value of Academic Libraries Toolkit*. Chicago: Association of College and Research Libraries, October 2010. http://www.ala.org/acrl/issues/value/valueofacademiclibrariestoolkit.

Association of Research Libraries. "About." Association of Research Libraries. Accessed February 7, 2018. http://www.arl.org/about#.VQHAco5v8g4.

———. "Statistics & Assessment." Association of Research Libraries. Accessed February 7, 2018. http://www.arl.org/focus-areas/statistics-assessment#.VRBaBo7F98E.

Bound, John, Michael Lovenheim, and Sarah Turner. "Why Have College Completion Rates Declined? An Analysis of Changing Student Preparation and Collegiate Resources." NBER Working Paper No. 15566. National Bureau of Economic Research, Cambridge, MA, December 2009. http://www.nber.org/papers/w15566.

Malenfant, Kara J., and Karen Brown. *Creating Sustainable Assessment through Collaboration: A National Program Reveals Effective Practices*. Occasional Paper No. 31. Urbana, IL: University of Illinois and Indiana University, National Institute for Learning Outcomes Assessment (NILOA), November 2017. http://learningoutcomesassessment.org/documents/Occasional_Paper31.pdf.

Malenfant, Kara J., Lisa Janicke Hinchliffe, and Debra Gilchrist. "Assessment as Action Research: Bridging Academic Scholarship and Everyday Practice." *College and Research Libraries* 77, no. 2 (March 2016): 140–43. https://doi.org/10.5860/crl.77.2.140.

Miao, Kysie. "Performance-Based Funding of Higher Education: A Detailed Look at Best Practices in 6 States." Center for American Progress, Washington, DC, August 2012. https://cdn.americanprogress.org/wp-content/uploads/issues/2012/08/pdf/performance_funding.pdf.

Mitchell, Michael, Michael Leachman, and Kathleen Masterson. "Funding Down, Tuition Up: State Cuts to Higher Education Threaten Quality and Affordability at Public Colleges." Center on Budget and Policy Priorities, Washington, DC, last updated August 15, 2016. https://www.cbpp.org/research/state-budget-and-tax/funding-down-tuition-up.

Mortenson, Thomas G. "State Funding: A Race to the Bottom." *Presidency*, 15, no. 1 (Winter 2012): 26.

National Conference of State Legislatures. "Performance-Based Funding for Higher Education." National Conference of State Legislatures, Denver, CO, July 31, 2015. http://www.ncsl.org/research/education/performance-funding.aspx.

OECD. "United States—Country Note." Education at a Glance 2012: OECD Indicators. OECD Publishing, 2012, https://www.oecd.org/unitedstates/CN%20-%20United%20States.pdf.

Orr, R. H. "Developing a Measure of Library Goodness." *Journal of Documentation* 29, no. 3 (1973): 315–32.

Shapiro, D., A. Dundar, P. Wakhungu, X. Yuan, and A. Harrel. *Completing College: A State-Level View of Student Attainment Rates*. Signature Report No. 8a. Herndon, VA: National Student Clearinghouse Research Center, February 2015.

Weston, Liz. "OECD: The US Has Fallen Behind Other Countries in College Completion." *Business Insider*, September 9, 2014. http://www.businessinsider.com/r-us-falls-behind-in-college-competition-oecd-2014-9.

Ziskin, Mary B., Don Hossler, Karyn Rabourn, Osman Cekic, and Youngsik Hwang. *Outcomes-Based Funding: Current Status, Promising Practices and Emerging Trends*. Toronto: Higher Education Quality Council of Ontario, 2014. http://www.heqco.ca/SiteCollectionDocuments/Outcomes-Based%20Funding%20ENG.pdf.

Section 1

Seeding the Initiative

Introduction

This book is intended to inform and enlighten you—librarians, professional staff, administrators, and others working in academic libraries—who are at all levels of experience and assessment skills, at all stages of implementation of assessment initiatives, and with varying access to expertise and resources. Accordingly, the four sections of this publication are organized to reflect a continuum of case studies of individuals and academic institutions at different points in their assessment journey in articulating their library's impact and value.

This first section, Seeding the Initiative, as the section title reflects, examines eight cases of academic libraries at the beginning stages of their library's assessment initiative and are considered "works-in-progress" where no outcomes or results are yet available. The value in these cases rests in the process of creating and planning the initial design of the initiative and the reporting of initial progress, which collectively can provide beneficial knowledge to those of you who may be considering embarking down a similar path.

This section involves chapters covering a wide range of topics including measuring archives as high-impact practices (chapter 1, Ainsworth, Helmke, and Reynolds), using the Gemba Kaizen principle from LEAN methodology to assess a print collection (chapter 6, Ram Nath), the use of logic models as a framework to develop measures for a library's strategic plan (chapter 7, Spears, Shelton, Dinsmore, and Elrod), and the application of succession planning to develop a sustainable information literacy assessment program (chapter 2, Folk), to name a few.

Each chapter is prefaced by a one-page summary profile. The purpose of this summary profile is to give you a quick overview of the chapter by providing fourteen salient items of descriptive information for the case study. The summary profile page will help you decide if the subsequent case study is of interest to you and thus warrants a deeper investigation and thorough read.

We hope you enjoy the variety of interesting case studies of academic libraries in the initial phases of their assessment activities found in the eight chapters in this first section, Seeding the Initiative.

Title: High-Impact Practices and Archives

Abstract: High-impact practices are increasingly used as a measurement tool to assess the efficacy of university programs as they relate to student retention and graduation rates. There is some literature on high-impact practices being used in libraries, but not in archives. This chapter explores the application of high-impact practice frameworks to archives. In a student success–driven atmosphere, the value of old archival paradigms like collection development, description, and access are less important. Archives providing internships, contributing to capstone projects, and facilitating undergraduate research are more valuable to administrators.

Keywords: assessment, high-impact practices, student success, higher education budgets, student retention

Project focus: assessment methodologies, techniques, or practices; organizational practices (i.e., strategic planning); assessment concepts and/or management

Results made or will make case for: a strategic plan or process, how money or resources may be directed

Data needed: survey respondent demographics

Methodology: qualitative, evaluation or survey

Project duration: less than 6 months

Tool(s) utilized: Qualtrics

Cost estimate: < $100

Type of institution: university—public

Institution enrollment: 5,000–15,000

Highest level of education: doctoral

Chapter 1

High-Impact Practices and Archives

Kyle Ainsworth, Jonathan Helmke, and Linda Reynolds

Introduction

Over the course of a month in May and June 2016, the provost of Stephen F. Austin State University (SFA) held four hour-long sessions with the faculty and staff of the Ralph W. Steen Library. The meetings were unprecedented; for the first time in memory, the provost of the university wanted to sit down with faculty and staff at all levels of the library operation. It was clear that this was a fact-finding mission for the provost, but the purpose and potential outcomes were unclear. The air of uncertainty influenced the library's response. Services and personnel were described as robust and reflexive, able to meet changing demands and student needs for study space, digital resources, reference, and tradition print materials. The provost listened, took notes, and asked questions, but it was only during discussion about the library's archives, the East Texas Research Center (ETRC), that librarians began to understand the overarching purpose for his visit.

The archives have excellent collections and valued public resource, but it also needs more space to store collections. There was a wide consensus that the prestige of the ETRC's collections merited its expansion. The provost listened, appreciated, but in the end asked one question: *How do the archives provide "transformative student learning experiences"?* The archivists noted that they offered graduate class internships and graduate assistantships, but their answers were incomplete because they were not familiar with the pedagogy of high-impact practices and thus not able to effectively communicate their answer to the provost.[1]

Constrained by tight budgets, administrators in higher education are looking at how their institutions gauge student success. Archives are not above reproach and are being asked to articulate the high-impact practices they have that contribute to transformative student experiences.[2] Thinking and measuring the value of academic archives in terms of their value to students, versus the diversity, quality, and organization of their collections, is a new paradigm for the academic archives. In this model, the university might value outreach to bring high school students on campus, working with underclassmen on document analysis and critical-thinking skills, or teaching upperclassmen through capstone projects and internships more than the number of new collections processed each year. If archives are not considering these high-impact practices, where do they fit in the long-range plans of libraries and universities?

High-Impact Practices

The phrase "high-impact practice" is relatively new in the academic pedagogy lexicon, only having been in existence since 2007.[3] It is the product of more than forty years of scholarly inquiry about student retention in higher education. The research shows that a combination of sociological and psychological factors heavily contribute to academic success. Students have to have individual motivation and a sense of community to learn. Universities can very directly and uniquely create their own school spirit with a welcoming and socially vibrant campus environment—residence halls, student centers, recreation centers, libraries, athletics, and so on—but recognizing a cohesive and salient core of programs, across the incredible diversity of higher education institutions, that would stimulate students and foster excellence from the very beginning of their university experience may prove much more difficult.[4] High-impact practices shift the definition of student success beyond "access, retention, graduation, and… grade point average" to students' tangible achievements and how those experiences prepare them for postgraduate life.[5]

The two organizations that have been at the forefront of this research are the Association of American Colleges and Universities (AACU) and the National Survey of Student Engagement (NSSE) project. In 2007, Appendix A of AACU's *College Learning for the New Global Century* report identified ten "effective educational practices" which were concluded to be "especially well-suited for assessing students' cumulative learning." These were first-year seminars and experiences, common intellectual experiences, learning communities, writing-intensive courses, collaborative assignments and projects, undergraduate research, diversity/global learning, service learning, community based learning, internships, and capstone courses and projects.[6] Later that year George D. Kuh examined these practices within the auspices of the NSSE survey and found that what the "report authors initially described—with self-conscious caution—as 'effective' can now be appropriately labeled 'high-impact' because of the substantial educational benefits they provide to students."[7]

NSSE was created in 1998 to assess higher education based on responses from undergraduates instead of relying on traditional "quality" metrics like accreditation processes and media rankings.[8] NSSE further distinguished its methodology from other entities by being a credible third-party survey organization, administering its survey at public and private four-year institutions to freshmen and seniors with at least two semesters experience, requiring an adequate sample from each participating college or university, and having a flexible survey that could be modified as needed. In 2007, 313,000 freshman and senior students from 610 four-year colleges and universities in the United States and Canada conducted NSSE surveys. Five hundred fifty-seven institutions participated in 2016.[9]

NSSE defines student engagement as "the amount of time and effort students put into their studies and other educationally purposeful activities… [and]… how the institution deploys its resources and organizes the curriculum and other learning opportunities to get students to participate in activities… that are linked to student learning."[10] From 2000 to 2012, NSSE assessed its survey results within five benchmark areas—level of academic challenge, active and collaborative learning, student-faculty interaction, supportive campus environment, and enriching educational experiences.[11] In 2014, it revised the benchmarks, breaking down the first four themes into ten "engagement indicators" and dividing the benchmark *enriching educational experiences* into six high-impact practices: participate in a learning community, complete a community-based project (service learning), research with faculty, complete an internship or field experience, study abroad, and complete a culminating senior experience.[12]

What is it that these transformative student learning experiences all have in common that make them so effective? First, high-impact practices entail that students be proactive and participatory in their own education. Writing-intensive courses and undergraduate research require time, dedication, and sustained effort. Many high-impact practices (e.g., internships and service learning) are outside the classroom. Students working closely with faculty, staff, their peers, or the local community "makes anonymity impossible, fosters face-to-face interaction, and fuels feedback."[13] High-impact practices are often experiential and students can see how their learning will benefit them long-term. Transformational learning exposes students to different cultures, gets students to collaborate with multifarious peoples, and in many cases are truly life-changing experiences.[14] In summary, Kuh writes, "The engagement premise is deceptively simple, even self-evident: The more students study a subject, the more they learn about it. Likewise, the more students practice and get feedback on their writing, analyzing, or problem solving, the more adept they become," and the more likely students are to develop good habits for lifelong learning.[15]

These kinds of programs are designed to be complementary and collaborative so that a student realizing success with a first-year seminar or collaborative learning could also participate in additional high-impact activities as an upperclassman. Promoting high-impact practice courses is one of the goals of AACU's Liberal Education and

America's Promise (LEAP) initiative. As Kuh notes, "to engage students at high levels, these practices must be done well." Programs need to be conceptualized, implemented and assessed at a local level and then scaled so that all undergraduates can avail themselves of these opportunities. In the best scenario, "institutions would structure the curriculum and other learning opportunities so that one high-impact activity is available to every student every year."[16]

Literature Review

The Association of College & Research Libraries (ACRL) defines information literacy as "the set of integrated abilities encompassing the reflective discovery of information, the understanding of how information is produced and valued, and the use of information in creating new knowledge and participating ethically in communities of learning."[17] This definition is a striking cognitive corollary to NSSE's definition of student success. ACRL also notes that information literacy "is not designed to be implemented in a single information literacy session in a student's academic career; it is intended to be developmentally and systematically integrated into the student's academic program at variety of levels," which closely parallels Kuh's feelings about high-impact practices.[18] Despite the obvious similarities between the objectives of high-impact practices and information literacy, the literature suggests that archivists have not done much to engage the high-impact practice aspects of the NSSE and AACU frameworks.[19]

Instead, the scholarship is narrowly focused on the services and programs libraries and archives implement to engage students at various levels. Some archival professionals might argue, "Well, what's the difference?" The difference is effective communication, and potentially much more. If archivists are writing about student engagement and assessment in one way and provosts and other higher education administrators are thinking about it another way, there is a chance meaningful information is being lost in translation. Academic libraries and archives need to disseminate reports of their activities in the language of high-impact practices. The risk if they do not do this is that decision-makers may not truly understand or realize the tremendous impact archives have on student success. With budgets, staffing, and other resources often on the line, it is in the best interests of libraries and archives to transition how they describe themselves within the context of the larger academic institution. Many of the student engagement tactics described in the literature below are embedded or standalone high-impact practices but are not identified as such.

There is a growing literature about archival classroom instruction for undergraduates.[20] Authors focus on bridging the gaps in students' understanding of critical-thinking skills, primary sources, and research methods. Many undergraduates have "archival anxiety" and are intimidated by the prospect of visiting and using academic archives.[21] Other scholars are focused on the expanding role that digital archives can have in archival instruction.[22] All of these studies could be transposed into *first-year seminars, writing-intensive courses, collaborative assignments and projects, undergraduate research,* and *capstone courses and projects.* By couching it within any of these high-impact practices, archivists can connect what they are doing to their administrators.

There are some excellent high-impact collaborative assignments and projects that have come out of archives. At Eastern Washington University "the History Librarian, Government Documents Librarian and University Archivist… provided separate, subject specific instruction sessions for the CSBS 331 course in multiple academic quarters."[23] In another example, the Louie B. Nun Center for Oral History at the University Kentucky Libraries developed an oral-history metadata synchronizer software that allowed first-year students to create content by indexing the oral histories and making them available to the general public. These indexes encouraged students to "think critically about what and how they write, which causes them to reflect upon and be more aware of the ways writing is epistemic."[24]

Even basic archival reference services can be recast to be support high-impact practices. As noted earlier, faculty engagement is critical for meaningful student engagement. In any of the AACU or NSSE high-impact practices, it could be a faculty librarian, individually or as part of a team, that fills the quintessential role as mentor, collaborator, or inspiration to one or many undergraduate students. Many archivists possess a great degree of historic, context, artifact, and collection-specific knowledge as well as strong understandings of the local archival organization and description. These competencies are incredible assets to students.[25]

James Madison University's Dean of Libraries and Educational Technologies Adam Murray is one of the very few to specifically cite high-impact practices. He surveyed sixty-eight library administrators to assess their institutions' alignment with ten high-impact practices from the 2007 AACU framework. He found that roughly one-third of the respondents worked at libraries with a "high alignment." In the quantitative analysis, *collaborative assignments and learning* had the highest library correlation of all the high-impact practices. Library instruction was closely tied to *learning communities* and *collaborative assignments and learning*. Some libraries provide office or study spaces to international programs, tying them into the *diversity and global learning* initiative. Murray's qualitative results showed that with the exception of common intellectual experiences and service learning, library administrators at "high alignment" institutions identified many examples of libraries contributing to high-impact practices. Most respondents agreed on literacy classes as being the most applicable; these were the major theme of their answers under first-year seminars, learning communities, writing-intensive courses, and capstone courses and projects. Murray's only mention of archives was for internships and abstractly in undergraduate research and capstone courses and projects as the gateway to the institutional repository.[26]

Some academic institutions are applying high-impact practice internships more directly. Gettysburg College's Musselman Library has had eleven music students intern in reference and special collections since 2005.[27] At Brigham Young University (BYU), the internship program is "specifically designed to give undergraduates the chance to explore their research and career interests and to provide opportunities for mentored learning outside a classroom setting."[28] The archives are intentional in their focus on undergraduate students, accepting eight to twelve students per year. Interns receive academic credit and "typically spend the bulk of their time working with a single curator on one or more projects throughout the semester."[29] Students become familiar with core archival competencies through readings and experience. Importantly, BYU students see the internships as beneficial even if they do not intend to study archives in the future, noting the hands-on experience they get working with primary sources and the diversity of archival content is applicable for many career interests.[30] The authors do not cite the AACU or NSSE frameworks, but a close organic alignment is clear.

It can be difficult to implement a rigorous, high-impact archival internship. The issues are finding the right balance of academic learning and labor, student reflection, faculty supervision and feedback, and professional experience to make the internship a substantial and worthwhile experience for the participant. Internships must be "deliberative" and act as a setting where students can apply their course work as well as "contribute rich material to students' academic experience that they can and should draw on in the context of their learning with faculty, staff and peers."[31] Internships go sideways for students when their educational and mentoring components devolve to the task labor of volunteers and student workers. Too often, Nancy O'Neill suggests, there is not the right symmetry of "learning goals and career development goals."[32]

Research Methodology

From November 2016 to February 2017, the authors surveyed provosts, library directors and deans, and archivists to discover their perceptions of archives and knowledge of high-impact practices. The purpose of the survey was to look for linkages; were archivists and administrators aware of high-impact practices, had they made any connections between these practices and archives and, if so, what were these connections? The intent of the survey was qualitative versus quantitative, seeking examples and opinions from respondents instead of statistics.

Initially, the authors emailed the survey to each provost, library director or dean, and head archivist at sixty-three institutions within the Southern Association of Colleges and Schools (SACS) accreditation region that had archives at their institution with full-time enrollment (FTE) ranging from 8,000 to 20,000.[33] SFA's enrollment is roughly at the midpoint (about 13,000) and it was logical to seek comparative results from colleges and universities of similar size. There was a low response rate from these SACS schools early on, however, so the authors widened the scope of their inquiry. The survey was also emailed to the Society of American Archivists Archives and Archivist email discussion list. This made an impact, as there were seventy-two total responses, of which twenty-six came from SACS schools and forty-six came from the SAA discussion list.[34]

Larger sample sizes (especially from provost set, see table 1.1) would have been preferred and would have allowed for stronger conclusions, but the authors' intent was always to conduct a preliminary investigation. As a result, the authors were very pleased with the survey response. Qualtrics Survey Software was used to create a survey with fifteen questions. The first four concerned a participant's demographics. The investigative portion of the survey was only ten questions. Questions 5 and 6 lead into to the survey's main section of inquiry, which was covered in questions 7 to 14. The final question gave survey-takers privacy options for their responses.

Table 1.1
High-Impact Practices Survey Participation

	Archivists	Directors/ Deans	Provosts	Other	Total
Started Survey	31	18	3	20	72
Completed Survey	13	11	3	0	27

Survey Results and Analysis

The main conclusion of the survey was that there is not effective communication about the value of archives within higher education. The responses to different survey questions illustrated this dissonance. Question 5 addresses the issue of internal communications directly. It asked survey participants, "Has the role of the archives been discussed at your school in the context of student success, transformative learning experiences, high-impact practices, student retention, graduation rates, or the first semester freshman experience? Table 1.2 suggests that the majority of survey-takers may not have had this discussion at their institution. Notably, thirteen archivists and two library directors or deans quit the survey after this question.

Table 1.2
Archives in the Context of High-Impact Practices

Survey Question 5	Answered	
	Yes	No
Provosts	0	3
Library Directors/Deans	8	10
Archivists	14	17

Question 6 (table 1.3) sought qualitative personal insights and asked the remaining survey participants their perception of the archives as it pertains to high-impact practices. For this question, all three provosts, fifteen of sixteen library directors or deans, and seventeen of eighteen archivists gave substantive responses. Augustana College in Illinois has gotten broad buy-in, but even there the work is not done. Special Collections Librarian Samantha Crisp at Augustana College wrote:

> In the wake of a complete redesign of our library space, which was converted to a center for student life in 2013, we worked actively to communicate to our President and administration that what sets a 21st century library apart from its peers are its unique collections—special collections, university archives, digital collections, etc. We also

attempted to communicate the role of special collections as liberal arts laboratories. In light of this, I think administrators are more aware of the important role special collections play in impacting the student experience; however, I feel there is more work to be done and that they only have a basic understanding of this concept.

Table 1.3

Assessing How University Administrators Value Archives.

Survey	
Q6	For library directors/deans and archivists:
	What is your perception of the value of archives as it pertains to "student success," "transformative learning experiences," "high-impact practices," and student retention?
	For provosts:
	What is your perception of the administration's value of the archives as it pertains to "student success," "transformative learning experiences," "high-impact practices," and student retention?

Other answers ranged from very positive to very negative. One provost, four library directors or deans, and one archivist wrote about archives and primary sources. Their sentiments were best summed up by a library director or dean who wrote, "I think some administrators recognize that the archives can play a role in helping students understand the use and importance of primary sources. By using primary sources students can learn synthesis and critical thinking skills."

Most survey participants did not draw such positive correlations, however. One library director or dean wrote that "I don't think that university administration perceives any direct link between the archives and student success." Three library directors or deans and one archivist echoed this sentiment. Similarly, another library director or dean wrote that archives are "a necessary component of any successful, similar institution of higher education," but that they have "limited academic relevance, mostly to majors and faculty in History and English." One archivist thought the university ascribed more of an administrative role than an academic role to the archives. That person wrote, "My perception is that the Administration sees our value more in placing the University and the surrounding community into a historical context… i.e., providing photos or historical narrative to commemorate events, people, and activities."

The thoughts of two participants really sum up the ambivalence most survey-takers had about the intersection of archives and high-impact practices. An archivist commented, "I don't think they single it out. To be honest, I'm not sure they have a good sense of the libraries' general contribution to student success, retention, etc. They suspect we are a good and helpful thing, so it's not that they think we aren't playing a role, it's just not clear what our impact is." This questioning is mirrored by a provost at another university, who stated: "I have a positive impression on the value, but I don't have evidence."

Question 7 (table 1.4) directed participants to indicate whether they were familiar with the AACU or NSSE framework so that they could continue taking the survey using a familiar model. Table 1.5 demonstrates that while the majority of provosts and library directors or deans had knowledge of AACU or NSSE, only four out of the eighteen archivists indicated they were acquainted with the two student success frameworks. Only six of eighteen archivists and seven of the sixteen library directors or deans continued the survey beyond this point. What this suggests is that there was a willingness to engage the survey when the focus was general and high-impact practices were ill-defined. But as the survey got into the specific and qualitative examination, the majority of participants possibly realized they did not understand the pedagogy and its terminology as well as they might have thought.

Table 1.4
Frameworks for Measuring Student Success in Archives.

Survey	
Q7	There are a pair of frameworks commonly used to inquire about "student success" initiatives at colleges and universities. We want to know how the archives fits into the model used at your institution. Please choose from the following options: a. Answer questions based on the **Association of American Colleges & Universities (AACU)** *High-Impact Educational Practices: What They Are, Who Has Access to Them, and Why They Matter,* 2008 b. Answer questions based on the **National Survey of Student Engagement (NSSE)** *From Benchmarks to Engagement Indicators and High-Impact Practices,* January 2014 c. Not familiar with either framework, but I will answer questions based on **AACU**. d. Not familiar with either framework, but I will answer questions based on **NSSE**.

Table 1.5
Archives in the Context of Models for High-Impact Practices.

	Provosts	Library Directors/Deans	Archivists
AACU	1	6	0
NSSE	1	4	4
Don't Know, use AACU	0	1	5
Don't Know, use NSSE	1	5	9
Total	3	16	18

The bulk of the survey, and where the authors really hoped to get qualitative examples of high-impact practices, were questions 8 through 14 (see table 1.6). Unfortunately, only seventeen individuals answered questions from this block of questions. The results mirrored earlier responses and demonstrated that many libraries and archives are passive and reactive versus proactive and intentional when it comes to student learning. Most responses were not high-impact practices at all and affirmed that there are minimal academic expectations for archives: to provide generic class tours and orientation sessions as a service point. Survey-takers indicated that students used the archives for undergraduate research and capstone projects, but that it was on a case-by-case basis and not done in any formal capacity.

Table 1.6
Archival Benchmarks and Effective Educational Practices.

Survey	NSSE	AACU
Q8	Academic Challenges: Please provide examples of how your archives engages students in higher-order learning, reflective & integrated learning, learning strategies, and/or quantitative reasoning.	Please give examples if your archives provides first-year seminars and experiences.
Q9	Learning with Peers: Please provide examples of how your archives engages students in collaborative learning and/or discussions with diverse others	Please provide examples if your archives creates archival learning communities, in which students in the same year of college take archival courses together and may live together on campus.
Q10	Experiences with Faculty: Please provide examples of how your archives engages students with student-faculty interaction and/or effective teaching practices.	Please provide examples if your archives is used for writing-intensive courses.
Q11	High-Impact Practices: Please provide examples if your archives creates archival learning communities or some other formal program where groups of students take two or more classes together.	Please provide examples if your archives is used for collaborative assignments and projects.
Q12	High-Impact Practices: Please give examples if your archives provides archival internships to students	Please provide examples if your archives helps create opportunities for undergraduate research.
Q13	High-Impact Practices: Please provide examples if your archives gives students the opportunity to work with an archives faculty or staff member on a research project.	Please give examples if your archives provides archival internships to students.
Q14	High-Impact Practices: Please provide examples if your archives gives students the opportunity to have an archival focus for their culminating senior experience (capstone course, senior project or thesis, comprehensive exam, etc.)	Please provide examples if your archives gives students the opportunity to have an archival focus for their capstone courses and projects "that is, culminating courses or final projects in a student's major, usually done in the senior year."

There were exceptions. Collectively, survey-takers from all three administrative units—archivists, library directors or deans, and provosts—expressed opinions that there are three high-impact practices where archives excel: the development of critical thinking with primary sources, undergraduate and capstone research, and experiential or service learning. The majority of respondents (12 of 17) indicated that they offer some kind of internship program (question 13). These were predominantly available to upperclassmen and graduate students, usually in the history department, and consisted of work on digital humanities, oral history, or collections development projects. The best developed internship program mentioned was that of Nadia Nasr, Head of Archives and Special Collections at Santa Clara University. Their archives is in the second year of a formal apprentice program. The purpose of the apprenticeship is to

> Train selected students in the basics of working in an archives and special collections department. Interns first work on processing collections with the University Archivist. Following that, there is a rotation component in which the intern works on different projects with various staff members.... Finally, the interns complete a final project that incorporates materials from [the archives].[35]

Nasr also noted that their archives is working to increase faculty-student interaction within the archives. There was a pilot class in the spring of 2017, English 103: Topics in Writing and Rhetoric—Analyzing and Composing Archives, which heavily incorporated archival materials and class visits into the curriculum. There was also one survey response that indicated some archives are making inroads collaborating with first-year seminars. Samantha Crisp, Special Collections Librarian at Augustana College, noted that her archives provides embedded instruction to about 25 percent of the first-year rhetoric program as well as some underclassman research method classes.

Case Study

Going back to the introduction, the question asked by SFA's provost challenged the archivists to reconsider the entire mission and purpose of their department. First, the archivists completely redesigned their model for class-based instruction. Historically, faculty brought students to the archives for class tours. The tour would visually expose students to the collections with a walk through the closed stacks and the reading room, as well as a basic tutorial on microfilm and requesting archival collections. The archivists did not teach students any archival information literacy—that was something they had to figure out on their own. Looking at table 1.7, you can see that 27 percent of the East Texas Research Center's (ETRC) users (141 undergraduate students) were not helped in a meaningful way when they received class tours. The elementary education students (105 total), on the other hand, worked on collaborative projects with a highly energetic and engaged professor. Working with the elementary education students provided ETRC faculty with their first experience with high-impact practices.

Table 1.7
Students at the East Texas Research Center, 2015–2016.[a]

Student Users and Workers	Visitors	Level	Notes
Elementary Education 302	46	Undergraduate	2 classes for TEKS module[b]
Elementary Education 352	59	Undergraduate	2 classes for TEKS module[b]
Class Tours	141	Undergraduate	8 classes
Individual Research Visits	213	Both	
History 535 Internship	8	Graduate	30 hours each
History 570 Internship	11	Graduate	15 hours each
Class Tours	38	High School	2 classes
Student Assistants (2)	n/a	Graduate	20 hours per week
Student Workers (9)	n/a	Undergraduate	10–20 hours per week
Total Visits[c]	516		

a. The academic year was September 1, 2015–August 30, 2016.
b. Texas Essential Knowledge and Skills
c. Students were counted for each individual visit.

The ETRC shifted its approach to class tours in August 2016 to combine them with instructed document analysis—showing students the variety of records in archives and then helping them learn how to decipher primary source materials. Another modification to the ETRC's standard class tour was to work closely with faculty to tailor the archives' primary sources directly to the current class module or project. This was a lot of work for the archivists, but there was a greater return on investment as the faculty members also embedded archival instruction into their syllabi and lesson plans.

Document analysis is easily adapted to host high-impact practices. The critical-thinking skills that it encourages—questioning complex ideas and subjects, understanding historical contexts and biases, deciphering and identifying arguments, formulating questions, and describing the content lucidly—underpin almost every aspect of student collegiate success. Early exposure and success at the ETRC using document analysis could give students the comfort level to return to the archives for their own research and creative activities.

A successful example was the History of the Written Word (English 342) class that came to the archives three times during the fall 2016 semester. The collaboration between archivists, students, and professor was excellent from start to finish. The class syllabus outlined each archival session in detail, including the purpose of the visit, a list of questions, and the expected learning outcomes. The professor took the ETRC's document analysis worksheet, compared it to those recommended by the Library of Congress and other archival entities, and then made a modified version that better fit the requirements for the class. It was so well written that the ETRC now uses the professor's revision with other classes.

Students were engaged and interested when they came to the ETRC for this class. They knew what they were supposed to be doing, asked many questions, and were confident in their research topic. They pored over love letters from the Civil War, World War I, World War II, and the Vietnam War, looking at changes to language and syntax over time. Where many students would be frustrated by the cursive writing, these students worked in teams to read the text. The professor walked among them, asking questions and helping the students understand their documents.

As part of their final paper, students had to select an archival collection and complete five document analysis worksheets from that collection. Most students were comfortable enough with archival research from their class visits that they had already selected documents to work with. Two students used the papers they wrote to present at a women and gender studies conference at SFA in March 2017.

The ETRC, like many of those in the survey results, has missed many chances in recent years to demonstrate to administrators the transformative learning techniques that it already practices. Archives must describe their instruction and outreach within student success frameworks to demonstrate their impact on student learning to administrators and other key constituencies. The ETRC is trying to do this with several innovative ideas. One way is to write about high-impact practices occurring in the archives in the library's strategic plan, which funnels into the university's strategic plan. This creates program awareness when administrators make decisions. A second avenue is for ETRC faculty to be elected or appointed as the library representatives on university committees and programs that look at student learning and teaching effectiveness. Currently the director of the archives is on the University Research Council and the Special Collections Librarian is the elected library representative to Faculty Senate. They can meaningfully contribute to the conversations at the university by sharing and demonstrating the value of the archives to student learning.

A strategy for the 2016–17 annual ETRC library department report is to prominently highlight the high-impact practices it engaged in that academic year. Archivists also encouraged the faculty they collaborated with to mention the ETRC in their own administrative reports. The long-term strategy is to integrate archival activities into many academic units.

There are a number of things that the ETRC wants to do or already does that it can brand or rebrand as high-impact practices:

Learning Communities (AACU, NSSE)—There is not an interdisciplinary research methods class for undergraduates at the university. The archives would be a perfect location to embed several class modules or even prepare an entire class in preparation for writing-intensive courses and capstone courses and projects. The ability to construct an argument and decipher different sources of information are skills needed by undergraduate students in every field, be it finance, chemistry, prelaw, history, or art. Document analysis is just the tip of the iceberg. The director of the ETRC supervises records management for the university. She also has training in digital forensics. This archival knowledge is especially applicable to undergraduates getting degrees in accounting, general business, computer science and mass communications.

Collaborative Assignments and Projects (AACU)—The ETRC hopes to entice faculty from a variety of disciplines besides history to incorporate the archives into their curriculum. Over the last five years, classes of majors from art, art history, criminal justice, English, geography, government, interior design, and social work have all used the archives.

Internships (AACU, NSSE)—The ETRC offers 150-hour internships to undergraduate students. Like most academic archives, the ETRC hires undergraduate student workers to do simple archival processing. For certain workers, applying some of the learning objectives of internships might produce high-impact results.

Capstone Courses and Projects (AACU, NSSE)—The director of the ETRC became graduate faculty in 2013 even though SFA does not have a library science program. This has raised the profile of the archives significantly, with the director having served on five masters' theses.

First-Year Seminars and Experiences (AACU)—SFA offers a first-year experience called SFA 101 that "promotes active learning, personal growth and achievement." Over 80 percent of incoming freshmen take the one-credit class voluntarily. There are sixty sections of SFA 101 offered every fall, and generally only one or two come to the archives for a brief orientation. The ETRC is actively working to get more involved. In the fall 2017 semester, for instance, the university archivist collaborated with three SFA 101 classes from the School of Honors. Students were broken into small groups and assigned a research topic about SFA history that they had to investigate at the archives and then present in poster format at the Student Center. This project introduced freshmen to the archives and enhanced critical thinking skills through the analysis of primary sources and peer collaboration. The project created a connection between students and the history of SFA and provided an opportunity for students to present their research in an academic setting to peers, professors and university administrators. The ETRC is working with the Honors program to build on this initial success and hopes to soon embed itself into other classes' introductory modules on information literacy and research methods. There is also the potential for an ETRC faculty member to instruct a SFA 101 section.[36]

Undergraduate Research (AACU)—For the 2017–18 academic year, all three archivists at the ETRC will also be responsible for subject areas as department liaison librarians. While this will be more work added to an already busy schedule, it is also an opportunity to be proactive and go to students and faculty and demonstrate archival resources.

The goal of the ETRC is to continue to develop high-impact practices at the archives. Although the acquisition of subject areas will help introduce the archivists to more faculty than they might otherwise meet, much of the impetus for teaching and learning activities to occur at the ETRC still depends on faculty and academic departments being interested. Scalability is also a major issue. There are only three faculty members in the archives: the director, the special collections librarian, and the university archivist. Incorporating high-impact practices into the archives is time-consuming and difficult to balance with traditional archival duties. The one truth that is certain is that the language of high-impact practices, student engagement, transformative student learning experiences, and intentionality is here to stay. It is in their own best interest that archives and libraries adapt their practices to match the pedagogy.

Conclusion

In light of the changing nature and structure of funding for higher education, archivists need to start translating their student instruction and reference activities into the language of high-impact practices. Traditional metrics, like visitor statistics and the number of archival collections acquired and described, do not adequately demonstrate the archives' value in the only currency of the twenty-first century: student success. As both the survey results and the dearth of archival literature on NSSE and AACU suggest, archivists have been slow to recognize and apply high-impact practices to their archives. The purpose of this article is to catalyze discussion and additional research. There needs to be quantitative and qualitative assessment data collected to provide evidence that these high-impact practices are effective in archives. We encourage others to write on this subject, contributing journal articles and conference presentations to a critically important, but poorly understood, archival pedagogy. There are great avenues for critical inquiry and assessment in the study of archives and high-impact practices.

Although it has been a full year since the library-wide meetings, and the role the provost wants the ETRC to play in teaching and learning remains uncertain, the archives is charging ahead to implement high-impact practices. The AACU and NSSE models outline ways that are successful not only for teaching and learning, but also for getting students and faculty to use the archives. Even if there is not administrative pressure to demonstrate transformative student learning, high-impact practices make sense for archives to implement. They give structure and a path forward to accomplish the mission and vision statements at the core of every archives' purpose. At SFA, this includes helping "students achieve academic success, develop critical thinking skills, and become life-long learners" by serving as "a gateway to information discovery, knowledge creation, and cultural preservation, fostering an atmosphere that encourages research and creativity, critical thinking, experiential learning, and collaborative partnerships."[37]

Notes

1. The library meetings were held in the context of the 2015–2023 Strategic Plan, *SFA Envisioned*. Driving the university-wide discussion on student engagement and success was one book in particular, *The Undergraduate Experience: Focusing Institutions on What Matters Most*. The provost discussed the book at the university's all-faculty meeting at the beginning of the fall 2016 semester. Afterwards, every faculty member on campus that wanted a copy received one. Discussions, first in small groups and then in faculty-wide plenary sessions, were convened to talk about the major themes and how they impacted the university. Final recommendations were made in April 2017 in time to influence the 2017–18 budget. High-impact practices are discussed in chapters two and three: see Peter Felten, John H. Gardner, Charles C. Schroeder, Leo M. Lambert, and Betsy O. Barefoot, *The Undergraduate Experience* (San Francisco: Jossey-Bass, 2016): 20–30, 48–51.
2. George D. Kuh and Robert M. Gonyea, "The Role of the Academic Library in Promoting Student Engagement in Learning," *College & Research Libraries* 64, no. 4 (2003): 256.
3. Carol Geary Schneider, "Liberal Education and High-Impact Practices: Making Excellence—Once and for All—Inclusive," introduction to *High-Impact Educational Practices: What They Are, Who Has Access to Them, and Why They Matter*, by George D. Kuh (Washington, DC: Association of American Colleges and Universities, 2008): 1,
4. Vincent Tinto, "Dropout from Higher Education: A Theoretical Synthesis of Recent Research,"

Review of Educational Research 45, no. 1 (1975): 89–125; John Bean, "Dropouts and Turnover: The Synthesis and Test of a Causal Model of Student Attrition," *Research in Higher Education* 12, no. 2 (1980): 155–87; Alberto Cabrera, Maria Castaneda, Amaury Nora, and Dennis Hengstler, "The Convergence between Two Theories of College Persistence," *Journal of Higher Education* 63, no. 2 (1992): 143–64; Adam Murray, "Academic Libraries and High-Impact Practices for Student Retention: Library Deans' Perspectives," *Libraries and the Academy* 15, no. 3 (July 2015): 472–73, https://doi.org/10.1353/pla.2015.0027.

5. Schneider, "Liberal Education and High-Impact Practices," 2.
6. National Leadership Council for Liberal Education and America's Promise (LEAP), *College Learning for the New Global Century, Appendix A: A Guide to Effective Education Practices* (Washington, DC: Association of American Colleges and Universities, 2007), 53–54. https://www.aacu.org/sites/default/files/files/LEAP/GlobalCentury_final.pdf.
7. Schneider, "Liberal Education and High-Impact Practices," 1.
8. National Survey of Student Engagement, *Our Origins and Potential* (Bloomington: Indiana University Center for Postsecondary Research, 2001), http://nsse.indiana.edu/html/origins.cfm.
9. George D. Kuh, "If We Could Do One Thing… ," Director's Message, in *Experiences That Matter: Enhancing Student Learning and Success—Annual Report 2007* (Bloomington: National Survey of Student Engagement, Indiana University, 2007), 10, http://nsse.indiana.edu/NSSE_2007_Annual_Report/docs/withhold/NSSE_2007_Annual_Report.pdf; National Survey of Student Engagement, "Quick Facts from NSSE 2016," in *Engagement Insights: Survey Findings on the Quality of Undergraduate Education—Annual Results 2016* (Bloomington: Indiana University Center for Postsecondary Research, 2016), http://nsse.indiana.edu/NSSE_2016_Results/pdf/NSSE_2016_Annual_Results.pdf.
10. "About NSSE," National Survey of Student Engagement, accessed February 7, 2018, http://nsse.indiana.edu/html/about.cfm.
11. "High-Impact Practices Boost Learning, Involved Parents No Problem," news release. National Survey of Student Engagement, November 5, 2007, http://nsse.indiana.edu/NSSE_2007_Annual_Report/docs/withhold/PressRelease2007.pdf
12. National Survey of Student Engagement, *From Benchmarks to Engagement Indicators and High-Impact Practices* (Bloomington: Indiana University Center for Postsecondary Research, January 2014), http://nsse.indiana.edu/pdf/Benchmarks%20to%20Indicators.pdf.
13. See George D. Kuh, *High-Impact Educational Practices* (Washington, D.C.: Association of American Colleges and Universities, 2008), 14, or Kuh, "If We Could Do One Thing… ," 7.
14. The effective practices in this paragraph are paraphrased from Kuh, *High-Impact Educational Practices*, 14-15, 17; Kuh, "If We Could Do One Thing…"; and Susan Albertine and Tia Brown McNair, "Seeking High-Quality, High-Impact Learning: The Imperative of Faculty Development and Curricular Intentionality," *Peer Review* 14, no. 3 (Summer 2012), https://www.aacu.org/publications-research/periodicals/seeking-high-quality-high-impact-learning-imperative-faculty.
15. George D. Kuh, "What We're Learning about Student Engagement from NSSE," *Change* 35, no. 2 (March/April 2003): 25.
16. Kuh, *High-Impact Educational Practices*, 20.
17. Association of College & Research Libraries, *Framework for Information Literacy for Higher Education* (Chicago: Association of College & Research Libraries, January 11, 2016), 3, http://www.ala.org/acrl/standards/ilframework.
18. Association of College & Research Libraries, *Framework for Information Literacy*, 10.
19. An "Experiences with Information Literacy" module was added to the NSSE survey in 2014. Neither archives nor high-impact practices are assessed in the module. See Kevin Fosnacht, "Information Literacy and NSSE: Introducing the Experiences with Information Literacy Module," *College & Research Libraries News* 75, no. 9 (October 2014): 490–91, 500; Kate Zoellner, "Exploring Undergraduate Student Experiences with Information Literacy," *Performance Measurements and Metrics* 17, no. 3 (2016): 241–51, https://doi.org/10.1108/PMM-07-2016-0032; and Kevin Fosnacht, "Information Literacy's Influence on Undergraduates' Learning and Development: Results from a Large Multi-institutional Study," in *At the Helm: Leading Transformation: Proceedings of the ACRL 2017 Conference, March 22–25, 2017, Baltimore, Maryland*, ed. Dawn M. Mueller (Chicago: Association of College & Research Libraries, 2017), 348–60. Several scholars used NSSE data before high-impact practices conceptually existed. Scott Bennett used NSSE benchmarks to look at library study space; see Scott

Bennett, "Designing for Uncertainty: Three Approaches," *Journal of Academic Librarianship* 33, no. 2 (March 2007): 165–79. Mark and Boruff-Jones created survey questions for the *active and collaborative learning* benchmark, correlated it to ACRL standards for information literacy, and assessed the responses of college and university freshman and seniors; see Amy E. Mark and Polly D. Boruff-Jones, "Information Literacy and Student Engagement: What the National Survey of Student Engagement Reveals about Your Campus," *College & Research Libraries* 64, no. 6 (November 2003): 480–93.

20. Marcus C. Robyns notes that there are still conflicting views about the archivist's role in instruction. Some archivists believe that "being a teacher goes beyond the mandate of archival management and that the responsibility for teaching thinking and research skills should be left to properly trained faculty." There is another cadre of archivists in the profession, however, that feels differently and is "promot[ing] archives as centers of learning and themselves as educators"; See Marcus C. Robyns, "The Archivist as Educator: Integrating Critical Thinking Skills into Historical Research Methods Instruction," *American Archivist* 64 (Fall/Winter 2001): 364.

21. The term "archival anxiety" comes directly from Greg Johnson, "Introducing Undergraduate Students to Archives and Special Collections," *College and Undergraduate Libraries* 13, no. 2 (2006): 96, https://doi.org/10.1300/J106v13n02_07. For more on undergraduates using the archives, see Jeanine Mazak and Frank Manista, "Collaborative Learning: University Archives and Freshman Composition," *Reference Librarian* 32, no. 67–68 (2000): 225–42, https://doi.org/10.1300/J120v32n67_16; and Magia G. Krause, "Undergraduates in the Archives: Using an Assessment Rubric to Measure Learning," *American Archivist* 73 (Fall/Winter 2010): 507–34.

22. "Digital archives eliminate many temporal and spatial obstacles to archival research," which is ideal for many undergraduate researchers; see James P. Purdy, "Three Gifts of Digital Archives," *Journal of Literacy and Technology* 12, no. 3 (November 2011): 40. In addition, these repositories give students the ability not only to "study primary materials collected in existing archives, but also [to] use digital technologies to contribute and even create new archives;" see Pamela VanHaitsma, "New Pedagogical Engagements with Archives: Student Inquiry and Composing in Digital Spaces," *College English* 78, no. 1 (September 2015): 38. Another excellent article is Matthew A. Vetter, "Archive 2.0: What Composition Students and Academic Libraries Can Gain from Digital-Collaborative Pedagogies," *Composition Studies* 42, no. 1 (2014): 35–53.

23. Paul Victor Jr., Justin Otto and Charles Mutschler, "Assessment of Library Instruction on Undergraduate Student Success in a Documents-Based Research Course: The Benefits of Librarian, Archivist and Faculty Collaboration," *Collaborative Librarianship* 5, no. 3 (2013): 154.

24. Douglas A. Boyd, Janice W. Fernheimer, and Rachel Dixon, "Indexing as Engaging Oral History Research: Using OHMS to 'Compose History' in the Writing Classroom," *Oral History Review* 42, no. 2 (2015): 364, https://doi.org/10.1093/ohr/ohv053.

25. Wendy Duff and Allyson Fox, "'You're a Guide Rather Than an Expert': Archival Reference from an Archivist's Point of View," *Journal of the Society of Archivists* 27, no. 2 (October 2006): 129–53; Wendy M. Duff, Elizabeth Yakel and Helen Tibbo, "Archival Reference Knowledge," *American Archivist* 76, no. 1 (Spring/Summer 2013): 68–94.

26. Murray, "Academic Libraries and High-Impact Practices," 477–82.

27. Timothy Sestrick and Lina Terjesen, "Changing Lives, One Note at a Time: Library Internships for Undergraduate Students," *Pennsylvania Libraries: Research & Practice* 2, no. 1 (Spring 2014): 38-47, https://doi.org/10.5195/palrap.2014.50.

28. Maggie Gallup Kopp and John M. Murphy, "Mentored Learning in Special Collections: Undergraduate Archival and Rare Books Internships," *Journal of Library Innovation* 3, no. 2 (2012): 51.

29. Kopp and Murphy, "Mentored Learning in Special Collections," 55.

30. Kopp and Murphy, "Mentored Learning in Special Collections," 59.

31. Nancy O'Neill, "Internships as a High-Impact Practice: Some Reflections on Quality," *Peer Review* 12, no. 4 (Fall 2010): 6, https://www.aacu.org/publications-research/periodicals/internships-high-impact-practice-some-reflections-quality.

32. O'Neill, "Internships as a High-Impact Practice," 7.

33. There are seventy-four SACS institutions with an FTE between 8,000 and 20,000, but eleven do not have archives.

34. Twenty people opened the survey but never answered a single question. Their median engagement was thirty-two seconds, or about enough time to read the survey introduction and close the tab.

35. "Training Future Archivists," *Santa Clara University Library Newsletter*, Fall 2016, https://www.scu.edu/library/newsletter/2016-04/training-future-archivists/.
36. "SFA 101," Stephen F. Austin State University, accessed August 25, 2017, http://www.sfasu.edu/sfa101/.
37. Excerpted from the mission statement and vision statements; see "Help," Ralph W. Steen Library, Stephen F. Austin State University, accessed August 20, 2017, https://library.sfasu.edu/help.

Bibliography

Albertine, Susan, and Tia Brown McNair. "Seeking High-Quality, High-Impact Learning: The Imperative of Faculty Development and Curricular Intentionality." *Peer Review* 14, no. 3 (Summer 2012). https://www.aacu.org/publications-research/periodicals/seeking-high-quality-high-impact-learning-imperative-faculty.

Association of College & Research Libraries. *Framework for Information Literacy for Higher Education.* Chicago: Association of College & Research Libraries, January 11, 2016. http://www.ala.org/acrl/standards/ilframework.

Bean, John. "Dropouts and Turnover: The Synthesis and Test of a Causal Model of Student Attrition." *Research in Higher Education* 12, no. 2 (1980): 155–87.

Bennett, Scott. "Designing for Uncertainty: Three Approaches." *Journal of Academic Librarianship* 33, no. 2 (March 2007): 165–79.

Boyd, Douglas A., Janice W. Fernheimer, and Rachel Dixon. "Indexing as Engaging Oral History Research: Using OHMS to 'Compose History' in the Writing Classroom." *Oral History Review* 42, no. 2 (2015): 352–67. https://doi.org/10.1093/ohr/ohv053.

Cabrera, Alberto, Maria Castaneda, Amaury Nora, and Dennis Hengstler. "The Convergence between Two Theories of College Persistence." *Journal of Higher Education* 63, no. 2 (1992): 143–64.

Duff, Wendy, and Allyson Fox. "'You're a Guide Rather Than an Expert': Archival Reference from an Archivist's Point of View." *Journal of the Society of Archivists* 27, no. 2 (October 2006): 129–53.

Duff, Wendy M., Elizabeth Yakel, and Helen Tibbo. "Archival Reference Knowledge." *American Archivist* 76, no. 1 (Spring/Summer 2013): 68–94.

Felten, Peter, John H. Gardner, Charles C. Schroeder, Leo M. Lambert, and Betsy O. Barefoot. *The Undergraduate Experience: Focusing Institutions on What Matters Most.* San Francisco: Jossey-Bass, 2016.

Fosnacht, Kevin. "Information Literacy and NSSE: Introducing the Experiences with Information Literacy Module." *College & Research Libraries News* 75, no. 9 (October 2014): 490–91, 500.

———. "Information Literacy's Influence on Undergraduates' Learning and Development: Results from a Large Multi-institutional Study." In *At the Helm: Leading Transformation: Proceedings of the ACRL 2017 Conference, March 22–25, 2017, Baltimore, Maryland.* Edited Dawn M. Mueller, 348–60. Chicago: Association of College & Research Libraries, 2017.

Johnson, Greg. "Introducing Undergraduate Students to Archives and Special Collections." *College and Undergraduate Libraries* 13, no. 2 (2006): 91–100. https://doi.org/10.1300/J106v13n02_07.

Kopp, Maggie Gallup, and John M. Murphy. "Mentored Learning in Special Collections: Undergraduate Archival and Rare Books Internships." *Journal of Library Innovation* 3, no. 2 (2012): 50–62.

Krause, Magia G. "Undergraduates in the Archives: Using an Assessment Rubric to Measure Learning." *American Archivist* 73 (Fall/Winter 2010): 507–34.

Kuh, George D. *High-Impact Educational Practices: What They Are, Who Has Access to Them, and Why They Matter.* Washington, DC: Association of American Colleges and Universities, 2008.

———. "If We Could Do One Thing…" Director's Message. In *Experiences That Matter: Enhancing Student Learning and Success—Annual Report 2007*, 7–10. National Survey of Student Engagement, Indiana University Bloomington, 2007. http://nsse.indiana.edu/NSSE_2007_Annual_Report/docs/withhold/NSSE_2007_Annual_Report.pdf.

———. "What We're Learning about Student Engagement from NSSE." *Change* 35, no. 2 (March/April 2003): 24–32.

Kuh, George D., and Robert M. Gonyea. "The Role of the Academic Library in Promoting Student Engagement in Learning." *College & Research Libraries* 64, no. 4 (2003): 256–82.

Mark, Amy E., and Polly D. Boruff-Jones. "Information Literacy and Student Engagement: What the National Survey of Student Engagement Reveals about Your Campus." *College & Research Libraries* 64, no. 6 (November 2003): 480–93.

Mazak, Jeanine, and Frank Manista. "Collaborative Learning: University Archives and Freshman Composition." *Reference Librarian* 32, no. 67–68 (2000): 225–42. https://doi.org/10.1300/J120v32n67_16.

Murray, Adam. "Academic Libraries and High-Impact Practices for Student Retention: Library Deans' Perspectives." *Libraries and the Academy* 15, no. 3 (July 2015): 471–87. https://doi.org/10.1353/pla.2015.0027.

National Leadership Council for Liberal Education and America's Promise (LEAP). *College Learning for the New Global Century*. Washington, DC: Association of American Colleges and Universities, 2007. https://www.aacu.org/sites/default/files/files/LEAP/GlobalCentury_final.pdf.

National Survey of Student Engagement. "About NSSE." National Survey of Student Engagement. Accessed February 7, 2018. http://nsse.indiana.edu/html/about.cfm.

———. *Engagement Insights: Survey Findings on the Quality of Undergraduate Education—Annual Results 2016*. Bloomington: Indiana University Center for Postsecondary Research, 2016. http://nsse.indiana.edu/NSSE_2016_Results/pdf/NSSE_2016_Annual_Results.pdf.

———. *From Benchmarks to Engagement Indicators and High-Impact Practices*. Bloomington: Indiana University Center for Postsecondary Research, January 2014. http://nsse.indiana.edu/pdf/Benchmarks%20to%20Indicators.pdf.

———. "High-Impact Practices Boost Learning, Involved Parents No Problem." News release. National Survey of Student Engagement, November 5, 2007. http://nsse.indiana.edu/NSSE_2007_Annual_Report/docs/withhold/PressRelease2007.pdf.

———. *Our Origins and Potential*. Bloomington: Indiana University Center for Postsecondary Research, 2001. http://nsse.indiana.edu/html/origins.cfm.

O'Neill, Nancy. "Internships as a High-Impact Practice: Some Reflections on Quality." *Peer Review* 12, no. 4 (Fall 2010): 4–8. https://www.aacu.org/publications-research/periodicals/internships-high-impact-practice-some-reflections-quality.

Purdy, James P. "Three Gifts of Digital Archives." *Journal of Literacy and Technology* 12, no. 3 (November 2011): 24–49.

Robyns, Marcus C. "The Archivist as Educator: Integrating Critical Thinking Skills into Historical Research Methods Instruction." *American Archivist* 64 (Fall/Winter 2001): 364.

Santa Clara University Library. "Training Future Archivists." *Santa Clara University Library Newsletter*, Fall 2016. https://www.scu.edu/library/newsletter/2016-04/training-future-archivists/.

Schneider, Carol Geary. "Liberal Education and High-Impact Practices: Making Excellence—Once and for All—Inclusive." Introduction to *High-Impact Educational Practices: What They Are, Who Has Access to Them, and Why They Matter*, by George D. Kuh, 1-8. Washington, DC: Association of American Colleges and Universities, 2008..

Sestrick, Timothy, and Lina Terjesen. "Changing Lives, One Note at a Time: Library Internships for Undergraduate Students." *Pennsylvania Libraries: Research & Practice* 2, no. 1 (Spring 2014): 38–47. https://doi.org/10.5195/palrap.2014.50.

Stephen F. Austin State University. "Help." Ralph W. Steen Library. Accessed August 20, 2017. https://library.sfasu.edu/help.

———. "SFA 101." Accessed August 25, 2017. http://www.sfasu.edu/sfa101/.

Tinto, Vincent. "Dropout from Higher Education: A Theoretical Synthesis of Recent Research." *Review of Educational Research* 45, no. 1 (1975): 89–125.

VanHaitsma, Pamela. "New Pedagogical Engagements with Archives: Student Inquiry and Composing in Digital Spaces." *College English* 78, no. 1 (September 2015): 34–55.

Vetter, Matthew A. "Archive 2.0: What Composition Students and Academic Libraries Can Gain from Digital-Collaborative Pedagogies." *Composition Studies* 42, no. 1 (2014): 35–53.

Victor, Paul Jr., Justin Otto, and Charles Mutschler. "Assessment of Library Instruction on Undergraduate Student Success in a Documents-Based Research Course: The Benefits of Librarian, Archivist and Faculty Collaboration." *Collaborative Librarianship* 5, no. 3 (2013): 154–76.

Zoellner, Kate. "Exploring Undergraduate Student Experiences with Information Literacy." *Performance Measurements and Metrics* 17, no. 3 (2016): 241–51. https://doi.org/10.1108/PMM-07-2016-0032.

Section 1

Title: Growing Our Field Evidence: Succession Planning for Sustainable Information Literacy Assessment

Abstract: Succession planning is not an unfamiliar concept in libraries. We often develop members of our profession to take the helm when it's time for the current leaders to step down or move on. However, the concept of succession planning is also useful for thinking about information literacy assessment tools. What works now might not work in a few years, and we need to be ready to move swiftly and strategically. This chapter will provide a case study of how one small regional campus of a large research university applied the concept of succession planning to information literacy assessment tools.

Keywords: planning, collaboration, assessment tools, agility

Project focus: information literacy assessment

Results made or will make case for: a strategic plan or process, improvements in teaching

Data needed: student demographics, responses to an information literacy assessment tool

Methodology: quantitative, evaluation or survey

Project duration: between 1 and 3 years

Tool(s) utilized: proprietary transition survey, proprietary information literacy assessment tool, data analysis software (STATA)

Cost estimate: $2,000–$5,000

Type of institution: regional campus of a large, state-related research university

Institution enrollment: < 5,000

Highest level of education: bachelor's

CC BY NC ND

Chapter 2

Growing Our Field Evidence

Succession Planning for Sustainable Information Literacy Assessment

Amanda L. Folk

Succession planning is a familiar concept in libraries. At both the institutional and national levels, we often think about how we can encourage and develop members of our profession to take the helm when it is time for the current leaders to step down or move on. However, the concept of succession planning is also useful for thinking about information literacy assessment tools. What works now might not work in a few years, and we need to be ready to move swiftly and strategically when it is time to rely on a new and sustainable assessment tool. This chapter will provide a case study of how one small regional campus of a large research university applied succession planning as a heuristic for proactively thinking about the sustainability of information literacy assessment.

Context

For several years, the University of Pittsburgh, including its four regional campuses, relied on a single proprietary information literacy assessment tool. Despite the focus on assessment at all of the university's campuses, it was unclear that the use of this tool provided any return on the University Library System's (ULS) investment, and there were preliminary discussions about whether to continue assessing information literacy in this way. Ultimately, the ULS decided to stop using the proprietary assessment tool for several reasons, including the response rate at each campus, the cost of the tool, the currency of the questions, the length of time it took the students to complete, and the fact that the ULS was able to access the resulting data only in the aggregate. This created an interesting situation in which the ULS decided to stop using the proprietary assessment tool, but the Pitt-Greensburg campus,* among other schools and regional campuses, valued the assessment data that resulted from its implementation.

With this in mind, the ULS agreed to work with interested librarians across the university to examine alternative information literacy assessment tools for a pilot. After reviewing several tools, the ULS opted to pilot the Higher Education Data Sharing Consortium (HEDS) Research Practices Survey because it would take the students about fifteen to twenty minutes to complete, had different survey administration options, asked current questions, and examined both information literacy skills and research behaviors, and the ULS would have access to the raw data.

Given that this was a pilot, it was not clear if this information literacy assessment tool would be supported in the long term, particularly on an annual basis. The Pitt-Greensburg campus, however, wanted to have some kind of information literacy assessment data collected on an annual or regular basis, even if it was on a smaller scale. At the same time, the Millstein Library librarians† at Pitt-Greensburg were interested in developing a more programmatic approach to our information literacy teaching and learning activities, including the development of a campus-specific definition of information literacy and the identification of tiered learning outcomes.[1] We knew that the availability of current information literacy assessment data would be critical to developing learning outcomes that were appropriate for our student population, as well as for revising and refining them over time. This meant that the Millstein Library librarians needed to find a scalable and sustainable method of capturing assessment data that would be meaningful to the library, the campus administration, and the faculty. In terms of sustainability and scalability, a small-scale survey seemed to be the best way to capture this kind of data across all levels of undergraduate students. However, having seen low response rates, particularly from upper-level students, for the proprietary assessment tool year after year, we knew that motivating the students to respond would be difficult. Although we had some funds to purchase incentives, that was not necessarily the best route to take for continued sustainability. At this point, we knew we needed to start thinking about what would succeed the HEDS survey if it was

---

*According to 2016–2017 provisional release data from the Integrated Postsecondary Education Data System (IPEDS), Pitt-Greensburg's student enrollment head count was just over 1,600 (about 1,550 FTE) undergraduate students. The campus reported employing seventy-six faculty. Pitt-Greensburg is an undergraduate-only campus.

†The Millstein Library employees four librarians, including the director, and four paraprofessional staff.

no longer available as an assessment tool so we could move swiftly and strategically if and when the time came.

Around the same time that we were piloting the implementation of the HEDS survey and brainstorming sustainable alternatives, the Association of College and Research Libraries (ACRL) was accepting applications for its third cohort of the Assessment in Action (AiA): Academic Libraries and Student Success program, which was part of the association's Value of Academic Libraries initiative. The purpose of this program was to support collaborative assessment projects between academic librarians and non-library colleagues. Each team consisted of a librarian team leader and at least two non-library colleagues, preferably one of whom was an administrator. The Millstein Library added some information literacy assessment questions to MAP-Works surveys that the campus administered annually in previous years, so the AiA program seemed to be a great opportunity to pitch a more formal and long-term collaboration with the campus for smaller-scale, sustainable information literacy assessment.

MAP-Works is an interactive student success tool that helps students make a successful transition to college, creates opportunities for early intervention, connects students to campus resources, and realigns students' expectations to improve their learning experience. MAP-Works uses survey, institutional data, and input by staff and faculty to create individualized risk indicators and reports for each student.[2] MAP-Works provides transition and checkup surveys that can be administered in both the fall and spring semesters to all levels of undergraduate students. The surveys include questions related to academic behaviors, campus involvement, institutional commitment, and living situation, and institutions also have the opportunity to add institution-specific questions. Students get a customized report based on their answers to the survey questions that highlight strengths and weaknesses and provide some guidance, which can be used to discuss with instructors or advisors.

When Pitt-Greensburg first implemented MAP-Works several years earlier, it used the tool only with incoming first-year students. Over time, however, the campus expanded the use of the tool, including the surveys, to all students. Since the campus was already administering MAP-Works surveys to all students and offering incentives for participation, it seemed to be a practical way to ask information literacy assessment questions using the available spaces for institution-specific questions. In addition, the MAP-Works surveys would allow us to think about analyzing students' basic information literacy skills with the other data collected in the survey, as well as looking at participating students' responses longitudinally.

Initial conversations with Sheila Confer, the colleague in charge of coordinating MAP-Works activities at Pitt-Greensburg, revealed that despite offers, other departments were not taking advantage of the institution-specific questions. Because of this, we negotiated using about ten of the available questions. I previously developed a handful of information literacy questions for a study that I conducted with library student employees, and we decided to review these questions, revise them when appropriate, and then add them to the MAP-Works survey.[3] We ended up adding nine questions to the fall 2015 first-year transition survey and the fall 2015 checkup survey for non-first-year students (see appendix 2.1). Once we had a plan of action in place, we completed an institutional review board (IRB) expedited application so we could share the results publicly. After collected data throughout the fall 2015 semester, I analyzed the data using Stata in the spring 2016 semester.

The HEDS Research Practices Survey was also administered on the Pitt-Greensburg campus, as well as other regional campuses, in fall 2015 to incoming first-year students and second-year students. The ULS assessment team analyzed the results of the survey for all of the participating campuses, but I analyzed the Greensburg-specific answers using Stata.

Communicating Results and Impact

The ULS assessment team analyzed the data collected from the fall 2015 administration of the HEDS survey at several regional campuses and compiled a report based on the analysis of the aggregated data. The ULS made these reports publicly available,[4] but I also sent them directly to Pitt-Greensburg campus administrators and to the Millstein Library librarians. This is how the results of the previous information literacy assessment tool were disseminated, and so this method of communication was expected. The report included an executive summary that included the major findings of the survey administration, including overall performance and students' information literacy strengths and weaknesses. The remainder of the report included many bar graphs that compared the University of Pittsburgh students to students from the other HEDS sample institutions.

In addition to the multi-campus reports, I developed two reports, one for incoming first-year students and another for second-year students, based on the Greensburg-specific results of the HEDS survey administration, since this was the data in which the Greensburg campus administrators were most interested. These reports also contained executive summaries that included information about the samples, as well as the salient findings related to participants' library usage habits, their research practices, their information literacy self-perceptions, and the results of the information literacy skills assessments. In the remainder of the reports, I presented detailed information about students' responses to each question, and I created a grading scale for performance on the information literacy skills assessment portion with a graph depicting the distribution of grades (see table 2.1). As with the ULS assessment team's report, I also sent these reports directly to Pitt-Greensburg campus administrators and the Millstein librarians.[*]

---

[*]For both the MAP-Works and Greensburg-specific HEDS survey reports, it was not unusual for either the Vice President of Academic Affairs (VPAA) or the Assistant Vice President of Academic Affairs (AVPAA) to call and briefly discuss the findings. Both the VPAA and AVPAA used the findings in their own assessment reports, including reports related to accreditation.

Table 2.1

HEDS Fall 2015 First-Year Student Information Literacy Assessment Grades

		# of Students	% of Students
A	(95–100%)	0	0.0%
A–	(90–94%)	0	0.0%
B+	(87–89%)	0	0.0%
B	(84–86%)	1	0.4%
B–	(80–83%)	0	0.0%
C+	(77–79%)	3	1.2%
C	(74–76%)	5	1.9%
C–	(70–73%)	7	2.7%
D+	(67–69%)	7	2.7%
D	(64–66%)	16	6.2%
D–	(60–63%)	20	7.7%
F	(below 60%)	240	77.2%

Note: Incoming first-year students could score a possible 29 points on the information literacy skills assessment portion of the HEDS survey. The mean score for incoming first-year students was 14.4 points, which is a 50%. Just over 77% of the incoming first-year students would have received an F grade (below 60%). No incoming first-year students received more than 25 points or an 86%.

Since the use of the MAP-Works survey for information literacy assessment was limited to Pitt-Greensburg, I was solely responsible for analyzing the data and communicating the findings. Given that this was a new initiative, the format of the report was slightly different from the HEDS reports. This report gave a brief introduction to the partnership and the initiative, as well as a summary of how I analyzed the data and some of the limitations of this assessment of skills. I felt that transparency regarding limitations was particularly important if we were going to consider this as a potential long-term replacement or supplement to the use of a proprietary assessment tool. Three different student cohorts were included in the MAP-Works assessment—first-year students (cohort 1), second-year students (cohort 2), and third- and fourth-year students (cohort 3). I provided a mean score for each cohort and indicated that the progressive increase in scores from the first-year students to the upper-level students was statistically significant based on hypothesis testing. I also included data on how each cohort answered each of the questions included on the MAP-Works survey (see table 2.2). This report, like the HEDS survey reports, was shared directly with Pitt-Greensburg administrators.

Table 2.2
Example of Question-Level Reporting for MAP-Works Assessment
Question 2. Which of the following is characteristic of a peer-reviewed or scholarly article?

	Cohort 1	**Cohort 2**	**Cohort 3**
A lot of glossy, colorful pictures	3 (0.80)	1 (1.85)	1 (0.76)
Easy to read using simple, everyday language	122 (32.36)	12 (22.22)	23 (17.56)
A bibliography or reference list	*159 (42.18)*	*39 (72.22)*	*101 (77.10)*
I don't know	90 (24.06)	1 (1.85)	6 (4.58)
No answer	3 (0.80)	1 (1.85)	9 (0.00)
N =	377	54	131

I felt that there would be wider interest in the findings of both the HEDS survey and the MAP-Works assessment, particularly among the Pitt-Greensburg faculty. With the support of the faculty-driven Community for the Advancement of Teaching (CAT), I proposed a session related to information literacy for the annual May faculty development programming, which campus administrators also attend. The contextual frame for this workshop was the work that the Millstein Library librarians had been doing related to developing a local and programmatic approach to information literacy, including the development of a campus-specific definition and a statement of philosophy and practice.[5] I then used salient findings from both the HEDS survey and the MAP-Works assessment to talk about what we know about our students' information literacy skills and beginning a conversation about how teaching faculty and librarians can collaborate around information literacy. Even though the Millstein Library librarians felt engaged with the faculty and students already, this session was intended to spark deeper conversations about information literacy collaborations.

In terms of succession planning, it was important to present the results of both surveys and talk about the differences between the two so that faculty and administrators understood the strengths and weaknesses of the data gathered through the administration of each survey. I was transparent about the fact that the HEDS survey may not be administered annually in the future and that the MAP-Works data would be used in its place. In addition, I asked attendees to sign up if they wanted to be added to a shared folder on Box that contained the Millstein Library's documentation related to information literacy, including the assessment reports for both the HEDS and MAP-Works surveys. This would provide wider distribution of the assessment work we were doing targeted initially at a captive audience. Almost every participant signed up to be added to this folder.

In addition to sharing our findings at the campus level, we presented a poster at the American Library Association (ALA) Annual Conference in June 2016 through our participation in the AiA program. This was an opportunity to share our experience using MAP-Works as a medium for information literacy assessment.[6]

Leveraging the Findings

After the fall 2015 semester, I intended to continue collecting data through both MAP-Works and the HEDS surveys for as long as possible. A benefit of both of these assessment tools was that we could collect longitudinal data on individual students. Even though a longitudinal sample would have been small and the participants would have been self-selected, it would have provided some insight into whether or not individual students' information literacy skills progressively develop and by how much. In addition to gaining some insight into information literacy skill development, the Millstein Library librarians intended to not only use these results for targeted outreach and lesson planning, but also to begin developing tiered, programmatic information literacy learning outcomes. In other words, we wanted to use this data to help us think about what we could reasonably expect our students to do and know after their first year of college and upon graduation. Developing these kinds of learning outcomes would help to guide our outreach to faculty, inform decisions about which courses we wanted to partner with and how we would partner with them, and allow us to develop course-level learning outcomes for instruction with appropriate activities. Due to the departure of two librarians, including the library's director, this goal currently remains unfulfilled.

During the 2015–16 academic year, Pitt-Greensburg decided to start looking at other retention and student success tools and ultimately decided to switch to Beacon to better fit the long-term needs of the campus. Although this would not ultimately affect the Millstein Library's ability to ask information literacy assessment questions through this medium, the surveys that Beacon offered were different from the ones that the campus had been using through MAP-Works. In the grand scheme of things, the major consequence of this would be the Millstein Library's ability to examine the development of information literacy skills in conjunction with other non-library-related variables of interest, such as academic self-efficacy or study skills. Although this was of interest to us down the road, the primary purpose for using a tool like MAP-Works for information literacy assessment was not affected by this change in tool.

Reflection

One reason that we were able to partner with the campus to use MAP-Works as a tool for information literacy assessment was that the Millstein Library was already viewed as a trusted partner. Built through several decades of collaborative work around student success, the Millstein Library already had a great reputation with administrators, faculty, and staff at Pitt-Greensburg. In other words, this collaboration was an extension of existing relationships; this was not a new relationship that we were attempting to establish or to build with campus partners. Furthermore, both the campus administration and faculty recognized information literacy as a key competency that was relevant to the campus's liberal arts mission, and the phrase "information-based, global society" appears in the Pitt-Greensburg mission statement.[7]

On the other hand, the Millstein Library needed to maintain this status as a trusted partner. The campus wanted students' information literacy skills to be assessed on a regular basis, but there was no guarantee that the ULS would be willing to invest in proprietary assessment tools for each campus, particularly on an annual basis. Using succession planning as a heuristic for thinking about the future allowed the Millstein Library to be proactive and responsive to the campus's needs, while also giving us time to explore several options before being in a situation in which we had to quickly or hastily react with minimal resources.

In terms of long-term sustainability, I think it would be critical to evaluate the questions that we included on the MAP-Works survey. In particular, it would be helpful to recruit colleagues at the University of Pittsburgh who are trained in designing valid and reliable assessments of learning to ensure that we are asking the right kinds of questions and that they are high-quality. Because I have no training in designing assessments of learning, I was not comfortable completely relying on this method of assessment and wanted to continue using the HEDS survey to complement the locally developed questions that we added to the MAP-Works surveys for as long as possible.

In addition, multiple-choice assessments of learning are appropriate and helpful tools, but they are not the be-all and end-all in terms of assessing learning. Though time is always a limiting factor, reflecting upon this experience and how we intended to use the data we collected, it would be appropriate to think about how to integrate authentic assessments of students' work into our information literacy assessment portfolio. For example, beginning a conversation with English composition colleagues about codeveloping an information literacy rubric to apply to final papers in College Composition 2 courses would be an excellent complement to the data that we were gathering with the HEDS and MAP-Works surveys. One advantage of this kind of authentic assessment is that it is not tool-based, and we would need to garner support from only a handful of instructors. If this endeavor was successful, we could push for applying a similar strategy to capstone projects, which all Pitt-Greensburg students are required to complete prior to graduation. While the monetary cost might be low, there is a significant cost in terms of time when using authentic assessments.

Appendix 2.1

Information Literacy Questions Added to the MAP-Works Surveys

Which of these options best describes what a peer-reviewed or scholarly article is?

___ An article that your peers said was interesting and helpful for their papers.

___ An article written by an expert in his/her field reviewed by other experts prior to publication.

___ An article that your professor recommends that you use for your assignment.

___ I don't know.

Which of the following is characteristic of a peer-reviewed or scholarly article?

___ A lot of glossy, colorful pictures

___ Easy to read using simple, everyday language

___ A bibliography or reference list

___ I don't know

Your professor says that you may not cite an encyclopedia as a source in your paper. Why might you still consult an encyclopedia?

___ Because encyclopedias give background information on many topics.

___ Because encyclopedias aren't written by scholars or experts.

___ Because encyclopedias aren't available online, so the information is credible.

___ I don't know.

Your professor assigned a 3–5 page paper about health care reform. The topic "health care reform" is…

___ too broad for the assigned page length.

___ just right for the assigned page length.

___ too narrow for the assigned page length.

___ I don't know.

In which of the following cases would you use "OR" to combine search terms when searching for articles?

___ In order to find articles that address either of my search terms

___ In order to find articles that address both of my search terms

___ In order to find articles that discuss one of my search terms but not the other

___ I don't know.

From the options below, which questions should you ask yourself when evaluating the quality of an article?

___ Who is the author? How old is the article? Does the author cite the sources used?

___ How long is the article? Does the article have pictures? Does the information match what is written on Wikipedia?

___ Can I get this article on Google? How small is the print? Is the article easy to understand?

___ I don't know.

When writing a paper, if you take another person's idea and put it into your own words but don't directly quote it, do you still need to cite it?

___ Yes

___ No

___ Sometimes

___ I don't know.

When you take another person's idea and summarize it in your own words, what it is called?

___ Paragraphing

___ Paraphrasing

___ Paraquoting

___ I don't know.

You are writing a paper about the Civil War. Which of the following is NOT a primary source?

___ A diary of a Civil War soldier

___ An article written in 2001 about the Civil War

___ A newspaper article written during the Civil War

___ I don't know.

Notes

1. "Ask Your Librarians—Greensburg Campus: Information Literacy," last updated February 27, 2018, University of Pittsburgh Course and Subject Guides, http://pitt.libguides.com/millsteinlib/infolit. (Note: In addition to the author of this chapter, Anna Mary Williford, Kelly Safin [née Bradish], Renee Kiner, and Amanda E. Miller were integral in developing the definition of information literacy, as well as the statement of philosophy and practice.)
2. This text was written by Sheila Confer for a poster presented at the 2016 ALA Annual Conference. See Amanda Folk, Jackie Horrall, and Sheila Confer, "Assessing Students' Information Literacy Skills Using MAP-Works" (poster presented at the American Library Association Annual Conference, Orlando, FL, June 23–28, 2016), https://www.slideshare.net/millsteinlib/information-literacy-pittgreensburg.
3. Amanda L. Folk, "How Well Are We Preparing Them? An Assessment of First-Year Library Students Assistants' Information Literacy Skills," *College & Undergraduate Libraries* 21, no. 2 (2014): 177–92.

4. "Assessment," University of Pittsburgh Library System, accessed May 15, 2017, http://www.library.pitt.edu/assessment.
5. "What Do We Know about the Information Literacy Skills of Pitt-Greensburg Students," accessed May 15, 2017, https://www.slideshare.net/millsteinlib/assessing-students-information-literacy-skills-using-mapworks.
6. Folk, Horrall, and Confer, "Assessing Students' Information Literacy Skills."
7. "Mission and History," University of Pittsburgh Greensburg, accessed May 15, 2017, http://www.greensburg.pitt.edu/about/mission-statement-and-campus-history.

Bibliography

"Ask the A Team @ Pitt-Greensburg: Information Literacy." February 27, 2018, University of Pittsburgh Course and Subject Guides. http://pitt.libguides.com/millsteinlib/infolit.

Folk, Amanda L. "How Well Are We Preparing Them? An Assessment of First-Year Library Students Assistants' Information Literacy Skills," *College & Undergraduate Libraries* 21, no. 2 (2014): 177–92.

Folk, Amanda, Jackie Horrall, and Sheila Confer. "Assessing Students' Information Literacy Skills Using MAP-Works." Poster presented at the American Library Association Annual Conference, Orlando, FL, June 23–28, 2016. https://www.slideshare.net/millsteinlib/assessing-students-information-literacy-skills-using-mapworks.

University of Pittsburgh Greensburg. "Mission and History." University of Pittsburgh Greensburg. Accessed May 15, 2017. http://www.greensburg.pitt.edu/about/mission-statement-and-campus-history.

University of Pittsburgh Library System. "Assessment." University of Pittsburgh. Accessed May 15, 2017. http://www.library.pitt.edu/assessment.

"What Do We Know about the Information Literacy Skills of Pitt-Greensburg Students." Accessed May 15, 2017. https://www.slideshare.net/millsteinlib/information-literacy-pittgreensburg.

Title: Connecting Student Success and Library Services

Abstract: The University of South Florida Sarasota-Manatee (USFSM) is a regional campus of the University of South Florida system. At the end of each library instruction session, students complete a one-minute paper highlighting what they learned in the session. Librarians met with USFSM Institutional Effectiveness to discuss using three years' worth of this collected qualitative data to determine the impact of library instruction on student success. This study will be ongoing, with an initial determination of impact within the next year. The proposed study is similar to a recent study by Mary O'Kelly at Grand Valley State University.

Keywords: assessment, qualitative data, student success, library instruction

Project focus: assessment methodologies, techniques, or practices; information literacy assessment; data use and technology; assessment concepts and/or management

Results made or will make case for: proof of library impact and value

Data needed: course demographics (title, section, instructor, etc.)

Methodology: qualitative, evaluation or survey

Project duration: ongoing (continuous feedback loop)

Tool(s) utilized Google Forms

Cost estimate: < $100

Type of institution: university—public

Institution enrollment: < 5,000

Highest level of education: master's/professional degree

Chapter 3

Connecting Student Success and Library Services

Diane Fulkerson and Jessica Szempruch

Context

The University of South Florida Sarasota-Manatee (USFSM) is a regional campus of the University of South Florida (USF) system with an enrollment of approximately 2,000 students. As of the 2015–2016 academic year, USF Sarasota-Manatee has 1,801 undergraduate students, 182 graduate students, and 88 non-degree-seeking students. The campus employees 85 full-time faculty and 62 adjuncts in addition to 12 graduate assistants, 53 student assistants, and 129 administrative and staff positions.[1] Library staffing consists of two librarians and two part-time employees. The USFSM campus does not have its own physical library, but students, faculty, and staff have access to the physical and electronic collections of the USF Library System, which serves over 50,000 students over its three campuses.

In September 2013, USFSM hired a new Faculty Coordinator of Library Services, Diane Fulkerson, to oversee and improve the library services offered on the campus. One area determined to be in need of significant improvement was library instruction. Unfortunately, few statistics were available to determine library instruction coverage for dates prior to Fulkerson's appointment, and assessment data was missing. This missing information posed an immediate concern for Fulkerson as the Association of College and Research Libraries (ACRL) *Value of Academic Libraries* report stresses the importance for academic and research libraries to develop documentation to demonstrate their value to their respective institutions.[2] With this in mind, improvement plans were immediately set in place, and spring semester of 2014 offered the first full semester of opportunities to promote library instruction to faculty.

At the time Fulkerson was hired to oversee library services at USFSM, the campus did not have a library instruction program in place. As the campus's sole librarian, she began building the instruction program by soliciting faculty to voluntarily include library instruction sessions within their courses. At USFSM, faculty request library instruction for their classes; in-class library instruction is not mandated. At the start of each semester, an email is sent to all faculty, including adjuncts, inviting them to include a library instruction session for their class. Spring semester of 2014 resulted in ten instruction sessions, reflecting faculty who understood the value of including a library instruction session for their course. This small number of instruction sessions, led by a solo librarian, was a crucial first step to building a well-regarded library instruction program at USFSM. The number of sessions has continued to grow each semester following these first sessions.

At present, USFSM has two librarians actively involved in library instruction. The basic assessment process developed from the first sessions in 2014 has remained consistent to today. At the end of each instruction session, students complete an anonymous "one-minute paper" evaluation. The librarian or the professor collects the one-minute paper at the end of the session. In these evaluations, students provide written feedback to the presenting librarian with answers to three prompts: three things they learned during the session; a personal reflection on how they will incorporate what they learned into their studies; and a final question using a five-point Likert scale (strongly agree to strongly disagree) to indicate they understand what was taught during the session. The Likert scale is shown in figure 3.1.

I am confident I understand most of the material presented in this session.

○ Strongly Agree

○ Agree

○ Neutral

○ Disagree

○ Strongly Disagree

Figure 3.1
Likert scale used in "one-minute paper" assessment.

The USFSM librarians continued to collect the evaluation forms every semester and used the responses to make immediate improvements to instruction. For example, as evidenced in figure 3.2, a breakdown by percentages indicated the majority of students strongly agree or agree they are confident they understand most of the material presented in the library instruction session. Once the librarians were able to determine the percentage of students who felt they understood the material covered in library instruction sessions, the librarians were able to confirm that library instruction sessions were effective.

I am confident I understand most of the material presented in this session

1,300 responses

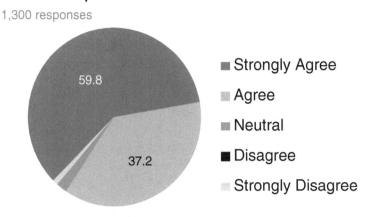

- ■ Strongly Agree
- ■ Agree
- ■ Neutral
- ■ Disagree
- ■ Strongly Disagree

Figure 3.2
Student confidence findings from "one-minute paper" assessments.

However, the librarians were still unsure how to analyze the results more formally to determine long-term trends. Semester improvements were implemented by the librarians; much of the qualitative data was used anecdotal. The completed evaluation forms sat in a box until the librarians could determine how to best analyze the results.

Due to the qualitative nature of students' responses, the data needed coding prior to analysis. A small librarian staff and limited funding meant that creative exploration of options was necessary. USF has an institutional license for ATLAS.ti qualitative analysis software; however, it proved to be extremely time-consuming to code the data using the ATLAS.ti software. The librarians found the solution in a 2016 article by Vaughn and Turner: how a thematic coding scheme and SurveyMonkey software could be used to analyze qualitative data.[3]

Inspired by this article, the USFSM librarians created a survey in Google Forms to code the data. Based on a review of the handwritten student assessments, the librarians created broad thematic categories to code the data. The broad thematic categories used included both items and actions, such as databases, citations, critical thinking, and evaluating sources. The coding for the data was fairly basic, based on the free responses from students who attended the instruction session. A small sample of the broad categories is provided in figure 3.3. Using these broad categories allowed for quicker processing of the assessment forms.

Three things you learned

☐ Databases   ☐ Developing research question
☐ Searching   ☐ Truncation
☐ RefWorks   ☐ Find It@USF
☐ Keywords   ☐ Citations

Figure 3.3
Thematic categories for coding "one-minute paper" responses.

An analysis of the survey responses indicated databases and developing search strategies were two of the top three things students learned in our library instruction sessions. Table 3.1 lists the top ten responses from the assessment forms.

Table 3.1
Top Ten Responses in Rank Order

Databases	55.5%
Searching	56%
Accessing Library Resources	29.3%
RefWorks	25.9%
ILL	14.7%
Evaluating Sources	14.6%
Citations	14.1%
Library Services @ USFSM	11.6%
Peer-Reviewed Articles	9.2%
Find It@USF	7.5%

The librarians manually entered the information from each of the one-minute paper evaluations. This was the most time-consuming part of the project as there were only two librarians to input the three-year backlog of data; however, the creation of the survey made data entry much easier and faster. With all of the historical data processed, staff now enters data from current instruction sessions immediately following each session. To date, the Google Forms survey contains almost 1,400 evaluation entries. Starting from the small number of sessions (ten) in the inaugural semester, the number of instruction sessions each year has grown. USFSM averages thirty-three instruction sessions per academic year with an average of 457 student participants. Table 3.2 lists the data for the academic years 2013–2016.

Table 3.2
2013–2016 Data by Academic Year, Sessions, and Participants

Academic Year	Number of Sessions	Number of Participants
2013–14	32	450
2014–15	31	378
2015–16	35	544

Overall, Google Forms proved to be a tool well-suited to the needs of this project. It is currently free for use; functional for multiple users working simultaneously; and, like Survey Monkey, provided the capability for an in-depth analysis of the data, which could be shared with university stakeholders, including USFSM's Office of Institutional Research and Effectiveness (OIRE).

In addition to the one-minute paper evaluation data, the librarians created a supplemental spreadsheet to record the course information, course reference number, date and time of the instruction session, librarian who taught the session, professor teaching the course, material covered in the session, and number of students in attendance. Due to privacy concerns, librarians do not take attendance to indicate presence of specific students at instruction sessions, and students complete the assessment form anonymously. Table 3.3 shows a sample of the data shared with OIRE.

Table 3.3
Supplemental Course and Training Data Provided

Session date	CRN	Course	Section	Professor	Librarian	Content	Surveys completed
10/31/13	88501	ENL 3251	521	Cavedo	Fulkerson	Library databases and citations	8
1/4/14	23653	MAR 6158	521	Lennon	Fulkerson	Library databases for International Marketing and citations	6
1/6/14	17389	MAR 3823	591	Lennon	Fulkerson	Library databases for Marketing Research and citations	21
1/9/14	15880	CCJ 3701	521	Ngo	Fulkerson	Citations, library databases and annotated bibliography	14
1/14/14	13815	PSY 3213	521	Aurilio	Fulkerson	Concept mapping, developing a topic, and databases	16
1/16/14	23069	PSY 3213	522	Reich	Fulkerson	Developing a topic and databases	6
1/21/14	13028	CCJ 3024	591	Scott	Fulkerson	Developing a topic and databases	21
1/28/14	19766	ENG 4934	521	Lipscomb	Fulkerson	Databases	5
1/30/14	23467	EVR 2001	522	Freeman	Fulkerson	Environmental studies databases and developing a topic	32
1/30/14	23148	EVR 2001	521	Freeman	Fulkerson	Environmental studies databases and developing a topic	11

With coding completed, the USFSM librarians then explored how to make connections between library instruction and student success. On September 28, 2016, the librarians attended a webinar presented by Mary O'Kelly from Grand Valley State University wherein she discussed her quantitative research on the connection between student retention and library instruction. O'Kelly's study found the highest retention correlations in freshman and graduate student populations who received library instruction compared to those who did not receive any library instruction. By comparing three years of data (current enrollment, academic course ± library instruction, and next semester enrollment), she demonstrated a small but statistically significant increase ($p = .0001$) in retention of students who received library instruction with their courses, with results continuing to grow in magnitude as the study continued. O'Kelly provided slides on the data collection, methodology, and results of the Grand Valley State University study to the attendees.[4]

Inspired to develop a similar study based on the quantitative data collected from the USFSM library instruction sessions, the USFSM librarians met with the USFSM OIRE to explore the possibility of replicating the study on the USFSM campus. After reviewing O'Kelly's protocol from the Grand Valley State University study and meeting with the librarians, the USFSM OIRE determined O'Kelly's study was statistically reliable and the USFSM librarians had collected the necessary comparative data to replicate the study using USFSM's reenrollment data, academic courses, and students who did and did not receive library instruction. We believe analysis of USFSM's quantitative data will show similar correlations to that at Grand Valley State University.

Communicating Results and Impact

The librarians scheduled a second appointment with two key players from USFSM OIRE, Laura Hoffman (Director) and Dr. Bonnie Jones (Assistant Vice President). During this meeting, Hoffman and Jones asked questions regarding the methods USFSM used to collect data about their instruction sessions. Hoffman also requested a detailed spreadsheet of supplementary information regarding the instruction sessions to complement the USFSM library's qualitative data. Using the historical information from Springshare's LibAnalytics (utilized from March 2016 to present) and Compendium's Desk Tracker (utilized from September 2013 through February 2016), librarians provided detailed library instruction data on course code, number, and section; professor name; librarian name; date; location; duration; content; and number of students present. The information provided by the librarians matched the data collected by OIRE. OIRE found this data especially appealing at this time as USFSM is poised to confer degrees upon its first class of first-time-in-college (FTIC) students. USFSM has tracked the FTIC students heavily since their enrollment at USFSM in fall 2013, and the information collected from the library sessions can be compared to the already collected OIRE data. OIRE is particularly interested in the FTIC student population as they are a first for the university, which has traditionally served only transfer student populations, and thus may be at greater risk for issues with persistence, timely completion, and retention. Comparing the information from library instruction sessions with other data points collected by OIRE will allow USFSM to establish a correlation between student retention and library instruction.

USFSM OIRE was very excited about the opportunity of working on the data analysis for this project. USFSM Library Services provides OIRE with the data and is not involved in the analysis, as OIRE already has institutional review board (IRB) approval to analyze student data and the staff to conduct the analysis. OIRE saw it as an extension of its work on assessment for accreditation by the Southern Association of Colleges and Schools (SACS), the regional body for accreditation of degree-granting higher education institutions in the southern states, and meeting metrics of the Performance-Based Funding Model required by the State University System of Florida Board of Governors. The library instruction data, combined with a variety of data points the USFSM OIRE gathers each academic year, will help the university to create a more complete picture on how it may improve retention and continue to deliver necessary programs for students determined to be at-risk. The benefits to the USFSM campus could lead to additional funding through achievement of specific Performance-Based Metrics and increased retention through collaboration between Library Services and Student Services.

Leveraging the Findings

Using a process similar to the one used by O'Kelly,[5] OIRE analysis is currently ongoing with no stated time line for completion. Once it is analyzed, the inclusion of the library assessment data with other OIRE reports will provide senior leadership with a better understanding of the role of library instruction in student retention and help illustrate a potentially meaningful correlation between the library and student academic success.

As the USFSM campus continues to grow, this data will support expanding Library Services to increase the depth of available services. As an example, one area of current university-wide concern surrounds engaging and supporting distance-learning students. Although USFSM offers a number of courses and programs online, Library Services currently has little interaction with the students in either discrete online courses or primarily online programs. USFSM librarians have created robust LibGuides to share with distance-learning students. These LibGuides are linked directly through Canvas LMS course modules by individual professors. In addition, librarians are available for one-on-one consultations virtually or face-to-face with students and faculty. Otherwise, interaction is limited.

The SACS *Principles of Accreditation*, which stress the importance of equitable access provided at the same level for distance-learning students and on-campus students,[6] provide the impetus for our next study. Since USFSM Library Services hopes to continue to increase library instruction to online students, inclusion of data collected from participants in online library instruction sessions with face-to-face instruction sessions would assist USFSM librarians to determine next steps towards increasing valuable connections to students on and off campus. Further, comparison of outcomes of students who have library instruction in a face-to-face class versus online students who did not have an instruction session would help USFSM librarians advocate for the resources necessary to increase outreach to online faculty and students. The online instruction study, currently in its planning process, will use a similar model as our "one-minute paper" project and provide another component of a 360 degree assessment of the relationships between library instruction and student outcomes.

The one-minute paper requires students to identify the three most important concepts discussed in the library instruction session that are relevant to their research and how they will incorporate those ideas into their research. The majority of students indicate they will use the information shown during the instruction session for their research projects. Table 3.4 shows the five most common responses.

Table 3.4
Top Five "One-Minute Paper" Responses

Use information shown in class	45.2%
Research for course assignments	28.8%
Use databases shown in class	25.6%
Find reliable, useful, and credible sources	20.1%
How to cite information	14.4%

Students also identify concepts they did not completely understand and provide their contact information to schedule a research consultation. Our goal for the online "one-minute paper" study mirrors the face-to-face "one-minute paper" study: to determine if there is a correlation between students receiving library instruction and academic success. We will know more once OIRE has completed its analysis.

In addition, this type of data will help USFSM librarians play a larger role in meeting campus-wide strategic goals. The USFSM campus is in the implementation stage of its Quality Enhancement Plan (QEP) with SACS; the focus of the QEP is critical thinking. The ACRL Assessment in Action (AiA) projects clearly demonstrate that student retention improves with library instructional services, which assists students in establishing critical-thinking and problem-based learning skills necessary for academic coursework.[7]

Data from the one-minute evaluation project and new library projects currently underway will make it possible for Library Services to work with campus administrators to develop and support campus strategic goals and initiatives to meet the Florida Board of Governors Performance Based Funding Metrics. Supporting the connection between academic libraries and the role of high-impact practices on student retention, Adam Murray states that library deans or directors "tend to view library instruction as the element of the academic library most involved in high-impact practices, particularly for learning communities and collaborative assignments and projects."[8]

Results from this current study could provide USFSM Library Services with the opportunity and ability to integrate selected high-impact practices from the Association of American Colleges and Universities (AAC&U) into their library services and instruction. The USFSM librarians could collaborate with faculty to integrate library instruction into high-impact practices in writing-intensive courses, collaborative assignments and projects, undergraduate research, service learning and community-based learning, and capstone courses and projects.[9] In addition to meeting student success goals for the campus, such as critical thinking, that data will reinforce the earlier evidence of the effectiveness of library instruction to improve student retention. This in turn can provide new opportunities to work with faculty to design course assignments and incorporate library instruction into their syllabi.

Reflection

The most challenging aspect of the project thus far was determining the best method to code the raw data. After a search of the literature, the article by Vaughn and Turner stood out as the best option for a study of this scope and a data set of this size. Creating an online survey with broad categories made it easier for librarians to enter, code, and analyze the data. Coding was a time-consuming effort, as two librarians took the initiative to input data from the three-year backlog. Slight variations of student handwriting and meaning of word choice were overcome by the librarians, who had worked together to develop an effective game plan. Vaughn and Turner described how they created a well-defined code dictionary with their project team in order to ensure consensus regarding the coding process.[10] The small team processing the USFSM data did not require a full-scale code dictionary; rather, they created a robust controlled-vocabulary list in the Google Form. No matter the approach, this process showed the importance of having a small, dedicated contingent who have a full understanding of the goals of the project and the meaning of each code.

This study demonstrated the potential value of collecting qualitative assessment data from instruction sessions, even if there is not a specific plan yet in place on how to use that data or apply the findings. Though the qualitative survey information had not been collated formally and compared to other institutional data, librarians did not let the information go to waste. The librarians used the raw assessment data twice: first by reviewing the "one-minute papers" after every session to make immediate improvements following the specific instruction sessions, and then by saving the completed papers for further analysis, such as that of this ongoing study. Qualitative data is important to making short- and long-term improvements to services and programs. It often provides additional information not easily obtained through quantitative data. Qualitative data provides researchers with information regarding beliefs, values, feelings, and motivations that underlie behaviors, whether these behaviors reflect information-seeking models, information behavior models, or critical-thinking models. Qualitative data may also help illuminate the relationships between cognitive processes, actions, and knowledge acquisition.[11]

ACRL's *Value of Academic Libraries* report notes, "In many cases, data exists that can link libraries to retention and graduation rates, but these correlations are not easily investigated."[12] A review of the literature indicates there is not a standard tool kit of evaluation and outcomes measures by which libraries collect and evaluate nonnumerical data related to library services. Thorpe, Lukes, Bever, and He suggest that standardization across library institutions could prove beneficial to understanding the continued impact of our work on student success.[13] Standardizing data collection would help academic libraries replicate studies that focus on the library's role in student success. Steven Scheuler in his article states, "By actively participating in assessment initiatives, librarians can offer their services and improve student engagement in higher education."[14]

The study and analysis of qualitative library assessment gathered by the USFSM librarians and analyzed by OIRE will help Library Services to expand its collaboration with Student Services and Student Engagement. As stated previously, this is slated to be an ongoing study. For the USFSM librarians to have the ability to run analyses with discrete student, course, and registration data may require specific permissions and training that may require negotiation with OIRE and the Registrar's Office, among others.

Recently, the campus created a Persistence Committee to reach out to at-risk students who are in jeopardy of being placed on academic probation or not persisting toward timely graduation; campus focus thus far has been on the aforementioned FTIC population. Library Services is a member of the committee, and other members of the committee refer students who need research assistance to the librarians for additional support. Participation in this committee helps Library Services to connect with students but also indicates that the campus understands the value of the services it provides to students.

OIRE is currently most interested in following the data from the fall 2013 FTIC cohort. Future research opportunities include evaluating the success of upper-level students completing capstone courses within their major, comparing those who did and did not receive library instruction. Including the capstone courses would provide an additional level of analysis with our FTIC cohort because students in the cohort in all likelihood had library instruction in their lower-level classes.

Many of the senior seminars at USFSM include a capstone project that includes a research component. Faculty teaching the senior seminars, especially in the social sciences, frequently include a library session as part of their classes. While many of the students may have had previous library instruction, the faculty understands the importance of additional instruction sessions for the course to focus on the capstone project. They feel it is essential for students to have a "refresher" instruction session to help them develop their topics and identify resources. As stated previously, including capstone projects in the analysis will provide the USFSM librarians the opportunity to integrate high-impact practices into courses and library instruction and to assess the pedagogical components of library instruction.

Even though the "one-minute paper" project is a work in progress, it serves as an example of analyzing data from library instruction sessions to determine a correlation between student retention and library services. The USFSM study replicates the work of Mary O'Kelly at Grand Valley State University on a smaller scale that did not require any financial resources. It was time-consuming to input the data from the one-minute papers, but it resulted in the librarians being able to use the data to develop future studies and directions for the library instruction program. This study also provides OIRE with additional data to track the retention of the campus's first cohort of FTIC freshman students.

Librarians at USFSM see this as an opportunity to share their work with other librarians who may be in a similar situation with qualitative data but unsure how to analyze it in order to make the connection between the value of library instruction and student success. At USFSM, the librarians will be able to expand their role in student success initiatives taking place on campus. It will also provide opportunities to support key initiatives from the campus strategic plan. Further, the campus Library Services can position themselves to increase and solidify their role as an integral part of the campus.

Although the review of current literature indicates much of the research on academic libraries and student retention examines various service points throughout the library, there are a small number of articles focused on student retention and library instruction. The study from Grand Valley State University Libraries is one of a few studies focused specifically on connecting library instruction and student retention. Replicating the Grand Valley study at USFSM provides smaller institutions with a how-to guide to replicate the study at their campus. The librarians at USFSM continue to collect data from their instruction sessions and forward it to OIRE. After the data is analyzed, it will be shared with the senior leadership at USFSM in addition to our Student Services office that oversees student retention, progression, and graduation. More importantly, we are exploring ways in which our data may be incorporated into additional institutional initiatives. Studies of this nature give libraries the ability to provide campus administrators with the data to indicate the relevance and importance of academic libraries and librarians in the twenty-first century.

Notes

1. University of South Florida, *USF System Facts 2016–2017* (Tampa: University of South Florida, Office of Decision Support, 2016), http://www.usf.edu/ods/documents/system-facts/usf-system-facts-2016-17.pdf.
2. Association of College and Research Libraries, *The Value of Academic Libraries*, researched by Megan Oakleaf (Chicago: Association of College and Research Libraries, 2010), 12, http://www.ala.org/acrl/sites/ala.org.acrl/files/content/issues/value/val_report.pdf.
3. Porcia Vaughn and Cherie Turner, "Decoding via Coding: Analyzing Qualitative Text Data through Thematic Coding and Survey Methodologies," *Journal of Library Administration* 56, no. 1 (2016): 44–45.
4. Mary O'Kelly, "Correlation between Library Instruction and Student Retention" (presentation, Southeastern Library Assessment Conference, Atlanta, GA, November 15, 2015), http://scholarworks.gvsu.edu/library_presentations/55/.
5. O'Kelly, "Correlation between Library Instruction and Student Retention."
6. Southern Association of Colleges and Schools Commission on Colleges, *The Principles of Accreditation: Foundations of Quality Enhancement*, 5th ed. (Decatur, GA: Southern Association of Colleges and Schools Commission on Colleges, last modified December 2011), http://www.sacscoc.org/pdf/2012PrinciplesOfAcreditation.pdf.
7. Association of College and Research Libraries, *Academic Library Impact on Student Learning and Success: Findings from Assessment in Action Team Projects*, prepared by Karen Brown with contributions by Kara J. Malenfant (Chicago: Association of College and Research Libraries, 2017), http://www.ala.org/acrl/sites/ala.org.acrl/files/content/issues/value/findings_y3.pdf.
8. Adam Murray, "Academic Libraries and High-Impact Practices for Student Retention: Library Deans' Perspectives," *portal: Libraries and the Academy* 15, no. 3 (July 2015): 485.
9. George D. Kuh, "High-Impact Educational Practices: A Brief Overview," excerpt from George D. Kuh, *High-Impact Educational Practices: What They Are, Who Has Access to Them, and Why They Matter* (Washington, DC: American Association of Colleges and Universities, 2008), https://www.aacu.org/leap/hips.
10. Vaughn and Turner, "Decoding via Coding," 45.
11. Mariaelena Bartesaghi and Ardis Hanson, "Understanding Social Networking: The Benefit of Discourse Analysis," in *Using Qualitative Methods in Action Research: How Librarians Can Get to the Why of Data*, ed. Doug Cook and Lesley Farmer (Chicago: Association of College and Research Libraries, 2011), 47–63.
12. Association of College and Research Libraries, *Value of Academic Libraries*, 14.
13. Angie Thorpe, Ria Lukes, Diane J. Bever, and Yan He, "The Impact of the Academic Library on Student Success: Connecting the Dots," *portal: Libraries and the Academy* 16, no. 2 (April 2016): 388.
14. Steven Andrew Scheuler, "Retention and Student Success: An Action Plan for Academic Librarians," *Library Leadership and Management* 30, no. 2 (2015): 4.

Bibliography

Association of College and Research Libraries. *Academic Library Impact on Student Learning and Success: Findings from Assessment in Action Team Projects*. Prepared by Karen Brown with contributions by Kara J. Malenfant. Chicago: Association of College and Research Libraries, 2017. http://www.ala.org/acrl/sites/ala.org.acrl/files/content/issues/value/findings_y3.pdf.

———. *The Value of Academic Libraries: A Comprehensive Research Review and Report*. Researched by Megan Oakleaf. Chicago: Association of College and Research Libraries, 2010. http://www.ala.org/acrl/sites/ala.org.acrl/files/content/issues/value/val_report.pdf.

Bartesaghi, Mariaelena, and Ardis Hanson. "Understanding Social Networking: The Benefit of Discourse Analysis." In *Using Qualitative Methods in Action Research: How Librarians Can Get to the Why*

Section 1

of Data. Edited by Doug Cook and Lesley Farmer, 47–63. Chicago: Association of College and Research Libraries, 2011.

Kuh, George D. "High-Impact Educational Practices: A Brief Overview." Excerpt from George D. Kuh, *High-Impact Educational Practices: What They Are, Who Has Access to Them, and Why They Matter*. Washington, DC: American Association of Colleges and Universities, 2008. https://www.aacu.org/leap/hips.

Murray, Adam. "Academic Libraries and High-Impact Practices for Student Retention: Library Deans' Perspectives." *portal: Libraries and the Academy* 15, no. 3 (July 2015): 471–87. https://doi.org/10.1353/pla.2015.0027.

O'Kelly, Mary. "Correlation between Library Instruction and Student Retention." Presentation, Southeastern Library Assessment Conference, Atlanta, GA, November 16, 2015. http://scholarworks.gvsu.edu/library_presentations/55/.

Scheuler, Steven Andrew. "Retention and Student Success: An Action Plan for Academic Librarians," *Library Leadership and Management* 30, no. 2 (2015).

Southern Association of Colleges and Schools Commission on Colleges. *The Principles of Accreditation: Foundations of Quality Enhancement*, 5th ed. Decatur, GA: Southern Association of Colleges and Schools Commission on Colleges, last modified December 2011. http://www.sacscoc.org/pdf/2012PrinciplesOfAcreditation.pdf.

Thorpe, Angie, Ria Lukes, Diane J. Bever, and Yan He. "The Impact of the Academic Library on Student Success: Connecting the Dots." *portal: Libraries and the Academy* 16, no. 2 (April 2016): 373–92.

University of South Florida. *USF System Facts 2016–2017*. Tampa: University of South Florida, Office of Decision Support, 2016. http://www.usf.edu/ods/documents/system-facts/usf-system-facts-2016-17.pdf.

Vaughn, Porcia, and Cherie Turner. "Decoding via Coding: Analyzing Qualitative Text Data through Thematic Coding and Survey Methodologies." *Journal of Library Administration* 56, no. 1 (2016): 41–51.

Title: Our "Special Obligation": Library Assessment, Learning Analytics, and Intellectual Freedom

Abstract: Best practices in library assessment reflect the core library values of patron privacy and confidentiality. This chapter reviews fundamental principles of intellectual freedom in light of academic library assessment and parent institutions' learning analytics initiatives. Privacy by Design, a framework for data governance that balances organizational mission with individual choice in personal data collection, is introduced. PbD presents an application of the broader concept of data governance and can inform library assessment and patron data use policies. Privacy audit techniques can then be used to evaluate the library's adherence to its data governance plan and identify areas for improvement.

Keywords: library assessment, learning analytics, privacy, intellectual freedom, confidentiality, ethics, data governance, Privacy by Design, quantitative assessment, patron data, personally identifiable information, privacy audit, surveillance

Project focus: assessment methodologies, techniques, or practices; organizational practices (i.e., strategic planning); user behaviors and needs; data use and technology; assessment concepts and/or management; concepts/theory; professional ethics

Results made or will make case for: changes in library policy, proof of library impact and value, a strategic plan or process

Data needed: Library assessment data (as defined by library)

Methodology: qualitative

Project duration: ongoing (continuous feedback loop)

Tool(s) utilized: N/A

Cost estimate: < $100

Type of institution: community college

Institution enrollment: 5,000–15,000

Highest level of education: associate's

CC BY NC

Chapter 4

Our "Special Obligation"

Library Assessment, Learning Analytics, and Intellectual Freedom

Sarah Hartman-Caverly

Librarians claim a special obligation to intellectual freedom.[1] Our instruction and information services, and our assessment of that work, must preserve patron privacy and confidentiality as the necessary conditions for free inquiry. Contemporaneous methods of institutional and academic library assessment, coupled with the data analytics capabilities of best-in-breed library and educational technology, challenge librarians' ethical commitment to intellectual freedom. This case study highlights the "unfreezing" stage of a community college librarian's organizational change efforts directed at redesigning library assessment in order to restore patron privacy in assessment practices and at advocating for students' intellectual freedom in institutional governance.[2] The methods and activities proposed highlight the role of the academic librarian in advocating and teaching intellectual freedom and of intellectual freedom as a subject of library assessment.

Context

Delaware County Community College (DCCC) is the open-admission institution of higher education serving Delaware and Chester counties in the metropolitan Philadelphia area of southeastern Pennsylvania. DCCC confers associate degrees and career credentials across a wide range of academic disciplines and skilled vocations to a diverse population of direct-from-high-school and post-traditional students. Nearly half of our students identify as people of color, and approximately two hundred international students study at the college each year. More than two-thirds of the college's 12,000 credit students attend part-time, many of them balancing family and work responsibilities with their pursuit of higher education or skills training. Financial aid funds the learning pursuits of 67 percent of our students. More than half of incoming students prepare for college-level courses by completing developmental reading, writing, or math curricula. After their studies at DCCC, 62 percent of our students avail themselves of the more than fifty agreements the college maintains with baccalaureate programs and transfer to continue their studies.[3]

DCCC Library Services is comprised of five full-time faculty librarians and adjunct library faculty providing information literacy instruction and research services at the college's primary Marple Campus and five of its eight satellite teaching sites. The college renovated the library footprint and opened the Marple Learning Commons in January 2013. Over the past five years, Library Services experienced significant changes in our physical plant, knowledge collection and collection development practices, and in organization and staffing. To create space for tutoring and writing services, more than one hundred desktop computers, group study spaces, and the comfortable seating areas that characterize learning commons facilities, librarians weeded the physical knowledge collection, halving it from approximately 40,000 volumes to 20,000 volumes. Titles were considered for deaccession based on circulation statistics dating from the implementation of the integrated library system, publication date and content currency, and curricular relevance; the need to reduce the footprint of the collection drove the weeding initiative. College administration increased the library acquisition budget for electronic materials to supplement the remaining physical collection with e-books, patron-driven acquisition collections, and article databases.

The transition to a learning commons transformed library staffing as well; a 2013 reorganization replaced the library director position with a director of the learning commons and expanded the responsibilities of circulation and technical services clerks to include customer service, triage reference, and technical support duties at an integrated information desk. Subsequent staffing changes jettisoned the learning commons director and further restructured support staff positions. During this transition, faculty librarians reported to an acting dean; in 2015, the college conducted a national search and hired a dean of educational support services with prior experience overseeing library, writing services, and technology services in a similar community college setting.

The period of transition from library to learning commons paralleled a significant college-wide curriculum revision. In 2014, DCCC faculty ratified nine learning goals developed in response to recommendations in the college's self-study report for Middle States Commission on Higher Education (MSCHE) reaccreditation.[4] The learning goals updated the competency-based curriculum model and include assessment plans that seek to quantify students' attainment of the goals upon academic program completion. Curriculum and assessment committees within the college's shared governance system processed hundreds of course and program change proposals over two academic years to align the entire curriculum with the new learning goal and assessment paradigm, and the college reported this accomplishment in its MSCHE Periodic Review Report. Information literacy is one of the learning goals, and library faculty collaborated with subject matter faculty across the disciplines to integrate information literacy into program curricula and to develop assessment plans to measure student learning outcomes. Library faculty also scaffolded information literacy outcomes, identifying competencies to be achieved at college orientation, in developmental reading and writing courses, in courses designated as meeting the information literacy learning goal, and in advanced academic and discipline-specific courses. In reference to the "Information Has Value" frame of the *Framework for Information Literacy for Higher Education* developed by the Association of College and Research Libraries (ACRL),[5] DCCC library faculty articulated a learning goal that requires students to "identify the legal, ethical, economic, and social issues (including privacy...) associated with the use of information."[6]

Enrollment, retention, and program completion concerns also assumed new significance for the college during this time frame. Community college enrollment trends tend to indirectly correlate with economic growth;[7] thus, as the "green shoots" of economic recovery emerged, DCCC's enrollment declined from its Great Recession peak.[8] Likewise, community colleges struggle to sustain thresholds measuring student retention and program completion, as they inherently serve diverse student populations with a wide range of personal educational goals, competing life priorities, and other obstacles to higher learning.[9] The development of quantitative institutional assessments like the American Association of Community College's Voluntary Framework of Accountability (VFA), Hobson's Predictive Analytics Reporting (PAR) Framework, and the College Scorecard under then-President Obama's Department of Education placed new urgency on metrics like enrollment, semester-to-semester and year-to-year retention, course pass rates, and credential completion.[10] DCCC implemented a variety of initiatives, including an early alert student tracking software that integrates with the college's new learning management system, which increased the institution's capability to track, monitor, and influence student progress to credential completion through a variety of automated and individualized student support interventions. With the adoption of these systems and concomitant services aimed at increasing enrollment, retention, and completion, DCCC entered the domain of learning analytics.

Renewed interest in library assessment emerged from these parallel restructurings of the learning commons, the college curriculum, and institutional assessment. Library faculty and administrators completed an assessment cycle in 2013 utilizing a method predicated on transactional statistics and analysis of an anonymized sample of student research assignments. However, the learning commons transition, onboarding of new leadership, significant college-wide curricular changes, increased emphasis on accountability for student success to inform institutional resource allocation, and adoption of new technologies—including a library services platform with enhanced patron analytics capabilities—to measure and track achievement of institutional metrics, contributed to a sense that the current library assessment approach did not serve emerging assessment needs. In November 2016, the dean charged the library faculty with developing new assessment methods that would demonstrate the library's contributions to student retention and success and circulated highly cited materials[11] describing library assessment practices at the University of Minnesota,[12] which are promoted by ACRL's Value of Academic Libraries initiative.[13]

Reading "Library Use and Undergraduate Student Outcomes" brought the three strands of institutional assessment, learning analytics, and library assessment into new relief. A particular claim in Soria, Fransen, and Nackerud's article captured my attention: "Privacy concerns are valid, but data can be gathered, stored, and aggregated without compromising individual privacy. We recommend putting infrastructure in place to begin gathering data as soon as possible, even if staff are not readily available to immediately analyze the data."[14]

Soria, Fransen and Nackerud go on to cite Megan Oakleaf, a significant proponent of library assessment, seminal figure of ACRL's Value of Academic Libraries initiative, and developer of the influential *Academic Library Value: The Impact Starter Kit*. Oakleaf explicitly elevates assessment above patron privacy and confidentiality in the talking points of *Impact Starter Kit* "Activity #24: To Assess or Not to Assess" and asserts that deidentified patron data must be partnered with student outcome metrics in order to demonstrate the library's contribution to institutional goals.[15]

This data collection posture substantiates my concerns regarding the library assessment methods described in Soria, Fransen, and Nackerud's article and promoted in other ACRL VAL initiatives. I perceive academic library assessment trends as emerging in stark contrast to fundamental library values regarding patron privacy and confidentiality as conditions for intellectual freedom. By abdicating our "special obligation" to intellectual freedom in response to the perceived existential threats posed by accountability-based funding and increasingly technocratic methods of institutional assessment,[16] academic libraries are producing an actual existential threat in the abandonment of our ethical bearings and professional identity.

Ethics in the academic library are, in fact, at an inflection point.[17] We face the ethical dilemma of tracking students' library use and correlating it with institutional outcomes in order to justify budget proposals, staffing levels, and, in some cases, our very existence on campus.[18] We identify privacy as a knowledge practice inherent to our discipline, yet compromise student privacy to demonstrate the degree to which this and other information literacy learning outcomes are achieved. We steward, and are in danger of exploiting, a silo of student learning data that is in high demand by institutional and higher education researchers, software and content vendors, government agencies, and other third parties. We operate within parent institutions increasingly preoccupied with the bottom line, answering to administrators and colleagues who do not always understand or share our commitment to intellectual freedom.

This challenge is multifaceted; so must be its resolution. Academic libraries must examine and reaffirm our ethical commitment to intellectual freedom; share our knowledge of privacy, confidentiality, and data governance with our parent institutions; model best practices in confidentiality and privacy policy-making, privacy disclosures, patron data collection, and privacy-aware assessment methods; and elucidate intellectual freedom concepts in our research instruction and reference consultations. In so doing, we will not only realize our commitment to safeguarding intellectual freedom, but also enhance the quality and utility of our assessment data.

Communicating Results and Impact

Rediscovering Our Roots: Librarian Self-Reflection, Scholarly Communication, and Library Policy

Library assessment practices that utilize patron data or data exhaust implicate the conditions of privacy and confidentiality that underpin a librarian's relationship with and information service to her patron.[19] Thus, questions of academic library assessment using learning analytics methods, or for purposes of correlating library use with individual student outcomes, are first and foremost ethical questions. The American Library Association's (ALA) Committee on Professional Ethics identifies intellectual freedom as the foundation for the profession's ethical principles and invokes privacy and confidentiality in the third statement of the Code of Ethics.[20]

Adopted in 1939 and amended three times (most recently in 2008), the ALA Code of Ethics interprets our shared disciplinary knowledge and values and reduces them to practice. It provides guiding principles for reasoning ethical dilemmas to resolution, and it is a living document, modifiable to reflect emerging ethical challenges and value positions. As currently interpreted in the Library Bill of Rights, Privacy Toolkit, Library Privacy Guidelines, and ALA policy,[21] the functional definition of privacy in librarianship is conceptually broad, encompassing autonomy privacy: "having to do with the ability of individuals to be free of actual or potential observation."[22] By contrast, contemporary discourse about privacy in the discipline, such as that in the excerpt from Soria, Fransen, and Nackerud, is bound by an implicit acceptance of conditions of constant data capture and reuse for data mining as normative, necessary, and resource-efficient in light of the availability of low-cost web-scale data storage services. In other words, the current conversation is focused narrowly on patrons' data privacy, but omits the larger context of autonomy privacy as prerequisite to intellectual freedom.[23]

Academic librarians are reopening a discursive space to bring autonomy, privacy, and intellectual freedom to the forefront of scholarly communication regarding assessment and patron data. My own entry point to this space was a systematic self-observation project[24] as part of a 2015–17 learning community of academic librarians.[25] Accompanied by interdisciplinary scholarship on privacy, data mining, learning analytics, and library assessment, this experience culminated in my renewed commitment to promoting intellectual freedom as a community college librarian. At the time that the call for proposals for this volume was announced, I was further synthesizing that scholarship to develop a counterproposal to the University of Minnesota model of library assessment that was slated for discussion at my library's department meeting. The assessment considerations first presented to colleagues on the library faculty at DCCC in January 2017 served as the basis for a presentation about learning analytics and student privacy offered during our college's faculty in-service professional development program in February 2017, were refined in a webinar presented for Tri-state College Library Cooperative,[26] are independently validated by Jones and Salo in "Learning Analytics and the Academic Library: Professional Ethics Commitments at a Crossroads" (in preprint at time of writing),[27] and unfold now as you read (see figure 4.1).

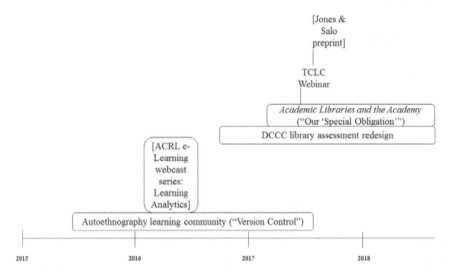

Figure 4.1
A time line of the author's scholarly communication activities within the academic library community regarding library assessment, learning analytics, and intellectual freedom.

The library assessment process I propose adds two preliminary steps to the conventional assessment cycle: a privacy audit, and a critical examination of the library's privacy policy. A privacy audit identifies the library's current patron data governance practices: what personal data is collected, when and where data collection occurs, who has access to the data collected, why the data is collected, and how the data is stored, secured, transferred, and destroyed. Specific privacy audit techniques are detailed in the ALA Privacy Tookit;[28] "Activity #12: Library Data Audit" in Oakleaf's *Impact Starter Kit* is also easily adapted for the purpose of a privacy audit.[29]

The results of a privacy audit then inform the development, amendment, reconfirmation, or enforcement of a library privacy policy. Library privacy policies should be predicated on data minimization,[30] "collecting the minimum amount of personal information required to provide a service or meet a specific operational need" and disposing of data once that need is met.[31] The ALA Privacy Toolkit and

Library Privacy Guidelines are invaluable resources in the implementation of a library privacy policy.[32] The library's assessment process can then be planned or reexamined and adapted, as necessary, to achieve alignment with the library's privacy policy (see figure 4.2). Moreover, the advancement of professional values, including privacy and confidentiality, should be assessed as a core function of the academic library.[33]

Privacy audit	• Document patron data collection
Privacy policy	• Guidelines for patron data collection and use
Identify outcomes	• Include intellectual freedom indicators
Determine methods	• Patron data use complies with privacy policy • Incorporate qualitative as well as quantitative instruments
Collect data	• Provide and comply with patron privacy choices
Analyze results	• Contextualize quantitative patron analytics and transactional data with qualitative findings
Improve library performance	• Apply findings to improve instruction, information services, and knowledge collections

Figure 4.2
The author's proposed library assessment cycle for DCCC Library Services.

As librarians, we have staked our claim to intellectual freedom as the special obligation of our profession.[34] What definition of privacy guides us to fulfillment of that obligation? Have changes in the information environment—for instance, the widespread use of data mining practices in applications such as learning analytics—fundamentally reshaped privacy as a cultural value, or rendered it obsolete? If so, is it not incumbent on us to reexamine and amend our professional ethics? By contrast, assessment itself is not mentioned in the code. Should assessment be included among the profession's core values? These questions go to the root of what it means to be a librarian and can be answered only by professional self-reflection, scholarly communication and good-faith debate, and renewed commitment to library policy-making consistent with our shared core values. As our professional ethics currently stand, privacy should be a forethought, and a subject, of assessment initiatives—not an afterthought.

Strengthening Our Trunk: Engaging Our Parent Institutions

Academic libraries are dependent upon parent institutions for resources, from staffing, to operating and acquisitions budgets, to the allocation of physical space. This dependence renders us accountable to administrative priorities that are increasingly framed in neoliberal terms and lend themselves to assessment methods derived from business metrics, like return-on-investment (ROI).[35] The ethical dilemma of library assessment that implicates patron privacy emerges when institutional assessment values and library intellectual freedom values conflict.

Academic libraries' primary value is, unarguably, our role in developing students' information literacy and in providing the raw material for the research and knowledge creation function of the university. Our library assessment initiatives must measure these impacts in ways consistent with our core values of privacy and confidentiality. In addition, we can do more to leverage our unique expertise in intellectual freedom, information systems management, structured data, and data governance to advise our institutions on risk management with respect to student data. Introducing system configuration and privacy audit methods, such as the Privacy by Design framework,[36] creates common ground with campus information technology and institutional research departments to ensure student privacy is a primary consideration in technology and assessment practices. Framing student data as a liability as well as an asset,[37] and advocating data governance planning on campus, allows libraries to establish privacy as our strategic differentiator and expert contribution in the domain of institutional information services.

Strategic planning and assessment cycles, accreditation self-studies, changes in executive administration, collective bargaining negotiations, and learning management and student information system deployments are all institutional activities that present opportunities to initiate the conversation about student data governance and intellectual freedom (see figure 4.3). The academic tradition of institutional decision-making through shared governance is an inclusive process,[38] in letter if not in spirit. Librarians can join committees in elected or amicus capacities to raise questions about the use of student data and to contribute our expertise on system configuration and interoperability, data flow analysis, FERPA regulations, data minimization, and other best practices in data governance.

In my experience, the same questions that guide data governance planning can be posed to raise institutional awareness of the need for data risk management:

- What data are we collecting and retaining about students?
- How is this data collected? How is it stored and secured? What is our breach response plan?
- How are students informed of this data collection? What opt-in or opt-out mechanisms are in place?
- How is this data used?
- Who has access to this data? Under what conditions is this data shared with third parties, including content and system vendors, financial institutions, and law enforcement?
- When and how, if ever, is this data destroyed?

The technopositivism advanced by the educational technology industry and educational policy organizations leaves little room for technoskepticism[39]—critical questioning of how technology serves higher learning, which instances of higher education's adaptation to emerging technology represent evolution, and which adaptations are suggestive of devolution. Librarians should assume the role of thought leaders in this discussion through informed questioning of the role of technology in education and research.

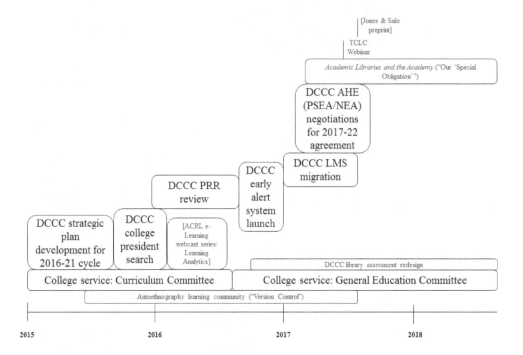

Figure 4.3
An updated time line of the author's scholarly communication activities within her parent institution, presenting a sample of college service and institutional changes presenting opportunities to raise awareness of data governance and intellectual freedom.

Librarian participation in institutional assessment presents another opportunity to demonstrate expertise in critical information evaluation. We teach students to examine sources as artifacts bearing the figurative fingerprints of the authors' information creation process, to reflect on those elements as indicators of information quality, to consider whether the information presented fulfills an information need,[40] and to navigate an increasingly complex terrain of authority and bias.[41] Applying these same techniques to the examination of institutional assessment data and reports revealed, in my experience, a creeping confirmation bias in institutional assessment and decision-making. Reports that seek to present the institution in the best possible light are one thing; at issue are institutional decisions validated by skewed internal data or data analysis. A dialogic technique that seeks test cases—examples, information, or analysis—contrary to the prevailing wisdom is a posture librarians can effectively assume in our contributions to institutional assessment and governance. Under examination, evidence-based or data-driven decision-making practices may be revealed as decision-driven data-making.

Engaging subject matter faculty on questions of student data governance, classroom confidentiality, and academic freedom is another important arena for librarian activity at the institutional level. At DCCC, the coincident implementation of a new learning management system and student early alert system created natural opportunities to discuss the impact that student progress monitoring, intrusive "nudge" advising,[42] and interdepartmental student data sharing might have on faculty-student interactions and the academic freedom of the classroom.

Anecdotal observation suggests that many faculty recognize the pervasive collection and analysis of students' clickstream data as antithetical to academic and intellectual freedom, but they lack the lexicon to articulate these concerns. All-faculty meetings and professional development in-service days present opportunities for librarians to share information and best practices around student privacy and intellectual freedom. When a configuration issue with the college's new early alert system became the subject of discussion at a fall 2016 faculty meeting, faculty members' frustration with the software could be reframed as a concern of trust in the adoption of new technology that intermediated faculty-student communications and produced a digital record of automated transactions that sometimes undermined and even contradicted individual professors' grading and course policies. Probing further with questions about learning data capture, storage, and sharing prompted another faculty member to wonder, "What is the institution's goal with all of this surveillance, exactly?" During another software training session, a faculty member in the ESL program asked about the implications of attendance data capture for international students' visa status. These and other practical questions provide openings to raise accompanying theoretical and ethical questions about the possible long-term implications and unintended consequences of learning data capture for academic and intellectual freedom.

A librarian colleague and I leveraged DCCC's learning management and early alert system implementations to introduce the umbrella concept of learning analytics,[43] and the student privacy and academic freedom challenges it poses, as the subject of an in-service session and the topic of a semester-long faculty learning community.[44] Framing learning analytics as a form of surveillance,[45] communicating emerging research on the chilling effect of surveillance that hampers free inquiry,[46] and discussing the disparate impact of structural surveillance on minority populations[47]—social identity groups to which many DCCC and other community college students belong[48]—proved a powerful point of departure for debating the appropriate context and role of student data capture in the academy. Subject matter faculty contributed their own examples, such as a career program in which students are required to achieve a percentage likelihood of passing the occupational licensure exam as estimated by a test preparation software prior to approval to sit for the exam. Likewise, we discussed the implications of perpetual storage and text analysis performed by services like TurnItIn, which retain a persistent digital copy and assign an originality score to students' written work. Many participants in the in-service session and learning community expressed a sense that certain student data capture practices crossed a line of intrusiveness in the institution's relationships with students. Few were surprised to learn of the billions of dollars of public and private investment in educational technology featuring analytics capabilities and of the public-private partnerships that promote use of this software in the education system. All shared a concern for how these technologies would impact faculty-student interactions and pedagogical prerogatives in the classroom, both in person and online. At least two participants are considering learning analytics as a potential topic for investigation as part of graduate coursework (see figure 4.4).

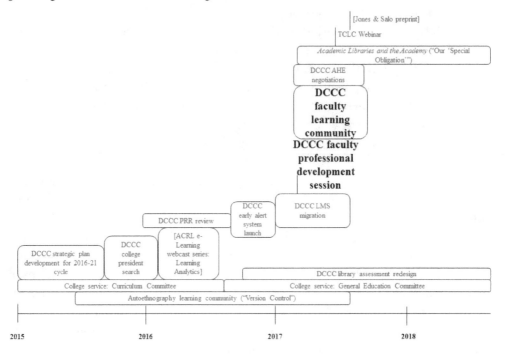

Figure 4.4
An updated time line of the author's scholarly communication activities within her parent institution, presenting work with subject matter faculty to raise awareness of learning analytics, data governance, student privacy, and intellectual freedom.

If we believe in the broad applicability of information literacy knowledge practices and dispositions, including the fundamental role of privacy as a condition for intellectual freedom, we must model these intellectual behaviors in our work beyond the library classroom threshold. Increasing capabilities for student data capture are producing institutional data hoards in search of a purpose[49]—a state opposed by emerging best practices of data minimization and governance posited both within and without the academic library.[50] Librarians are uniquely positioned to bring these issues to the fore of institutional initiatives involving assessment, system configuration, and strategic planning. In applying our disciplinary knowledge to the realization of academic freedom in our parent institutions, librarians demonstrate value beyond that of our research instruction and information services. Our consistent and unwavering advocacy for intellectual freedom also contextualizes library assessment practices that prioritize student privacy and agency. This full spectrum of value we contribute to our parent institutions should serve as the basis for library assessment and institutional investment in the library.

Extending Our Branches: Enacting Library Ethics in Assessment

The academic library mission should serve institutional priorities in ways that are consistent with our professional code of ethics and the guidelines, standards, and frameworks advanced by ACRL.[51] By extension, library assessment initiatives should not only reflect these principles, but also effectively evaluate our enactment of them.[52] Affirming the library's privacy policy and engaging in institutional privacy advocacy serve as the foundation for ethical, effective, and meaningful library assessment. Academic libraries must recognize our qualitative value as well as our quantitative value and give voice to those qualities that tell the whole story of the library and its contributions to institutional goals. If intellectual freedom is the primary motif of that story, it must not be compromised in the telling; to the contrary, upholding intellectual freedom and protecting privacy and confidentiality are library activities we should assess.[53]

Contemporary library assessment trends are explicitly derived from business metrics and prioritize the library's impact on individual student achievement,[54] weakening our ability to convey our value as a common good.[55] Moreover, quantitative academic library assessment practices overly rely on the surreptitious retention of students' clickstream data and data exhaust, and on correlational methods yielding findings of questionable practical significance. As academic libraries design, implement, and update assessment practices, we must take special notice when these practices involve the retention of patron-generated data beyond its primary purpose of enabling the core library functions of circulation and authentication to electronic content. Is it truly worth compromising our commitment to intellectual freedom and our core values of privacy and confidentiality to discover that the number of databases students use correlates with the number of e-journals they access and with their enrollment in introductory library research courses?[56] Academic librarians must apply a critical cost-benefit analysis to the use of patron analytics in assessment.

Oakleaf asserts that "the data we collect represents what we value about ourselves and how others will judge us."[57] I propose a corollary: the *manner* in which we collect data represents what we value about ourselves and how others will judge us. While I am critical of an overreliance on the low-hanging fruit of patron data capture for purposes of library assessment, I am not opposed to patron analytics in total; rather, I simply suggest that we seek students' informed consent for this data capture and endeavor to contextualize transactional statistics with qualitative information.

Privacy by Design provides a useful framework for the design of library assessment practices and configuration of library systems that retain and make use of students' library data. Privacy by Design is a positive-sum approach that prioritizes individuals' privacy and agency, ensures transparency and accountability in data collection, enacts data governance strategies that support data security across the data life cycle, and provides mechanisms for users to consent to or opt out of data capture and to seek redress of privacy concerns.[58] Enabling students to opt out of data collection certainly impacts the integrity and "bigness" of the resulting data set; however, the cost-benefit analysis of opt-out mechanisms is surely in favor of preserving intellectual freedom and informed patron choice in the face of statistical validity of assessment data.[59] Acknowledging participants' self-selection bias resulting from informed consent to contribute data to library assessment is an acceptable way to qualify the limitations of the resulting data capture. I applied the Privacy by Design framework to library assessment indicators to propose a system that seeks qualitative as well as quantitative input (see table 4.1).

Table 4.1
Privacy by Design and Fair Information Practices for Library Assessment

Principles of Privacy by Design[a]	PbD Fair Information Practices for Library Assessment
Proactive, not reactive; preventive, not remedial	Library assessment plan complies with library privacy policy and data governance plan.
	Privacy, confidentiality, and intellectual freedom performance indicators are evaluated in library assessment.
Privacy as the default	Patron data used or collected is for specific, limited purposes (beyond core library operations, such as circulation and authentication).
	The purposes of data collection are communicated to patrons in privacy disclosures.
	Patron data collection is limited, and collection of personally identifiable information is subject to data minimization procedures.
	Patron data is securely destroyed when the specific, limited purpose is achieved.
Privacy embedded into design	Systems are configured to restrict patron data retention, access, and sharing to specific, limited, disclosed purposes and user roles.
	Cybersecurity mechanisms, such as encrypted data storage and communication over https, are in place.
Full functionality—positive-sum, not zero-sum	Library assessment methods are designed to promote and respect patrons' privacy choices, including active (opt-in) or passive (opt-out) consent mechanisms.
	Creative assessment strategies, including qualitative methods, complement patron analytics.
End-to-end security—life cycle protection	Retained patron data is stored, and eventually destroyed, securely.
	The library has a breach response plan to notify affected patrons of patron data security breaches.

Principles of Privacy by Design[a]	PbD Fair Information Practices for Library Assessment
Visibility and transparency	Patron data collection complies with posted library privacy policies. Summary library assessment results and plans for improvement are shared with patrons and other stakeholders. Sharing of patron data with third parties outside the library is disclosed. Patrons are able to opt out of data sharing.
Respect for user privacy	Active (opt-in) or passive (opt-out) consent is secured for patron data use, retention, and sharing beyond core library operations. Care is taken to ensure the accuracy of patron data. Patrons have the ability to access, review, amend, and request destruction of their individual data.[b] Mechanisms are in place to facilitate redress of patron privacy concerns.

a. Ann Cavoukian, "Privacy by Design: The Seven Foundational Principles: Implementation and Mapping of Fair Information Practices," Internet Architecture Board, accessed May 24, 2017, https://iab.org/wp-content/IAB-uploads/2011/03/fred_carter.pdf.

b. American Library Association, "Questions and Answers on Privacy and Confidentiality," last modified July 1, 2014, http://www.ala.org/advocacy/privacy/FAQ.

Prevailing library assessment data, including transactional data, library survey instruments like LibQUAL+, institutional survey instruments like NSSE and CCSSE,[60] student and graduate satisfaction surveys, and even anonymized and aggregated librarian evaluation data serve to convey the "what" of library activity, but fall short of elucidating the "why." Qualitative data is integral to our ability to tell the whole story of the academic library; it allows us to interpret quantitative data and conveys the humanist meaning and value of our work with students and within our institutions. Furthermore, qualitative data gathered from focus groups, testimonials, advisory committees, feedback forms, and self-studies results from transparent data collection practices free of the taint of surreptitious clickstream data capture. Resolving the ethical conflict between intellectual freedom and patron analytics inspires us to more transparent, qualitative assessment practices that not only inform patrons of and respect their privacy choices, but also produce more nuanced, interesting, meaningful, and actionable library assessment data.

The Fruit Does Not Fall Far: Intellectual Freedom for and with Our Students

Underpinning my concern about academic library assessment practices is a deep-seated commitment to students' intellectual freedom. I assign a broad definition to intellectual freedom as the right to nonconformity,[61] ensured practically by library professionals' "long-standing commitment to an ethic of facilitating, not monitoring, access to information."[62] Patrons entrust their research interests, curiosities, untested hypotheses, knowledge gaps, and other information habits to us; our stewardship of their epistemological and ontological development, in keeping these activities in confidence,[63] is what differentiates our information services from those offered by commercial entities in exchange for the ability to exploit users' behavioral data.

Privacy and intellectual freedom are values born of a particular individualist sociocultural legacy;[64] consequently, they are dynamic, evolving dialectically with developments in technology and shifts in social expectations. The academic library community has proposed that learning analytics in the K–12 education system have primed postsecondary students to be "well adjusted to predictative analysis."[65] Within two years of this supposition, accounts from the UK's Open University indicate that some students are "horrified" by the extent of learning data capture[66]—in spite of access to disclosures about the institution's learning analytics initiatives. Furthermore, professional guidance explicitly cautions librarians against the assumption that patrons no longer value privacy,[67] compels us to share "the truth and some options" about patron data use,[68] and charges us to teach and advocate for intellectual freedom in the academy.[69]

Concurrent with my advocacy for student privacy in library assessment and college-wide learning analytics initiatives at DCCC is an intentional effort to incorporate intellectual freedom concepts in my lesson plans and reference consultations with students. I use the filter bubble phenomenon, big data consumer profiling, workplace monitoring, Internet of Things, electronic domestic surveillance, and the chilling effect of self-censorship as sample topics or case studies in information literacy sessions; offer stand-alone workshops on big data, learning analytics, FERPA and student privacy rights, and First Amendment considerations for college students; and coordinate DCCC Library Services' observation of Banned Books Week in September and Choose Privacy Week in May. I seek opportunities to explain differences in relevancy ranking between library databases and commercial search engines during reference service; acknowledging that, while a subscription database might fail to place the most useful article on the first page of results, it will not engage in the kind of user profiling, search engine bias, and Internet censorship that characterize commercial web search tools.[70] Students appreciate this behind-the-curtain insight into the inner workings of communication and research technologies; some are even inspired to investigate these phenomena in their research assignments.

Our purpose as academic librarians is to cultivate students' information autonomy; to encourage the habits of mind that underpin conscious observation of the world, the capacity to question the natural and social forces shaping one's experience of reality, the facility for seeking credible information and applying it to interpret these experiences, the self-efficacy to induce abstract concepts and deduce reasoned conclusions, and the will to engage with the world so as to shape it for the better. My informal contact with students on campus provides a constant reminder that there are as many teachable moments beyond the classroom as inside it; students observe our behaviors and decipher our institutional policies for evidence of whether we embody the values we espouse from the lectern, of whether the principles and skills we teach are, in fact, applicable in the "real" world outside the ivory tower. The dispositions we shape as academic librarians decide the fate of intellectual freedom and the future viability of the participatory political system it underpins.[71]

Leveraging the Findings

The professional self-reflection, intra- and interdisciplinary scholarly communication, library assessment planning, institutional service, and instructional strategies described in this case study constitute preparation for the "moving" phase of adoption[72] and implementation of practical library assessment methods, and for development of library-specific and college-wide student data governance plans, that prioritize intellectual freedom. In consultation with the dean of educational support services, I developed a multiyear professional action plan (table 4.2) that brings these initiatives to fruition. This plan leverages the library and Learning Commons as a pilot site for privacy-aware assessment and patron analytics initiatives, providing proof-of-concept and a model for scaling student privacy initiatives up and across the institution.

Table 4.2
Intellectual Freedom Organizational Change Action Plan

Year	Initiatives	Outcomes	Collaborators
2017–18	Library assessment plan Learning Commons professional development on FERPA and student privacy Learning Commons privacy audit	Propose library assessment practices that are consistent with the core library values of privacy, confidentiality, and intellectual freedom. Propose opt-in or opt-out mechanisms for collection of patron data to be used in library assessment or for purposes beyond core library operations. Develop and implement FERPA and student privacy training with Learning Commons faculty and staff to build a culture of privacy awareness. Convene a representative, cross-functional working group to document student data used and collected by Learning Commons functions, including library services, tutoring and writing services, and facility and network security apparatus.	Dean of Educational Support Services Coordinator of Tutoring Services Faculty librarians Learning Commons support staff Learning Commons student workers

Year	Initiatives	Outcomes	Collaborators
2018–19	Learning Commons patron data governance plan Learning Commons privacy guidelines Alignment of library assessment plan	Convene a representative, cross-functional working group to derive a Learning Commons data governance plan from the results of the privacy audit (this may, or may not, be the same working group that performed the privacy audit). Interpret the internal data governance plan as patron-facing Learning Commons privacy guidelines. Amend the library assessment plan for compliance with the Learning Commons data governance plan, as needed.	Dean of Educational Support Services Coordinator of Tutoring Services Faculty librarians Learning Commons support staff Learning Commons student workers
2019–20	Library assessment implementation	Conduct data collection and analysis phase of library assessment plan.	Dean of Educational Support Services Faculty librarians
Long-term goals	Promote student privacy as a strategic initiative for the college. Implement college-wide professional development about FERPA and student privacy. Coordinate a college-wide student privacy audit. Develop a student data governance plan for DCCC. Update the college's Policy on Student Confidentiality.[a]	Engage the strategic planning cycle to situate student data security as an institutional "threat" and privacy as an "opportunity" in SWOT analysis and goal planning. Propose student privacy as a subject of professional development; develop FERPA and privacy training internally, or identify, evaluate, and recommend external privacy training services. Using the Learning Commons privacy audit as a model, leverage campus partnerships to conduct a college-wide student data audit. Derive an institutional data governance plan from the results of the privacy audit. Propose changes to the college's Policy on Student Confidentiality through the College Advisory System of shared governance, as indicated by the privacy audit and data governance plan.	Office of the President, including Assistant to the President for Strategic Planning DCCC College Advisory System Professional Development Committee DCCC Office of Information Technology DCCC Institutional Effectiveness DCCC Office of the Provost, including student success initiatives utilizing learning analytics

Year	Initiatives	Outcomes	Collaborators
Long-term goals	Advocate for student privacy as an object of institutional action and assessment.	Work with Institutional Effectiveness to implement methods of assessing the college's compliance with its data governance plan, and share results with the college community.[b]	DCCC College Advisory System, including Assessment Processes Committee, Institutional Resources Technology Advisory Subcommittee, and the Student Affairs Committee Board of Trustees

a. Delaware County Community College, "Policy on Student Confidentiality," Student Handbook—Academic Information and Policies, accessed May 24, 2017, https://www.dccc.edu/campus-life/helpful-links/student-handbook/academic-info-policies#StudentConfidentiality.

b. Office of Ethics, University of California Berkeley, "Transparency Report," accessed May 24, 2017, https://ethics.berkeley.edu/privacy/transparency.

Reflection

The recognition of learning analytics as a form of surveillance,[73] and the conviction that surreptitious retention and use of patron data for library assessment is antithetical to librarianship's promotion of intellectual freedom, culminates a decade of my working in academic libraries and constitutes a pivotal actualization of my professional identity as a librarian. These opinions, formed through reflective analysis of the impact of technology on community college librarianship, directly substantiated by scholarly communication in library science, the humanities, social sciences, and computer and information sciences and validated by the principles and guidance produced by the American Library Association and Association of College and Research Libraries, nevertheless regularly put me at odds with my colleagues in the library, my supervisor's and parent institution's assessment priorities, many projects promoted through the Value of Academic Libraries initiative, and the prevailing technopositivism of higher education. My scholarship and commentary on student surveillance in academic libraries and the academy have been characterized as alarmist, anachronistic, antagonist, blunt, curmudgeonly, impractical, and politicized—nevertheless, the ideas persist. Colleagues I turn to for mentorship have advised greater moderation, political sensibility, and self-censorship in my advocacy for student privacy and intellectual freedom. Allusions to my tenure progress, institutional fit, and inadequacy as a cultural change agent force me to acknowledge that the stakes—professionally and personally—are high.

But ethics and cultural value systems frame our individual efforts in a bigger picture, connecting us to something larger than ourselves, situating our present efforts at the nexus of past and future, and imbuing our lived experiences with deeper meaning. I feel I have no choice but to uncompromisingly fulfill the core values of librarianship in my instruction and information services—and in the manner in which I assess my work to achieve continuous improvement. I remain "explicitly committed to intellectual freedom" and to fulfillment of my "special obligation to ensure the free flow of information and ideas to present and future generations."[74] In an information environment characterized by algorithmic censorship, politicized journalism and propaganda, and ubiquitous state-sponsored, corporate, and social surveillance,[75] the stakes—socially and culturally—are even higher.

There is much work to be done in restoring the public's awareness and value of intellectual freedom, and it begins at home—in our own libraries. Surveillance in and by the academic library is the professional crisis and opportunity of our time. As librarians, we are called to advocate, educate, and evaluate for intellectual freedom. Our collective response to this call indicates the well-being of the informed citizenry[76] we serve today, and its prospect in the future.

Notes

1. American Library Association, "Professional Ethics," last modified January 22, 2008, http://www.ala.org/tools/ethics.
2. Jean M. Bartunek and Richard W. Woodman, "Beyond Lewin: Toward a Temporal Approximation of Organizational Development and Change," *Annual Review of Organizational Psychology and Organizational Behavior,* no. 2 (2015): 157–82, https://doi.org/10.1146/annurev-org-psych-032414-111353.
3. "Fast Facts about Delaware County Community College," Delaware County Community College, accessed May 24, 2017, https://www.dccc.edu/about/news-information/fast-facts; Institutional Effectiveness, Delaware County Community College, "2016 Fall Third Week Credit Enrollment Report," Institutional Effectiveness, Delaware County Community College, "Student Financial Aid 2015–16," Integrated Postsecondary Education Data System (IPEDS).
4. "College Academic Learning Goals," Delaware County Community College, accessed May 24, 2017, https://www.dccc.edu/academics/resources/college-academic-learning-goals.
5. Association of College and Research Libraries, "Information Has Value," *Framework for Information Literacy for Higher Education* (Chicago: Association of College and Research Libraries, 2016), http://www.ala.org/acrl/standards/ilframework#value.
6. "General Information Literacy Learning Competencies—College Academic Learning Goals," Information Literacy Faculty Toolkit, Delaware County Community College, last modified March 27, 2017, http://libguides.dccc.edu/c.php?g=386844&p=2903065.
7. Victor M. H. Borden, "Down Means Up," *Community College Week* 23, no. 8 (November 29, 2010): 7–11, EBSCOhost MasterFILE Premier; Victor M. H. Borden, "A Downward Trend," *Community College Week* 26, no. 14 (2014): 7–10, Academic Search Premier, EBSCOhost.
8. Caitlin Kenney, "Bernanke Sees Green Shoots," *Planet Money,* National Public Radio, March 16, 2009, http://www.npr.org/sections/money/2009/03/bernanke_sees_green_shoots.html.
9. Community College Research Center, "Community College FAQs," Teachers College, Columbia University, accessed May 24, 2017, http://ccrc.tc.columbia.edu/Community-College-FAQs.html; American Association of Community Colleges, "College Completion Challenge Resources," accessed May 24, 2017, http://www.ccsse.org/center/about_cccse/college_completion_challenge.cfm#resources ; Center for Community College Student Engagement, *Expectations Meet Reality: The Underprepared Student and Community Colleges,* annual report, 2016, https://www.ccsse.org/docs/Underprepared_Student.pdf.
10. American Association of Community Colleges, Voluntary Framework of Accountability website, accessed May 24, 2017, http://vfa.aacc.nche.edu/Pages/default.aspx; Hobsons Education Advances, PAR Framework website, accessed May 24, 2017, http://www.parframework.org/about-par/; US Department of Education, "College Scorecard Data," accessed May 24, 2017, https://collegescorecard.ed.gov/data/.
11. Krista M. Soria, Jan Fransen, and Shane Nackerud, "Library Use and Undergraduate Student

Outcomes: New Evidence for Students' Retention and Academic Success," *portal: Libraries and the Academy* 13, no. 2 (April 2013): 147–64, https://doi.org/10.1353/pla.2013.0010 was cited 114 times in Google Scholar at time of writing; see https://scholar.google.com/scholar?q=soria+%22library+use+and+undergraduate+student+outcomes%22, accessed May 24, 2017; second most downloaded *portal: Libraries and the Academy* article in April 2017: https://muse.jhu.edu/frequently_downloaded?filter=journal&filter_id=159, accessed May 24, 2017.

12. Soria, Fransen, and Nackerud, "Library Use and Undergraduate Student Outcomes."

13. "ACRL Value of Academic Libraries Bibliography," Association of College and Research Libraries, accessed May 24, 2017, http://acrl.ala.org/valueography/.

14. Soria, Fransen, and Nackerud, "Library Use and Undergraduate Student Outcomes," 160.

15. Megan Oakleaf, "Activity #24: To Assess or Not to Assess," in *Academic Library Value: The Impact Starter Kit* (Syracuse, NY: Dellas Graphics, 2012).

16. American Library Association, "Professional Ethics."

17. Kyle M. L. Jones and Dorothea Salo, "Learning Analytics and the Academic Library: Professional Ethics Commitments at a Crossroads," *College and Research Libraries*, preprint, accessed May 24, 2017, http://crl.acrl.org/index.php/crl/article/view/16603/18049.

18. Sarah Childs, Graham Matthews, and Graham Walton, "Space, Use and University Libraries: The Future?" in *University Libraries and Space in the Digital World*, ed. Graham Matthews and Graham Walton (Farnham, UK: Ashgate, 2013), 201–16, https://dspace.lboro.ac.uk/dspace-jspui/handle/2134/11496.

19. American Library Association, "Privacy: An Interpretation of the Library Bill of Rights," last modified July 1, 2014, http://www.ala.org/advocacy/intfreedom/librarybill/interpretations/privacy.

20. American Library Association, "Professional Ethics."

21. American Library Association, "Privacy: An Interpretation of the Library Bill of Rights"; American Library Association, "Privacy Tool Kit," last modified January 2014, http://www.ala.org/advocacy/privacy/toolkit; American Library Association, "Library Privacy Guidelines," accessed May 24, 2017, http://www.ala.org/advocacy/privacy/guidelines; American Library Association, "Policy Concerning Confidentiality of Personally Identifiable Information About Library Users," last modified June 30, 2004, http://www.ala.org/advocacy/intfreedom/statementspols/otherpolicies/policyconcerning.

22. Sol Bermann, "Free to Be You and Me: Autonomy Privacy in Higher Education," *EDUCAUSE Review*, January 17, 2017, http://er.educause.edu/blogs/2017/1/free-to-be-you-and-me-autonomy-privacy-in-higher-education.

23. American Library Association, "Privacy Tool Kit"; Bermann, "Free to Be You and Me."

24. Noelie Rodriguez and Alan Ryave, *Systematic Self-observation* (Thousand Oaks, CA: Sage, 2002).

25. Anne-Marie Deitering, "CFParticipation: Autoethnography Learning Community," info-fetishist, May 22, 2015, https://info-fetishist.org/2015/05/22/cfparticipation-autoethnography-learning-community/.

26. Sarah Hartman-Caverly, "Our 'Special Obligation': Library Assessment, Learning Analytics, and Intellectual Freedom" (presentation, Tri-state College Library Cooperative, April 3, 2017), YouTube video, 1:12:20, published by TCLC Libraries, April 7, 2017, https://youtu.be/bKiTR9TNdf8.

27. Jones and Salo, "Learning Analytics and the Academic Library."

28. American Library Association, "A Privacy Audit," last modified April 2017, http://www.ala.org/advocacy/privacy/toolkit/policy#privacyaudit.

29. Megan Oakleaf, "Activity #12: Library Data Audit," in *Academic Library Value: The Impact Starter Kit* (Syracuse, NY: Dellas Graphics, 2012).

30. Bernard Marr, "Why Data Minimization Is an Important Concept in the Age of Big Data," *Forbes*, March 16, 2016, https://www.forbes.com/sites/bernardmarr/2016/03/16/why-data-minimization-is-an-important-concept-in-the-age-of-big-data/.

31. American Library Association, "Library Privacy Guidelines for Library Management Systems," last modified June 24, 2016, http://www.ala.org/advocacy/privacy/guidelines/library-management-systems.

32. American Library Association, "Developing or Revising a Library Privacy Policy," last modified April 2017, http://www.ala.org/advocacy/privacy/toolkit/policy; American Library Association, "Library Privacy Guidelines."

33. Association of College and Research Libraries, *Standards for Libraries in Higher Education: Prin-*

ciples and Performance Indicators (Chicago: Association of College and Research Libraries, 2011), http://www.ala.org/acrl/standards/standardslibraries.

34. American Library Association, "Professional Ethics."

35. Sheila Slaughter and Gary Rhoades, *Academic Capitalism and the New Economy* (Baltimore: Johns Hopkins University Press, 2004); John Lehner, "Return on Investment in Academic Libraries Research," ACRL SE09 Doc 4.0, memo to Executive Committee of the ACRL Board of Directors, April 4, 2009, http://connect.ala.org/files/61784/doc_4_0_roi_memo_pdf_49f626bc94.pdf.

36. Ann Cavoukian, "Privacy by Design: The Seven Foundational Principles: Implementation and Mapping of Fair Information Practices," Internet Architecture Board, accessed May 24, 2017, https://iab.org/wp-content/IAB-uploads/2011/03/fred_carter.pdf.

37. Office of Ethics, "Information Risk Governance Committee (IRGC)," University of California Berkeley, accessed May 24, 2017, https://ethics.berkeley.edu/privacy/irgc.

38. American Association of University Professors, "Statement on Government of Colleges and Universities," last modified April 1990, https://www.aaup.org/report/statement-government-colleges-and-universities; Mark Taylor, "Shared Governance in the Modern University," *Higher Education Quarterly* 67, no. 1 (2013): 80–94, https://doi.org/10.1111/hequ.12003, Academic Search Premier, EBSCOhost.

39. EDUCAUSE, "Teaching and Learning," accessed May 24, 2017, https://www.educause.edu/focus-areas-and-initiatives/teaching-and-learning; Achieving the Dream, "Technology in Education," accessed May 24, 2017, http://achievingthedream.org/focus-areas/technology-in-education.

40. Association of College and Research Libraries, "Information Creation as a Process," *Framework for Information Literacy for Higher Education* (Chicago: Association of College and Research Libraries, 2016), http://www.ala.org/acrl/standards/ilframework#process.

41. Association of College and Research Libraries, "Authority Is Constructed and Contextual," *Framework for Information Literacy for Higher Education* (Chicago: Association of College and Research Libraries, 2016), http://www.ala.org/acrl/standards/ilframework#authority.

42. Jeffrey Fletcher, Markeisha Grant, Marisol Ramos, and Melinda Mechur Karp, "Integrated Planning and Advising for Student Success (iPASS): State of the Literature," CCRC Working Paper No. 90, Community College Research Center, Teachers College, Columbia University, October 2016, http://ccrc.tc.columbia.edu/media/k2/attachments/ipass-state-of-the-literature.pdf.

43. "Learning Analytics," EDUCAUSE accessed May 24, 2017, https://library.educause.edu/topics/teaching-and-learning/learning-analytics.

44. "Learning Analytics," Delaware County Community College, last modified April 12, 2017, http://libguides.dccc.edu/learning_analytics.

45. Sharon Slade and Paul Prinsloo, "Learning Analytics: Ethical Issues and Dilemmas," *American Behavioral Scientist* 57, no. 10 (2013): 1510–29, https://doi.org/10.1177/0002764213479366.

46. American Library Association, "Privacy: An Interpretation of the Library Bill of Rights"; Jon Penney, "Chilling Effects: Online Surveillance and Wikipedia Use," *Berkeley Technology Law Journal* 31, no. 1 (2016): 117–82, https://doi.org/10.15779/Z38SS13; Alex Matthews and Catherine E. Tucker, "Government Surveillance and Internet Search Behavior," SSRN, February 17, 2017, https://doi.org/10.2139/ssrn.2412564; Pen American Center, *Chilling Effects: NSA Surveillance Drives U.S. Writers to Self-censor* (New York: Pen American Center, November 12, 2013), https://pen.org/sites/default/files/2014-08-01_Full%20Report_Chilling%20Effects%20w%20Color%20cover-UPDATED.pdf.

47. Sorelle Friedler, Carlos Scheidegger, and Suresh Venkatasubramanian, Algorithmic Fairness website, accessed May 24, 2017, http://fairness.haverford.edu/index.html; Neil M. Richards, "The Dangers of Surveillance," *Harvard Law Review* 126, no. 1934 (May 20, 2013): 1934–65, https://harvardlawreview.org/2013/05/the-dangers-of-surveillance/; Dorothy Roberts and Jeffrey Vagle, "Racial Surveillance Has a Long History," The Hill, January 4, 2016, http://thehill.com/opinion/op-ed/264710-racial-surveillance-has-a-long-history; Jeffrey L. Vagle, "The History, Means, and Effects of Structural Surveillance," Penn Law: Legal Scholarship Repository, paper 1625, University of Pennsylvania Law School, February 7, 2016, accessed May 24, 2017, http://scholarship.law.upenn.edu/cgi/viewcontent.cgi?article=2626&context=faculty_scholarship.

48. See Context section, above.

49. EDUCAUSE, *Seven Things You Should Know About… How Learning Data Impacts Privacy* (Lou-

isville, CO: EDUCAUSE Learning Initiative, 2017), https://library.educause.edu/~/media/files/library/2017/5/eli7144.pdf.

50. American Library Association, "Library Privacy Guidelines for Library Management Systems"; Marr, "Why Data Minimization Is an Important Concept."

51. Association of College and Research Libraries, "Guidelines, Standards, and Frameworks," accessed May 24, 2017, http://www.ala.org/acrl/standards.

52. Association of College and Research Libraries, *Standards for Libraries in Higher Education.*

53. Association of College and Research Libraries, "Intellectual Freedom Principles for Academic Libraries: An Interpretation of the Library Bill of Rights," last modified July 12, 2000, http://www.ala.org/acrl/publications/whitepapers/intellectual; Association of College and Research Libraries, *Standards for Libraries in Higher Education*; American Library Association, "Professional Ethics."

54. Lehner, "Return on Investment in Academic Libraries Research"; Association of College and Research Libraries, *Academic Library Impact on Student Learning and Success*, prepared by Karen Brown with contributions by Kara J. Malenfant (Chicago: Association of College and Research Libraries, April 2017)http://www.ala.org/acrl/sites/ala.org.acrl/files/content/issues/value/findings_y3.pdf.

55. Deanna B. Marcum, "Defining 'Common Good' in the Digital World" (paper presented at the symposium The Diffusion of Knowledge in the Digital Age, Philadelphia, PA, November 13, 1999, accessed May 24, 2017, https://www.jstor.org/stable/1558326

56. Soria, Fransen, and Nackerud,, "Library Use and Undergraduate Student Outcomes," 154.

57. Oakleaf, "Activity #12: Library Data Audit."

58. Cavoukian, "Privacy by Design."

59. American Library Association, "Privacy: An Interpretation of the Library Bill of Rights."

60. "LibQUAL+," Association of Research Libraries, Statistics and Assessment, accessed May 24, 2017, http://www.arl.org/focus-areas/statistics-assessment/libqual; "About NSSE," National Survey of Student Engagement, accessed May 24, 2017, http://nsse.indiana.edu/html/about.cfm; "Why CCSSE?" Community College Survey of Student Engagement, accessed May 24, 2017, http://www.ccsse.org/.

61. Hartman-Caverly, "Our 'Special Obligation.'"

62. American Library Association, "Privacy: An Interpretation of the Library Bill of Rights."

63. American Library Association, "Privacy and Confidentiality," accessed May 24, 2017, http://www.ala.org/Template.cfm?Section=ifissues&Template=/ContentManagement/ContentDisplay.cfm&ContentID=25304#.

64. Dorothy J. Glancy, "The Invention of the Right to Privacy," *Arizona Law Review* 21, no. 1 (1979): 1–39, http://law.scu.edu/wp-content/uploads/Privacy.pdf.

65. Steven J. Bell, "Keeping up with… Learning Analytics," Association of College and Research Libraries, last modified October 2014, http://www.ala.org/acrl/publications/keeping_up_with/learning_analytics.

66. Goldie Blumenstyk, "As Big Data Comes to College, Officials Wrestle to Set New Ethical Norms," *Chronicle of Higher Education*, June 28, 2016, http://www.chronicle.com.libdb.dccc.edu/article/As-Big-Data-Comes-to-College/236934 (requires login).

67. American Library Association, "Developing or Revising a Library Privacy Policy."

68. American Library Association, "Developing or Revising a Library Privacy Policy."

69. Association of College and Research Libraries, "Information Has Value"; American Library Association, "Advocating for Intellectual Freedom," last modified July 1, 2014, http://www.ala.org/advocacy/intfreedom/librarybill/interpretations/advocating-intellectual-freedom.

70. Electronic Privacy Information Center, "Privacy and Consumer Profiling," accessed May 24, 2017, https://epic.org/privacy/profiling/; Eric Goldman, "Search Engine Bias and the Demise of Search Engine Utopianism," *Yale Journal of Law and Technology*, 2005–2006, Santa Clara University Legal Studies Research Paper No. 06-08, Marquette University Law School Legal Research Paper No. 06-20, https://ssrn.com/abstract=893892; Electronic Frontier Foundation, "Content Blocking," accessed May 24, 2017, https://www.eff.org/issues/content-blocking; Julia Greenberg, "When Tech Giants Deliver the News, They Decide What News Is," *Wired*, June 10, 2015, https://www.wired.com/2015/06/apples-news-app-gives-power-decide-whats-news/.

71. Association of College and Research Libraries, "Information Has Value"; American Library Asso-

ciation, "Professional Ethics."

72. Bartunek and Woodman, "Beyond Lewin."

73. Phillip Long and George Siemens, "Penetrating the Fog: Analytics in Learning and Education," *EDUCAUSE Review*, September/October 2011, 30–40, http://er.educause.edu/articles/2011/9/penetrating-the-fog-analytics-in-learning-and-education; Chris Barker, *The Sage Dictionary of Cultural Studies,* s.v. "surveillance" (London: Sage UK, 2004), Credo Reference; Slade and Prinsloo. "Learning Analytics."

74. American Library Association, "Professional Ethics."

75. Internet Policy Observatory, "Censorship," accessed May 24, 2017, http://globalnetpolicy.org/research_tags/censorship/; Onlinecensorship.org, "What Is Online Censorship?" accessed May 24, 2017, https://onlinecensorship.org/; Fairness and Accuracy in Reporting, "FAIR Studies," accessed May 24, 2017, http://fair.org/fair-studies/; Reporters without Borders, "2017 World Press Freedom Index: Detailed Methodology," accessed May 24, 2017, https://rsf.org/en/detailed-methodology; Justin Coler, "A Former Fake News Creator on Covering Fake News," NiemanReports, Nieman Foundation at Harvard, May 1, 2017, http://niemanreports.org/articles/a-former-fake-news-creator-on-covering-fake-news/; Jay Stanley, *The Surveillance-Industrial Complex* (New York: American Civil Liberties Union, August 2004), https://www.aclu.org/other/surveillance-industrial-complex.

76. American Library Association, "Professional Ethics."

Bibliography

Achieving the Dream. "Technology in Education." Accessed May 24, 2017. http://achievingthedream.org/focus-areas/technology-in-education.

American Association of Community Colleges. "College Completion Challenge Resources." Accessed May 24, 2017. http://www.ccsse.org/center/about_cccse/college_completion_challenge.cfm#resources

———. Voluntary Framework of Accountability website. Accessed May 24, 2017. http://vfa.aacc.nche.edu/Pages/default.aspx.

American Association of University Professors. "Statement on Government of Colleges and Universities." Last modified April 1990. https://www.aaup.org/report/statement-government-colleges-and-universities.

American Library Association. "Advocating for Intellectual Freedom." Last modified July 1, 2014. http://www.ala.org/advocacy/intfreedom/librarybill/interpretations/advocating-intellectual-freedom.

———. "Developing or Revising a Library Privacy Policy." Last modified April 2017. Accessed May 24, 2017. http://www.ala.org/advocacy/privacy/toolkit/policy.

———. "Library Privacy Guidelines." Accessed May 24, 2017. http://www.ala.org/advocacy/privacy/guidelines.

———. "Library Privacy Guidelines for Library Management Systems." Last modified June 24, 2016. http://www.ala.org/advocacy/privacy/guidelines/library-management-systems.

———. "Policy Concerning Confidentiality of Personally Identifiable Information About Library Users." Last modified June 30, 2004. http://www.ala.org/advocacy/intfreedom/statementspols/otherpolicies/policyconcerning.

———. "Privacy: An Interpretation of the Library Bill of Rights." Last modified July 1, 2014. http://www.ala.org/advocacy/intfreedom/librarybill/interpretations/privacy.

———. "Privacy and Confidentiality." Accessed May 24, 2017, http://www.ala.org/Template.cfm?Section=ifissues&Template=/ContentManagement/ContentDisplay.cfm&ContentID=25304#.

———. "A Privacy Audit." Last modified April 2017. http://www.ala.org/advocacy/privacy/toolkit/policy#privacyaudit.

———. "Privacy Tool Kit." Last modified January 2014. http://www.ala.org/advocacy/privacy/toolkit.

———. "Professional Ethics." Last modified January 22, 2008. http://www.ala.org/tools/ethics.

———. "Questions and Answers on Privacy and Confidentiality." Last modified July 1, 2014. http://www.ala.org/advocacy/privacy/FAQ.

Section 1

Association of College and Research Libraries. *Academic Library Impact on Student Learning and Success: Findings from Assessment in Action Team Projects*. Prepared by Karen Brown with contributions by Kara J. Malenfant. Chicago: Association of College and Research Libraries, April 2017. http://www.ala.org/acrl/sites/ala.org.acrl/files/content/issues/value/findings_y3.pdf.

———. "ACRL Value of Academic Libraries Bibliography." Accessed May 24, 2017. http://acrl.ala.org/valueography/.

———. *Framework for Information Literacy for Higher Education*. Chicago: Association of College and Research Libraries, 2016. http://www.ala.org/acrl/standards/ilframework.

———. "Guidelines, Standards, and Frameworks." Accessed May 24, 2017. http://www.ala.org/acrl/standards.

———. "Intellectual Freedom Principles for Academic Libraries: An Interpretation of the Library Bill of Rights." Last modified July 12, 2000. http://www.ala.org/acrl/publications/whitepapers/intellectual.

———. *Standards for Libraries in Higher Education*. Chicago: Association of College and Research Libraries, 2011. http://www.ala.org/acrl/standards/standardslibraries.

Association of Research Libraries. "LibQUAL+." Association of Research Libraries, Statistics and Assessment. Accessed May 24, 2017. http://www.arl.org/focus-areas/statistics-assessment/libqual.

Barker, Chris, *The Sage Dictionary of Cultural Studies*, s.v. "surveillance." London: Sage UK, 2004. Credo Reference.

Bartunek, Jean M., and Richard W. Woodman. "Beyond Lewin: Toward a Temporal Approximation of Organizational Development and Change." *Annual Review of Organizational Psychology and Organizational Behavior*, no. 2 (2015): 157–82. https://doi.org/10.1146/annurev-orgpsych-032414-111353.

Bell, Steven J. "Keeping up with… Learning Analytics." Association of College and Research Libraries. Last modified October 2014. http://www.ala.org/acrl/publications/keeping_up_with/learning_analytics.

Bermann, Sol. "Free to Be You and Me: Autonomy Privacy in Higher Education." *EDUCAUSE Review*. January 17, 2017. http://er.educause.edu/blogs/2017/1/free-to-be-you-and-me-autonomy-privacy-in-higher-education.

Blumenstyk, Goldie. "As Big Data Comes to College, Officials Wrestle to Set New Ethical Norms." *Chronicle of Higher Education*. June 28, 2016. http://www.chronicle.com.libdb.dccc.edu/article/As-Big-Data-Comes-to-College/236934 (requires login).

Borden, Victor M. H. "Down Means Up." *Community College Week* 23, no. 8 (November 29, 2010): 7–11. MasterFILE Premier, EBSCOhost.

———. "A Downward Trend." *Community College Week* 26, no. 14 (2014): 7–10. Academic Search Premier, EBSCOhost.

Cavoukian, Ann. "Privacy by Design: The Seven Foundational Principles: Implementation and Mapping of Fair Information Practices." Internet Architecture Board. Accessed May 24, 2017. https://iab.org/wp-content/IAB-uploads/2011/03/fred_carter.pdf.

Center for Community College Student Engagement (CCCSE). *Expectations Meet Reality: The Underprepared Student and Community Colleges*. Annual report, 2016. https://www.ccsse.org/docs/Underprepared_Student.pdf.

Childs, Sarah, Graham Matthews, and Graham Walton, "Space, Use and University Libraries: The Future?" In *University Libraries and Space in the Digital World*. Edited by Graham Matthews and Graham Walton, 201–16. Farnham, UK: Ashgate, 2013. https://dspace.lboro.ac.uk/dspace-jspui/handle/2134/11496.

Coler, Justin. "A Former Fake News Creator on Covering Fake News." NiemanReports. Nieman Foundation at Harvard. May 1, 2017. http://niemanreports.org/articles/a-former-fake-news-creator-on-covering-fake-news/.

Community College Research Center. "Community College FAQs." Teachers College, Columbia University. Accessed May 24, 2017. http://ccrc.tc.columbia.edu/Community-College-FAQs.html.

Community College Survey of Student Engagement. "Why CCSSE?" Accessed May 24, 2017. http://www.ccsse.org/.

Deitering, Anne-Marie. "CFParticipation: Autoethnography Learning Community." info-fetishist, May 22, 2015. https://info-fetishist.org/2015/05/22/cfparticipation-autoethnography-learning-community/.

Delaware County Community College. "College Academic Learning Goals." Accessed May 24, 2017. https://www.dccc.edu/academics/resources/college-academic-learning-goals.

———. "Fast Facts about Delaware County Community College." Accessed May 24, 2017. https://www.dccc.edu/about/news-information/fast-facts.

———. Information Literacy Faculty Toolkit. Accessed May 24, 2017. http://libguides.dccc.edu/ilfaculty-toolkit.

———. "Learning Analytics." Delaware County Community College. Last modified April 12, 2017. http://libguides.dccc.edu/learning_analytics.

———. "Policy on Student Confidentiality." Student Handbook—Academic Information and Policies. Accessed May 24, 2017. https://www.dccc.edu/campus-life/helpful-links/student-handbook/academic-info-policies#StudentConfidentiality.

EDUCAUSE. "Learning Analytics." Accessed May 24, 2017. https://library.educause.edu/topics/teaching-and-learning/learning-analytics.

———. *Seven Things You Should Know About… How Learning Data Impacts Privacy.* Louisville, CO: EDUCAUSE Learning Initiative, 2017. https://library.educause.edu/~/media/files/library/2017/5/eli7144.pdf.

———. "Teaching and Learning." Accessed May 24, 2017. https://www.educause.edu/focus-areas-and-initiatives/teaching-and-learning.

Electronic Frontier Foundation. "Content Blocking." Accessed May 24, 2017. https://www.eff.org/issues/content-blocking.

Electronic Privacy Information Center. "Privacy and Consumer Profiling." Accessed May 24, 2017. https://epic.org/privacy/profiling/.

Fairness and Accuracy in Reporting. "FAIR Studies." Accessed May 24, 2017. http://fair.org/fair-studies/.

Fletcher, Jeffrey, Markeisha Grant, Marisol Ramos, and Melinda Mechur Karp. "Integrated Planning and Advising for Student Success (iPASS): State of the Literature." CCRC Working Paper No. 90. Community College Research Center, Teachers College, Columbia University. October 2016. http://ccrc.tc.columbia.edu/media/k2/attachments/ipass-state-of-the-literature.pdf.

Friedler, Sorelle, Carlos Scheidegger and Suresh Venkatasubramanian. Algorithmic Fairness website. Accessed May 24, 2017. http://fairness.haverford.edu/index.html.

Glancy, Dorothy J. "The Invention of the Right to Privacy." *Arizona Law Review* 21, no. 1 (1979): 1–39. http://law.scu.edu/wp-content/uploads/Privacy.pdf.

Goldman, Eric. "Search Engine Bias and the Demise of Search Engine Utopianism." *Yale Journal of Law and Technology,* 2005–2006. Santa Clara University Legal Studies Research Paper No. 06-08; Marquette University Law School Legal Research Paper No. 06-20. SSRN. https://ssrn.com/abstract=893892.

Greenberg, Julia. "When Tech Giants Deliver the News, They Decide What News Is." *Wired.* June 10, 2015. https://www.wired.com/2015/06/apples-news-app-gives-power-decide-whats-news/.

Hartman-Caverly, Sarah. "Our 'Special Obligation': Library Assessment, Learning Analytics, and Intellectual Freedom." Presentation, Tri-state College Library Cooperative, April 3, 2017. YouTube video, 1:12:20. Published by TCLC Libraries, April 7, 2017. https://youtu.be/bKiTR9TNdf8.

Hobsons Education Advances. PAR Framework website. Accessed May 24, 2017. http://www.parframework.org/about-par/.

Institutional Effectiveness, Delaware County Community College. "2016 Fall Third Week Credit Enrollment Report.".

———. "Student Financial Aid 2015–16." Integrated Postsecondary Education Data System (IPEDS).

Internet Policy Observatory. "Censorship." Accessed May 24, 2017. http://globalnetpolicy.org/research_tags/censorship/.

Jones, Kyle M. L., and Dorothea Salo. "Learning Analytics and the Academic Library: Professional Ethics Commitments at a Crossroads." *College and Research Libraries*, preprint, accessed May 24, 2017, http://crl.acrl.org/index.php/crl/article/view/16603/18049.

Kenney, Caitlin. "Bernanke Sees Green Shoots." *Planet Money,* National Public Radio. March 16, 2009. http://www.npr.org/sections/money/2009/03/bernanke_sees_green_shoots.html.

Lehner, John. "Return on Investment in Academic Libraries Research," ACRL SE09 Doc 4.0. Memo to Executive Committee of the ACRL Board of Directors, April 4, 2009. http://connect.ala.org/files/61784/doc_4_0_roi_memo_pdf_49f626bc94.pdf.

Section 1

Long, Phillip, and George Siemens. "Penetrating the Fog: Analytics in Learning and Education." *EDU-CAUSE Review*, September/October 2011, 30–40. http://er.educause.edu/articles/2011/9/penetrating-the-fog-analytics-in-learning-and-education.

Marcum, Deanna B. "Defining 'Common Good' in the Digital World." Paper presented at the symposium The Diffusion of Knowledge in the Digital Age, Philadelphia, PA, November 13, 1999. Accessed May 24, 2017. https://www.jstor.org/stable/1558326

Marr, Bernard. "Why Data Minimization Is an Important Concept in the Age of Big Data." *Forbes*, March 16, 2016. https://www.forbes.com/sites/bernardmarr/2016/03/16/why-data-minimization-is-an-important-concept-in-the-age-of-big-data/.

Matthews, Alex, and Catherine E. Tucker. "Government Surveillance and Internet Search Behavior." SSRN, February 17, 2017. https://doi.org/10.2139/ssrn.2412564.

National Survey of Student Engagement. "About NSSE." Accessed May 24, 2017. http://nsse.indiana.edu/html/about.cfm.

Oakleaf, Megan. *Academic Library Value: The Impact Starter Kit*. Syracuse, NY: Dellas Graphics, 2012.

Office of Ethics, University of California Berkeley. "Information Risk Governance Committee (IRGC)." Accessed May 24, 2017. https://ethics.berkeley.edu/privacy/irgc.

———. "Transparency Report." Accessed May 24, 2017. https://ethics.berkeley.edu/privacy/transparency.

Onlinecensorship.org. "What is Online Censorship?" Accessed May 24, 2017. https://onlinecensorship.org/.

Pen American Center. *Chilling Effects: NSA Surveillance Drives U.S. Writers to Self-Censor*. New York: Pen American Center, November 12, 2013. https://pen.org/sites/default/files/2014-08-01_Full%20Report_Chilling%20Effects%20w%20Color%20cover-UPDATED.pdf.

Penney, Jon. "Chilling Effects: Online Surveillance and Wikipedia Use." *Berkeley Technology Law Journal* 31, no. 1 (2016): 117–82. https://doi.org/10.15779/Z38SS13.

Reporters without Borders. "2017 World Press Freedom Index: Detailed Methodology." Accessed May 24, 2017. https://rsf.org/en/detailed-methodology.

Richards, Neil M. "The Dangers of Surveillance." *Harvard Law Review* 126, no. 1934 (May 20, 2013): 1934–65. https://harvardlawreview.org/2013/05/the-dangers-of-surveillance/.

Roberts, Dorothy, and Jeffrey Vagle. "Racial Surveillance Has a Long History." The Hill, January 4, 2016. http://thehill.com/opinion/op-ed/264710-racial-surveillance-has-a-long-history.

Rodriguez, Noelie, and Alan Ryave. *Systematic Self-observation*. Thousand Oaks, CA: Sage, 2002.

Slade, Sharon, and Paul Prinsloo. "Learning Analytics: Ethical Issues and Dilemmas." *American Behavioral Scientist* 57, no. 10 (2013): 1510–29. https://doi.org/10.1177/0002764213479366.

Slaughter, Sheila, and Gary Rhoades. *Academic Capitalism and the New Economy: Markets, State, and Higher Education*. Baltimore: Johns Hopkins University Press, 2004.

Soria, Krista M., Jan Fransen, and Shane Nackerud. "Library Use and Undergraduate Student Outcomes: New Evidence for Students' Retention and Academic Success." *portal: Libraries and the Academy* 13, no. 2 (April 2013): 147–64. https://doi.org/10.1353/pla.2013.0010.

Stanley, Jay. *The Surveillance-Industrial Complex: How the American Government Is Conscripting Businesses and Individuals in the Construction of a Surveillance Society*. New York: American Civil Liberties Union, August 2004. https://www.aclu.org/other/surveillance-industrial-complex.

Taylor, Mark. "Shared Governance in the Modern University." *Higher Education Quarterly* 67, no. 1 (January 2013): 80–94. https://doi.org/10.1111/hequ.12003. Academic Search Premier, EBSCOhost.

US Department of Education. "College Scorecard Data." Accessed May 24, 2017. https://collegescorecard.ed.gov/data/.

Vagle, Jeffrey L. "The History, Means, and Effects of Structural Surveillance." Penn Law: Legal Scholarship Repository, paper 1625. University of Pennsylvania Law School. February 7, 2016. http://scholarship.law.upenn.edu/cgi/viewcontent.cgi?article=2626&context=faculty_scholarship.

Section 1

Title: Research and Writing in the Discipline: A Model for Faculty-Librarian Collaboration

Abstract: This study assessed the impact of partnership between faculty teaching Writing in the Discipline courses with subject librarians on all three groups: students, faculty, and librarians. Partnering pairs were asked to develop interventions through which librarians could support students in achieving specific learning outcomes. To determine the effectiveness of the collaborations, pre- and post-course surveys were conducted of the students and post-course surveys of the faculty and librarians. Overall, better relationships developed between faculty, librarians, and students as a result of the collaboration. The chapter concludes with a protocol of best practices developed for future WID faculty-librarian collaborators.

Keywords: faculty-librarian collaboration, assessment, learning outcomes, Writing in the Discipline

Project focus: information literacy assessment; services (i.e., customer service at reference desk); user behaviors and needs; assessment concepts and/or management

Results made or will make case for: improvements in services, proof of library impact and value, a strategic plan or process, decisions about library staffing

Data needed: benefits of faculty-librarian collaboration; impact on undergraduate students, faculty, and librarians while supporting institutional values, specifically disciplinary writing and critical thinking.

Methodology: qualitative, quantitative, mixed method, evaluation or survey

Project duration: greater than 1 year

Tool(s) utilized: Qualtrics, staffing for reading and analyzing qualitative data and for preparing presentation materials as well as developing subsequent materials and documentation

Cost estimate: < $100

Type of institution: university—private

Institution enrollment: 5,000–15,000

Highest level of education: master's/professional degree

Chapter 5

Research and Writing in the Discipline

A Model for Faculty-Librarian Collaboration

Talia Nadir and Erika Scheurer

Context

The University of St. Thomas is a medium-sized private Catholic comprehensive university in Saint Paul, Minnesota. While its core curriculum is substantial, the university currently has no first-year experience or other official means of embedding information literacy into the curriculum. The library staff has worked hard for years to forge connections with faculty, reaching out at academic department meetings and to individual faculty members. Success has been spotty and somewhat limited to a handful of long-term librarian-faculty collaborations.

In 2009, St. Thomas began a Writing across the Curriculum (WAC) initiative that relies on a five-day faculty certification seminar. The seminar, limited to cohorts of twenty faculty members (full-time as well as adjunct), focuses on writing as a process as well as a product, the relationship of writing to critical thinking and learning, effective ways to support writing in progress, and course alignment with assignment scaffolding. By

2015, enough faculty had completed the seminar to implement a four-course graduation requirement in WAC: two Writing Intensive courses (usually in the core curriculum), one Writing to Learn course (any level or discipline), and one Writing in the Discipline (in the student's major field of concentration).

Because the goals of WAC mesh so well with library instruction and information literacy, Talia, a research and instruction librarian and Assessment in Action (AiA) participant, invited Erika Scheurer, WAC director and associate professor of English, to join her to conduct a research study in 2015–2016 assessing the effects of librarian-faculty collaborations in WID courses.

Our Case Study

In our study—for which Talia received a grant from the Association of College and Research Libraries (ACRL) program Assessment in Action: Academic Libraries and Student Success—we chose to focus on the third-tier WAC requirement, Writing in the Discipline (WID), for two main reasons. First, library research to complete high-stakes assignments is often a key element of these courses and faculty are motivated to teach majors research skills specific to their academic disciplines. Second, the WAC certification seminar emphasizes the importance of supporting high-stakes writing projects through a process that includes identifying key learning goals, discerning which parts of the project students struggle with the most, and developing support activities to teach students the information and skills they need to complete these more difficult parts. For many faculty members, this process reveals that students need support in learning how to conduct disciplinary research.

The goal of our study was to determine the impact of faculty-librarian partnerships on students, faculty, and librarians and to discern which forms of collaboration were viewed by the participants as most effective. We utilized surveys (see appendix 5.1 for all the survey questions and appendix 5.2 for the quantitative results of the student surveys) to obtain this information: pre- and post-course surveys for the students and post-course surveys for faculty and librarians. The content of the surveys was developed in collaboration with library staff. We wanted to learn about students' prior library experience and knowledge and gain insight into their levels of confidence with research before and after the course. For all three constituencies—students, librarians, and faculty—we developed questions to elicit their perceptions of what was most beneficial about the faculty-librarian collaboration and how they might do things differently in the future.

We also aimed to increase collaboration between subject librarians and faculty, especially in those disciplines where collaboration is lacking. In the end, we had volunteer participants from five academic departments in the fall semester of 2015, and seven in the spring semester of 2016. In all, approximately 166 students were assessed over both semesters (see table 5.1).

Table 5.1
Number of Survey Responses by Class

	Pre-Fall 2015	Pre-Spring 2016	Post-Fall 2015	Post-Spring 2016
Freshman	3	6	3	4
Sophomore	0	45	0	36
Junior	23	24	16	16
Senior	25	40	19	20
N =	51	115	38	76

Formats of library intervention ranged from one-shot instruction sessions to multiple meetings, including one-on-one work with students. We left it to the faculty-librarian team to determine their level of collaboration.

Students in participating courses were surveyed online at the beginning and end of the semester, with the surveys including both quantitative and qualitative questions; surveys were voluntary and anonymous. The pre-survey aimed to assess previous exposure to library research and comfort level in conducting research. The post-survey asked students to reflect on their experience of working with a librarian/faculty team during the course and its impact, if any, on their comfort level with research as well as the usefulness of the collaboration and influence on their writing.

Our findings indicate a significant shift from low or neutral to high levels of confidence in students between the beginning and end of each semester. Specifically, students' confidence using the library and its resources for general academic research rose by 16 percent; for research specifically oriented towards their major, their confidence rose by 25 percent. Table 5.2 represents the combined fall 2015 and spring 2016 responses to the questions about confidence.

Table 5.2
Levels of Confidence Using Library Resources: Pre- and Post-Course
Using the scale below, how would you rank your level of confidence in...

Question		Not at all confident 1	2	Somewhat confident 3	4	Very confident 5
Using the library and its resources for general academic research	PRE N=165	9 5.5%	10 6.1%	59 35.8%	62 37.6%	25 15.2%
	POST N=108	1 0.9%	1 0.9%	32 29.6%	49 45.4%	25 23.1%
Using the library and its resources for research in your major	PRE N=165	11 6.7%	21 12.7%	50 30.3%	60 36.4%	23 13.9%
	POST N=107	2 1.9%	1 0.9%	24 22.4%	40 37.4%	40 37.4%

Also, the percentage of agreement and strong agreement with the following statements was extremely high:

- The library instruction related directly to the course: 86 percent
- Materials presented or covered were relevant to the course: 87 percent
- The library instruction was helpful or worthwhile: 83 percent

In their comments, students expressed enthusiasm about learning about tools such as RefWorks as well as about practical skills, as expressed by the following: "[how] to access the different databases that fall under each class category. It was applicable to all my classes and even some work I did outside of class." Many found meeting with the librarian one-on-one extremely useful. One noted, "I would recommend having every class meet with you if you have the time. It was incredibly helpful to meet at the library and learn about resources in relation to my topic." Finally, some comments revealed a deeper appreciation of the connection between research and writing: "Research is key, make sure to take a lot of time doing it. The more in-depth the research, the easier the writing process will be."

At the end of each semester, librarians and faculty members completed surveys in which they reflected on their experience; they made observations about the collaboration and their perceptions of the impact it had on students' work. Faculty pointed to a greater number of resources gathered by students and appreciated the higher quality of research due to the librarian's intervention: "The quality of their research also is vastly different, of course, and they walk away with valuable skills in navigating online databases and citation skills, as well as in finding sources related to their topics."

Faculty also valued broader benefits of their collaboration with librarians, commenting on their enjoyment of the process and how much they learned. As one stated, "I think this type of collaboration is vital for students… having a librarian available to assist students is a great benefit to them and to me." A faculty member with more experience with library pairing explained his or her choice to do so this way: "I try whenever possible to collaborate with [the librarian] in my core classes, and I appreciate that many students seem to become energized about their research topics after our library instruction sessions, more so than other classes where we haven't had the session."

Librarians, for their part, found the collaboration with faculty members enabled them to teach information literacy more effectively: "It was valuable for me to be able to see where the needs were/adapt my teaching style to help students where they were instead of where I thought they might be, and for the students to understand all of the various ways I could be of assistance throughout the research process," and "I am better able to tailor my instruction sessions and the individual research appointments I have with students to meet those goals." Also, they perceived better relationships between themselves, faculty, and students. Indeed, for some, working with faculty proves an essential point of access to students; as one librarian noted, "Collaborating with faculty is often the only way we, as librarians, can reach students so it's crucial we partner with them."

Conclusions

In their comments, both faculty and librarians identified the quality of communication and coordination between them as essential for success. As one faculty member commented, "It is essential to discuss what goals the faculty member has for the collaboration and provide the librarian with a syllabus copy, and specific course assignments if the research librarian will be actively involved in assisting students." Librarians found frequent communication vital (and lacking in less successful pairs). One noted, "I think the biggest 'Do' is to make sure to keep honest and open communication flowing throughout. Set expectations and goals beforehand about what you each see your role to be, and stay positive."

Overall, from the perspectives of both faculty and librarians and from our reading of student feedback on more and less collaborative pairs, the following elements are key to success:

- Faculty and librarians are on the same page regarding outcomes for student learning in the area of research.
- Early on, librarians and faculty communicate about the nature of the research assignment and then continue to communicate often.
- At the outset, teams clarify where the roles of librarian and faculty are distinct and where they overlap.

In addition, the comments from faculty, librarians and students highlighted the importance of individualized instruction. A single presentation from the librarian—especially when it was more generic and not specific to the assignment—was not enough; students were less satisfied in those courses, especially when they had seen the presentation before. Group presentations were more effective when tailored to the specific assignment and when they were part of a scaffolded series of interventions, including one-on-one instruction. Finally, as can be expected, students were more likely to take advantage of one-on-one library instruction when it was required or offered for extra credit than when it was simply encouraged.

One area of possible friction we observed between faculty and student comments and the perspectives of librarians—both in our study and in the broader research[1]—is that many of the faculty and student survey respondents mentioned how much working with the librarian saved time and energy, made life easier, and so on. For students, for example, this was reflected in frequent references to the utility of learning about tools such as RefWorks. However, as we know, what librarians have to offer goes far beyond providing tools, extending into teaching critical thinking about research. The following comment from a faculty member points to his or her understanding of the larger teaching role of the librarian partner: "Personally, I love collaborating with other teachers because I think that we provoke each other into more extended or in-depth discussions, with each other and with students. I thought this was true for this experience with [the librarian]." Clearly this faculty member sees his or her librarian partner as a fellow instructor, not as someone providing a time-saving service; however, this level of understanding was not common in faculty comments.

Finally, our study reinforced a larger issue at our university frequently discussed in the literature:[2] lack of systematic introduction and extension of IL skills for students throughout the curriculum. Although these were WID courses and usually fell somewhat later in students' academic careers, 19 percent of the fall semester students and 24 percent of the spring semester students reported no prior experience doing library research. In addition, while almost three quarters of the students had experienced library instruction sessions before in other courses (fall: 72 percent; spring: 73 percent), the remaining quarter had received no instruction of any kind up to that point. Therefore, what should have been a fine-tuning and focusing of research skills at the WID level was in reality a first exposure for a significant portion of the students.

Communicating Results and Impact

Talia shared our findings in a poster session at the annual meeting of the Association of American Libraries in Orlando in summer 2016. The following fall we offered a Faculty Development workshop aimed at University of St. Thomas (UST) faculty and librarians. Our presentation, "Supporting Student Research through Faculty-Librarian Partnerships," was attended primarily by UST librarians, including the libraries' director; a single faculty member attended, one who had participated in the study. Later that semester we presented at the Sixth Biennial International Conference on Critical Thinking and Writing "Creative Connectivity: Thinking, Writing and the Translation of Information to Understanding," sponsored by Quinnipiac University. Our audience consisted of primarily writing program faculty from across the country.

Our presentations, which included equal speaking time for both of us, consisted of PowerPoint slides that detailed our study and its findings and also provided best practices. In addition to the presentations, Erika wrote a column in *Synergia*, UST's online faculty development newsletter, where she shared our research as well as "A Guide for Faculty-Librarian Collaboration" that we have developed together following our study (see appendix 5.3). Our aim for the guide was to take what we learned about effective faculty-librarian collaboration both in our case study and in our research in the field and produce a concise step-by-step guide for how to proceed, along with helpful tips.

Both the faculty members and the librarians with whom we shared our research results agreed that students benefit from close faculty-librarian collaboration and from one-on-one support from librarians. Indeed, our study reinforced scholarship on this point, specifically in library science.[3] Although the results were not necessarily new, conducting this study in the context of our university and making the results public has been a crucial step in the overall effort of the library to gain recognition for the benefits librarians can provide for students. As the faculty and librarian survey comments we have shared demonstrate, the benefits of collaboration are well known among librarians and the faculty who work with them. The challenge remains persuading the rest of the faculty to take part—and to follow through once they agree to collaborate.

While we had always known about this challenge of inducing faculty to work more closely with their subject librarians, we learned it anew in spring 2017, when we attempted to build on the results of our study and forge new WID faculty-librarian collaborations. In January, Erika individually contacted the thirty-three faculty scheduled to teach WID courses, sharing our research and guide and inviting them to collaborate with their subject librarians. Of these, eight initially responded in the affirmative; of these, four had already built working collaborations with their subject librarians. Before the semester began, one of the faculty members who had no experience working with his subject liaison librarian had accepted Erika's invitation to meet one-on-one and developed an extensive plan for scaffolding librarian intervention into his students' research project.

By the point of Erika's mid-term check-in, of the four participating faculty, two had dropped out: one because he did not think the primary research he assigned required help from a librarian, the other because she was teaching an overload and had no time (despite being interested). Of the remaining two, at their end-of-semester check-ins, the first had managed to fit in only one chance for the librarian to meet with the class and hoped to do more next time; the second, with whom Erika had met extensively in January, had scheduled only late-semester interventions, and these consisted mainly of the librarian's offering feedback on near-final drafts of the research projects. The faculty member expressed eagerness to do a more thoroughly scaffolded IL intervention in the next iteration of the course.

Leveraging the Findings

The minimal results of our attempt to personally support WID faculty through one-on-one contact and through the guide we had developed reinforced for us the need for system-wide change. As the research indicates, information literacy needs to be formally scaffolded into the curriculum;[4] the "scattershot" approach, dependent as it is on the personal motivation of individual faculty, will not ensure that all of our students are information-literate upon graduation. Our university is currently undergoing a major core curriculum review, providing an opportunity for systemic change in how we teach IL. We have both been in contact with a key administrative member of the review committee, sharing our research and our conviction that IL should be formally included in the new curriculum. While at this writing a formal proposal has not been presented to the faculty, we have learned that the inclusion of IL is part of the plan and currently expressed in the following way:

> Information literacy is an important requirement that will be fulfilled partially by the core but also within the majors. We envision a series of touchpoints infused throughout a student's experience that includes:
>
> - A module in the co-curricular FYE [First Year Experience]
> - Connections in core courses
> - Robust partnerships with library, CFD [Center for Faculty Development], and Student Affairs to provide training, workshops, activities, etc.
> - Connection in majors with required assessment element (mandatory objective in TK20 [assessment system])
> - For all faculty, intentional identification of IL-related coursework in syllabi, assignments

While this list is certainly ambitious and a clear departure from the university's current scattershot approach to IL, it is also quite vague. In order for the goal of IL-across-the-curriculum to become a reality, we will need to offer—and probably insist upon—our leadership and expertise every step of the way. Ideally, although they do not enjoy faculty status at UST, librarians, too, will be invited to curricular discussions. A key part of this process involves identifying key supporters and enlisting them in the implementation. First among these supporters will be the faculty across the curriculum who already have forged successful collaborations with their subject liaison librarians. As we share our research results, these faculty will need to step up and share their personal experiences working with their library colleagues.

Second, while no mandate succeeds without support from the faculty, we also will need to have strong support from the upper administration.[5] Evidence that this will be forthcoming has appeared in a recent proposal for A Year of Information Literacy, an effort recently launched by the office of Academic Affairs and the Vice Provost of Undergraduate Studies for 2017–2018. This coming year of focus on IL, if executed in close collaboration with the university libraries, may provide us much-needed momentum and a clear mandate for robust inclusion of IL in the new core curriculum.

Reflection

By far, the most gratifying aspect of our case study was our collaboration as researchers, presenters, and writers. Because, as a librarian and a faculty member, we were representatives of two of the constituencies we studied, we were able to offer each other valuable insights into our perspectives on faculty-librarian collaboration—all while we ourselves collaborated!

For example, when Erika asked Talia why some librarians in our study deployed the one-shot lecture method of collaboration instead of a more embedded approach, Talia reminded her that librarians do not enjoy the power and prestige of faculty members and therefore are likely to do what the faculty member wants, even if they personally would prefer to do more. Talia also reflected on the frustration shared by some librarians who feel as though they're not taken seriously and are treated by faculty as merely tool providers. Likewise, when Talia expressed frustration at faculty members' lack of follow-through in our spring 2017 attempt to build on what we learned in our study, Erika described how the increasing pressures on faculty to embed new pedagogical approaches into their teaching (not only WAC, but also community engagement, sustainability, diversity, etc.) lead them to feel overwhelmed. These are only two examples of many we could cite illustrating how not only the outcomes of our research, but also the process of collaborating on it led us to deeper insights into the dynamics of librarian-faculty pairings. This experience was definitely gratifying to us both personally and professionally.

Connected to our differing perspectives as faculty member and librarian, a key insight we gained from our study centered on how the hierarchical and "siloed" nature of the academy leads to obstacles that seem insurmountable at times. After all, the main result of our case study—that students, faculty, and librarians all benefit from faculty-librarian collaboration—is not a revelation. Our study confirmed what we already knew, and we hoped that having local data showing the benefits of faculty-librarian collaboration and providing support for faculty (in the form of the guide as well as access to Erika as WAC director) would encourage more pairings. But in our follow-up, this seemingly commonsense expectation did not become a reality.

Why? One reason we did not see dramatic increases in faculty-librarian pairings as a result of our case study is that because, as we have mentioned, at our university librarians do not hold faculty status (as they do at some);[6] they are pushed into a "service" role that leads them to an often-frustrating position of passively waiting for faculty members to choose to collaborate with them. And even when they do, faculty often fail to take full advantage of the librarian's potential role as a teacher of critical thinking about the research process, holding to the view of librarians as providers of useful tools such as RefWorks. The problem here is that because of the existing hierarchy, faculty need to take the initiative in forging productive collaborations; however, they are not inclined to do this if they are uninformed about or afraid of what a productive collaboration looks like.

Aside from the problem of hierarchy—seeing librarians as providing a service for faculty and students—another obstacle to productive librarian-faculty collaboration rests in the idea of teaching as a solo occupation. Any faculty members who have cotaught courses—as Erika has done many times—know that there are both pleasures and challenges to coteaching. One of the main challenges faculty must overcome is the assumption that teaching—and the position of authority that comes with it—is ideally done alone. Just as the field of composition studies in recent decades has replaced the image of the isolated writer composing in solitude with that of writing as a social act, so our image of the isolated professor must become adjusted in order for faculty to be open to sharing their authority with librarians.

This difference in perspective became extremely evident in the follow-up semester when Erika sent our guide to faculty for feedback. We originally had suggested that the faculty member and librarian develop learning outcomes for research together. Our first step read, "Develop shared outcomes for assessment of the learning goals connected to disciplinary research." After hearing back from a faculty member who felt strongly that faculty need to have learning goals in place *before* working with the librarian, we revised the first step to read, "Work with your librarian to hone outcomes for assessment of the learning goals connected to disciplinary research." While we thought it was entirely appropriate for faculty and librarians to develop assessment outcomes for disciplinary research together, we realized that the suggestion may be off-putting to some faculty, as it was in this case.

Aside from the need to debunk the myth that writing and teaching are best done solo, another similarity between the areas of library-faculty collaboration and writing studies is the issue of time as it is perceived by faculty. Erika continues to do research in WAC studies on faculty perceptions of "coverage" of course content.[7] In the early days of building our university WAC program (and still today), faculty told her that they could not possibly bring in more writing to their courses because they needed to use the time to "cover" course content. We have noticed a similar perception among some faculty when it comes to embedding the librarian more deeply into their courses—scheduling multiple interventions, for example, instead of the "one-shot" library session (which itself feels like a sacrifice of course time to some). As WAC director, Erika has worked to convince faculty to see writing as a *means* of covering course content—that students learn the content *through* the writing process. In the same way, we must encourage faculty to see the process of learning information literacy not as an isolated activity, but as a *means* of covering their goal of students being able to conduct research in their field.

Going into our case study, we knew that faculty-librarian collaboration enabled student learning. We wanted to learn specifically *how* it was useful for students, librarians, and faculty. When we learned that and translated it into our guide, the obstacles before us became clearer. For faculty and librarians to effectively collaborate across the curriculum in a concerted, non-scattershot way, we need first to address fundamental assumptions about hierarchy and the roles of faculty and librarians. Our case study, then, turned out to be a crucial springboard for what now will prove to be a tremendous undertaking for the two of us: using what we have learned in order to effectively collaborate with faculty, administrators, and librarians as the university formally scaffolds IL instruction into the core curriculum. At this point, we have participated in a summer 2017 working group aimed at clarifying IL goals for the new curriculum and submitted a detailed proposal for scaffolding IL in the proposed core curriculum. Also, we have agreed to participate in a faculty learning community focused on IL, leading one of the meetings.

Despite our efforts to date, given the immensity and complexity of the curriculum revision currently underway, it would be easy for the IL piece to become sidelined in the name of moving forward to meet the fall 2018 deadline for approval of the new core curriculum. If this happens, we will continue to be proactive: facilitating faculty-librarian pairings through our research, sharing the best practices we have developed, and standing poised to advance IL's inclusion in the curriculum in both formal and informal ways wherever we see an opportunity. We will need to persist and continue to work as a team, not only calling for faculty-librarian collaboration, but also modeling it in our joint advocacy.

Appendix 5.1

Survey Questions

Pre-survey/Students

1. Have you had any library research experience prior to this semester?
2. Have you attended a library instruction session in any (other) classes before? If yes, which class/course(s) was it for?
3. Do you have any experience using library databases for research?
4. Have you ever checked out a book from the UST library?
5. Have you ever requested a book from another CLIC library via the catalog?
6. Have you ever requested a book or an article from another library using our Interlibrary Loan service?
7. Have you ever visited the Media collection at the OSF library?
8. Have you been asked to evaluate information sources for any research you have previously done?
9. Are you familiar with RefWorks (online bibliographic management tool)?
10. Have you ever used RefWorks for creating a bibliography (Works Cited)?
11. Using the scale below, how would you rank your level of confidence in:

	Not at all confident (1)	2	Somewhat confident (3)	4	Very confident (5)
using the library and its resources for general academic research	O	O	O	O	O
using the library and its resources for research in your major	O	O	O	O	O
evaluating resources you find on the Web	O	O	O	O	O

Post-survey/Students

1. Using the scale below, how would you rank your level of confidence in:

	Not at all confident (1)	2	Somewhat confident (3)	4	Very confident (5)
using the library and its resources for **general academic** research	O	O	O	O	O
using the library and its resources for **research in your major**	O	O	O	O	O

2. Please rate your level of agreement regarding library instruction (experience) in this course:

	Strongly Disagree	Disagree	Neither Agree nor Disagree	Agree	Strongly Agree	N/A
The library instruction related directly to the course.	O	O	O	O	O	O
Materials presented or covered were relevant to the course.	O	O	O	O	O	O
The library instruction was helpful or worthwhile.	O	O	O	O	O	O

3. Was there anything you wish the librarian had done differently?
4. What is the most important thing you learned or gained from the library research experience this semester?
5. Do you have any suggestions or comments for the librarian that you think would help make your future research experience better or more useful?
6. Is there something you learned about research this semester that you wish you knew as a first-year student? If so, what?
7. Do you have any other comments about your research process/experience that you would like to share?

Post-semester Reflections/Faculty

1. What did the librarian do that was least effective? Why, in your view, was this not particularly helpful?
2. What, from your perspective, are the advantages of collaborating with a librarian (for you, for your students)?
3. Please compare this course, in which you collaborated with a librarian, to other sections you have taught but without collaborating with a librarian. Have you noticed differences in your students' writing (process and/or product) related to research?
4. What advice would you give to other faculty (yourself included) on "do's and don'ts" for librarian-faculty collaborations of this kind?
5. If there is anything else that you would like to say that is not covered above, please do so here.

Post-semester Reflections/Librarians

1. In your collaboration, what did the professor do that was most effective? Why, in your view, was this particularly helpful?
2. In your collaboration, what did the professor do that was least helpful? Why, in your view, was this not particularly helpful?
3. What, from your perspective, are the advantages of collaborating with a teaching faculty (for you, for the students)?
4. Please compare this course to other courses in which you collaborated with a professor. What was similar and different? Have you connected any differently with the students in this class?
5. What advice would you give to other librarians (yourself included) on "do's and don'ts" for librarian-faculty collaborations of this kind?
6. If there is anything else you would like to say that is not covered above, please do so here.

Appendix 5.2

Survey Data

Assessment in Action Student Pre-survey Fall 2015 (Quantitative Data)

Please select the course name and number

#	Answer	%	Count
1	EXSC 449	20.75%	11
2	HIST 465	0.00%	0
3	JPST 365	22.64%	12
4	GERM 300	15.09%	8
5	SOWK 380	41.51%	22
6	SOCI 480	0.00%	0
	Total	100%	53

Class Status

#	Answer	%	Count
1	Freshman	5.88%	3
2	Sophomore	0.00%	0
3	Junior	45.10%	23
4	Senior	49.02%	25
	Total	100%	51

Have you had any library research experience prior to this semester?

#	Answer	%	Count
1	Yes	81.13%	43
2	No	18.87%	10
	Total	100%	53

Have you attended a library instruction session in any (other) classes before?

#	Answer	%	Count
1	Yes	71.70%	38
2	No	28.30%	15
	Total	100%	53

Do you have any experience using library databases for research?

#	Answer	%	Count
1	Yes	90.57%	48
2	No	9.43%	5
	Total	100%	53

Have you ever checked out a book from the UST library?

#	Answer	%	Count
1	Yes	39.62%	21
2	No	60.38%	32
	Total	100%	53

Have you ever requested a book from another CLIC library via the catalog?

#	Answer	%	Count
1	Yes	32.08%	17
2	No	67.92%	36
	Total	100%	53

Have you ever requested a book or an article from another library using our Interlibrary Loan service?

#	Answer	%	Count
1	Yes	47.17%	25
2	No	52.83%	28
	Total	100%	53

Have you ever visited the Media collection at the OSF library?

#	Answer	%	Count
1	Yes	16.98%	9
2	No	83.02%	44
	Total	100%	53

Have you been asked to evaluate information sources for any research you have previously done?

#	Answer	%	Count
1	Yes	43.40%	23
2	No	56.60%	30
	Total	100%	53

Are you familiar with RefWorks (online bibliographic management tool)?

#	Answer	%	Count
1	Yes	50.94%	27
2	No	49.06%	26
	Total	100%	53

Have you ever used RefWorks for creating a bibliography (Works Cited)?

#	Answer	%	Count
1	Yes	42.31%	22
2	No	57.69%	30
	Total	100%	52

Using the scale below, how would you rank your level of confidence in:

#	Question	Not at all confident (1)	2	Somewhat confident (3)	4	Very confident (5)	Total
1	using the library and its resources for general academic research	3.77% 2	7.55% 4	41.51% 22	35.85% 19	11.32% 6	100% 53
2	using the library and its resources for research in your major	7.55% 4	9.43% 5	32.08% 17	39.62% 21	11.32% 6	100% 53
3	evaluating resources you find on the Web	1.88% 1	11.32% 6	37.74% 20	37.74% 20	11.32% 6	100% 53

Assessment in Action Student Pre-survey Spring 2016 (Quantitative Data)

Please select the course name and number.

Answer	%	Count
BIOL 365	0.00%	0
COJO 340	9.57%	11
ENGL 482	6.09%	7
EXSC 449	8.70%	10
HIST 463	0.87%	1
NSCI 398	0.00%	0
JPST 355	9.56%	11
JPST 375	15.65%	18
PSYC 212.1	20.00%	23
PSYC 212.2	16.52%	19
SPAN 301	13.04%	15
Total	100%	115

Class Status

#	Answer	%	Count
1	Freshman	5.22%	6
2	Sophomore	39.13%	45
3	Junior	20.87%	24
4	Senior	34.78%	40
	Total	100%	115

Have you had any library research experience prior to this semester?

#	Answer	%	Count
1	Yes	75.9%	85
2	No	24.1%	27
	Total	100%	112

Have you attended a library instruction session in any (other) classes before?

#	Answer	%	Count
1	Yes	73.2%	82
2	No	26.8%	30
	Total	100%	112

Do you have any experience using library databases for research?

#	Answer	%	Count
1	Yes	89.3%	100
2	No	10.7%	12
	Total	100%	112

Have you ever checked out a book from the UST library?

#	Answer	%	Count
1	Yes	61.6%	69
2	No	38.4%	43
	Total	100%	112

Have you ever requested a book from another CLIC library via the catalog?

#	Answer	%	Count
1	Yes	37.5%	42
2	No	62.5%	70
	Total	100%	112

Have you ever requested a book or an article from another library using our Interlibrary Loan service?

#	Answer	%	Count
1	Yes	42.0%	47
2	No	58.0%	65
	Total	100%	112

Have you ever visited the Media collection at the OSF library?

#	Answer	%	Count
1	Yes	31.0%	34
2	No	69.0%	76
	Total	100%	110

Have you been asked to evaluate information sources for any research you have previously done?

#	Answer	%	Count
1	Yes	31.3%	35
2	No	68.7%	77
	Total	100%	112

Are you familiar with RefWorks (online bibliographic management tool)?

#	Answer	%	Count
1	Yes	45.5%	51
2	No	54.4%	61
	Total	100%	112

Have you ever used RefWorks for creating a bibliography (Works Cited)?

#	Answer	%	Count
1	Yes	31.3%	35
2	No	68.7%	77
	Total	100%	112

Using the scale below, how would you rank your level of confidence in:

#	Question	Not at all confident (1)	2	Somewhat confident (3)	4	Very confident (5)	Total
1	using the library and its resources for general academic research	6.25% 7	5.36% 6	33.04% 37	38.39% 43	16.96% 19	100% 112
2	using the library and its resources for research in your major	6.25% 7	14.29% 16	29.46% 33	34.82% 39	15.18% 17	100% 112
3	evaluating resources you find on the Web	5.36% 6	20.53% 23	29.46% 33	31.25% 35	13.39% 15	100% 112

Assessment in Action Student Post-survey Fall 2015 (Quantitative Data)

Please select the course name and number

#	Answer	%	Count
1	EXSC 449	31.58%	12
2	HIST 465	2.63%	1
3	JPST 365	0.00%	0
4	GERM 300	23.68%	9
5	SOWK 380	34.21%	13
6	SOCI 480	7.89%	3
	Total	100%	38

Class Status

#	Answer	%	Count
1	Freshman	7.89%	3
2	Sophomore	0.00%	0
3	Junior	42.11%	16
4	Senior	50.00%	19
	Total	100%	38

Please rate your level of agreement regarding library instruction (experience) in this course:

Question	Strongly Disagree	Disagree	Neither Agree nor Disagree	Agree	Strongly Agree	Total
The library instruction related directly to the course.	0.00% 0	2.86% 1	14.29% 5	37.14% 13	45.71% 16	100% 35
Materials presented or covered were relevant to the course.	0.00% 0	2.94% 1	11.77% 4	52.94% 18	32.35% 11	100% 34
The library instruction was helpful or worthwhile.	2.86% 1	5.71% 2	8.57% 3	48.57% 17	34.29% 12	100% 35

Using the scale below, how would you rank your level of confidence in:

#	Question	Not at all confident (1)	2	Somewhat confident (3)	4	Very confident (5)	Total
1	using the library and its resources for general academic research	0.00% 0	0.00% 0	40.00% 14	40.00% 14	20.00% 7	100% 35
2	using the library and its resources for research in your major	2.86% 1	0.00% 0	25.71% 9	34.29% 12	37.14% 13	100% 35

Assessment in Action Student Post-survey Spring 2016 (Quantitative Data)

Please select the course name and number

Answer	%	Count
COJO 340	3.95%	3
ENGL 482	9.21%	7
EXSC 449	1.32%	1
JPST 355	17.11%	13
JPST 375	15.79%	12
PSYC 212.1	28.95%	22
PSYC 212.2	15.79%	12
SPAN 301	7.89%	6
Total	100%	76

Class Status

#	Answer	%	Count
1	Freshman	5.26%	4
2	Sophomore	47.37%	36
3	Junior	21.05%	16
4	Senior	26.32%	20
	Total	100%	76

Using the scale below, how would you rank your level of confidence in:

Question	Not at all confident (1)	2	Somewhat confident (3)	4	Very confident (5)	Total
using the library and its resources for general academic research	1.37% 1	1.37% 1	24.66% 18	47.95% 35	24.65% 18	100% 73
using the library and its resources for research in your major	1.39% 1	1.39% 1	20.83% 15	38.89% 28	37.50% 27	100% 72

Please rate your level of agreement regarding library instruction (experience) in this course:

#	Question	Strongly Disagree	Disagree	Neither Agree nor Disagree	Agree	Strongly Agree	Total
1	The library instruction related directly to the course.	8.22% 6	0.00% 0	4.11% 3	41.09% 30	46.58% 34	100% 73
2	Materials presented or covered were relevant to the course.	8.22% 6	0.00% 0	2.74% 2	41.09% 30	47.95% 35	100% 73
3	The library instruction was helpful or worthwhile.	8.22% 6	2.74% 2	5.48% 4	39.73%	43.83% 32	100% 73

Appendix 5.3

Talia Nadir, Research and Instruction Librarian
Erika Scheurer, Director of Writing Across the Curriculum

Writing in the Disciplines: A Guide For Faculty-Librarian Collaboration

Faculty:

Develop a research project (or projects) that includes specific learning goals for disciplinary research. Break down the project into scaffolded smaller assignments and steps. Think about specific learning goals connected to disciplinary research.

Librarian + Faculty

Meeting 1:

- Work with your librarian to hone outcomes for assessment of the learning goals connected to disciplinary research.
- Develop an assessment tool whereby you together will judge whether the goals were met. This may be a student survey or other opportunity for students to reflect on their learning. It may also involve assessment of the writing: What will you look for in the final products in order to determine the degree to which students have met the goals?
- Look at assignment together. Where do students typically struggle when it comes to disciplinary research in general and/or this project (if assigned before)? Where will students need the most support?

Meeting 2:

- Together develop a plan for supporting students—ideally some blend of whole-group and small-group presentation with one-on-one meetings and in-class work time with the librarian present for individual assistance.
- Put group presentations and in-class work days on the course syllabus; the faculty member should be present on these days. Also, schedule dates when the faculty member will check in with the librarian on student progress.
- Make individual meetings with the librarian either required or optional (extra credit), but either way, require students to write brief reflections after each visit that are graded in some low-stakes way.

Sample reflection for students on meeting with the librarian:

BEFORE THE MEETING:

List specific goals for this session with the librarian:

AFTER THE MEETING:

1. Describe your meeting with the librarian in as much detail as possible:
2. Did you meet the goals you set for this meeting? If so, how? What did you learn? If not, why not?
3. List some specific action steps you will take (and when) as a result of this meeting.. *It is important that these action steps be specific.*

Some points to keep in mind for successful faculty-librarian collaborations:

- Research and writing are both developmental processes, not one-shot fixes. This is why the stand-alone presentation on library resources is not as effective as multiple targeted interventions at different points in the research process.
- It is important for faculty to allow librarians (and librarians to allow themselves) to go beyond showing tools and focus on critical thinking. The goal for students as writers is to encourage them to see the writing process in a more complex way (not just about correctness). Likewise, we want to encourage students to see the research process in a more complex way (not just citation tools such as RefWorks).
- For this partnership to work, it is important for the faculty member to maintain an open attitude toward the educational process and to sharing expertise with the librarian.
- Timing is key! Don't bring in the librarian when there is no specific assignment connected to what students will be doing just because it fits in the syllabus that day. Target interventions for maximum impact.
- Incorporating support for the writing process requires faculty to change their ideas about "coverage" of course material: Writing becomes seen as a *means* of covering material rather than as an obstacle. In the same way, it helps for faculty to see support for the research process not as something that takes valuable class time, but as time invested in meeting important course goals connected to students learning disciplinary research concepts and skills.

Notes

1. Association of College and Research Libraries, *Academic Library Impact on Student Learning and Success*, prepared by Karen Brown with contributions by Kara J. Malenfant (Chicago: Association of College Research Libraries, 2017). http://www.ala.org/acrl/sites/ala.org.acrl/files/content/issues/value/findings_y3.pdf.
2. Barbara Junisbai, M. Sara Lowe, and Natalie Tagge, "A Pragmatic and Flexible Approach to Information Literacy: Findings from a Three-Year Study of Faculty-Librarian Collaboration," *Journal of Academic Librarianship* 42, no. 5 (September 2016): 604-611, https://doi.org/10.1016/j.acalib.2016.07.001.
3. William Badke, "Can't Get No Respect: Helping Faculty to Understand the Educational Power of Information Literacy," *Reference Librarian* 43, no. 89–90 (2005): 63–80, https://doi.org/10.1300/J120v43n89_05.

4. Margaret Artman, Erica Frisicaro-Pawlowski, and Robert Monge, "Not Just One Shot: Extending the Dialogue about Information Literacy in Composition Classes," *Composition Studies* 38, no. 2 (2010): 93–110.
5. Glenn Johnson-Grau, Susan Gardner Archambault, Elisa Slater Acosta, and Lindsey McLean, "Patience, Persistence, and Process: Embedding a Campus-wide Information Literacy Program across the Curriculum," *Journal of Academic Librarianship* 42, no. 6 (November 2016): 750–56, https://doi.org/10.1016/j.acalib.2016.10.013.
6. Yvonne Nalani Meulemans and Allison Carr, "Not at Your Service: Building Genuine Faculty-Librarian Partnerships," *Reference Services Review* 41, no. 1 (2013): 80–90, https://doi.org/10.1108/00907321311300893; William H. Walters, "Faculty Status of Librarians at U.S. Research Universities," *Journal of Academic Librarianship* 42, no. 2 (March 2016): 161–71, https://doi.org/10.1016/j.acalib.2015.11.002.
7. Erika Scheurer, "What Do WAC Directors Need to Know about 'Coverage'?" *WAC Journal* 26, no. 1 (Fall 2015): 7–21, https://wac.colostate.edu/journal/vol26/scheurer.pdf.

Bibliography

Artman, Margaret, Erica Frisicaro-Pawlowski, and Robert Monge. "Not Just One Shot: Extending the Dialogue about Information Literacy in Composition Classes." *Composition Studies* 38, no. 2 (Fall 2010): 93–110.

Association of College and Research Libraries. *Academic Library Impact on Student Learning and Success: Findings from Assessment in Action Team Projects.* Prepared by Karen Brown with contributions by Kara J. Malenfant. Chicago: Association of College and Research Libraries, 2017. http://www.ala.org/acrl/sites/ala.org.acrl/files/content/issues/value/findings_y3.pdf.

Badke, William. "Can't Get No Respect: Helping Faculty to Understand the Educational Power of Information Literacy." *Reference Librarian* 43, no. 89–90 (2005): 63–80. https://doi.org/10.1300/J120v43n89_05.

Johnson-Grau, Glenn, Susan Gardner Archambault, Elisa Slater Acosta, and Lindsey McLean. "Patience, Persistence, and Process: Embedding a Campus-wide Information Literacy Program across the Curriculum." *Journal of Academic Librarianship* 42, no. 6 (November 2016): 750–56. https://doi.org/10.1016/j.acalib.2016.10.013.

Junisbai, Barbara, M. Sara Lowe, and Natalie Tagge. "A Pragmatic and Flexible Approach to Information Literacy: Findings from a Three-Year Study of Faculty-Librarian Collaboration." *Journal of Academic Librarianship* 42, no. 5 (September 2016): 604–11. https://doi.org/10.1016/j.acalib.2016.07.001.

Meulemans, Yvonne Nalani, and Allison Carr. "Not at Your Service: Building Genuine Faculty-Librarian Partnerships." *Reference Services Review* 41, no. 1 (2013): 80–90. https://doi.org/10.1108/00907321311300893.

Scheurer, Erika. "What Do WAC Directors Need to Know about 'Coverage'?" *WAC Journal* 26, no. 1 (Fall 2015): 7–21. https://wac.colostate.edu/journal/vol26/scheurer.pdf.

Walters, William H. "Faculty Status of Librarians at U.S. Research Universities." *Journal of Academic Librarianship* 42, no. 2 (March 2016): 161–71. https://doi.org/10.1016/j.acalib.2015.11.002.

Title: Thinking LEAN: The Relevance of Gemba-Kaizen and Visual Assessment in Collection Management

Abstract: The Gemba-Kaizen, a Japanese concept of continuous improvement, is a simple qualitative assessment tool using "visual management" to assess the root cause of the gap between the current state and the desired state and enable deliberations on countermeasures to close the perceived gap. In Singapore Management University, the Gemba assessment is applied to the value stream of the library's print collection. Using a set of metrics, assessors went to the place of action, observed the collection, reported on problem areas, and followed up on suggestions to eliminate wastes. This is essentially the content of the Gemba-Kaizen LEAN method of assessment. We found the Gemba to be a sustainable tool to drive continuous assessments of the print collection, where visual management is used to observe and quickly determine problems at the source.

Keywords: Gemba, Kaizen, LEAN, process improvement, assessment, continuous improvement, qualitative methodology, collection assessment, visual management, collection management, analytics, data driven assessment.

Project focus: assessment methodologies, techniques, or practices; collections; assessment concepts and/or management

Results made or will make case for: improvements in services, improvements in collections, changes in library policy, how money or resources may be directed

Data needed: age of collection, usage of collection

Methodology: qualitative, mixed method

Project duration: less than 3 months

Tool(s) utilized: in-house metrics, rubric for assessment, and library staff

Cost estimate: $100–$500

Type of institution: university—public

Institution enrollment: 5,000–15,000

Highest level of education: doctoral

cc BY ND

Chapter 6

Thinking LEAN
The Relevance of Gemba-Kaizen And Visual Assessment in Collection Management

Nazimah Ram Nath

Summary

The Singapore Management University (SMU) Libraries' have used the LEAN and Six Sigma methodologies in recent years to plan and push for continuous process improvement in their operations. In one assessment project, the Gemba-Kaizen principle from LEAN was adapted and applied to an initiative centered on assessing the library's Lifestyle print collection. This strategy became a prime agent for change, which resulted in some marked improvements in collection management activities within the SMU Libraries. This case study at SMU Libraries will describe key principles of Gemba-Kaizen and how it was found to be a sustainable tool to drive continuous assessment of the print collection, where visual management is mostly used to observe and determine problems at the source of the value stream. As an assessment tool, Gemba is one of the "low-hanging fruit," which is within reach, quick to plan for and to implement. It is a course of action that can be undertaken quickly and easily, as part of a wider range of changes or solutions to a problem. This study will also show that a simple, basic assessment tool like the Gemba can have impact and add value to services, while remaining painless to plan, execute, and implement.

Introduction

A review of library literature suggests that there has been a gradual shift in academic libraries, over the years, in how they evaluate their productivity and how they demonstrate value to their stakeholders. Heath mentioned the strides the library community has made in the past decade and discussed how assessment has gradually evolved from initially being "quantitative" before addressing the current climate, where libraries practice continuous assessment and engage various different methods and tools to assess the value of services provided to library user communities.[1] Kinman, in a five-year study, discussed how e-metrics can be incorporated into a broader assessment of a library's success in meeting the needs of its users.[2] According to Taylor and Heath, the Association of Research Libraries (ARL) also made a similar observation when it released a survey report in which assessment was highlighted as an integral part of a strategic plan to monitor trends and change in library processes.[3] Hiller, Kyrillidou, and Oakleaf had reflected on the diverse range of assessments taking place in libraries as well as changes in the types of assessment activities taking place in these institutions over time.[4] These and other recent studies suggest that assessment in libraries has moved beyond being merely an indicator of productivity or simply being a measure of input and output.

In keeping with the general trend in academic libraries, Singapore Management University Libraries (SMU Libraries) have made assessment a critical component of its strategic plans. Over recent years, the SMU Libraries have been building and encouraging a culture of assessment and continuous improvement, where decisions and new initiatives were carried out based on data, statistics, and analysis. The library management felt that assessment helps the library demonstrate its value and its place within the university, especially when it involves new services and products. In addition, data-driven assessment and continuous process improvement initiatives allow the library to resolve issues as they arise.

This chapter will present a case study of one instance of data-driven, continuous improvement activity using LEAN principles, tools and techniques to assess the library's print Lifestyle collection with a view to improve collection quality and end-user experience. This will be followed by the reasons for using the Gemba-Kaizen methodology and the purpose and structure of the Gemba Walk, these being the techniques adopted to carry out assessment of the collection. An analysis of assessment as a transformative process is then provided, and the chapter concludes with reflections on the sustainability of the Gemba as an assessment tool.

Background: SMU Libraries and the Culture of Assessment

The Singapore Management University (SMU) was established on January 2000 as a university specializing in business and management studies. SMU and the campus is the academic home to the university's 8,000 undergraduate and postgraduate students[5] and offers courses in business administration, accountancy, economics, information systems management, law, and the social sciences. The SMU Libraries consist of two locations; the Li Ka Shing Library at Stamford Road, which houses all print and audiovisual collections, except for the Law print collection, which resides at the Kwa Geok Choo Law Library situated at Armenian Street. Both libraries, as well as the various schools, make up the City Campus, with a collective collection size of 60,000 print resources and about 400,000 electronic resources. For the purpose of this chapter, references will be made to the Li Ka Shing Library, where the assessment took place.

The library is driven based on our mission and vision to provide high-quality resources, facilities, and customer-focused services that support multidisciplinary research and holistic education. It is supported by thirty-nine staff members, of whom twenty-three are professional librarians, and sixteen are para-professionals, technical and administrative staff. In 2013, the library embarked on an aggressive "continuous improvement" initiative, by training all staff members in the LEAN—Six Sigma Green Belt program. The intention behind the training was to promote a culture of assessment among staff members as well as to equip them with the necessary language, knowledge, and tools to champion a data-driven environment. The training and knowledge gained would enable them to use both qualitative and quantitative data to assess the current state of a value stream and, from there on, to drive improvement projects after identifying service gaps. Before the establishment of "culture of assessment" as a strategic goal of the library, most assessment projects in the library were spontaneous, the activities were short-term, and they were largely contained within silos of individual library working units. After the LEAN—Six Sigma Green Belt training, all library staff bought into the concept that assessment is everyone's responsibility and future assessment initiatives were planned with involvement and collaboration among members of different library working groups.

Ammos Lakos and Shelley Phipps defined a culture of assessment as an "organizational environment in which decisions are based on facts, research, and analysis, and where services are planned and delivered in ways that maximize positive outcomes and impacts for customers and stakeholders."[6] Continuous improvement via continuous assessment became a strategic direction and part of every library staff member's work goals in SMU Libraries, and the various departments in the library would regularly discuss areas of focus and processes that could benefit from an improvement.

In one of our brainstorming sessions, it was proposed that the library carry out an assessment of the Lifestyle collection at the Li Ka Shing Library to check for its relevance, value, and impact to stakeholders and to seek areas where improvements can be made using some of the LEAN tools.

Defining the Problem

To allow the reader to understand the problem presented in this case study, some context should be provided. The Lifestyle collection in the Li Ka Shing Library was started in 2008 and consisted of unregulated mix of titles, without a policy to guide its growth. In 2013, the collections team in SMU Libraries drafted a policy paper, which provided guidelines on what should be included or excluded from the Lifestyle collection. The collection had to be vibrant, up-to-date, contemporary, and of value to end users. The Lifestyle collection serves as a recreational reading collection of popular works, supporting the university's holistic education approach. The collection acquires contemporary bestsellers, award-winning fiction titles, and other popular works, including self-help titles and travel guides, according to the guidelines and parameters set in the policy. As the Lifestyle collection occupied a prime location within the library spaces, it was important to the library management that the collection be visually appealing, invite browsing, have popular titles, meet user expectations, and be well used.

Usage data had been analyzed as a preliminary assessment of the popularity of titles in the collection. Checkout statistics however, had their limitations. While usage numbers inform assessors on the usability of a collection, they do not do as well in providing a context to understand the root cause of any problem that might exist, nor do they present additional data to facilitate improvements in required areas of that value stream. To make better judgements on how effective the current collection is in satisfying the purpose for which it is intended, a different type of assessment and analysis was needed, one that would measure the collection's quality as well as its utility. A LEAN assessment tool that enabled analysis beyond numerical data was considered ideal

The project team first decided on the goals of this assessment and outlined what we wanted to determine from the assessment of the Lifestyle collection. The goals were

- Assessment should be able to give an indication if the collection has up-to-date titles, is well used, does not have gaps, and concurs with the collection policy.
- The assessment should allow assessors to record shortfalls, issues, and concerns with the collection.
- The time needed for the assessment exercise should not exceed forty-five minutes.
- The tool used should be sufficiently flexible for assessors to record improvements and for the library project team to develop an action plan.

The project team also wanted the selected assessment methodology to be able to provide answers to the following questions:

- Do we have the right/relevant books?
- Is the space being used as it should?
- Are the books accessible?
- Is the display attractive to users?
- Is the collection aligned to the library's policy?
- What is the average age of the collection?
- Has regular weeding been done?
- Could we do better?

Besides the general use and non-use of the collection, the agenda behind the assessment was to elicit information, among other things, on the duplication of titles, age and condition of the materials, breadth and depth of the coverage, and impact of the Lifestyle collection on the SMU user community.

Path to LEAN Assessment, Gemba, and Kaizen

In examining other industries for best practices, we came across varied assessment methodologies. Fault Trees, Fishbone Diagrams, and Swim Lane analysis, as well as a Plan-Do-Check-Act (PDCA) problem-solving cycle were commonly used methods that were reported in industry literature. After some discussion and considering the training we have had, the project team began to focus on LEAN manufacturing methodology, based on the Toyota Production System. The principles in LEAN manufacturing were increasingly being adopted in service organizations, which faced many of the same challenges as manufacturers. A common challenge was the need to improve service quality and the reduction of customer complaints. The LEAN philosophy promises dramatic changes in these areas within a short period of time. Before we delve deeper into the case study, a summary of the principles behind the LEAN Gemba-Kaizen philosophy may be useful to allow the reader to understand the reasons behind the choice of this tool for the assessment of the Lifestyle collection.

LEAN is a management philosophy focused on creating value when delivering a product or service to customers. In Womack and Jones's *LEAN Thinking*, five principles of the LEAN system were outlined:[7]

1. Defining value for each product/service
2. Eliminating all unnecessary steps in each value stream
3. Making value flow to the customer
4. Knowing that the customer pulls all activities, products, and services
5. Pursuing perfection continuously

Giovanni De Zan and colleagues summarized LEAN as an integrated sociotechnical system whose main objective was to eliminate waste by concurrently reducing or minimizing internal variability. The LEAN management method uses less effort, less space, a lower level of investments, and shorter time duration for new products development.[8] In LEAN assessment, assessors study, explore, and learn the "as-is state" and identify the gaps that can take the service or product toward the ideal "to-be state." To determine the diagnosis of the as-is state, assessors will focus on imperfections, problems, and inefficiencies of the process, collecting them and documenting them, usually by using rubrics or templates for evaluation. This will be carried out with assessors concretely moving through the value stream to diagnosis the main issues related to the productive process.

The team formed a consensus that the LEAN Gemba-Kaizen method would be most effective in meeting our assessment needs and decided to adopt the "Gemba Walk" as our specific assessment tool. A Gemba Walk is the Check component in the Plan-Do-Check-Act problem-solving model. It involves going to the place where the value stream resides and checking to make sure that standards are being followed, that problems are getting corrected, that processes are working the way they were intended to, and if not, to find out why.[9]

Gemba and Kaizen are Japanese concepts that feature largely in LEAN management. In Japanese, *kaizen* means "continuous improvements" that entail relatively little expense.[10] Kaizen focuses on improvements in quality, cost, and delivery, and, according to Imai, although improvements under kaizen are small and incremental, the kaizen process brings about dramatic results over time.[11] Kaizen also stresses cross-functional collaborations with various stakeholders.

Gemba, in Japanese, means "real place."[12] Within a business environment, *Gemba* refers to the place where value is created. It is also the place where data can be found. Thus "going to the Gemba" is considered, in LEAN, to be a basic assessment methodology, involving a visit to the site of the value stream or the site of action and observing what goes on and asking questions until the root cause of the problem is determined. As iterated by Imai, "one of the most useful tools for finding the root cause in the Gemba is to keep asking 'Why' until the root cause is reached. This process is sometimes referred to as the 'Five Whys' because chances are, that asking 'why' five times will uncover the root cause."[13]

The Lifestyle Collection and the Gemba Walk

Gemba relies heavily on visual assessment and is used in production and manufacturing processes to assess the root cause of the gap between the current state and the desired state and to subsequently deliberate on the most promising countermeasures to close the gap.

The Gemba assessment is applied to an area that is part of a larger value stream. A Gemba Walk enables a deep dive into respective value streams in order to understand what really happens day-to-day and to guide corrective actions.[14] It's like looking in from the outside, according to Nestle, and helps teams better understand the value of their services and gain a fresh perspective of their work.[15]

To start with, Gemba Walks must be done where the value is created or where it "resides." Petruska notes that "by staying in one spot for a very long period of time observing, listening and training all your senses in one repetitive process, you develop a very deep understanding,"[16] and this understanding will help toward the identification of value propositions and determination of products and services that would delight customers. Petruska describes these as "service delighters."[17] Gemba Walks encourage direct observation, engagement with stakeholders, and working on improvements. This visual assessment strategy is encouraged for the purpose of maximizing customer value, identifying and eliminating wastes in the process, solving problems along the way, and empowering stakeholders to make decisions. At SMU, we applied this assessment tool to the Lifestyle collection in a pioneering attempt to introduce a culture of continuous assessment to the library's print collection.

The project team, which is comprised of four librarians and headed by the head of the Information Resources and Access department, started the project by selecting a group of stakeholders as assessors. In keeping with the spirit of LEAN and Gemba-

Kaizen, which encourage collaboration, the pilot collection assessment project included participation from technical service paraprofessionals, subject librarians, and collection specialists. A total of six assessors, with two assessors from each of the stated domains, formed the assessment team. One of the aims of the exercise was also to engage more members of the collections and technical services team in understanding LEAN concepts and increase their ability to be involved in improvement processes in their area of work. To guide the Gemba assessors, a set of metrics was selected as a reference point for assessment and a scoring rubric was created based on those metrics. A rubric is a scoring tool that lists the criteria for a piece of work, or "what counts"; it also articulates gradations of quality for each criterion, from excellent to poor.[18] A scoring rubric enables assessors to score based on their expectations of quality around a task, service, or product in a consistent manner. Rubrics facilitate assessment and feedback and help assessors envision what can be done in terms of improvement. Both criteria and performance level descriptions are present in scoring rubrics, and they particularly work in instances where the evaluation criteria are especially subjective.[19]

Assessors were then given a scorecard based on the rubric, on which to score their assessment (see table 6.1). A review of LEAN principles, the SMU Libraries Collection policy, and the Lifestyle collection usage statistics were also shared with the assessors prior to their assessment exercise, as points of reference.

Table 6.1
The Lifestyle Collection Gemba Walk Scorecard

Criteria		Excellent (5)	Good (4)	Satisfactory (3)	Needs Improvement (4)	Poor- Needs an Overhaul (5)
Meets demand	Collection has the books I want to read					
	Suggestions and user requests have been considered					
Appropriateness of titles	Collection meets criteria indicated in policy					
	All relevant authors and titles are in the collection					
Shelving location	Books are shelved according to classification number indicated in catalogue					
	There is no need for extensive shelf reading					

New titles	There is regular addition of new titles					
	Latest bestsellers are on the shelves					
	Award winning fiction titles are in the collection					
Circulation[a]	Collection is well used					
Appearance	Books are in good condition					
	Worn and torn books are not on the shelves					
	Older titles have been weeded out					
	Displays are attractive					
a. Based on usage statistics						

With this scorecard in hand, the assessors independently went to the Gemba, accompanied by a librarian from the project team. The role of the librarian was to provide the assessor with any contextual information or clarification that she might need as she raised questions as part of her assessment. The various assessors went to the place of action (the Lifestyle collection); they observed the collection; asked questions about the various acquisition, processing, and circulation workflows; and scored the collection as they observed. They then individually presented their assessment to the project team:

THE GEMBA WALK: FINDINGS AND OUTCOME

The qualitative assessment carried out of the Lifestyle collection found that the collection was up-to-date as befitting a collection for recreation reading. The assessors noted that recommended classics, award-winning titles, as well as contemporary best sellers had equal representation in the collection, to cater for the diverse reading interests of the user community. It was also noted that the size and the content of the collection closely adhered to the guidelines in the collection policy. The assessors also highlighted areas for improvement pertaining to the following:

1. Shelf labels
It was found that the shelves were not labeled according to the classification numbers on the spine labels of the books. This made it a little tiresome for users, as there was no visual prompt to act as a finding aid if they were looking for a specific title within a specific call number range. It was also suggested that categorizing the collection by sections like Fiction, Poetry, Hobbies, Self-Help, or "Our Most Popular" and labeling the shelves accordingly would help users and attract more browsing of the collection.

2. Call number labels
Spine labels on books need replacement as a few were faded and not easily readable, thus compromising on retrieval and access.

3. Increased shelf reading activity
As this was a highly circulated and browsed collection, books were not always shelved in the correct order by users after browsing. Increase in the frequency of shelf reading in this collection was recommended. Based on further evidence from search request results and user enquiries, it was established that books were not always where they should be.

4. Review processing standards
As the labels on the cover of books marking them for Lifestyle tended to peel off, making them look unsightly, there was a recommendation for the physical items processing team to review processing standards and improve the quality of the labels used to label the books and book jackets.

5. Special collection
Assessors put forward the suggestion of designating a special place in the Lifestyle collection for Singapore literature so as to encourage access, browsing, and reading of local literary works.

The project team analyzed the assessment and shared the findings with the line managers in charge of various library operations within the value stream for follow-up on rectification of problem areas and for consideration of implementing the suggestions for improvements. Countermeasures were implemented where feasible. One immediate follow-up activity was to increase shelf reading frequency to ensure that the books were always neat and arranged in sequence. Books with faded and damaged labels were repaired and labels replaced. Following the first Gemba Walk of the Lifestyle collection, we implemented a regular Gemba follow-up every quarter. Subsequent Gemba assessments have shown that the collection has improved in the areas indicated in the scorecard and that initial problem areas were rectified.

Discussion and Next Steps

The Gemba Walk is usually carried out by management executives to evaluate a process at the place of action, typically in a manufacturing industry setting. In SMU Libraries, however, the process was carried out by a mixed group of senior librarians, assistant librarians, and library para-professionals. The principle of the Gemba is that to understand the problem, one must go to the actual place where it is happening, get the facts, ask questions about the process, and experience the effects for oneself. Doing so will help process owners or managers to grasp the entire situation and not just one small subset or snapshot of it, and this will enable better and more informed decision-making.[20] Understanding what is happening, where it is happening, and why it is happening helps to generate countermeasures and corrective actions to eliminate the problems observed. Gemba also enables one to check if countermeasures are effective and to use the new information to generate new countermeasures, if existing ones were found to be ineffective. What Gemba does is to aid in continuous monitoring of the value stream and serves as a simple, yet powerful, methodology to drive continuous improvement.

When a report of the assessment was shared with the Information Access and Resources team, this being the library's technical services department, it was acknowledged that the Gemba as an assessment tool had helped the library to become aware of any existing abnormalities in the Lifestyle collection, to verify established standardized processes, to solve problems as they occurred, and to correct errors quickly. Going to the Gemba promoted a deep curiosity to what was going on and took away the assumption of what we *thought* was going on. This created a more efficient work environment, which directly contributed to a more effective service to end users.

The collections team found the Gemba Walk to be very useful in informing them of what needed to be fixed immediately and helped to implement continuous improvement in collections services. The collections team voted to roll out the Gemba Walk assessment methodology to other collections within the library. The project team also suggested that for assessment to be more effective and valuable, other end-user stakeholders, for example, students and academic staff, can also be invited to participate in the assessment, as stakeholders' assessment of the library collection is also important in gauging if their needs and expectations are being met.

Reflections

In our continuous improvement journey, we realized that assessment and assessment tools need not be complicated or overly sophisticated. Simple tools like the Gemba work well toward quality improvement efforts, as it is not complex, tedious, or time consuming. There is not much preliminary planning involved in implementing the Gemba, and it can be planned for and carried out quickly, within a short period of time, incurring little cost and utilizing less manpower. It is the Gemba's simplicity that gives it its repetitive value. The Gemba assessment can be done often, is easy to measure and assess, and is sustainable, due to it not being resource-intensive. It is also flexible enough to be applied across other services within the library context. Doing the Gemba for the Lifestyle collection has helped the library understand the gaps in the collection and improve its processing standards. We have since used the Gemba to assess other physical collections in the library, like the Media collection, and put in measures to address the problem areas. Some of the measures included commissioning a weeding and relocation exercise so that the shelf space can be freed to include new and current resources. By using the Gemba, the library is able to work on continuous improvements in the management of our physical collection. The end result is a fresher, vibrant, and up-to-date library collection.

Conclusion

This case study has illustrated that LEAN principles, even when isolated to one process, can produce significant improvements in impact and quality. LEAN, Gemba, and Kaizen are philosophies that can create dramatic improvements in an organization through the application of the Go See and Ask Why principles. "Go See" refers to the ability for everyone involved in the work to see what actually happens, by visually observing the value stream. In this project, taking a step back enabled work teams to look at their processes differently and provided a better understanding of their customer needs. "Ask Why" is a technique to determine the root cause of a problem. By asking "why" repeatedly, LEAN enables service providers to come closer to providing customers with what they want.

As a change management tool, LEAN has far-reaching impact on both library staff and patrons. In SMU Libraries, we found that going to the Gemba helped those involved in the value stream to better understand their process interactions and learn to see what was not working while it was happening. Because the Gemba allows for as many process owners and stakeholders to be engaged as possible, it has the potential to tap all their experiences and creativity, which will generate more improvement ideas. Indirectly, it also helps to build stake in their improvements and pride in what they have done.[21]

For library patrons, the solution has come just in time. Since visual management is used to observe and determine problems at the source, this in turn drives continuous improvement in the process, and end users are receiving better, superior service and products, as early detection of issues and concerns means services can be continuously enhanced and problem areas eliminated.

Nestle writes, "When mining for productivity improvement, you may strike gold almost anywhere but you really must go to the Gemba to understand what is happening and why it is happening,"[22] and because of that, as he appropriately puts it—Gemba Is Gold.[23]

Notes

1. Fred Heath, "Library Assessment: The Way We Have Grown," *Library Quarterly* 81, no. 1 (2011): 7, https://doi.org/10.1086/657448.
2. Virginia Kinman, "E-Metrics and Library Assessment in Action," *Journal of Electronic Resources Librarianship* 21, no. 1 (2009): 15, https://doi.org/10.1080/19411260902858318.
3. Meredith Taylor and Fred Heath, "Assessment and Continuous Planning: The Key to Transformation at the University of Texas Libraries," *Journal of Library Administration* 52, no. 5 (2012): 426, https://doi.org/10.1080/01930826.2012.700798.
4. Steve Hiller, Martha Kyrillidou, and Megan Oakleaf, "The Library Assessment Conference: Past, Present, and Near Future!" *Journal of Academic Librarianship* 40, no. 3–4 (May 2014): 410–12, https://doi.org/10.1016/j.acalib.2014.05.013.
5. Wikipedia, s.v. "Singapore Management University," accessed May 1, 2017, https://en.wikipedia.org/w/index.php?title=Singapore_Management_University&oldid=775980850.
6. Amos Lakos and Shelley E. Phipps, "Creating a Culture of Assessment: A Catalyst for Organizational Change," *portal: Libraries and the Academy* 4, no. 3 (July 2004): 352, https://doi.org/10.1353/pla.2004.0052.
7. James P. Womack and Daniel T. Jones, *Lean Thinking* (New York: Free Press, 2003), 16-26.
8. Giovanni De Zan, Alberto Felice De Toni, Andrea Fornasier, and Cinzia Battistella, "A Methodology for the Assessment of Experiential Learning Lean: The Lean Experience Factory Case Study," *European Journal of Training and Development* 39, no. 4 (2015): 332–54.
9. Tom Southworth, "Gemba Walks," Printing Lean, Label and Narrow Web, March 8, 2012, 38, http://www.labelandnarrowweb.com/issues/2012-03/view_printing-lean/gemba-walks.
10. Masaaki Imai, *Gemba Kaizen*, 2nd ed. (New York: McGraw Hill, 2012), 1.
11. Imai, *Gemba Kaizen*, 2.
12. Imai, *Gemba Kaizen*, 13.
13. Imai, *Gemba Kaizen*, 30.
14. Southworth, "Gemba Walks," 39.
15. Mark Nestle, "Gemba Is Gold," *ASQ Six Sigma Forum Magazine* 13, no. 1 (November 2013): 34.
16. Robert Petruska, *Gemba Walks for Service Excellence* (Boca Raton, FL: CRC Press, 2012), 13.
17. Petruska, *Gemba Walks*, 13.
18. Heidi Goodrich Andrade, "Understanding Rubrics," Saddleback College, June 20, 2014, https://www.saddleback.edu/uploads/goe/understanding_rubrics_by_heidi_goodrich_andrade.pdf.
19. Susan M. Brookhart and Fei Chen, "The Quality and Effectiveness of Descriptive Rubrics," *Educational Review* 67, no. 3 (August 2015): 344, https://doi.org/10.1080/00131911.2014.929565.
20. Southworth, "Gemba Walks," 39.
21. Nestle, "Gemba Is Gold," 36.
22. Nestle, "Gemba Is Gold," 36.
23. Nestle, "Gemba Is Gold," 32.

Bibliography

Andrade, Heidi Goodrich. "Understanding Rubrics." Saddleback College, June 20, 2014. https://www.saddleback.edu/uploads/goe/understanding_rubrics_by_heidi_goodrich_andrade.pdf.

Brookhart, Susan M., and Fei Chen. "The Quality and Effectiveness of Descriptive Rubrics." *Educational Review* 67, no. 3 (August 2015): 343–68. https://doi.org/10.1080/00131911.2014.929565.

De Zan, Giovanni, Alberto Felice De Toni, Andrea Fornasier, and Cinzia Battistella. "A Methodology for the Assessment of Experiential Learning Lean: The Lean Experience Factory Case Study." *European Journal of Training and Development* 39, no. 4 (2015): 332–54.

Heath, Fred. "Library Assessment: The Way We Have Grown." *Library Quarterly* 81, no. 1 (2011): 7–25. https://doi.org/10.1086/657448.

Hiller, Steve, Martha Kyrillidou, and Megan Oakleaf. "The Library Assessment Conference: Past, Present, and Near Future!" *Journal of Academic Librarianship* 40, no. 3–4 (May 2014): 410–12. https://doi.org/10.1016/j.acalib.2014.05.013.

Imai, Masaaki. *Gemba Kaizen: A Commonsense Approach to a Continuous Improvement Strategy*, 2nd ed. New York: McGraw Hill, 2012.

Kinman, Virginia. "E-Metrics and Library Assessment in Action." *Journal of Electronic Resources Librarianship* 21, no. 1 (2009): 15–36. https://doi.org/10.1080/19411260902858318.

Lakos, Amos, and Shelley E. Phipps. "Creating a Culture of Assessment: A Catalyst for Organizational Change." *portal: Libraries and the Academy* 4, no. 3 (July 2004): 345–61. https://doi.org/10.1353/pla.2004.0052.

Nestle, Mark. "Gemba Is Gold." *ASQ Six Sigma Forum Magazine* 13, no. 1 (November 2013): 32–36.

Petruska, Robert. *Gemba Walks for Service Excellence: The Step-by-Step Guide for Identifying Service Delighters*. Boca Raton, FL: CRC Press, 2012.

Southworth, Tom. "Gemba Walks." Printing Lean, Label and Narrow Web, March 8, 2012. http://www.labelandnarrowweb.com/issues/2012-03/view_printing-lean/gemba-walks.

Taylor, Meredith, and Fred Heath. "Assessment and Continuous Planning: The Key to Transformation at the University of Texas Libraries." *Journal of Library Administration* 52, no. 5 (2012): 424–35. https://doi.org/10.1080/01930826.2012.700798.

Wikipedia, s.v. "Singapore Management University."Accessed May 1, 2017. https://en.wikipedia.org/w/index.php?title=Singapore_Management_University&oldid=775980850.

Womack, James P., and Daniel T. Jones. *Lean Thinking: Banish Waste and Create Wealth in Your Corporation*. New York: Free Press, 2003.

Section 1

Title: Delivering on the Institution's Mission: Developing Measures for a Research Library's Strategic Plan

Abstract: The growth of academic library assessment positions demonstrates the focus on strategic planning, financial accountability, and academic impact sought by today's university leaders. This case study describes the process used to facilitate the George A. Smathers Libraries' Institutional Effectiveness Plan, a goal-setting function that connects the libraries' value to the larger institutional mission.

This study describes this ongoing process employed by the assessment librarian and the libraries' statistics and assessment committee, presenting preliminary formative findings resulting from the first six months of this program. We highlight the "seeding the initiative" perspective and the library's experience with building a culture of assessment.

Keywords: strategic plan, logic model, assessment

Project focus: assessment methodologies, techniques, or practices; organizational practices (i.e., strategic planning); assessment concepts and/or management

Results made or will make case for: improvements in services, improvements in spaces, improvements in collections, proof of library impact and value, a strategic plan or process

Data needed: logic models, reflection essays, strategic plan

Methodology: qualitative, evaluation or survey

Project duration: ongoing (continuous feedback loop)

Tool(s) utilized: use of logic models and department chairs' time

Cost estimate: < $100

Type of institution: university—public

Institution enrollment: 30,000+

Highest level of education: doctoral

Chapter 7

Delivering on the Institution's Mission

Developing Measures for a Research Library's Strategic Plan

Laura I. Spears, Trey Shelton, Chelsea Dinsmore, and Rachael Elrod

Context

The George A. Smathers Libraries at the University of Florida have consistently utilized a measured approach to the delivery of information services and strong collection development and access. The libraries employ many of the innovative approaches academic libraries have used to demonstrate value, including balanced scorecards and LibQUAL+ surveys, all designed both to assess the libraries' place in their users' landscape and to evaluate the capacity of the libraries to meet these needs.[1] The libraries' adoption of LibQUAL+ in 2002 to provide measures for assessing library service quality placed them on a familiar path of many academic research libraries in which traditional indicators of library success were derived from the outputs of library transactional data.

However, as the context of the academic library has changed, with digital-heavy collections and collaborative, iterative, user-driven services, the libraries have created a strategic plan designed to meet the dynamic information needs of its university community. With the creation of *Strategic Directions: UF Libraries 2014–2017,*[2] the libraries have articulated plans to meet and exceed the demands of an "R1" institution, one with higher education's "highest research activity" designation.[3] The next step was for the libraries to assess program and project effectiveness, demonstrate student and faculty impact, and generate consensus about an academic library's place in the modern user's scholarly experience.

Academic library value is no longer simply the sum of its volumes and titles reported to organizational statistical data sets; moreover, given the digital nature of materials and many services, consensus on definitions of usage and clarity of the essential role of the librarian in a seemingly self-serve online information world are hard to delineate. Thus, the challenge has shifted from how to apply strategic thinking to the library environment to an emphasis on how to assess the value of services and materials, in their various forms, generate criteria from the object of study, and capture meaningful measures upon which the library community agrees.

This chapter summarizes the libraries' first year with an assessment librarian tasked to identify and describe the implementation of the libraries' *Strategic Directions*, to begin to assess the outcomes of projects and programs and create an understanding of the libraries' place within the larger university community. We proposed using logic models—a popular visualization of strategic goal achievement—to understand the contributions of the many library departments to the *Strategic Directions'* stated outcomes. We also build on Spears' recent research using Moore's *Creating Public Value* framework to examine if logic model use supports the libraries' messaging that demonstrates library value.[4]

Placing the Libraries into the University Community

The libraries participate in the Responsibility Center Management (RCM) budget model that the university has used since FY2010.[5] To communicate the extent to which annual appropriations may or may not support the libraries' ability to "meet the information needs of the University and appropriately support its teaching, research and clinical initiatives,"[6] the libraries formalized goals and objectives into the 2014–2017 *Strategic Directions*, and these were first communicated in the 2015 Smathers Libraries RCM Budget Review FY2015. Additionally, the libraries began to participate in the university Institutional Effectiveness Plans, using the *Strategic Directions* as the goals and objectives of the libraries' efforts.

Strategic Directions

In FY2011–2012, the libraries implemented a comprehensive compensation program to meet external market demands.[7] This effort was accompanied by the implementation of a new strategic plan, the George A. Smathers Libraries' *Strategic Directions: UF*

Libraries 2014–2017.[8] The process began with the creation of guiding principles and strategies (figure 7.1) for fulfilling and identifying the goals and objectives of the libraries' diverse departments. To assess the libraries' goal achievement, the assessment librarian first coded the text from the working principles into a simple logic model (table 7.1) to look at the intent of these statements through the logic model lens. Logic models exist in many variations and are often revised to suit individual contexts.

GUIDING PRINCIPLES FOR FULFILLING OUR MISSION AND VISION

- Foster an internal environment with equal partnership between all levels of staff, based on the principles and practice of courtesy, professionalism and mutual respect
- Consider the user experience as foundation for every decision to be made
- Promote a productive, diverse, and team-based working environment
- Be innovative, experimental and flexible
- Rely on evidence based decision making (assessment)
- Offer services that meet the evolving needs of the University enterprise
- Initiate and participate in collaboration and community building
- Assure effective, efficient and equitable access to information

GUIDING STRATEGIES

- The libraries will support the university's objective of becoming a Top 10 research institution by acquiring recurrent funding to develop sustainable collections
- The libraries will continue the print-to-online evolution that offers most library resources electronically, focusing on providing users improved ease of use, discoverability and seamless access to commercial and UF digitized content
- The libraries will develop tools and methods for ongoing assessment of holdings, usage and services so that librarians can make data-based decisions
- The libraries will develop a robust marketing plan to create a brand and better acquaint users with the expertise of library faculty and staff and the content offered to users
- The libraries will continue to advocate for a campus-wide Open Access (OA) initiative while providing ongoing education opportunities for staff and UF faculty and students on issues such as ownership rights, sustainability, and archiving of online resources
- The libraries will meet the informational needs of users with disabilities by ensuring that the libraries keep current with assistive technologies and make these widely known to our end users

Figure 7.1
Working principles and strategies for UF Libraries' *Strategic Directions.*
(Source: George A. Smathers Libraries, *Strategic Directions: UF Libraries 2014–2017* [Gainesville: University of Florida, 2014], p.3 http://ufdc.ufl.edu/IR00004144/00001?search=strategic+=directions.)

Librarian and statistician Ray Lyons wrote extensively in his blog, *Lib(rary) Performance* about the use of logic models. In his May 21, 2012 post, he remarked, "a [logic] model is a theoretical and, in a sense, artificial mindset applied to real-life situations."[9] But logic models also function as a time line that concretely identifies the inputs of a project or program, activities conducted, outputs delivered, and ultimately observable outcomes and potential or desired long-term impacts.[10]

Table 7.1 illustrates this logic model, extracting the inputs, activities, and outputs directly from the libraries 2014–2017 *Strategic Directions* working principles;[11] many of the indicators and outcomes were also derived from the working principles; however, the impacts were implied and derive from the goals expressed in the libraries' mission and vision. The libraries' planning effort resulted in the 2014–2017 *Strategic Directions,* which were fleshed out with more definitive objectives and strategies to support these goals.

Table 7.1
Smathers Libraries 2014–2017 *Strategic Directions* Expressed in a Logic Model

Inputs/Activities/ Outputs	Indicators	Outcomes	Impacts
Courtesy, professionalism, mutual respect	Measure the internal environment	Equal partnership between all levels of staff; diverse, team-based environment	Greater success in student academic achievements
Innovations	Services meet evolving needs	Effective, efficient, & equitable access	Greater success in faculty/researcher accomplishments
Flexibility	Services meet evolving needs	Effective, efficient, & equitable access	A library with the reputation for enhancing student/ faculty recruiting
Experiments	Services meet evolving needs	Effective, efficient, & equitable access	A library that enhances knowledge creation & scientific endeavor
Collaborations	Users acquainted with library expertise & content	Community-building capacity increased; diverse, team-based environment	A library with increased access to all materials
Evidence-based decisions	Developed tools and processes	Data-based decisions	
Acquisition of recurrent funding	Top 10 research institution	Sustainable collections	
Print to online evolution	More e-resources	Improved user discovery & access	
Robust marketing/ branding	Users are aware of collections & services	Users know the librarians & the collections	
Open access (OA) advocacy	Increase in open access publications	Increased understanding of ownership rights, sustainability, & archiving OA materials.	
Upgrade assistive technologies	Assistive technologies are current	Meet the needs of those with disabilities	

However, the final version of *Strategic Directions: UF Libraries, 2014–2017* does not define the inputs, outputs, activities, and indicators that will be used by each department, year by year, to plan, monitor, and measure their efforts toward accomplishing the libraries' mission and vision. As a means to identify these terms and to assess each department's efforts supporting them, the assessment librarian used the *Strategic Directions* as a framework to identify and examine the ways in which each department views and contributes to meeting the needs of the university community.

Institutional Effectiveness Plans

The purpose of the university's Institutional Effectiveness Plans (IE Plans) is to provide the UF administrative units a mechanism to systematically review program goals and outcomes, formatively assess unit quality, and demonstrate unit contributions to the overall UF mission.[12] The IE Plan breaks down into mission, vision, goals, action items, resources, measures of results, and time line for completion. In 2016, the assessment program, headed by the assessment librarian, acquired the task of completing the IE Plan, a document that should articulate the authentic, substantial efforts and outcomes of the libraries' faculty and staff and not simply result from an understanding of each unit's work. As can happen with any complex and busy organization, goals and objectives codified in strategic plans and institutional reporting are often not reviewed for their alignment with actual activities and results. So the approach was to begin deductively and ensure that the contents of the IE Plan reflected the libraries' deliverables as framed by the 2014–2017 *Strategic Directions*.

To achieve this, the assessment librarian first approached the libraries' Statistics and Assessment Committee (SAC) as the unit representatives who should facilitate the completion of the IE Plan as part of their committee's effort. But it became clear, after multiple presentations of the IE Plan structure and an additional presentation by faculty on operationalizing variables based on the libraries' *Strategic Directions*, that individuals were confused about how to articulate both the plan and their results, so a subcommittee, including library unit heads from the Digital Production Services and the Acquisitions and Collections Services units along with the Head of the Education branch library, was developed to adopt a new approach.

Logic Models

In a May 5, 2017 listserv message, Ray Lyons succinctly wrote about logic models, which have been in use in the library field since the 1970s. Logic models, very simply, "organize the library's thinking about program and service delivery and the accomplishment of desired outcomes."[13] And in my view, logic models can demonstrate the library staff's oft-hidden but necessary efforts to make information accessible, collaborative, digital, educational, and meaningful. Further, logic models are often used in grant writing, both to illustrate the ability of the grant applicant to follow through and complete the proposed project, and as a component of program or project evaluation. With the libraries' substantial record of grant funding applications and awards received, the assessment librarian anticipated that many of the library units would have individuals with experience in using logic models, so logic models were presented to the SAC to create awareness, and then the subcommittee was formed and agreed to train more intensively on logic model use with the objective of specifically articulating the resources and processes required to execute the action items listed in the IE Plan.

The subcommittee met for two group sessions, completing a pre- and post-training assessment, an analysis of logic model uses, and an exercise applying the logic model using the content from the IE Plan. The assessment librarian also met with each subcommittee member in a one-on-one meeting to discuss questions and review their attempts to place action items from the 2016–2017 IE Plan to which they could be expected to contribute into the logic model structure.

Communicating Results and Impact

Pre-exercise Survey

Together we conducted a pre-exercise survey to understand the knowledge of the libraries' *Strategic Directions*, their use as structure of the libraries' IE Plan, their prior use of logic models, and how each of the participants' units might be expected to contribute based on the current action items included in the IE Plan. All of the participants expressed no prior experience with logic models outside of the presentation to the SAC, and each was unaware of the extent to which the IE Plan was structured on the libraries' *Strategic Directions*.

As a result of this disconnection with the use of the *Strategic Directions* for the IE Plan, the IE Plan, as written, poorly describes an objective that can be measured by each unit. When asked to review the action items, which in the IE Plan represent the statements of each strategic direction, the participants struggled with how to operationalize each because they did not participate in writing them and each action item was not constructed to fully describe the program or project being measured.

This session also revealed that the proposed logic model that was initially provided for this use was not structured as well as it could be. The resulting logic model draws on Richard Orr's work with evaluation models, presenting five components—resources, capabilities, utilization, outcomes and impact—with corresponding measures for each (figure 7.2).[14]

Spears'own experience evaluating proposals for the Florida Division of Library Information Services from 2009 to 2013 provided a basis for applying this model to the libraries, and based on feedback from the first session, the logic model was modified specifically for operationalizing our own IE Plan, resulting in implementation of our libraries' *Strategic Directions* (table 7.2).

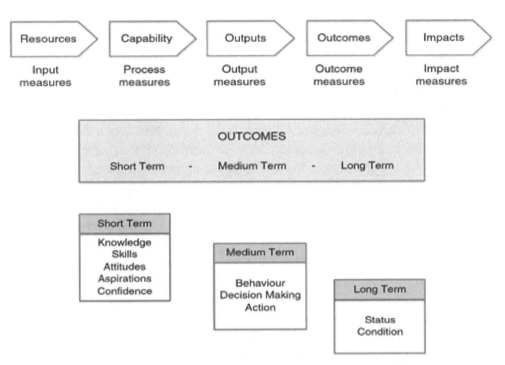

Figure 7.2
Breakdown of Orr evaluation model. (Source: Joseph Matthews,"Assessing Outcomes and Value: It's All a Matter of Perspective," *Performance Measurement and Metrics* 14, no. 3 [2015]: 211–33.)

Table 7.2
Smathers Libraries Logic Model

Context of the Area for Analysis	Goals Objectives					Intended Objectives		Intended Goals
	Action Item from IE Plan	Inputs	Activities	Participation	Measures	Outcomes		Impacts
						Short Term	Medium Term	Long Term
Problem/ Area		What we invest	What we do	Who we reach	Outputs	*learned*	*action*	*condition*
Priorities		**Assumptions** (list those from any section)				**External Factors** (issues or factors that influence outcomes that occur outside your department)		

Logic Model Exercises

Each participant was asked to select an action item from the Smathers Libraries 2016–2017 IE Plan for which they were listed as a resource and to which they could expect to contribute. After the first group session, they were asked to complete the logic model using their selected action item. However, given the feedback from the one-on-one sessions, it became clear that each participant needed to rewrite the action item into an objective with specific, measurable elements, as the original action items from the IE Plan were not specific enough for an individual department to reasonably work on.

At this point, the participants also had an opportunity to attend a meeting at which a colleague with research design expertise presented a workshop on operationalizing variables from an item, activity, or experience that they might need to measure. This was designed to support the completion of the Inputs-Resources-Outputs sections and is an important aspect of the culture of assessment. The libraries' assessment program has been designed to assess and evaluate all types of phenomena; accordingly, there are units for which measures are difficult to identify, so we have focused on "capturing" these. This can be a simple photo essay of daily library interactions or the concept of communities of practice evolving from digital humanities programs and projects. So for the UF Libraries, the culture includes assessment, evaluation, and capture.

We held our final group session, which covered specific questions about their logic models. The participants turned in their logic models, and they were also given the assessment questions again as prompts for their reflection essays. In reviewing the logic models, all three participants were able to construct the practical elements of inputs, activities, and outputs, albeit with varying degrees of specificity. For example, the logic model for the Digital Production Services unit includes a rewritten action item to make it more applicable to the unit's contribution to the objectives within the Digital and Digitized Collections strategic direction, which includes a broad spectrum of activities within the libraries. Each of the three participants' logic models follows, with explanations narrated by each about the model they created and how it was used within their unit.

Digital Production Services (DPS)

Our library spent over a year working collaboratively to develop a strategic directions document with the Digital Production Services looking at "digital directions." The interesting aspect of the term *digital* is that it turns out to be a very general term with broad implications. While Digital Projects had an entire strategic direction created for it, it seemed like a great many action items in the other sections also impacted or relied on support from the digital group. The *Strategic Directions* document is meant to provide guidelines for prioritizing projects and for guiding day-to-day work. Demonstrating that activities over the course of the year contributed to progress on the action items to support the larger goals of the institution is intended to factor into annual evaluations. DPS Chair Chelsea Dinsmore describes the use of logic models by her department.

The strategic direction that has the most obvious impact on DPS is written as "Strengthen the Libraries' capacity to create and curate scholarly content in a diverse range of digital formats and create scalable services/sustainable infrastructure to support digital." An action item attributed to this goal is "Increase internal capacity for digitization and expand collections." While some capacity can be gained by improving workflows and finding efficiencies in the process, our capacity for digitization is largely defined by staffing levels—more financial support means more available staff hours for scanning. Beyond the support already provided by the library, we rely on grants to extend our capacity.

Digital Services supports grant-writing efforts to obtain funding for digitization projects by providing technical process write-ups for inclusion in grants as well as cost estimates that substantiate budget requests. Staff salaries are often included as part of cost share. Additionally the department provides consulting services on best practices and work-arounds for helping the curator achieve his or her desired collection presentation, while overseeing and performing scanning and image processing, quality control, metadata review, and ingest; ensuring content and metadata are archived; and tracking all of those steps.

The baseline infrastructure for DPS is provided by the library and includes fifteen full-time benefitted staff (15 FTE) and 140 hours a week of hourly labor; five copybook scanners, two cradle scanners, one large-format overhead camera and table, assorted cameras and stands, one high-speed sheet-feed scanner, and twelve computers for image capture and processing. Office space and generous internet connections might also be considered since the unit is housed off-campus in leased space and is not connected to the internet infrastructure provided by the university. Technical support for our computers is provided by library IT; the Cataloging department provides cataloging support for digitization projects; and the Special and Area Studies department provides most of our content for scanning, thereby contributing to project planning and management. Additionally, Digital Production Services acts as the technical host for the Digital Library of the Caribbean (dLOC), and this provides another avenue for grant projects to support DPS as well as partnership opportunities for library faculty and staff.

The department is able to track the number of pages generated every month and how many collections are created or added to the digital library. However, those numbers do not really reveal our productivity. Successful capacity increases will be measured by an increased ability to digitize projects. Having a clear understanding of workflows that can be expressed through the visual representation of the logic model (table 7.3) will be one measure of success. It should answer the question "Do our colleagues understand how we develop time and cost estimates?" It will also make developing those estimates more straightforward.

A similar visual representation created for the structure of collections already in place will facilitate matching similar topics and collections early in the process, rather than discovering overlap after much of the work is complete. Finally, our department being involved in grant projects from the very beginning is a desired outcome, rather than being brought in as an afterthought. This will indicate that we have made our part of the process sufficiently transparent and have educated the larger library properly on our role and our partnering abilities.

Table 7.3
Digital Production Services Logic Model

	Definition	**Digital Productions Services**
Action Item from the IE Plan	The intervention, action, or program/project that responds to the context described.	Increase internal capacity for digitization and expand collaborations with external partners that include all types of content providers (Family Search, Newspaper.com, Digital Public Library [DPL], Adam Matthew Digital, Elsevier Ltd., etc.).
Inputs	The resources available to operate a program/process/intervention, including staff, organizations, communities, and finances.	Staff (15 FTE); equipment (scanners, computers, specialized furniture); technical support from other library departments.
Outputs	**Activities:** Specific things that the program/process/intervention is doing.	Staff supports grant-writing efforts to garner funding for digitization projects; provides consulting services on best practices and work-arounds; oversees and performs scanning.
	Participation: The variety of stakeholders reached by the program/process/intervention.	Researchers and scholars of all levels at UF and around the world.
	Measures: These are agreed upon indicators of activity by which a program/process/intervention can be observed.	An increasing rate of content added to UFDC—more pages scanned/loaded this month/year than last month/year; fewer errors found/reported; a regular number (or more) of grants applied for; (#) of internal library curator trainings held; existing relationships with external partners maintained with positive additions to UFDC resulting.
Outcomes	**Short-Term (Results):** These are generally the "learning areas" that demonstrate specific changes as a result of a program/process/intervention.	Gaining a clear understanding of work flows, one that can be expressed through visual representation; A similar visual representation created for the structure of collections already in place.
	Medium-Term (Results): These are generally the "action areas" that demonstrate specific changes as a result of a program/process/intervention.	Presentation of the workflow and collection layout as part of renewed training efforts leading to Digital Services department being involved in grant projects from the very beginning, rather than being brought in as an afterthought.
	Long-Term (Impacts): Long-term intended or unintended overall program effects occurring in the organization, community, or systems as a result of program/process/intervention activities.	An increased ability to support efforts to generate digitization projects.

	Definition	**Digital Productions Services**
Assumptions	Definitions of terms that provide specific indication of meaning or provide reference to an external source or standard. These can be any source to which your department refers or adheres.	Ongoing library support for digitization infrastructure (equipment, space, staff, maintenance, internet connection, etc.); state (FALSC) support for hosting digital collections and Florida Digital Archive (FDA).
External Factors	Organizations, authorities, pressures, events, or influences from outside the libraries that influence or mandate library operations.	Grant proposals often take a year to review and then are not always granted; funding for large-scale projects may not materialize, and the time frame is not always set (apply this year, rejected and reapply next year, funded the 3rd year). Our capacity is not always taken advantage of—sources of content may not be prepared to provide it.

Acquisitions and Collections Services (ACS)

The logic model created for the IEP objective geared towards expanding and assessing just-in-time collection-building efforts allowed the ACS department to clearly state what problem was being addressed, how the plan aligned with priorities and the strategic directions, actions that needed to be accomplished, what resources would be needed, who would be impacted, and how success would be measured. Many of these items are naturally assumed when building a new purchasing plan, but putting them in writing helps the person planning flesh out all areas that need considering and assists in explaining the plan to other stakeholders. The libraries *Strategic Directions* document is intended to guide library activities, but cannot be detailed enough to cover all initiatives. Although the logic model form may be somewhat intimidating to new users and require some in-depth explanation, use of the tool to align department-level activities to the *Strategic Directions* greatly assists in completing the necessary reporting documents required by the libraries and the university, such as the IEP (table 7.4).

As the relatively new chair of the ACS department, Trey Shelton relies on the *Strategic Directions* to guide recommendations to collection coordinators and library administrators regarding collections and material budget decisions. Aligning projects to the *Strategic Directions* can also help in understanding what priority a given project or initiative should receive. The ACS department's work primarily contributes to the Creative and Dynamic Content Management section of the *Strategic Directions*.

The department facilitates all materials-related purchases and licensing, administers all collections funds, plans and develops collection strategies, and performs analysis and assessment of collections and purchasing plans. The department is also responsible for managing all electronic resources, administering the access and discovery systems (e.g., discovery layer, link resolver, proxy server, A–Z database list), and coordinating batch catalog processes and reports, including batch MARC record loading. Regardless of format, the department supports traditional just-in-case and newer just-in-time purchasing models in order to balance both short-term user needs and the long-term collecting goals of the libraries.

All of the acquisition and collections activities the department is responsible for are intrinsically tied to the *Strategic Directions*, but this does not remove the need to plan initiatives intended to directly contribute toward these directions and assess their ultimate impact. With flat or shrinking material budgets, all new purchases are the result of canceling or not purchasing a different resource. Therefore, libraries must be diligent to ensure their purchase decisions are geared toward meeting their users' and institutional needs. Even with detailed analysis, it is often difficult to know if a given plan (just-in-case or just-in-time) is adequately and efficiently achieving its goals. Using benchmarking, based either on local data or data present in the literature, provides some level of assurance of the success of a plan. However, these activities can be time-consuming and may not result in particularly actionable information.

Table 7.4
Acquisitions and Collections Services Logic Model

	Definition	Acquisitions and Collections Services
Action Item from the IE Plan	The intervention, action, or program/project that responds to the context described.	Continue to expand "just-in-time" purchasing plans, including local and consortial models, including: State University Libraries consortial Evidence-Based Acquisition (EBA) plan with Taylor & Francis for monographs covering the Humanities & Social Sciences (to launch in the fall semester), a streaming video EBA plan with Docuseek2 (to launch in August 2016), an expansion of the music scores and monographs print Patron Driven Acquisition (PDA) plan (fall semester); piloting of a Germanic/Slavic and European Studies print PDA plan (spring semester), and Expansion of CRC Press NetBase EBA plan for STEM (August 2016).
Inputs	The resources available to operate a program/process/intervention, including staff, organizations, communities, and finances.	Allocation of funds for PDA/DDA/EDA plans and licensing desired course reserves; collaboration with State University Libraries, FALSC, and Taylor & Francis to structure shared EBA plan; use of assessment analytics to understand use and user patterns.
Outputs	**Activities:** Specific things that the program/process/intervention is doing.	Participate in a state-wide University Library shared EBA plan with Taylor & Francis; continue a variety of local use-driven acquisition plans; allocate funding, build/adjust plan parameters, load discovery records, monitor and assess usage and cost, make recommendations for future plans/revisions/cancellations.

	Definition	Acquisitions and Collections Services
Outputs	**Participation:** The variety of stakeholders reached by the program/process/intervention.	Users of State University Libraries, users of Smathers Libraries, selector/liaisons, Acquisitions & Collections services personnel, Access Services personnel, library administrators.
	Measures: These are agreed-upon indicators of activity by which a program/process/intervention can be observed.	Usage reports and resulting cost-usage analysis will provide ROI metrics. Benchmarks may be other local plans or analysis of plans from other institutions as found in the literature. Plan subject coverage and support based on the subject classification of the content in the discovery pool, the subject classification of the content, and the dollar value of the content
Outcomes	**Short-Term (Results):** These are generally the "learning areas" that demonstrate specific changes as a result of a program/process/intervention.	Acquire content in a cost-effective manner that meets users' immediate needs.
	Medium-Term (Results): These are generally the "action areas" that demonstrate specific changes as a result of a program/process/intervention.	Understand what content types and subject areas are best supported by PDA/DDA/EBA plans; participate in the plans that best meet user needs.
	Long-Term (Impacts): Long-term intended or unintended overall program effects occurring in the organization, community, or systems as a result of program/process/intervention activities.	The libraries will utilize cost-effective methods of meeting users' immediate needs, while continuing to build distinct and targeted collections that satisfy long-term goals.
Assumptions	Definitions of terms that provide specific indication of meaning or provide reference to an external source or standard. These can be any source to which your department refers or adheres.	It is impossible to meet all user information needs; content licensed for discovery is applicable to users' research/learning needs; State University Libraries have common collection interests that would be well served by shared-collection purchasing models; PDA/DDA/EBA plans are cost-effective; e-books and streaming video are key formats/material types for users.
External Factors	Organizations, authorities, pressures, events, or influences from outside the libraries that influence or mandate library operations.	Library funding can support these DDA/PDA/EBA plans; publisher/providers are fiscally stable and able to continue to offer these plans; users are interested in utilizing library services to meet their information needs.

Education Branch Library

One of the goals in the libraries' 2016–2017 IEP, "Integrate Space, Technology, and Service," fit into our renovation plans: "Provide multi-purpose library spaces which serve as inviting venues for a variety of functions and deliver diverse and up-to-date technology resources to foster innovation, enhance learning and improve collaboration."

The problem or area that we want to address is an outdated library facility. The priorities for the facility renovation are to install new carpet; perform asbestos abatement; purchase new furniture; wash and paint walls; provide ADA accessibility at the service desk; provide an ADA accessible restroom; update staff offices and staff lounge to enhance workflow; improve lighting; add a computer lab; and add an educational makerspace area.

The action item from the IEP that best addresses this project is "Integrate Space, Technology, and Services." The inputs, library resources, are faculty and staff time used to develop the renovation plans and assess user satisfaction. The activities involved in this project are collaborating with library, university, and outside personnel, such as architects, engineers, and designers, to create a blueprint of the proposed renovation, identify new furniture to replace existing furniture, and develop a time line of the renovation process including relocating staff and faculty during the renovation as well as a communication time line for communicating with our patrons about the process.

Participants, or "who we will reach," include students, faculty, staff, and the general public who use the library. The measurements or outputs that we will use to assess the renovation include gate counts, study room usage provided by the room reservation program, computer usage, and circulation numbers. Assumptions made in this project include the belief that money will be provided by the state to fund the project, that the renovation is wanted and needed, that library users will like the renovation, and that the renovation will increase usage and user satisfaction of the facility, technology, and materials.

A survey of our patrons shows that they desire a modern education library with increased technology, more power outlets, and new flexible furniture. The short-term results are that we will gain a better understanding of user satisfaction and hopefully increase user satisfaction, increase gate counts, increase study room usage, increase circulation of materials, and increase use of library technology that extends student learning and collaborative efforts. The medium-term results are that we will be able to use a post-survey to assess if user satisfaction has indeed been increased. The long-term, ultimate impact is that we will have an improved library space that users are satisfied with.

The external factors, outside of the control of the libraries, that influence this project are the state governor, who has the authority to veto funding for the project; architects, engineers, and designers who let us know what can and cannot be done with the building; and the administration of the College of Education, as the library is embedded within its building and it has some authority over the building, particularly the outside of the building including outdoor signage (table 7.5).

Table 7.5
Education Library Logic Model

	Definition	Education Library
Action Item from the IE Plan	The intervention, action, or program/project that responds to the context described.	Conduct space use assessment to include user perceptions, unobtrusive observations, and student use data.
Inputs	The resources available to operate a program/process/intervention, including staff, organizations, communities, and finances.	Faculty & intern time, survey software, discretionary funding for incentives, COE administration.
Outputs	**Activities:** Specific things that the program/process/intervention is doing.	IRB approval, study design, survey, unobtrusive observations, email, announcements.
	Participation: The variety of stakeholders reached by the program/process/intervention.	Primarily the students and faculty of the College of Education.
	Measures: These are agreed-upon indicators of activity by which a program/process/intervention can be observed.	Conducted focus groups.
Outcomes	**Short-Term (Results):** These are generally the "learning areas" that demonstrate specific changes as a result of a program/process/intervention.	Obtain student perceptions, user needs, and findings.
	Medium-Term (Results): These are generally the "action areas" that demonstrate specific changes as a result of a program/process/intervention.	Incorporate findings into renovation plans.
	Long-Term (Impacts): Long-term intended or unintended overall program effects occurring in the organization, community, or systems as a result of program/process/intervention activities.	Our students have a place that is innovative, welcoming, and research-supportive.
Assumptions	Definitions of terms that provide specific indication of meaning or provide reference to an external source or standard. These can be any source to which your department refers or adheres.	That we can get a representative sample of COE students/faculty.
External Factors	Organizations, authorities, pressures, events, or influences from outside the libraries that influence or mandate library operations.	State funding, COE, Student Government, Teacher Resource Lab.

Section 1

Leveraging the Findings

Part of this assessment exercise in the use of logic models included the questions asked prior to beginning the logic model exercise and then repeated during the reflection essays written by each participant. They were asked about their knowledge of the libraries' *Strategic Directions* and the related IE Plan as well as any knowledge or experience they had with logic models. Two participants indicated that they were involved in the "town halls" the libraries engaged in while creating the *Strategic Directions*:

> I was heavily involved in the process of developing the *Strategic Directions*. I participated in several town-hall style meetings that were facilitated by two associate deans and intended to gather input from all levels of staff and faculty. During the town hall meetings, the facilitators would pose a topic or issue and begin to write the thoughts and ideas posed by the staff, and these were grouped into general categories. Participants were asked to provide additional thoughts and ideas related to the categories. In the next stage, working groups were tasked with developing language from the categorized feedback for the strategic directions; each group was assigned a specific focus area based on our area of expertise. I was assigned to the working group charged with developing language for what ultimately became the Creative and Dynamic Content Management section of the *Strategic Directions*. The language that the group eventually developed attempted to balance both the tension between traditional selection methods and newer use-driven (Patron/Demand Driven Acquisition, Evidence Based Acquisition/Selection, Purchase on Demand) models and between print and electronic formats.

One participant arrived at the libraries after the creation of the *Strategic Directions* stated these "were shared with me shortly after I arrived and I then had to plug the needs of my branch into what had already been written, which were not necessarily a good fit." Finally, one participant who participated in the creation of the *Strategic Directions* "had not worked with logic models before, but was looking for some means of articulating what we actually needed 'to do' in order to make effective use of the Strategic Directions that we had created."

Reflection and Analysis of Public Value Contributions

According to Matthews, "Social impacts can be though [*sic*] of as the meaning of the library to the community in which the library exists."[15] Many studies have examined the positive contributions by stakeholders on personal, social, economic and community-building levels.[16] It is the experience and findings from Spears' own research that librarians often miss opportunities to fully communicate the ways in which they contribute to communities because they miss elements of messages that appeal and are important, especially to policy-making and funding decision-makers.[17] For this exercise, we examined the usefulness of logic models to illustrate value as framed by Moore's model of Creating Public Value, and considered the following:[18]

1. Do the participants' descriptions express the three issues associated in building public value for the university community (legitimacy and support, operational capabilities, public value goals and vision)?

    The development of the acquisitions department analysis of user-based acquisitions to examine one the highest expenses in the libraries, electronic resources, is an example of a practice that develops legitimacy for ongoing collection development. This process demonstrates the commitment the libraries have to the users, both students and faculty, as materials are directly related to their scholarly needs. Implementation and analysis of user-based acquisitions also provides the libraries with organic samples of our relationship to and value for scholars' ongoing research needs.

2. Do participants perceive this as a valid way to build legitimacy and support, operational capabilities, and public value as they communicate with stakeholders?

    The efforts of both the Education Library and the Digital Production Services demonstrate that building relationships with their communities, through library space needs assessment and collaborative grant development, can be enhanced by their use of tools that describe and visualize the resources, activities, and outputs that they contribute to ongoing development of public value and to building operational capacities that go beyond the daily operations in which they are involved.

3. In what ways, if any, do participants examine, build, or express public value in this exercise?

    Each department expressed how interrelated its activities and resources are with the greater libraries organization and to the larger university community. The DPS demonstrates the capacity building that leads to community building; the ACS department's focus builds value by establishing transparency in use of public funds to create community value; and the Education Library space assessment focuses on understanding what the community finds of value in the library space.

Finally, the participants commented on their view of the use of logic models both to describe project and program goal achievement and to demonstrate how logic models contributeto their ability to articulate library value to their diverse stakeholders. The Head of the Education Library remarked,

> The logic model has been a useful exercise to incorporate assessment into our renovation planning. Before I had heard of the logic model, library administrators and I had planned for a renovation based on our 'gut feeling' that it was time for change. The carpet was old, the

furniture hadn't been updated since the building opened thirty-seven years ago, and there were some accessibility features that could be added. One thing we had not considered was the feedback from our patrons. I had never used a logic model before, but in using the logic model, I was able to realize that assessment of user satisfaction was necessary to plan a successful renovation.

For the Acquisitions Department, "we needed to plan initiatives intended to directly contribute toward the strategic directions and assess their ultimate impact. With flat or shrinking materials budgets, all new purchases are the result of canceling or not purchasing a different resource. Therefore, libraries must be diligent to ensure their purchase decisions are geared toward meeting their users' and institutional needs."

Conclusion

This exercise was a project conducted by the assessment librarian and three unit heads that are responsible for managing departments in three areas: Acquisitions and Collections Services, Digital Production Services, and the Education Library Branch. While the responsibility for completing the libraries' IEP is purely the role of assessment, it seemed clear that we could not report goals, objectives, and results for a diverse group of departments. (This represents just a few of the more than twenty-five departments.) The IEP is where the libraries' value is communicated to a variety of stakeholders. Our IEP has been made a model for the UF community as an example of clear articulation of goal planning, strategizing, and achievement. But this process is a collaborative one in which a majority of unit heads—those accountable for the results—better understand what their work is and how to measure it.

The logic model process was used during the IEP 2017–2018 development. Seventeen different departments participated and created logic models to articulate their objectives for the upcoming academic year. The logic models completed demonstrate the complex nature of goal completion, with projects and programs involving anywhere from a single department to every department across the University Libraries. The departments were asked to participate using an online content-sharing system called Basecamp to encourage collaboration and sharing of ideas. However, no unit felt comfortable with the software, and it was not used.

The assessment librarian reviewed each logic model and requested revisions as needed. As soon as individuals were able to articulate an objective they personally created and will implement, understanding of the use of the logic model increased. However, most participants struggled to identify measures of their efforts and it required coaching for every participant to develop or identify meaningful indicators. This phenomenon of struggling with measuring library activity accomplishments continues to challenge librarians, but the process of using logic models may be an approach that helps clarify both how to do this and how to make it meaningful to librarians for whom this is a relatively new or strange task.

We learned a great deal about the distributed accountabilities that exist in the libraries' structure. We also realized that logic models, goal setting, and operationalization of a phenomenon are an articulation that is common to library research but not necessarily to library practitioners. We will definitely continue to work in small groups or one-on-one in establishing the useful logic model tool. As our information profession grows in its diversity, and our work behind the scenes continues to be little understood, the use of logic models makes transparent the resources and activities required to serve the needs of the academic community.

Notes

1. Stephen R. Shorb and Lori Driscoll, "LibQUAL+™ Meets Strategic Planning at the University of Florida," *Journal of Library Administration* 40, no. 3–4 (2008): 173–180.
2. George A. Smathers Libraries, *Strategic Directions, UF Libraries 2014–2017* (Gainesville: University of Florida, George A. Smathers Libraries, 2014), http://ufdc.ufl.edu/IR00004144/00001?-search=strategic+=directions.
3. Carnegie Classification of Institutions of Higher Education, "About Carnegie Classification," accessed May 24, 2017. http://carnegieclassifications.iu.edu/2010/.
4. Mark Moore, Creating Public Value (Boston: Harvard University Press, 1995).
5. George A. Smathers Libraries, Fiscal Services @ UF Libraries, University of Florida, accessed April 30, 2017, http://cms.uflib.ufl.edu/fiscalservices/rcm.
6. Judith Russell, Patrick Reakes, Brian Keith, Cecilia Botero, and Ben Walker, *Fiscal Year 2015–2016 Budget Review: The George A. Smathers Libraries* (Gainesville: University of Floriday, George A. Smathers Libraries, 2015), 2, http://ufdc.ufl.edu/AA00027538/00001/citation?search=keith+%3d-budget.
7. Russell et al., *Fiscal Year 2015–2016 Budget Review*.
8. George A. Smathers Libraries, *Strategic Directions*.
9. Ray Lyons, "Assessment's Top Models," *Lib(rary) Performance* (blog), May 21, 2012, https://libper-formance.com/2012/05/21/assessments-top-models/.
10. Joseph Matthews, "Assessing Outcomes and Value: It's All a Matter of Perspective," *Performance Measurement and Metrics* 14, no. 3 (2015): 211–33.
11. George A. Smathers Libraries, *Strategic Directions*, 3.
12. "Planning Resources," Institutional Assessment, University of Florida, accessed February 8, 2018, https://assessment.aa.ufl.edu/institutional-effectiveness/planning-resources/.
13. Ray Lyons, "Logic Models," ARL-ASSESS list-serv, May 5, 2017, https://mail.google.com/mail/u/0/#search/ray+lyons/15bd9195b7544fba
14. Matthews, "Assessing Outcomes and Value," 212.
15. Matthews, "Assessing Outcomes and Value," 220.
16. Matthews, "Assessing Outcomes and Value," 220.
17. Laura I. Spears "Using Social Networks for Library Funding Advocacy: A Discourse Analysis of the 'Save the Miami-Dade Public Libraries' Facebook Campaign" (PhD diss., The Florida State University, 2016).
18. Moore, *Creating Public Value*.

Bibliography

Carnegie Classification of Institutions of Higher Education. "About Carnegie Classification." Accessed May 24, 2017. http://carnegieclassifications.iu.edu/2010/.

George A. Smathers Libraries. "Fiscal Services @ UF Libraries. University of Florida. Accessed April 30, 2017. http://cms.uflib.ufl.edu/fiscalservices/rcm.

———. *Strategic Directions, UF Libraries 2014–2017.* Gainesville: University of Florida, George A. Smathers Libraries, 2014. http://ufdc.ufl.edu/IR00004144/00001?search=strategic+=directions.

Lyons, Ray. "Assessment's Top Models." *Lib(rary) Performance* (blog), May 21, 2012. https://libperformance.com/2012/05/21/assessments-top-models/.

Lyons, Ray. "Logic Models," ARL-ASSESS list-serv, May 5, 2017. https://mail.google.com/mail/u/0/#-search/ray+lyons/15bd9195b7544fba

Matthews, Joseph. "Assessing Outcomes and Value: It's All a Matter of Perspective." *Performance Measurement and Metrics* 14, no. 3 (2015): 211–33.

Moore, Mark. *Creating Public Value: Strategic Management in Government.* Boston: Harvard University Press, 1995.

Russell, Judith, Patrick Reakes, Brian Keith, Cecilia Botero, and Ben Walker. *Fiscal Year 2015–2016 Budget Review: The George A. Smathers Libraries.* Gainesville: University of Florida, George A. Smathers Libraries, 2015). http://ufdc.ufl.edu/AA00027538/00001/citation?search=keith+%3d-budget.

Shorb, Stephen R., and Lori Driscoll. "LibQUAL+™ Meets Strategic Planning at the University of Florida." *Journal of Library Administration* 40, no. 3–4 (2008): 173–80.

Spears, Laura I. "Using Social Networks for Library Funding Advocacy: A Discourse Analysis of the 'Save the Miami-Dade Public Libraries' Facebook Campaign." PhD diss., The Florida State University, 2016.

University of Florida. "Planning Resources." Institutional Assessment. Accessed February 8, 2018. https://assessment.aa.ufl.edu/institutional-effectiveness/planning-resources/.

Title: Begin Again

Abstract: One of the hallmarks of any assessment or evaluation is that it serves as an agent for improved change. However, not all changes are positive. In some cases, improvements in one area of library service delivery have negative effects in other areas of service delivery. In addition to this, no assessment is ever perfectly planned nor conducted. Each of these factors contributes to the need for library assessments to be periodically repeated.

This chapter begins with a description of an assessment planning guide and journal to chronicle how the assessment was planned and unfolded. From here it discusses factors of repeating assessment in terms of planning, conducting, and reporting repeat assessments. The chapter will focus on two repeat assessments as examples. One discusses the reshelving of checked-out books to determine if changed procedures following an employee change resulted in improved service delivery. The other discusses the examination of open-ended comments from several administrations of the LibQUAL+ survey. The chapter concludes with establishment of a reassessment schedule for library assessments.

Keywords: assessment planning, evaluation planning, repeated assessments, planning guide

Project focus: organizational practices (i.e., strategic planning); assessment concepts and/or management

Results made or will make case for: more funding, improvements in services, improvements in spaces, improvements in collections, proof of library impact and value, a strategic plan or process, how money or resources may be directed

Data needed: The data in the first of two examples was quantitative in that the assessment randomly removed books from library stacks and then tracked the time it took for each book to be reshelved. The second of two examples uses data collected from multiple administrations of the LibQUAL+ survey. This example focuses on the coding and tracking of positive and negative comments in six key categories. The tracking enables librarians to determine areas which that have improved over the years and the degree to which they have improved. It also highlights areas where continued emphasis is needed for improvement.

Methodology: quantitative, mixed method, evaluation or survey

Project duration: The reshelving assessment took place within 5 years. The the LibQUAL+ survey assessment is an ongoing assessment spanning 15 years.

Tool(s) utilized: The reshelving study used a great deal of manpower as books had to be pulled from stacks throughout the library and key information recorded so they could be tracked. Examination of book locations was tracked daily until all books were returned. No high tech was really needed, just a lot of record keeping.

The LibQUAL+ survey requires IRB approval, but there is very little adjustment as we have applied for virtually the same IRB over seven administrations of the survey. The survey requires complicated survey administration as participants are rerouted from the data collection survey to a survey to register for incentive prizes to protect anonymity. Identifying the initial categories took significant effort and was supported by a sociology class studying qualitative research methods. Since the protocols have been established for the categories, coding is fairly straightforward.

Cost estimate: $2,000–$5,000

Type of institution: college—private

Institution enrollment: 30,000+

Highest level of education: doctoral

Chapter 8

Begin Again

Holt Zaugg

Context

Successful assessments do not just happen. Each assessment needs careful planning at several levels that consider a variety of assessment elements. Some of the elements include the evaluators and their roles, rigor, institutional review board approval, methods, potentially a pilot study, the scope of the project, which people connect to the project, and dissemination of findings.

A key element often neglected in planning an assessment is when to repeat the assessment.[1] Reassessments enable those connected to the project or organization to determine how the organization changed following the initial assessment and subsequent changes.[2] Reassessments allow evaluators to re-examine program attributes of the initial assessment, to add methods to assess new program components or to subtract assessment procedures for discontinued or irrelevant program components. As the program evolves and changes, so do the subsequent assessments.

Using a dozen library assessments, including follow-up assessment, four components were identified to assist in the decision of if and when to conduct a reassessment. The four components are complexity, cost, interactions, and reporting. The components often interconnect with each other. For example, increasing or decreasing the complexity of the reassessment will influence the cost. Reporting overlaps with interactions as findings from one assessment may influence individuals to change practices. While each core component is connected, each is discussed independently here.

Complexity

The component of complexity considers anything that increases the difficulty of conducting the reassessment. It includes the number of methods used to conduct the assessment as well as the complexity of data collection and analysis. Often evaluators will combine data collection methods to gain greater insights or for triangulation of findings. Each method used to collect the data may be rather simple, in and of itself, but combining several methods increases the complexity of an assessment.

Similarly, a reassessment may use only one or two methods, but each method may be difficult to administer or to analyze. For example, in a wayfinding study in an academic library, participants were asked to find twelve people, places, or things. Each trip began at the library entrance, and participants found a pathway to the person, place, or thing. As participants moved through their library pathway, they were followed by two researchers who video recorded the participant. This single data collection method had considerable complexity in gaining needed approvals, ensuring cameras were working properly and had sufficient memory to record, and ensuring the safety of all involved—try following a participant running up stairs while recording!

Once collected, the analysis required researchers to view video recordings several times, with each viewing taking the full time of the actual pathway experience. This one data collection method had considerable complexity in both data collection and analysis.[3]

In reassessments, there is always the temptation to add new data collection methods or to increase the complexity of previous data collection methods. While the merits of doing so need to be considered with each reassessment project, evaluators need to ask what the gains and costs are of the increased complexity. It is always important to document all assessment procedures and any method changes made during the assessment. This documentation typically occurs in an assessment journal entry. It provides a context for why methods were used or changed and is helpful for reassessment decisions.

Cost

Costs are both tangible and intangible. There is a cost in terms of time and money associated with each assessment. Someone needs to conduct the study, whether that is full-time employees, students as a class assignment, or volunteers. While some costs may be lessened by using volunteers or student classes studying research methods, there is still a cost associated with finding and training the volunteers or teaching the research methods class.[4] Typically, these costs are covered in the form of employee salaries, but not all libraries have individuals hired to conduct assessments.

In addition, some assessments need specialized equipment. This equipment may range from cameras and recorders to rooms dedicated to conducting focus groups. It also includes data analysis software, such as transcription and statistical software. There may be travel costs associated with dissemination.

In addition to the monetary cost, there is also the cost of time. Each reassessment will take time. With each subsequent reassessment, the time needed to complete the assessment may diminish. For example, after the initial administration of the LibQUAL+ survey, subsequent IRB applications should need only minor adjustments instead of a total rewrite. With repeated administrations, best practices for data collection are better known. Learning from past assessments enables researchers to avoid previous errors. However, the reverse may also happen as evaluators reuse a method with a new group of participants who respond in new or different ways from the first assessment participants. Adding new data collection methods may also influence previously used methods.

Evaluators should consider and respect participant time. There needs to be consideration of participant time in the assessment and their activities outside of the assessment. Nobody wants to participate in an assessment while writing a major paper or preparing for an exam. Matching the assessment time with participant activities outside of the assessment eases the strain of a reassessment. Each of these costs influences when a reassessment can occur, especially in a time of budget restrictions and emerging projects that need assessment.

Interactions

Interactions include both people and things. Every assessment includes some aspect of people interacting with other people, an object, the surrounding environment or some combination of these three interactions. The interplay of person-to-person or person-to-object interactions within a specified environment needs to be considered.[5] For example, in designing new independent study carrels, the object of the assessment was the new study carrel and its features. However, these features would be meaningless outside of the context of students actually studying in a prototype of the new carrels in a study location in the library.

Similarly, a study on communication patterns within a library involves very few physical things, and it has greater emphasis on library employee interactions. While several modalities of communication are considered (face-to-face, email, social media, phone, etc.), the communication modalities only facilitate the communication interaction and the environment (friendly or antagonistic) in which the communication occurs. The actual intensity of the communication is the focus and of primary importance. A reassessment would focus on key elements of interest identified in the initial assessment, namely, the type of interaction, the participants involved in the interaction, and the environment surrounding the interactions. It would also consider how interactions between employees have changed between administrations. It would seek to answer questions regarding new policy and procedure changes.

Personnel interactions also play a role in deciding when to repeat assessments. Employee personalities may influence how processes happen and where services are located within a library. As people retire or leave a position, changes will occur. The change of personnel provides an opportunity to assess just how changes, implemented by the new employee, will affect processes. A similar situation occurs for new technology introduced into the library. The new technology provides an opportunity to improve services in the library. Imagine how cataloging has changed, from typing out card catalogues to using computers to catalogue items for discovery.

Changes in interactions signal an opportunity to reassess, but, prior to the reassessment, baseline data needs to be collected. Having the baseline data allows the library to determine if service delivery has improved; if changes have made things just different, but not necessarily better; or if changes made things worse. With a change in technology and personnel, there also needs to be a sufficient time following the change so those providing and using the services in new ways can adjust to the new processes. Either way, the change signals the opportunity for a reassessment.

Reporting

Reporting findings has a historical and a personal side. Historically, reassessments considered the background of previous assessments and how they inform strategic planning and decision-making in the library. They consider economic changes when library funding moves from being flush with cash to having to deal with funding cutbacks.

On the personal side, reassessments consider the atmosphere of assessment within the library. There is a vast difference between libraries that encourage and foster an atmosphere of assessment for planning and decision-making and those that deride assessments as interfering with the way things are done. The level of interest in the study may also come from those initiating the study. Whether it be university leadership, library leadership, or a supervisor requesting the assessment, strong interest in the study propels the reassessment of services forward. It is obvious that the broader the base of support or the higher the level of administrative interest in the reassessment, the faster it will move forward. This level of interest in the findings will not only provide support for conducting the reassessment, but it will also help efforts to share the findings and implement recommendations. It is clear that those conducting the reassessment (as with all assessments) need to frame the findings in ways that the stakeholders can understand.[6]

While these four components will influence when reassessments should occur, they will not carry the same weight with each reassessment. While each reassessment considers and influences other assessments, ultimately each assessment stands on its own. The context in which each reassessment occurs guides the degree to which each of the components will influence when the reassessment should be done.

Two Reassessments

With this in mind, I examine two reassessments in our library to better understand how these components influence when reassessments occurred. The first assessment is a localized reassessment examining a specific library service. It examines how quickly books were put back on library shelves once patrons returned them to the library. The second reassessment examines the factors for repeated administrations of a large, multi-library assessment (LibQUAL+ survey). It examines how open-ended comments from the LibQUAL+ survey were used to inform library services. I briefly describe each study with emphasis on the factors that determined the reassessment. In subsequent sections, I discuss how the study results were used to inform strategic planning and service delivery decisions.

Book Reshelving

The stacks management department is responsible for reshelving all materials returned to the library. It has a two-tiered system. Employees bring books to a central area for sorting into defined areas within the library. From there, they place books on sorting shelves near the book's location in the library. Originally, once there were sufficient books on the sorting stacks, student employees reshelved the books in their proper location in the library stacks. An initial assessment, initiated by library leadership, determined the length of time it took from when a book was returned to the library until it was reshelved in its proper place.

After the stacks manager retired and a new stacks manager was in place for almost a year, we conducted a reassessment to determine if changes initiated by the new stacks manager improved reshelving efforts. For example, the new manager had books reshelved as soon as possible once they were put on the sorting shelves instead of waiting for a sufficient number of books to be put on the sorting shelves. In the second assessment, we repeated all methods used in the first but added an additional step. When we took the books off shelves, instead of checking all of them out and returning them, we took half of the books and put them on the Return Books Here shelving. This method simulated those patrons who take a book off of the shelf and use it within the library without checking it out. This additional method allowed us determine any differences in how long it took books to be reshelved whether they were checked out and returned or used within the library.

Key reassessment components included a strong interest by library leaders to know if the service had improved and by how much. The study used a single data collection method. While we used only one method, it was quite complex and time-consuming. We chose random books from the shelves, but the areas in the library where books were chosen were on a specific schedule to ensure each library area was covered. We also randomized the location of where we placed books on the Return Books Here shelving. When we took books off of the shelf, we recorded the title, author, and call number of each book along with the date and time (morning or afternoon) each book was taken and where in the library it was returned. Once we started taking the books, we also began checking both the sorting shelves and the book's appropriate location twice a day, typically in conjunction with taking new books from the shelf.

The initial study used only one person, but the reassessment involved two full-time non-student employees and two part-time student employees to take and track books daily over a three-week period. This collaboration allowed for a greater number of books to be pulled and tracked over a shorter period of time. It also lessened the impact on any one employee of doing all of the data collection. A key factor in the reassessment was the interest by a library administrator and the new stacks manager. Other considerations included the complexity of the data collection and analysis. Most issues were resolved in the first assessment, so procedures for the second assessment went much smoother. There was a significant time commitment as each book had to be tracked back to its original location, but we expected anomalies and were prepared to deal with them. For example, at times books became "lost" as, upon return, they were pulled for repairs or other maintenance before being sent to stacks management. We needed additional tracking time to locate the path these books followed back to their shelf, but we were aware of where we could look so overall tracking time was lessened. There was a large time commitment, but with the extra staffing, the data collection and analysis went much smoother. Results from both studies were not broadly disseminated as the assessment focused on a specific library service. We informed all stakeholders of the results.

LibQUAL+ Survey Open-Ended Comments

The LibQUAL+ survey is a large-scale service perception survey administered by the Association of Research Libraries upon request by each library. In the last fifteen years, more than 1,300 libraries in thirty-three countries have used the survey to gauge patron perception of user experience. Our library administers the LibQUAL+ survey every two years in either the winter semester (January–April) or the fall semester (September–December). While most of the survey is selected choice, there is an option for an open-ended comment section on the survey. The reassessment described here focuses only on the responses to the open-ended questions.

Following several administrations, we had a substantial number of open-ended responses for each year of administration, but we had not fully coded them. We partnered with a Sociology 404 class studying advanced qualitative assessment methods to code the comments from each year of the LibQUAL+ survey administration. Working in teams and using standardized coding practices, student researchers from the class developed six broad categories used to code each comment. The categories include staff, building, on-site resources, web-based resources, communications, and policies. An "other" category was used for unique comments that did not fit within a defined category. Once placed in a category, each comment was coded as being positive, negative, or both. Because of the length and content of comments, some comments were split and placed into more than one category.

As with the small-scale study, many of the assessment issues were resolved within the first sorting of open-ended comments, so coding subsequent comments went both more smoothly and faster. The survey is well known and used by all in the library, so there was full support, from administration to front-line employees, for repeating the study. The survey's administration was straightforward, as administration practices (e.g., IRB application, sampling) were more consistent and standardized with each administration. Following the development of categories and the initial coding, two student employees coded each comment. When there was as a disagreement, they discussed the difference to reach consensus on where each comment should be placed. Non-student Assessment Office employees verified all codings. While this took a bit of time, the initial coding guide and examples lessened the time needed. The library administration paid the cost for the right to use the survey and for employee wages to administer, analyze, and report results.

There was broad support for the findings. The two-year time frame between administrations allowed the library time to identify needed changes and to implement new policies, practices, or services to improve patron comments. The time between reassessments was sufficient to determine if a change was meaningful. We reported results library-wide at the library town meeting and in the faculty meeting. We also put a final report on a wiki available to all library employees.

Communicating Results and Impact

The results of each assessment were communicated quite differently. It is standard practice to post all final reports of any assessment on the library's private wiki page (available to anyone within the library, but shared only upon request with those outside the library). Such was the case with both of these assessments, but initial dissemination efforts were quite different.

The reshelving study was very localized and specific to one department in the library. We shared the reassessment findings only with the stacks manager and the senior library administrator. In both cases, the stakeholders had a direct interest and responsibility to account for the efficacy of the service. The findings were largely positive, but identified key areas within the library and with overall practices that had and could make a difference. For example, the previous stacks manager had waited until there were a substantial number of books on the sorting shelves before putting each book back in its proper place. The new stacks manager did not wait for a sufficient number of books to be on the sorting shelves and restacked them at a much faster rate. The reassessment indicated that the reshelving change saved time. The reassessment also indicated areas within the library where reshelving times were still substantially slower than other areas for reshelving. This information helped the stacks manager target specific training to help student employees.

We took a more open approach to discussing the coding of open-ended responses from the LibQUAL+ survey. Using the trends and patterns discovered in the initial analysis, we openly presented on our findings from the reassessment and how they added to the trends and patterns in each category. Figures 8.1–8.3 show examples of three category trends from the initial and subsequent reassessments. The staff category trends (see figure 8.1) indicate mostly positive trends in patron comments but also show that the gap between positive and negative comments increased. The site resource category trends (see figure 8.2) indicates a pattern where most patron comments were initially negative and fewer positive, but, due to changes in services and materials, the gap was closed and now is exhibiting a similar pattern to the staff category where the gap between positive and negative comments is widening in a good way. Finally, the communication category trends (figure 8.3), indicates that, initially, virtually all patron comments were negative and any efforts to improve communication between the library and its patrons were largely ineffective. In each case, the initial assessment (2003 to 2011) provided strong trend data. The subsequent readministrations (2013 and 2015) continued the trends initially identified by the student researchers from the Sociology 404 Qualitative Methods class.

We reported findings from each category to senior library administration and related library committees. Following these presentations, we made a summary report to all library employees. This practice differed because of the history, familiarity, and respect the survey carried within the library. The library had already had multiple administrations of the survey. In addition to the quantitative analyses of the selected response questions, we had made other attempts at analyzing the open-ended responses. The student researchers' process was a simpler and a clearer method for coding. It was also easier for librarians to understand. As librarians were already familiar with other reports from the LibQUAL+ survey, the addition of a new report was easier to accept. The respect for previous findings transferred to the new findings.

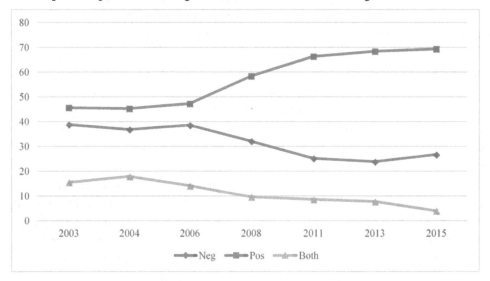

Figure 8.1
Positive and negative open-ended comment trends in the staff category from subsequent readministrations of the LibQUAL+ survey.

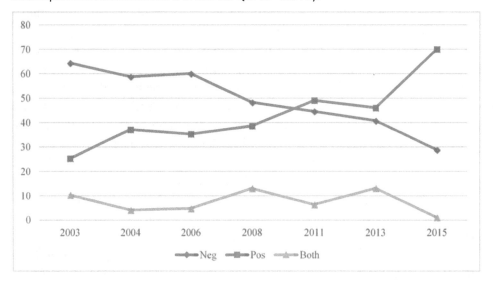

Figure 8.2
Positive and negative open-ended comment trends in the site resource category from subsequent readministrations of the LibQUAL+ survey.

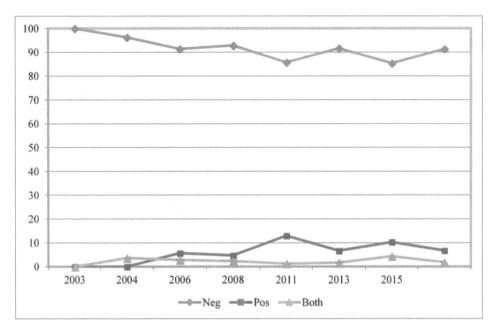

Figure 8.3
Positive and negative open-ended comment trends in the communications category from subsequent re-administrations of the LibQUAL+ survey.

Leveraging the Findings

Regardless of the size of the various assessments, the stakeholders connected to each assessment continue to use the reassessment data to improve service delivery. The stacks manager used the findings to refine service delivery and to adjust her training practices to meet the specific needs of student employees. In areas of the library that were lagging behind in reshelving time, she has examined the area for unique features of the collections that may slow reshelving. She also used the data to modify student employee training. She uses the reassessment to focus in on and hone her management practices.

In this case, the change in personnel resulted in the change of how books were reshelved, thus triggering the need to repeat the assessment. The stacks manager was greatly interested in examining her services and process, which lent support to the study. She has since submitted a proposal to alter the way returned books are processed. If the library accepts this proposal, then, after implementation, another reassessment would be triggered. If the proposal is not accepted, then we will conduct another reassessment about four years after the last one so all current student employees have left the university. The assessment will examine how well the new student employees are working on the process. If the manager leaves her position for another before this time, we will conduct a reassessment.

In the case of the LibQUAL+ survey, the trends and patterns substantiate changes to library policy and service delivery meant to address specific issues. The results in figures 8.1 and 8.2 help to substantiate that these efforts were successful. They offer encouragement to continue with improvement practices to continue these trends.

The communication category trends shown in figure 8.3 indicate that efforts to improve communication between the library and its patrons have been largely ineffective. While disappointing, the patterns provide evidence that what we were doing needs to change. As a result, new advertising and promotion initiatives are underway to increase the communication between the library and its patrons. The LibQUAL+ survey is also unique as its repetition every two years is part of expected library assessment practices.

Leveraging the findings of a reassessment, whether large or small, rests on the willingness of others (employees and library leaders) to act on assessment findings. Those who seek out the findings from initial and repeated assessments foster a culture of assessment that is enabling and empowering to initiate good change.

Reflection

Each of the components discussed helps to determine when an assessment should be repeated. While evaluators may understand the need to plan for repeated assessments, not everyone associated with the initial assessment does. Timing and presentation of this need become critical features in working with others to determine when a reassessment should happen. Those individuals who embrace and use assessment typically have no problem determining a reassessment at the outset of the initial assessment. Others who are more skeptical of assessments may need to be approached about a reassessment after the initial assessment is reported. The reporting allows evaluators to indicate what was and was not working well, but it also provides an opportunity to indicate what needs further study or repeated study. As skeptical users come to understand and use findings and see improvement in their service delivery, they become stronger supporters of initial and repeated assessments.

However, people are people! Not all library employees are able or willing to accept findings that indicate that change needs to occur, especially when the change involves them doing something in a different way. In these cases, it is critical to determine exactly what type of information or questions they want answered. Using their input and questions to cater the reassessment specifically to their needs makes the assessment findings more palatable. It also promotes the need for reassessment. Helping them to understand the thinking and processes used to design an assessment and determine when a reassessment should occur engages them in the process and encourages support of the evaluation process.

Notes

1. Larry Nash White, *Library Performance and Service Competition* (Oxford: Chandros, 2008), 99–106.
2. Martin Fojt, ed., "Strategies for Service Quality II," special issue, *Library Review* 44, no. 5 (1995): 13–15; Martin Fojt, "Capturing the Customer's Voice," in "Strategies for Service Quality II," special issue, ed. Martin Fojt, *Library Review* 44, no. 5 (1995): 22–23; Jeremy Garskof, Jill Morris, Tracie

Ballock, and Scott Anderson, "Towards the Collective Collection: Lessons Learned from PALCI's DDA Pilot Projects and Next Steps," Collaborative Librarianship 8, no. 2 (2016): 84–98.
3. Holt Zaugg, Curtis Child, Dalton Bennett, Jace Brown, Melissa Alcaraz, Alexander Allred, Nathaniel Andrus, et al., "Comparing Library Wayfinding among Novices and Experts," *Performance Measurement and Metrics* 17, no. 1 (2016): 70–82.
4. Liesbeth Baartman, Judith Gulikers, and Asha Dijkstra, "Factors Influencing Assessment Quality in Higher Vocational Education," Assessment and Evaluation in Higher Education 38, no. 8 (2013): 978–97; Holt Zaugg and Curtis Child, "Collaborating with Nonlibrary Faculty for Assessment and Improved Instruction," *Journal of Library Administration* 56, no. 7 (2016): 823–44.
5. Martin Fojt, "Can a Company Be Both Low-Cost and Service-Oriented?" in "Strategies for Service Quality II," special issue, ed. Martin Fojt, *Library Review* 44, no. 5 (1995): 18-19; Diana Pereira, Maria Assunção Flores, and Laila Niklasson, "Assessment Revisited: A Review of Research in Assessment and Evaluation in Higher Education," *Assessment and Evaluation in Higher Education* 41, no. 7 (2016): 1008–32.
6. Martin Fort, "The Kingdom of the Customer," in "Strategies for Service Quality II," special issue, ed. Martin Fojt, *Library Review* 44, no. 5 (1995): 41–42; Joseph R Matthews, Library Assessment in Higher Education (Westport, CT: Libraries Unlimited, 2007), 119–140.

Bibliography

Baartman, Liesbeth, Judith Gulikers, and Asha Dijkstra. "Factors Influencing Assessment Quality in Higher Vocational Education." *Assessment and Evaluation in Higher Education* 38, no. 8 (2013): 978–97.

Fojt, Martin. "Can a Company Be Both Low-Cost and Service-Oriented?" In "Strategies for Service Quality II," edited by Martin Fojt, (1995): 18–19.

———. "Capturing the Customer's Voice." In "Strategies for Service Quality II," edited by Martin Fojt, (1995): 22–23.

———. "The Kingdom of the Customer." In "Strategies for Service Quality II," edited by Martin Fojt, (1995): 41–42.

Fojt, Martin, ed. "Strategies for Service Quality II," special issue. *Library Review* 44, no. 5 (1995).

Garskof, Jeremy, Jill Morris, Tracie Ballock, and Scott Anderson. "Towards the Collective Collection: Lessons Learned from PALCI's DDA Pilot Projects and Next Steps." *Collaborative Librarianship* 8, no. 2 (2016): 84–98.

Matthews, Joseph R. *Library Assessment in Higher Education.* Westport, CT: Libraries Unlimited, 2007.

Pereira, Diana, Maria Assunção Flores, and Laila Niklasson. "Assessment Revisited: A Review of Research in Assessment and Evaluation in Higher Education." *Assessment and Evaluation in Higher Education* 41, no. 7 (2016): 1008–32.

White, Larry Nash. *Library Performance and Service Competition: Developing Strategic Responses.* Oxford: Chandros, 2008.

Zaugg, Holt, and Curtis Child. "Collaborating with Nonlibrary Faculty for Assessment and Improved Instruction." *Journal of Library Administration* 56, no. 7 (2016): 823–44.

Zaugg, Holt, Curtis Child, Dalton Bennett, Jace Brown, Melissa Alcaraz, Alexander Allred, Nathaniel Andrus, et al. "Comparing Library Wayfinding among Novices and Experts." *Performance Measurement and Metrics* 17, no. 1 (2016): 70–82.

Section 2

Low-Hanging Fruit

Introduction

This book is intended to inform and enlighten you—librarians, professional staff, administrators, and others working in academic libraries—who are at all levels of experience, assessment skills, and stages of implementation of assessment initiatives and with varying access to expertise and resources. Accordingly, the four sections of this publication are organized to reflect a continuum of case studies of individuals and academic institutions at different points in their assessment journey in articulating their library's impact and value.

This second section is called Low-Hanging Fruit. As the title implies, this section examines eleven cases of academic libraries involved in library assessment initiatives that were easy to launch and implement due to few constraints since they were low-cost and adequate support and expertise were already in place. These assessment projects tend to be shorter in length, typically under a year, and can be managed by one individual or a small group of individuals with limited financial and external resources. These cases are presented so others in similar situations can quickly and effectively replicate these assessment initiatives and hopefully with similar success.

This section involves chapters covering a useful range of topics. These include developing and implementing a library digital dashboard to display the library's contribution to student learning and faculty research (chapter 14, Kremer and Hoyt), holistic assessment measures that examine all aspects of library support to contribute to an academic program review (chapter 15, McCafferty and Harris), and Q-methodology as a quick and indirect assessment method in describing how a given population perceive an academic library's services and resources (chapter 18, Resnis and Shrimplin). In addition, Hoffman (chapter 12) writes about a participatory, transparent, and collaborative top-to-bottom and bottom-to-top process to triangulate an assessment plan, and Jones Architecture (chapter 13) describes how an academic library successfully redesigned its outdated library pace to revive its role as a vibrant hub of student and faculty activity. Several case studies focus on discovery access, such as a methodology of how to assess the ROI of web-scale discovery tools (McMullen, chapter 16) and an assessment of first-year students' use of the library's federated discovery tool (Viars and Slutskaya, chapter 19).

149

Each chapter is prefaced by a one-page summary profile. The purpose of this summary profile is to give you a quick overview of the chapter by providing fourteen salient items of descriptive information for the case study. The summary profile page will help you decide if the subsequent case study is of interest to you and thus warrants a deeper investigation and thorough read.

We hope you enjoy the interesting mix of eleven case studies of academic libraries involved in library assessment projects that were relatively easy to launch, implement, and measure in this second section, Low-Hanging Fruit.

Section 2

Title: Three Thousand Library Users Can't Be Wrong: Demonstrating Library Impact Using One Open-Ended Survey Question

Abstract: Librarians seeking to balance quantitative value measures with qualitative methods should consider the inclusion of critical incident technique (CIT) questions into their library value inquiries. Even the addition of one well-conceived CIT question in a larger survey question pool can provide valuable stories in users' own words describing the impact of the library's services, resources, and spaces on teaching, learning, and research at their institution. This chapter will discuss the CIT question used by one large, multi-campus public research library to elicit over 3,000 undergraduate student, graduate student, and faculty responses: "Tell us in a few sentences about a time that Libraries staff, services, resources, or spaces had a positive impact on your academic work." Taken as a whole, the comments point to the impact of library staff, spaces, and services on faculty and students, while individual responses can serve as callouts within larger reports and provide depth and description necessary to understand other quantitative results.

Keywords: assessment, value/impact, critical incident technique, survey, qualitative methods

Project focus: assessment methodologies, techniques, or practices; user behaviors and needs; data use and technology; assessment concepts and/or management

Results made or will make case for: more funding, improvements in services, improvements in spaces, improvements in collections, changes in library policy, proof of library impact and value, a strategic plan or process

Data needed: We collected status (faculty, grad, undergrad), level (title, degree, year in school, respectively), major or college/school, and whether they self-identified as part of a special population (e.g. international student, transfer student)

Methodology: qualitative, quantitative, evaluation or survey

Project duration: greater than 1 year

Tool(s) utilized: We used Qualtrics as our survey tool and did all of our coding in Excel. Visualization was done in Tableau. One part-time, hourly Assessment Research Analyst was hired out of the overall survey budget.

Cost estimate: $2,000–$5,000; the overall project budget was in the range specified, but the specific technique we are writing about, critical incident technique, does not require such a substantial investment.

Type of institution: university—public

Institution enrollment: 30,000+

Highest level of education: doctoral

Chapter 9

Three Thousand Library Users Can't Be Wrong

Demonstrating Library Impact Using One Open-Ended Survey Question

Jackie Belanger, Maggie Faber, and Megan Oakleaf

Introduction

Libraries nationwide are striving to capture, demonstrate, and communicate their value and impact on users. How do academic libraries help students learn, earn better course grades, and be retained through graduation? How do academic libraries aid faculty in their teaching, research, and grant-seeking efforts? Many libraries have engaged in quantitative approaches to answering these questions, perhaps because they appear more manageable and less time-consuming than other methods. However, quantitative approaches speak only to some library stakeholders and resource allocators, not all. In order to create a rich, detailed picture of library value and impact, qualitative strategies are key.

This case study explores how the University of Washington (UW) Libraries employed a critical incident technique question on a user survey to gather stories about the library's impact on teaching, learning, and research and used the resulting responses in communication, outreach, and fund-raising efforts. It also provides tips for working with qualitative impact data and describes ways to improve upon the critical incident technique (CIT) question and subsequent use of responses.

Context

The University of Washington is a large comprehensive research institution with three campuses (Seattle, Bothell, and Tacoma). The UW Libraries is a member of the Association of Research Libraries (ARL) and includes sixteen different libraries across the three campuses. The UW Libraries has run a large-scale user survey (the Triennial Survey) every three years since 1992. The Triennial Survey is distributed to all faculty and graduate students at all three campuses, to all undergraduates at the smaller Bothell and Tacoma campuses, and to a sample of 5,000 undergraduate students at the Seattle campus (a stratified sample based on year in school). Survey results are used to improve spaces, services, and resources, as well as for budget and advocacy purposes. Library assessment staff (the Director of Assessment and Planning, an Assessment Librarian, and a Data Visualization and Analysis Librarian) are responsible for survey design, implementation, and data analysis.

Beginning in 2007, the Triennial Survey included a question about the contribution the UW Libraries makes to research, teaching, and learning at the institution. The faculty and graduate surveys, for example, ask respondents to rate the library's contribution in areas such as keeping current in their field, enriching student learning experiences, getting research funding, and making efficient use of their time.[1] While this question provides rich quantitative data that enables UW Libraries to communicate how its services and resources support the campus community, assessment staff also recognized that there was a missing element in survey data: stories in users' own words describing the impact of library services, resources, and spaces on their work. Inspired by Oakleaf and Millet's deployment of a "help study" comprised of two CIT questions designed to elicit examples of library value,[2] assessment staff decided to include a new open-ended question on the 2016 Triennial Survey that could provide evidence of the value of UW Libraries to users and the institution. A CIT question involves asking respondents to describe a memorable interaction, with the aim of exploring moments of personal significance and gaining insights into those experiences in a respondent's own words.[3] Todd and Kuhlthau employed a critical incident question on a large-scale survey designed to understand how school libraries help students.[4] Drawing on the examples provided by Oakleaf and Millet, and by Todd and Kuhlthau, the following CIT question was asked of UW faculty, graduate students, and undergraduate students to draw out evidence of library impact: "Tell us in a few sentences about a time that Libraries staff, services, resources, or spaces had a positive impact on your academic work."

The 2016 survey was distributed to over thirty thousand faculty and students across all three UW campuses and was completed by more than 8,000 respondents. The response rates varied by population: 34 percent for faculty across all three campuses, 23 percent for graduate students, and 22 percent for undergraduate students. No incentives were offered to faculty and graduate students, but twenty university bookstore gift cards of $100 each were offered in a lottery for undergraduates who completed the survey. The CIT question received over 3,000 responses, the highest response of any qualitative question on the survey. These responses covered topics ranging from teaching and learning, to support for research and clinical work, study spaces, interlibrary loan services, collections, and technology. Many of the results made explicit the connection between a library service, resource, or space and what users were able to do or how they specifically benefited as a result of using the service. Some key examples include comments that highlight the time and money saved for faculty, clinicians, students, and the institution. One faculty member shared the following:

> I cannot stress how important and helpful the [Libraries' Active Learning Classroom] has been for my teaching. We are able to teach twice the number of students in this space as we would in another space—or put another way, we are able to increase access to our major without greatly increasing costs because this space is available.

A number of comments point to the value of liaison support for faculty and student work at various points in the research life cycle (including getting grants, finding research material, and communicating research). A graduate student noted:

> As a PhD student, I had a question about copyright issues involving my published article. UW Libraries was very helpful in allowing me to successfully navigate the complexities of copyright law and inform me about open access options that I was unaware of. As a result, my work has been cited more than I anticipated!

In addition, there were numerous examples of the critical importance of study space for student success and grades. An undergraduate student commented on the value of the study space in UW's Suzzallo Library:

> Every day, I sit at Suzzallo's big library, pull out my laptop, and am actually able to focus on my school work. This has been the single most important thing that has helped me turn my college career into a successful one.

Taken as a whole, the comments point to the positive impact of library staff, spaces, and services on faculty and students. Individual responses have served as callouts within larger reports and provide depth and description necessary to understand quantitative results. The specific ways in which these results can be used are discussed in more detail in the following section.

Communicating Results and Impact

In order to make sense of such a large volume of qualitative data and to communicate the comments as effectively as possible, responses to this question were coded using both content codes (e.g., spaces, teaching and learning, collections) and a single code for impact. This enabled comments reports to be generated quickly based on the needs of various individuals and groups, such as the Dean of UW Libraries or the library fundraising unit. In the first instance, results from this question were shared internally (via presentations and short reports) with library leadership and with all library employees at a large all-staff meeting at the start of the academic year. Results focusing on specific operational areas such as digital scholarship, IT, collections, and access services were also shared with a variety of library departments and stakeholder groups via targeted reports and interactive Tableau dashboards (figure 9.1). The dashboards provided staff with a flexible way to find comments by topic and impact. The approach to coding and the presentation of CIT question results in the dashboards were designed to empower library staff to identify for themselves the comments most relevant to their needs, both for internal reporting and for communicating with faculty, students, and other external stakeholders.

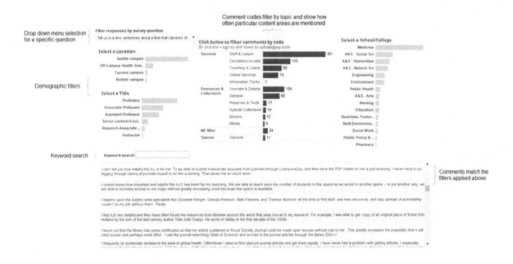

Figure 9.1
The Triennial Survey comments dashboard allows library staff to discover impact stories by filtering for demographic information, keywords within the comment, or general topic coding by Assessment staff.

To maximize the usefulness of quantitative and qualitative survey data for library staff, assessment staff also created a set of "impact snapshots" that include a key data point (drawn from either survey data or annual library statistics) coupled with a related quote elicited from the CIT question. These impact snapshots are particularly useful for advancement and fund-raising efforts. Impact comments were used at major fundraising events in fall 2016 and spring 2017. At the first event, the Dean of the UW

Libraries highlighted user stories in a presentation to donors. At the second event—focused on supporting preservation, programs, and student employee scholarships—key impact stories were featured on table tents on all guest tables (figure 9.2). For many audiences, like the community members and university administrators who often attend fund-raising events, hearing stories in users' own voices paints a compelling picture of the difference the library makes for students and faculty.

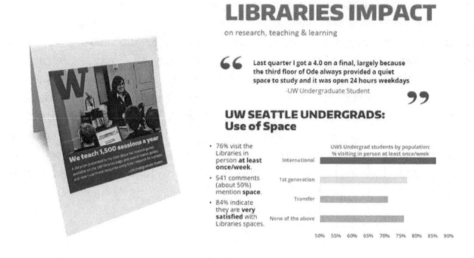

Figure 9.2
Two ways impact comments have been communicated with the campus community. (Left) Table tents from the 2017 Literary Voices fund-raising event paired images, annual statistics, and impact statements on each table. (Right) The Dean of UW Libraries shared slides with impact stories and contextual statistics at the 2016 Dean's Circle event.

User comments have been especially valuable when used in conjunction with quantitative data to provide a more holistic and meaningful picture of library value. For example, the dean's presentation to donors included survey data showing that 76 percent of undergraduate students use the library at least once per week, paired with a student comment about the impact using a library space had on the student's ability to get a good grade. Combining quantitative and qualitative data in this way helps to convey both the scope and the depth of library contributions in key areas such as student success.

These stories have also had unexpected and less obvious uses. For example, at large institutions, the ways in which staff work matters to users may not always be immediately or directly visible to staff themselves. While the focus in recent years has centered on demonstrating value to external audiences, making the value of staff work more visible within the library can be one important, if intangible, benefit. The impact comments have also been effective in gaining buy-in from staff in engaging with survey results more broadly. At a meeting with the UW Libraries Teaching and Learning

Group, for example, the discussion began with the comments about the impact of the instruction program on student learning and success, and then broadened to areas for possible improvement in terms of outreach to faculty and instructors in support of their teaching. In this case, starting with positive stories about what users value with regard to the library lays the groundwork for productive conversations about potential improvements.

Leveraging the Findings

In addition to the approaches above, the next steps for using impact comments involve partnerships between assessment staff and those responsible for library marketing and communication, as well as individual librarians and library units, to develop targeted marketing and outreach campaigns for specific services such as online chat reference, instruction, and liaison support. Going forward, various library units plan to use the comments and the impact snapshot template as the basis for working with library marketing staff to create tailored communication plans for different services and audiences. The aim of these campaigns will be to highlight the range of library services and resources available to students and faculty and to demonstrate the difference these services make to users' work. The snapshots may also be used as part of a new library website template, with pages about a specific service and space including a relevant comment about the impact they have on users. This approach would highlight the value of each service or space and also provide a consistent visual branding across different sites. Assessment staff can support these communication efforts by continuing to streamline the process of accessing and working with the data. This can involve the ongoing creation of tailored reports, as well as assisting with the creation of additional impact snapshots to provide library staff with a menu of options that they can readily draw upon for a variety of outreach and communication needs.

Reflection

One of the key successes of this approach to gathering qualitative impact data was the ability to reach thousands of users by including a single question on a large-scale survey. This method, or variations on it, is applicable to a variety of libraries and scalable to different contexts and needs: a CIT question can be distributed via an existing library survey or can be sent to users as a single question. In addition, this qualitative data can be powerful either independently or used in conjunction with quantitative data in the form of survey results or other routinely collected library statistics. The resulting impact data and story snapshots have the potential to create rich, detailed pictures of library value and impact that can appeal and be tailored to a wide variety of library stakeholders.

As this question was new on the 2016 UW Libraries Triennial Survey, there is still much that can learned and improved upon for future iterations of the survey. One possible area for improvement is the formulation of the critical incident technique question itself. While the single question produced over 3,000 comments, in reality many of the responses did not fully articulate the impact of the library or librarians: many described a service they liked or found useful but stopped short of providing full, concrete details of the *results* of using that particular service or resource. Approximately 20 percent of the responses to this question provided examples of what a library service or resource enabled them to do. In the help study that inspired this CIT question, Oakleaf and Millett suggested asking the question in two parts ("Think of a time when the library/librarians helped you. What help did you receive? What did that help enable you to do?"). However, because the question was embedded in a large, multipart survey, UW assessment staff decided that their users might be more inclined to answer a single, open-ended question. A more effective way to make impact explicit might be to use the two-part question formulation suggested by Oakleaf and Millet. This two-part reformulation has the potential to increase the number of usable impact stories from respondents, but there might be a tradeoff in requiring more time and effort for users to answer.

The use of a single CIT question on a user survey is a simple and scalable approach to understanding impact. Librarians seeking to emulate this approach should prepare for the high volume of comments resulting from this question and the additional effort required to code and report results. As discussed previously, responses to this question were coded both for content and for whether the comment articulated the library's impact. The authors used a single yes/no code for impact; others may wish to add additional codes to distinguish the type of impact, such as time or money saved, better grades, or getting research funding. Adding these codes might create additional challenges to coding. However, a greater level of detail could be valuable for communicating more targeted impact stories to different audiences.

While the meaning of "library impact" sounds intuitive, it was challenging to define what counted as impact and to distinguish when users actually articulated that impact, rather than merely implying it. The eventual defining criterion was that the comment mentioned what a service or resource enabled the user to do or how the user's behavior was changed. The authors looked for comments that indicated how the library helped users to complete or do better work, or to work faster or less expensively. Impact comments generally had two important elements: they identified the library space, service, or resource used, or the support provided by the library or a librarian, and gave a specific example of what the library or librarian helped them do (figure 9.3). This second element was the least likely to be fully articulated in the comment. For example, some students noted that using library quiet spaces helped them to feel more motivated or focused on their coursework. While this demonstrates the importance of library spaces, ultimately the authors decided that this didn't constitute an example of impact because it failed to describe what the user was able to do or how a specific behavior was changed. In other cases, the difference a service made was implied and not directly stated. For example, respondents occasionally implied that efficiencies resulted from using a library service or resource (e.g., that time was saved by using library resources), but the exact efficiencies were left vague. These cases were judged based on what was actually stated and typically not considered as articulated impact. The complexity of identifying impact in the CIT question comments means that additional time and attention to detail may be required in the coding process.

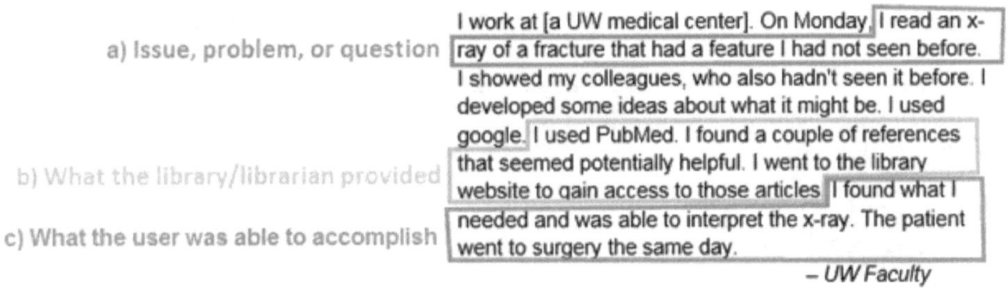

a) Issue, problem, or question

> I work at [a UW medical center]. On Monday, I read an x-ray of a fracture that had a feature I had not seen before. I showed my colleagues, who also hadn't seen it before. I developed some ideas about what it might be. I used google. I used PubMed. I found a couple of references that seemed potentially helpful. I went to the library website to gain access to those articles. I found what I needed and was able to interpret the x-ray. The patient went to surgery the same day.
> – UW Faculty

b) What the library/librarian provided

c) What the user was able to accomplish

Figure 9.3
Identifying impact within a comment required two key elements: what the library or librarian provided and what this enabled the respondent to accomplish (b and c in this figure). Many also identified a third element (a) of the issue, problem, or question, which typically led to stronger stories, but was not required to be considered impact.

Conclusion

A single open-ended CIT question on a large-scale survey can provide libraries with stories about their impact and value in users' own voices. The key benefit of this approach for libraries of various types and sizes is that is relatively easy to implement and scale; the question can be used on its own, or as part of a multiquestion survey. While an investment of time is required to code and communicate the comments, the rich data yielded by this question can be used effectively for a variety of outreach, fund-raising, and marketing purposes, and the data is powerful either on its own or in conjunction with quantitative data. Although improvements can be made to both the CIT question itself and use of the resulting data, the approach in the 2016 UW Triennial Survey yielded a large number of comments highlighting the impact of library services, resources, and spaces on faculty and students. New ways of sharing the results with staff allowed them to find and communicate the stories that are relevant to their work while also engaging them in other survey results and library statistics. Incorporating impact stories into communication plans, marketing materials, and library events have helped users recognize the services and resources available to them and helped stakeholders understand that the services and resources the library makes available have a profound, varied, and positive impact on the campus community.

Notes

1. UW Libraries Triennial Survey instruments and results are available at the University of Washington Libraries Assessment webpage: http://www.lib.washington.edu/assessment/surveys/triennial.
2. Megan Oakleaf and Michelle Millet, "Help Yourself to Student Impact Data: Conducting a 'Help'

Section 2

Study to Explore Academic Library Value," *ACRL Value of Academic Libraries* (blog), March 20, 2012, http://www.acrl.ala.org/value/?p=285.

3. William Borgen, Norman Amundson, and Lee Butterfield, "Critical Incident Technique," in *The SAGE Encyclopedia of Qualitative Research Methods*, vol. 1, ed. Lisa M. Given (Thousand Oaks, CA: SAGE Publications, 2008), 158–59. Gale Virtual Reference Library, GALE|CX3073600095, http://link.galegroup.com/apps/doc/CX3073600095/GVRL?u=wash_main&sid=GVRL&x-id=2dd5dc76.

4. Ross Todd and Carol Kuhlthau, "Student Learning through Ohio School Libraries, Part 1: How Effective School Libraries Help Students," *School Libraries Worldwide* 11, no. 1 (2005): 63–88. EBSCOhost.

Bibliography

Borgen, William, Norman Amundson, and Lee Butterfield. "Critical Incident Technique." In *The SAGE Encyclopedia of Qualitative Research Methods*, vol. 1. Edited by Lisa M. Given, 158–159. Thousand Oaks, CA: SAGE Publications, 2008. Gale Virtual Reference Library, GALE|CX3073600095. http://link.galegroup.com/apps/doc/CX3073600095/GVRL?u=wash_main&sid=GVRL&xid=2dd5dc76.

Oakleaf, Megan, and Michelle Millet. "Help Yourself to Student Impact Data: Conducting a 'Help' Study to Explore Academic Library Value." *ACRL Value of Academic Libraries* (blog), March 20, 2012, http://www.acrl.ala.org/value/?p=285.

Todd, Ross, and Carol Kuhlthau. "Student Learning through Ohio School Libraries, Part 1: How Effective School Libraries Help Students." *School Libraries Worldwide* 11, no. 1 (2005): 63–88. EBSCO-host.

Whelan, Debra Lau. "13,000 Kids Can't Be Wrong." *Library Journal,* February 1, 2004. http://lj.library-journal.com/2004/02/ljarchives/13000-kids-cant-be-wrong/.

Title: Rowan University Libraries' Head-Counting Study

Abstract: Many non-library administrators assume that library buildings are no longer needed because resources are online and students can study elsewhere. Rowan University Libraries' head count study began as a way to provide evidence for a pilot project to extend hours. The study identifies the number of people by area in the library as well as the use of technology. The benchmarking (evidence) results have been used for updating the building hours and adding specific types of study/collaboration spaces to better serve the students, as well as articulating how much the library space is used.

Keywords: head counting, space studies, data-driven decisions, user behavior and needs

Project focus: spaces; user behaviors and needs; data-driven decisions

Results made or will make case for: improvements in spaces, proof of library impact and value, how money or resources may be directed, adjustment to operation hours—information for project drove the need to adjust the operational hours of the building

Data needed: number of patrons using which spaces within the library and if they are using technology

Methodology: mixed method

Project duration: over 3 years, but less than the 5 years

Tool(s) utilized:

- One staff person at the top of the hour would walk the entire public area of the entire building.
- The staff person used a clipboard, pencil, and printed survey sheets that listed each of the areas of the library as well as the categories "Individuals without technology"; "Individuals with technology"; "Groups without technology"; and "Groups with technology."
- Survey sheets were then transferred into Microsoft Office Excel for calculations and creating graphs.
- Some staff would use their personal cell phone cameras to capture some observations.

Cost estimate: < $100

Type of institution: university—public

Institution enrollment: 5,000–15,000

Highest level of education: doctoral

CC BY ND

Chapter 10

Rowan University Libraries' Head-Counting Study

Susan Breakenridge

Introduction

Most academic libraries report information such as the number of volumes held, interlibrary loans processed, and instruction sessions offered. However, those numbers do not easily demonstrate direct impact on the students. For libraries that are new to assessment, a starting point is benchmarking the services that could add value or impact student patrons. Of the basic library services (providing access to collections, access to reference assistance, and access to study and collaboration spaces), space is a relatively easy and inexpensive area to demonstrate value.

Many non-library staff and administrators assume that library buildings are no longer needed because students will and want to study in other spaces since many library resources are available online. But just because students can and might study elsewhere, is that what is best for them? "AiA [Assessment in Action] library impact studies document that students who used the library in some way achieved higher levels of academic success."[1] A basic way to demonstrate that libraries are physically still being used by patrons is to capture usage. Gate counts are easy enough to capture, but they are not overly informative. Conducting head counts can be more accurate and informative than relying on gate counts when the building houses more offices and services than just the library.

Rowan University's Campbell Library began conducting head counts during the fall semester of 2013. The number of head counts have transitioned over the semesters to now include hourly head counts for a full week during the middle of the semester as well as the last three to ten days of the semester (including finals). The head counts were conducted for the purposes of (1) making decisions related to services and facility updates and (2) being able to articulate the library's value and impact on the students. The head counts identify the number of people by area in the library as well as their use of technology. Staff conduct the head counts, recording the usage on paper forms. The trend line shows the number of patrons using the library in the overnight hours has increased over time, as seen in figure 10.1. Only Rowan faculty, staff, and students are allowed access after 8:00 p.m. when the doors require users to swipe their university ID card. The benchmarking results were used for updating the building hours, adding specific types of study and collaboration spaces to better serve the students, and informing administrators. The library administration is now positioned to explore different assessment approaches to demonstrate impact, such as patron surveys and focus groups.

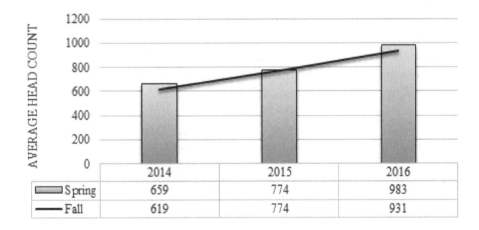

Figure 10.1
Average head count by year and semester.

Rowan's Head-Counting Study: Creating a Plan

In late 2013, the new Rowan University Library administration were requested by the student government organization to have the library open twenty-four hours during finals. The administrators were familiar with these types of requests from previous institutions and knew extending operational hours comes with a cost but not necessarily more building usage. Since the administrators were new, no evidence of need was available. Wanting to be responsive to students, they started with a conservative approach, added some late-night hours, and began collecting data on usage during the added hours as a pilot project.

The first part of the head-counting study plan was recruiting staff from across the library to provide coverage at the circulation desk during the extra hours. The library administration was allowed to offer staff the option of earning either overtime pay or compensatory time. (Two semesters later, the university required that only compensatory time be offered.) Not all circulation services were offered during the extended hours, but the staff from other departments were trained on basic circulation skills (e.g., checking out material and reserving study rooms). The second part of the head-counting study plan was recruiting staff to walk the building, recording the number of people using the facility, especially during the overnight hours. The library administration had the authority to adjust staff schedules with adequate notice to work the overnight hours, but due to concerns that a "required change" would cause poor morale and call-outs, the staff members were offered the option to volunteer to work extra hours for either overtime pay or compensatory time.-Over the semesters the most staff ever involved per semester in the overnight counting was four. Though these employees were supportive of the project, they were thankful for its temporary nature. Staffing the circulation desk during the overnights was more challenging even with incentives. The third part of the head-counting study plan was working with the facilities and security departments. Additional janitorial services were needed for restroom checks and trash removal, but coordination was also needed since most of the regular building cleaning happened on the third shift when the building was closed. The library administration also requested a dedicated security officer to be stationed in the building during the extended hours. This was an overtime expense for the officer's time, but the library was not charged for the service.

In the last ten to fifteen years, library space planning has become more prevalent, for example, the work conducted by Nancy Foster and Susan Gibbons at the University of Rochester's River Campus Libraries using anthropological and ethnographic methods.[2] Campbell Library was not prepared to do a project of that size, and thus started off simply. The tally sheet document used to record the usage listed all the unique locations in the building as well as four defining categories of how people might be using the space: individual without computer, individual with computer, group without computer, and group with computer. The library administration was curious to know the answers to these questions:

- In what areas of the building were patrons working? This would help to identify which physical aspects of the building patrons navigated to and some popular spots the library administration might consider replicating. Some other library space research includes physical aspects of the building during late hours, student behaviors in libraries, library space and furniture, and physical improvements to libraries.[3]
- Were patrons working alone or in groups? This would help to identify the physical needs of the patrons—single-seat tables, multiple-seat tables, or lounge furniture—and some of the popular configurations that the library administration might consider replicating. Though patron need (individual or group) might dictate the space used, sometimes patrons use spaces and furnishings

differently than expected. Library social space and informal social learning spaces in libraries can have an impact on how library space is developed.[4]
- Were patrons using computers? This would help the library administration identify if more library computer workstations were needed. Though college students are encouraged to have their own personal computers or laptops, that does not mean they would bring them to the library.[5]

Determining if people were working alone or in groups was easy but determining if the person was using a computer without appearing to be nosy required some tactful discretion. The staff doing the counts were to minimize disruption to users. However, in the early morning hours, sometimes the staff needed to be purposeful to check certain areas for security reasons. The tally sheet document locations were updated as changes to the building occurred. An example of the tally sheet document is in table 10.1.

Table 10.1
Example of Head-Counting Tally Sheet by Area and Activity

Second Floor	individual	indvidual with computer	group	group with computer	TOTAL
PAC, Rm 245 - tables					
PAC, Rm 245 - 2 computers					
Study Rm 242A					
Study Rm 242B					
Reference Computers -					
Reference Rm - tables					
Mircoform Reader					
Reference Area Scanner/Printer Alcove					
Reference - 240A (Purple)					

Tally sheets have been used for all the usage collection to date. A complete tally sheet consisted of three pages. Though it would have been more economical to use double-sided pages, it took time to flip sheets, so for the sake of speed and ease, one-sided pages were used. Though paper is relatively inexpensive, it is an expense to note. A staff member explored a digital application that would do the same thing, but it has not been adopted yet due to the multiple steps to record the different categories. Other libraries might find the digital application an option, and it was an open-access application at this writing, but it requires a device that the library might have to purchase.

The number of extended hours and how often the counts were conducted changed over the semesters as shown in table 10.2. Some of the change was due to the finals schedule or the library administration wanting to explore additional or different days before and during finals.

Table 10.2
Number of Head-Counting Hours by Semester

Semester	# of Nights with Extended Hours (Open Overnight)	# of Days Counted	Hours Counted	Conducted Mid-semester Counts (1 Week)
Fall 2013	6 (7th canceled due to storm)	5	5, 7, 9, 11 p.m. and 1 a.m.	No
Spring 2014	8 (no weekends)	6	Midnight–7 a.m.	No
Fall 2014	3 (no weekends)	3	Midnight–7 a.m.	No
Spring 2015	7	7	Midnight–6 a.m. (and most of the weekend hours)	No
Fall 2015	5 (no weekends)	8	All open hours	Yes
Spring 2016	7 (no weekends)	15 consecutive days	All open hours	Yes
Fall 2016	5 (no weekends)	10 consecutive days	All open hours	Yes

Communicating Results and Impacts

Initially the pilot project study results were shared internally with the library administration and staff. Though the administration did not identify any number at which to continue the extended hours, the results were adequate to continue the pilot the following semester. Due to the different dynamics (i.e., weather, holidays, and graduation ceremonies) between the end of the fall semester and the end of the spring semester, the pilot extension included being open twenty-four hours.

Besides informing and influencing the building hours during finals, facility decisions were made based in part on the usage numbers and staff's anecdotes from their head-counting experiences. Staff conducting the head counts noted noise problems near the public restrooms and elevators filtered into study areas. In March 2014, four doors were installed at room entrances to keep noise down near study areas on the third and fourth floors (see figure 10.2). Also in the spring of 2014, planning started for the renovation of the fourth floor study area funded by the library's endowment. Since patrons moved the heavy furniture around during finals, the new furniture for the space was selected knowing that patrons would likely rearrange it to make group settings. The space renovation received new carpet, paint, and furniture—tables, chairs, lounge furniture, and movable whiteboards (see figure 10.3).

Figure 10.2
New door installed near
elevator noise area.

Figure 10.3
Renovation reading room with way-finding
carpet.

The head-counting study during the spring 2014 finals continued to be informative. Group space was at a premium, so the library administration identified two spaces that could be turned into three study rooms. During the fall of 2014, a large room that housed a photocopy machine was renovated into two 6-person study rooms (see figures 10.4 and 10.5). During the spring of 2015, another, smaller photocopy room was transitioned into a third 6-person study room.

Figure 10.4
Former photocopy room.

Figure 10.5
Two new six-person study rooms.

The spring of 2015 library hours for finals included being open twenty-four hours over the weekend. Though the library administration predicted the counts would be low, it was agreed that having the data was important. The study results continued to show that most patrons in non–computer lab spaces had personal laptop computers or alternative technology. Due to the lines of patrons waiting to use the second floor desktop computers, the library administration acknowledged the need for more computer workstations.

The reference collection deselection project in the spring of 2015 dramatically decreased the collection's footprint on the second floor, so library administration began looking at alternatives for the space and the adjacent areas that had microforms. With the need for more collaboration rooms, desktop computer stations, and another printer, the 2015 Library Endowment Project started to take form. Each year, the administration has endowment funds to use as it sees appropriate. The 2015 Library Endowment Project was the redesigning and repurposing of the second floor reference area. The microforms were moved to other areas in the library, and then the architect was able to design a space that had four 5-person collaboration rooms, sixteen new desktop computer stations, and new tables for fifty users (see figure 10.6). The student printers were provided by the university IT department, so providing usage information was important to proposing that IT add another printer in the library. IT agreed, and it was added after the renovation project was complete.

The four new collaboration rooms included large-screen monitors that had wireless connections for laptops. The Facility Project Planner assigned to the renovation work was aware that two new university buildings being constructed on campus were planning similar group spaces, so this was an opportunity for the university IT department to experiment with less-expensive technology in preparation for those new building spaces. Some of the study tables in the reference area (a variety of two-, four-, and six-person tables) had electrical and USB power outlets available on the tabletops.

Figure 10.6
Reference area—computers, tables and study rooms.

In the fall of 2015, a week-long mid-semester count was started to capture a benchmark to compare to the end-of-semester counts. News of the library's head-counting study had spread through the university's Facilities Campus Planning department. This department is responsible for assigning or reassigning campus space. Campus space is at a premium, and no space is off limits for consideration. The library's study results showing usage in daily and hourly increments help keep the space planners from taking more library space for other academic needs. On a historical note, taking space from the library for university needs is not unheard of. Four large meeting rooms were taken years ago and made into university classrooms, and in the summer of 2013, the unfinished fifth floor of the library was completed for academic offices.

The renovated spaces have proven to be popular even after the newness wore off. As seen in table 10.3, the fourth floor reading room (Rm 425—Open Study Area—tables) continues to be busy three years after renovation, and the reference area renovation (Reference Computers) made the top list within less than a year after renovation completion.

Table 10.3
The Top Five Areas Used during Specific Semester

Fall Finals 2016		Spring Finals 2016		Fall Finals 2015	
Totals	Space	Totals	Space	Totals	Space
2741	Rm 425 - Open Study Area - tables	4283	Rm 425 - Open Study Area - tables	2832	Rm 425 -Open Study Area - tables
2271	Current Periodicals Rm - tables	3625	Current Periodicals Rm - tables	2354	Current Periodicals Rm - tables
2006	1st - individual desks	3419	4th Center - individual tables/desks	2269	1st - individual desks
1904	4th Center - individual tables/desks	3064	Reference Rm - tables	2156	4th Center - individual tables/desks
1598	Reference Computers	2598	1st - individual desks	2080	Reference Rm - tables

The pictures taken during spring 2016 finals (see figure 10.7) in the fourth floor reading room shows how popular the space has become.

Figure 10.7
Fourth floor reading room—spring 2016 finals.

Leveraging the Findings

Now that the library administration has a better understanding of which spaces are being used and to what degree, the next steps are to learn (1) more specifics about what the student patrons are doing in the space, (2) why they choose the library and the specific location within the library, and (3) why students are not using the physical library resources, services, and space. These three areas will require special user engagement with formal planning and preparation that includes human subject approval from the institutional review board. The library's assessment staff has begun developing a project plan that includes patron surveys (physical forms and online forms) during finals, student focus groups within the next year, and survey distribution

Section 2

to student populations not entering the library also within the next year. Depending on the types of questions, the library administration may need to use staff less directly involved with library services or project planning to ensure staff are not influencing the results.

The results of the next study should provide the library administration with information about how to market the library resources, services, and spaces. The results may provide more information about the type of spaces students would like that could be incorporated into renovation projects. The results may also assist the administration in fund-raising efforts because it will be information directly from students.

Reflection

This very basic assessment project of conducting head counts has proven to be very informative for the new library administration. This author personally conducted many of the head counts over the semesters and has observed unique behaviors and phenomena. An example of a regular occurrence was how groups of students, such as sorority or fraternity "study table" groups, had to have their tables touching. The individuals in the group were not necessarily studying the same subject or even working together, but they had a great need to move tables so everyone in their group was at a spot that touched the "group table." Being able to see one another was not sufficient. It also made no difference if the tables were rectangle or round, the tables just had to touch at one point.

Another interesting observation was the patrons' choice of technology. When the initial head count was conducted, it was assumed that patrons would have laptops to write papers or interact with the library's electronic resources. Though that was still a popular approach, this author came to appreciate how many patrons used tablets or iPads and even smartphones to do all these activities. Some users even had two or more electronic devices in front of them. Not all activity was scholarly in nature, but even from this author's quick glance observations, it cannot be assumed that the patrons' social media engagement was not with classmates on a course project.

Noise was an interesting issue. Though many library users understand that libraries should be moderately quiet, when groups of people gather, noise occurs. On occasion complaints were reported to the service desks, but they were typically related to spaces designated for group study. The staff that conducted the head counts discussed the noise issue on multiple occasions. One particular space was designated a quiet zone, but due to the furniture in the area, patrons regularly created large group tables. The staff was frustrated that the groups disregarded the quiet signs, but the patrons studying at individual tables in the vicinity rarely seemed affected. The staff concluded that most of the individual patrons were using headphones or earbuds and were not bothered by noise.

Consistency in how different staff might conduct a count was a minor concern. Each time a new person was added to the group conducting head counts, he or she was put through a minor training session that included a simulation. The person was shown the path through the library that is the most efficient, since during busy times, a single count (walk through the entire building) could take about thirty minutes. The person would be asked to conduct a head count while the trainer also completed one to determine how far off the trainee's counts were. Manual head counting is not perfect since the staff conducting the counts must always be looking for people who are walking as well as recording the location and activity of the patrons who are sitting. Other rules for the head counts included these:

- Count only patrons. Do not include library staff, university staff who are working in the area (e.g., custodial or facility staff) or library student staff who are working.
- When counting, continue on the designated path; never double back to "recount." Library users move around and will never stand still for a count, so stay on the path and count what is ahead, not behind.
- Be as inconspicuous as possible when trying to determine if technology is being used. Being too nosy could scare users out of the library.
- Patrons who are not sitting will be counted and recorded in the "walking through" category on the tally sheet.
- The head-counting staff will be asked by patrons about what they are doing since the counting activity is so systematic. Some patrons may be suspicious and concerned, while others will just be curious about why the staff member is walking by every hour.
- Remember that head counting in this fashion is not an exact science, but it can still be quite powerful.

The project collaborators included the university's Department of Public Safety and Facilities. Like most universities, the institution, as well as the city it is in, has its share of crime, so requesting a security presence was important to help make the staff and patrons feel safe. Though the library building's access in the late evenings and overnight was only via a card swipe for Rowan faculty, staff, and students, the security officer was stationed at the front desk and conducted periodic walks through the building. One of the security concern was fear that stressed patrons would have confrontations within the building. The facility department was not able to provide more dedicated staff during the extra hours. However, when the regular janitorial staff was not scheduled in the building, a campus janitorial floater checked the restrooms' toilet paper and hand towel supply and pulled trash. Luckily the amount of vandalism and theft over the eight semesters was minimal.

Lessons Learned

A major lesson learned was to take pictures—before, during and after! Pictures are critical to tell the library's story from multiple perspectives:

- space improvements—then and now photos
- space usage—document that the space is being used (take photos of users in the space)

- space usage—document how the space is being used (examples—study room windows being used as impromptu whiteboards; unplugging library equipment to plug in users' devices; movement of furniture, especially when furniture appears to be switched out—a likely sign the original furniture is broken or uncomfortable).

Another lesson in hindsight was to conduct the hourly daily and mid-semester counts. It seems so logical and immediately worthwhile, but for the library administration it took time with the interval steps to agree on the need for and value of such information. This author would highly recommend to other institutions that they do the hourly daily counts from the very beginning.

A final lesson is to decide whether to include a location of "book stacks" on the tally sheet to record patron activity that is specific to the library activity of looking at books on the shelf. That activity was not important to the library administration to capture, so those people were recorded as "walking through" in the appropriate area.

Challenges

Academic library usage is cyclical, with peaks typically happening around mid-semester and going into semester finals. Library usage can be different based on which semester and, to some degree, on the weather. Winter weather impacted Campbell Library during the first semester's head count—the institution had a snow closure. During a different semester, this author heard patrons discussing how they were staying at the library because it was raining outside, so if one patron was not leaving during a storm, it is reasonable to assume that others were not coming to the library from other locations for the same reason.

Another challenge of the project was arranging for staff to do the counts. In the first few semesters, it was only a few days with a few counts being done by two staff members, but by the spring of 2016, the number of hourly counts hit 280, requiring up to six staff. This came with a significant amount of compensatory time for the staff, which can have a monetary value calculated, but the library administration was committed to the project and assessment and deemed it worthwhile.

The Campbell Library has approximately 800 seats (tables, seats, lounge seats, single units, and multiple) and some of the highest head counts have reached over 500. A challenge is having enough of the seating the patrons want. As the number of users increases, the likelihood of users not finding the seating they want increases. The question is how many times users will tolerate no space before they do not return to the library.

This project can be done at any type and size of institution, with the primary issue being compensating staff conducting the head counts if they need to work overtime.

Notes

1. Association of College and Research Libraries, *Documented Library Contributions to Student Learning and Success*, prepared by Karen Brown with contributions by Kara J. Malenfant (Chicago: Association of College and Research Libraries, 2016), 13.

2. Nancy Foster and Susan Gibbons, *Studying Students* (Chicago: Association of College and Research Libraries, 2007).
3. Peg Lawrence and Lynne Weber, "Midnight–2:00 a.m.: What Goes On at the Library?" *New Library World* 113, no. 11/12 (2012): 528–48, https://doi.org/10.1108/03074801211282911; Doug Suarez, "What Students Do When They Study in the Library: Using Ethnographic Methods to Observe Study Behavior," *Electronic Journal of Academic and Special Librarianship* 8, no. 3 (Winter 2007), http://southernlibrarianship.icaap.org/content/v08n03/suarez_d01.html; Camille Andrews and Sara E. Wright, "Library Learning Spaces: Investigating Libraries and Investing in Student Feedback," *Creating Sustainable Community: The Proceedings of the ACRL 2015 Conference March 25–28, 2015*, ed. Dawn M. Mueller (Chicago: ACRL, 2015), http://www.ala.org/acrl/acrl/conferences/acrl2015/papers; Heather Cunningham and Susanne Tabur, "Learning Space Attributes: Reflections on Academic Library Design and Use," *Journal of Learning Spaces* 1, no. 2 (2012), http://libjournal.uncg.edu/jls/article/view/392/287; Harold Shill and Shawn Tonner, "Creating a Better Place: Physical Improvements in Academic Libraries, 1995–2002," *College and Research Libraries* 64, no. 6 (2003): 431–66.
4. Joanna Bryant, Graham Matthews, and Graham Walton, "Academic Libraries and Social and Learning Space: A Case Study of Loughborough University Library, UK," *Journal of Librarianship and Information Science* 41, no. 1 (2009), 7–18; Kelly Matthews, Victoria Andrews, and Peter Adams, "Social Learning Spaces and Student Engagement," *Higher Education Research and Development* 30, no. 2 (2011): 105–20.
5. Susan Thompson, "Are Desktop Computers Still Relevant in Today's Libraries?" *Information Technology and Libraries*, 31, no. 4 (2012): 20–33.

Bibliography

Andrews, Camille, and Sara E. Wright. "Library Learning Spaces: Investigating Libraries and Investing in Student Feedback." *Creating Sustainable Community: The Proceedings of the ACRL 2015 Conference March 25–28, 2015*. Edited by Dawn M. Mueller. Chicago: Association of College and Research Libraries, 2015. http://www.ala.org/acrl/acrl/conferences/acrl2015/papers.

Association of College and Research Libraries. *Documented Library Contributions to Student Success: Building Evidence with Team-Based Assessment in Action Campus Projects*. Prepared by Karen Brown with contributions by Kara J. Malenfant. Chicago: Association of College and Research Libraries, 2016.

Bryant, Joanna, Graham Matthews, and Graham Walton. "Academic Libraries and Social and Learning Space: A Case Study of Loughborough University Library, UK." *Journal of Librarianship and Information Science* 41, no. 1 (2009): 7–18.

Cunningham, Heather, and Susanne Tabur. "Learning Space Attributes: Reflections on Academic Library Design and Use." *Journal of Learning Spaces* 1, no. 2 (2012), http://libjournal.uncg.edu/jls/article/view/392/287.

Foster, Nancy, and Susan Gibbons. *Studying Students: The Undergraduate Research Project at the University of Rochester*. Chicago: Association of College and Research Libraries, 2007.

Lawrence, Peg, and Lynne Weber. "Midnight–2:00 a.m.: What Goes On at the Library?" *New Library World* 113, no. 11/12 (2012): 528–48. https://doi.org/10.1108/03074801211282911.

Matthews, Kelly, Victoria Andrews, and Peter Adams. "Social Learning Spaces and Student Engagement." *Higher Education Research and Development* 30, no. 2 (2011): 105–20.

Shill, Harold, and Shawn Tonner. "Creating a Better Place: Physical Improvements in Academic Libraries, 1995–2002." *College and Research Libraries* 64, no. 6 (2003): 431–66.

Suarez, Doug. "What Students Do When They Study in the Library: Using Ethnographic Methods to Observe Study Behavior." *Electronic Journal of Academic and Special Librarianship* 8, no. 3 (Winter 2007), http://southernlibrarianship.icaap.org/content/v08n03/suarez_d01.html.

Thompson, Susan. "Are Desktop Computers Still Relevant in Today's Libraries?" *Information Technology and Libraries,* 31, no. 4 (2012): 20–33.

Section 2

Title: Measuring Accessibility and Reliability of a Laptop-Lending Kiosk in an Academic Library

Abstract: This study assesses a laptop-lending kiosk in an academic library, a 24/7 self-service option from which easy access and consistent performance are required. In order to measure accessibility and reliability, quantitative transaction data from January 2013 to December 2016 are analyzed. First, the number of transactions by time and by distinct user are calculated and compared to the number of users entering the library to analyze percentage of users engaging the service. Second, transactions marked as problems are analyzed to find specific devices, time periods, or users experiencing issues affecting reliability.

Keywords: laptop-lending kiosk, academic library, self-service

Project focus: assessment methodologies, techniques, or practices (e.g., critical incident technique); services (i.e., customer service at reference desk); data use and technology

Results made or will make case for: more funding, improvements in services, changes in library policy, proof of library impact and value, decisions about library staffing, how money or resources may be directed

Data needed: service transaction

Methodology: quantitative

Project duration: 2 months

Tool(s) utilized: Microsoft Excel

Cost estimate: < $100

Type of institution: university—private

Institution enrollment: 15,000–30,000

Highest level of education: doctoral

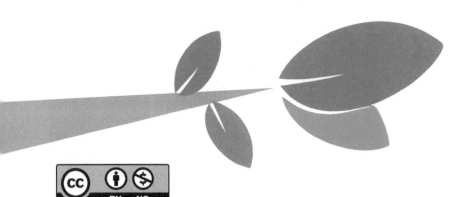

[cc] [BY] [NC]

Chapter 11

Measuring Accessibility and Reliability of a Laptop-Lending Kiosk in an Academic Library

Hae Min Kim

Introduction

This paper presents a case study of analyzing and visualizing usage data from a laptop-lending self-checkout service at Drexel University Libraries (DUL) to measure its accessibility and reliability. Although many universities, including Drexel, have required students to own a personal laptop for their studies, laptop-lending services in academic libraries are active. Since laptop-lending services were introduced in academic libraries in the late 1990s, the service has been provided at circulation desks under the supervision of library staff members. Studies reveal that device circulation has issues, including storage space, battery charging, and staff operations, but a laptop vending machine is considered to be a simple and secure self-service model.[1] It allows users to check out a computer by themselves without help through simple steps on a touch screen, and libraries can sustain computers in the kiosk. Ryerson University Library presented a paper considering its selection of a model of self-service laptop lending,[2] and some academic libraries, including Drexel University, Texas A&M University, Illinois State University, Georgia State University, and Georgia Institute of Technology, have adopted laptop vending machines. However, it is hard to find papers about the assessment of a laptop-lending kiosk with quantitative methods. In published literature, researchers have discussed the implementation of the lending programs and assessed services through user surveys, focus groups, and interviews.[3] Chapman and Woodbury conducted quantitative analysis using transactional data and added more laptops and modified workflows.[4]

DUL has provided the service for more than four years. Quantitative data analysis could uncover the objective status of the service, reveal the needs and expectations of users, and inform management decisions. Analysis based on transactional data and information related to kiosk usage helps libraries to establish their own continuous reports.

DUL implemented a laptop vending machine in December 2012 to provide 24/7 lending self-service to the Drexel community. The service was initiated at the request of Drexel students and student government organizations regarding interest in using laptops any time of day or night on campus. Although students have their own laptops, they mentioned that they are hesitant to carry them both because it was burdensome and it posed a security risk.

DUL launched a service providing twelve Apple MacBook (fifteen-inch) laptops through the kiosk. Drexel community members with a valid ID can borrow a laptop from the kiosk in the main library building for up to five hours. A laptop checkout requires four steps: tap the kiosk screen, swipe a user ID card, agree to terms and conditions, and grab to go. The kiosk is located in the main library's twenty-four-hour open space to Drexel members. The service became popular in a year, and eighteen laptops were added to the kiosk for a total of thirty available computers. While we have collected transactional records continually and had statistics including the numbers of checkouts and problems, the ratio of problems to successful checkouts is conspicuous and could affect usage and users' satisfaction. Problems are identified as transactions with any errors resulting in the unavailability of lending or use of a laptop. An example of a use issue is when the kiosk dispenses a laptop but the borrower finds the laptop has a problem such as proving unbootable.

A 24/7 self-service requires easy access and consistent performance. In order to measure those two factors—accessibility and reliability—three academic years' transaction data, from September 2013 to September 2016, was gathered and analyzed quantitatively. For accessibility, patterns in volume of checkouts were calculated over the year, term, week, day, and hour. User status and department were identified. Distinct users were quantified to reveal the number of individuals using the service. The data was compared to that library building's entrance data to analyze percentage of kiosk users. For reliability, transactions marked as "problem reported" were assessed. The number of problems occurring within a time period, number of distinct users who were confronted with problems, and number of devices with problems were analyzed to find specific times, users, and reliability issues.

The findings from this study make contributions to the current literature as a case study of identified user patterns and self-service kiosk problems to help libraries to manage their services and improve them for users. This study will help librarians and professional staff to anticipate the usage of self-service kiosks and to identify issues through transaction data analysis, and it will be a fundamental source for demonstrating the value and impact of the service.

Data Collection

For analyses in this paper, three different data sets were necessary: laptop transactional data, user information, and library entrance data. First, the laptop kiosk vendor provides an administration website for presenting the status of kiosk and laptops and transaction reports. On the transaction report webpage, the section "Transactions in Order" has a record of each transaction, including errors. Reasons for errors are marked in the section "Transactions Reporting Problems." The collected transactional data is in the range of September 23, 2013, through September 18, 2016, and the total number of records is 26,582. This range includes three academic years (AY): AY13–14, between September 23, 2013, and September 21, 2014; AY14–15, between September 22, 2014, and September 20, 2015; and AY15–16, between September 21, 2015, and September 18, 2016. Each academic year is composed of four terms at Drexel—Fall, Winter, Spring, and Summer—and each term has ten weeks of classes, one exam week, and one or more break weeks. The transactional data set from the admin website has five variables, including day, date, user, device tag, and duration. The user variable is the user's university identification number. In order to match the numbers with patron status and department information, user information was required as a second data set. The third data set is the library's card swipe (entrance) data to reveal the percentage of laptop users among the number of library users.

Data Preparation

One Microsoft Excel file was organized to contain transactional data and user information. Based on the five variables from the kiosk admin website, I added parsed date information and calendar and academic year, term, and week information to the file for easy and smooth pivot analysis in Excel. User status and college information were identified for each record and added to the file (table 11.1). The library's entrance data was prepared as separate files and calculated by different unit criteria to compare with the transactional data.

Table 11.1
Data Variables and Samples

Variables	Data Sample
Day	Monday
Date Time	9/22/2014 1:27:55 PM
User	00000
Device Tag	4C0094E83B
Duration	0:59:00
Error	(Marked as Error or Blank)
Date	9/22/2014
Month	9
Hour	13
Academic Year	AY 14-15
Calendar Year	2014
Term	Fall
Week	Week1
User Status	Undergraduate
User College	College of Computing & Informatics

Data Analysis

Accessibility

The main purpose of the self-service kiosk is to offer user access to borrowed laptops at any time. In this study, accessibility is defined as the laptop kiosk being in service with at least one laptop available to borrow. To examine the accessibility of the service, the number of transactions by different time units and distinct users was measured. The data was compared to the library's entrance data to analyze percentage of laptop service users. Distinct users were identified to reveal the proportion of individuals by college.

Checkout by Time Unit

The number of checkouts was analyzed by academic year, term, week of the term, day of the week, and hour to reveal usage patterns. The total number of checkouts for three academic years was 22,717. The average checkouts per month is 631, which is 21 per day (30 days per month). There is a clear trend of a decrease in borrowing during the three academic years. In AY13–14, the total number of checkouts was 10,991. However, in AY14–15, 6,580 checkouts occurred, which is a 40.1 percent decrease in usage compared to the previous year. In AY15–16, there was a 21.8 percent decrease from AY14–15; the total number of checkouts was 5,146 (table 11.2). In Drexel's academic year, the peak activity month is October when the first term (Fall) of a year is underway and many midterm exams are scheduled, and the second peak month occurs in May in the Spring term, which is the last time period of a year for majority of students and often includes final exam week (figure 11.1).

Table 11.2
Checkouts by Academic Year and Month

Academic Year\Month	Sep	Oct	Nov	Dec	Jan	Feb	Mar	Apr	May	Jun	Jul	Aug	Total	Average
AY 13–14	268	1,028	746	323	800	1,305	1,297	1,493	**1,575**	1,035	659	462	10,991	915.9
AY 14–15	399	**1,406**	1,013	438	206	324	572	627	642	428	270	255	6,580	548.3
AY 15–16	192	507	481	297	384	550	550	440	**633**	308	329	475	5,146	428.8
Total	859	2,941	2,240	1,058	1,390	2,179	2,419	2,560	2,850	1,771	1,258	1,192	22,717	–
Average	286.3	980.3	746.7	352.7	463.3	726.3	806.3	853.3	950.0	590.3	419.3	397.3	–	–

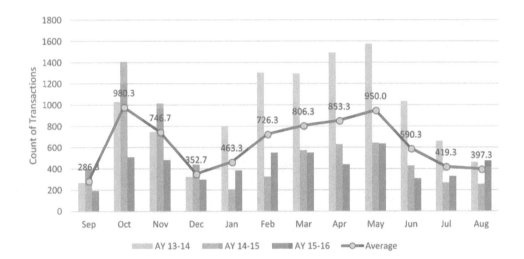

Figure 11.1
Checkouts by academic year and month.

Figure 11.2 and table 11.3 present usage patterns by term and week of the term. Spring terms totaled 7,094 checkouts, the most of the four terms, and week 10 was the busiest week in a term. The average of checkouts by week of a term shows that Week 5 and Week 10 had more usage than other weeks, which reflects students' academic life cycle for both midterm and final exam periods. For visualization, figure 11.2 illustrates the trends of checkouts, and table 11.3 shares more detailed data. In order to improve readability of table 11.3, grayscale has been applied to indicate maximum values within the area designated by the thick box border. A conditional format in Excel highlights the data to assist visualization of values from minimum to maximum in the range of cells.

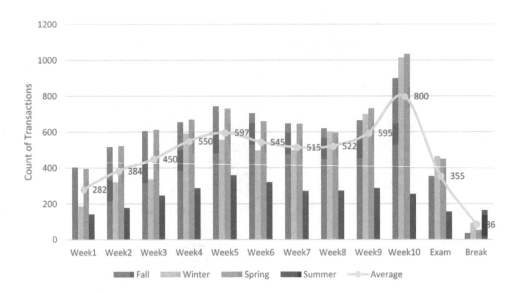

Figure 11.2
Checkout by term and week.

Table 11.3
Grayscales of Checkout by Term and Week

Term\Week	Week 1	Week 2	Week 3	Week 4	Week 5	Week 6	Week 7	Week 8	Week 9	Week 10	Exam	Break	Total
Fall	403	516	605	654	743	704	647	619	664	898	352	33	6,838
Winter	187	319	336	591	556	497	498	602	699	1,014	464	92	5,855
Spring	395	522	612	668	730	659	645	596	731	1,033	450	53	7,094
Summer	142	178	246	286	358	319	271	272	286	254	155	163	2,930
Total	1,127	1,35	1,799	2,199	2,387	2,179	2,061	2,089	2,380	3,087	1,21	294	22,717
Average	281.8	383.8	449.8	549.8	596.8	544.8	515.3	522.3	595.0	799.8	355.3	85.3	—

Table 11.4 shows the usage pattern by day of the week and hour. The same grayscale has been applied to this table. The results show that there are concentrated time periods: Monday at 2:00 p.m. is the darkest cell and busiest time period, and 2:00 p.m. on Wednesday and then 1:00 p.m. on Monday follow. Also, the patterns in lending volume depicted in table 11.4 show Sunday after 5:00 p.m. has more usage than Friday. These kiosk usage numbers reflect the influx pattern of library patrons and demonstrate the laptop service is approachable to them.

Table 11.4
Grayscales of Checkout by Day of the Week and Hour

Hour \ Day	Mon	Tue	Wed	Thu	Fri	Sat	Sun	Total
12 AM	36	59	43	66	40	20	21	285
1 AM	73	95	97	91	54	8	22	440
2 AM	32	42	49	48	32	10	6	219
3 AM	5	13	7	10	7	6	3	51
4 AM	11	5	10	10	4	5	2	47
5 AM	5	8	5	11	6	4	2	41
6 AM	14	24	15	21	9	3	2	88
7 AM	17	12	12	15	16	3	11	86
8 AM	10	13	10	11	11	13	11	79
9 AM	123	107	137	81	78	20	20	566
10 AM	228	186	221	197	140	42	50	1,064
11 AM	294	259	286	275	222	64	78	1,478
12 PM	332	372	362	373	231	93	83	1,846
1 PM	414	358	384	306	256	104	173	1,995
2 PM	459	401	431	396	273	118	176	2,254
3 PM	413	381	397	357	226	123	226	2,123
4 PM	376	366	375	294	195	121	185	1,912
5 PM	325	308	310	279	140	92	173	1,627
6 PM	294	302	239	220	107	93	151	1,406
7 PM	288	280	234	159	107	116	159	1,343
8 PM	276	277	269	165	112	115	162	1,376
9 PM	235	254	197	146	96	93	111	1,132
10 PM	143	151	145	87	79	85	96	786
11 PM	86	89	90	54	37	45	72	473
Total	4,489	4,362	4,325	3,672	2,478	1,396	1,995	22,717

Checkout by User

The checkout data was analyzed with users' college and status. Figure 11.3 shows colleges with the greatest number of laptop circulations by academic year. Users in Colleges of Engineering, Business, and Arts and Sciences together comprised 70 percent of all checkouts each academic year. Those three colleges enroll 44.3 percent of students at Drexel (AY15–16); thus I calculated the ratio of the number of distinct users compared to enrollment (full-time and part-time) in order to determine the proportion of individuals in each college and eliminate the size effect of colleges. Table 11.5 presents that ratio in the three academic years. Students from the College of Business demanded the most laptop service: 12.4 percent in AY 13–14 and 7.8 percent in AY 14–15 (that is, about 12 out of 100 students in the College of Business borrowed a laptop at least once in AY 13–14). The College of Medicine had a higher proportion of engaged users than other colleges in AY 15–16, its percentage having increased from 7.4 percent to 8.2 percent, while other colleges showed a decrease in engaged users compared to the previous year. In terms of user status, figure 11.4 demonstrates the majority user group is undergraduate students (87%) followed by graduate students (9%) and staff (2%, except library staff members). The greatest use of the kiosk has been by undergraduate students.

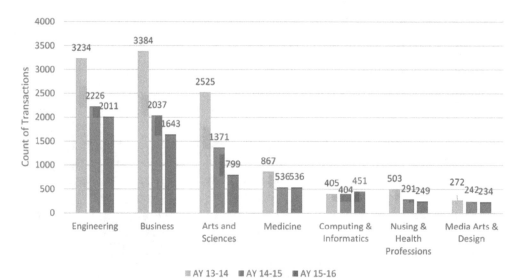

AY 13-14   AY 14-15   AY 15-16

Figure 11.3
Checkout by college and academic year.

Table 11.5
Ratio of Distinct Users to Enrollment by College

Academic Year	AY 13–14			AY 14–15			AY15–16		
College	Distinct User	Enrollment	%	Distinct User	Enrollment	%	Distinct User	Enrollment	%
Engineering	439	4,678	9.4%	356	4,649	7.7%	283	4,506	6.3%
Business	510	4,129	**12.4%**	324	4,151	**7.8%**	197	4,082	4.8%
Arts & Sciences	320	3,069	10.4%	214	3,005	7.1%	135	2,754	4.9%
Medicine	123	1,064	11.6%	80	1,083	7.4%	87	1,067	**8.2%**
Computing & Informatics	82	1,049	7.8%	69	1,818	3.8%	55	1,753	3.1%
Nursing & Health Prof.	88	4,604	1.9%	92	4,931	1.9%	51	4,846	1.1%
Media Arts & Design	75	2,024	3.7%	45	2,083	2.2%	42	2,092	2.0%

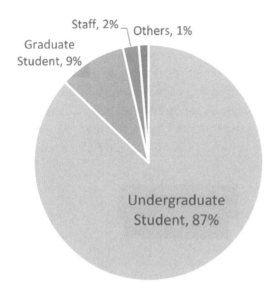

Figure 11.4
Laptop kiosk user groups.

Library Users and Laptop Checkouts

The number of distinct kiosk users has been compared to the distinct number of the library building visitors. This analysis reveals the percentage of library users who borrowed laptops via the self-checkout kiosk. Figure 11.5 shows declines in each academic year similar to the trend of decreasing numbers of checkouts. At the highest, about 6 out of 100 library visitors borrowed laptops via the kiosk in the Spring 13–14 term.

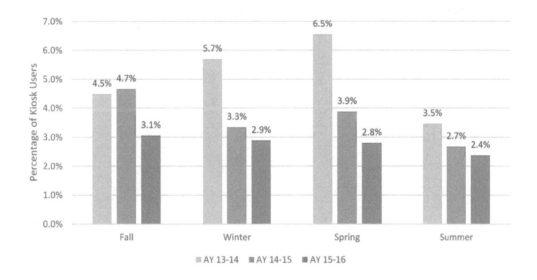

Figure 11.5
Ratio of distinct number of kiosk users to library users by term.

When it comes to week of the term, Week 10 has remarkably high ratio of kiosk users (figure 11.6), which indicates more individuals come to the library in order to check out a laptop than in other weeks. For example, 12 out of 100 library users borrowed computers via the kiosk, while only 1 out of 100 used it during the break week (table 11.6). The pattern of the distinct user ratio is similar to the one of the number of transactions through time periods. For three academic years, 3,185 users made 22,717 checkouts (without transactions marked as problems), averaging to 7 times per user. Out of total users, 1,162 users (36.5%) were one-time borrowers, while 14 (0.4%) users created 2,437 transactions, which is 10.7 percent of all checkouts.

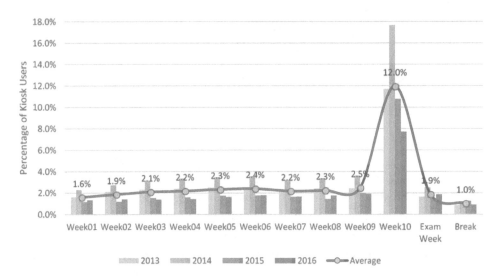

Figure 11.6
Ratio of distinct number of kiosk users to library users by week of the term.

Table 11.6
Grayscales of the Ratio of Distinct Number of Users to Library Users

Year\ Week	Week 1	Week 2	Week 3	Week 4	Week 5	Week 6	Week 7	Week 8	Week 9	Week 10	Exam	Break	Total
2013	1.6%	2.1%	2.3%	2.4%	2.5%	2.5%	2.3%	2.4%	2.4%	11.7%	1.6%	0.9%	6.1%
2014	2.3%	2.7%	3.2%	3.4%	3.5%	3.6%	3.2%	3.4%	3.6%	17.6%	2.5%	1.1%	7.4%
2015	1.2%	1.2%	1.5%	1.6%	1.7%	1.8%	1.6%	1.4%	2.0%	10.8%	1.5%	1.3%	4.5%
2016	1.3%	1.4%	1.4%	1.4%	1.6%	1.8%	1.6%	1.8%	1.9%	7.7%	1.9%	0.9%	4.1%
Total	1.6%	1.9%	2.1%	2.2%	2.3%	2.4%	2.2%	2.3%	2.5%	12.0%	1.9%	1.0%	5.5%

Reliability

Expectations of the self-service kiosk include consistent performance. To explore reliability, transactions marked as problem reports were investigated. The number of problems by academic year, distinct user, and devices were analyzed to find specific time, users, or devices having issues affecting reliability. The kiosk is set up to check out a laptop when the laptop has recharged to at least 70 percent battery life and after clearing data created by previous users. However, the kiosk lending procedures could experience errors resulting in user turn-aways, including user authorization issues at the kiosk, or on the laptop, malfunctions such as screen or keyboard issues or failed boot-up. Also, we considered a transaction of less than five minutes duration time as a problem, assuming that such a fast return implied there was no actual use of the laptop (the kiosk lending process from swiping user ID at the kiosk, then the boot-up time for the laptop, and the time spent taking the laptop to a seat and then carrying it back were assumed to take most of the short lending time period). The service identified different types of problems, which were tracked and assessable via the admin website with different error labels. However, it is hard to clarify exactly what kind of problem was encountered when a user experienced an issue resulting in a short circulation of a laptop.

Problem Transactions

The number of total transactions has decreased during the three academic years, but the number of transactions marked as error was steady at around 1,288. The percentage of error transactions doubled between AY13–14 and AY15–16 (figure 11.7), which means in one out of four transactions, problems occurred prohibiting regular use of a laptop during the most recent period analyzed.

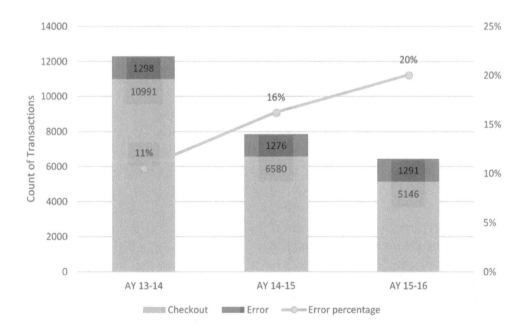

Figure 11.7
Checkout and problem transactions by academic year.

Problems and Users

During the three academic years, 3,355 patrons accessed the laptop kiosk. Among them, 1,313 (39.1%) people faced a problem at least once, and 170 (5.1%) people who encountered at least one error never checked out a laptop. Figure 11.8 demonstrates the distinct numbers of total users, users who encountered errors, and error percentage by academic year. The percentage has increased since AY13–14 and reached 45 percent in AY15–16, which indicates that almost a half of all kiosk users faced at least one problem in the use of the self-checkout service.

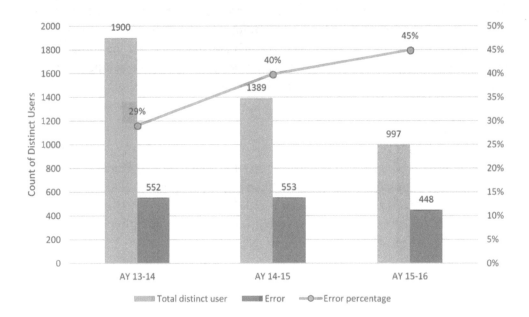

Figure 11.8
Distinct users and errors encountered by academic year.

Problems and Devices

The kiosk contained thirty laptops as of 2014. The lending machine decides which device among them to dispense to a user based on a laptop's condition, such as battery charging and data cleaning work. It is possible that specific laptops have more issues than others, so error transactions were analyzed by device. Table 11.7 shows the percentage of errors for each device in three academic years. The color scale applied to each group of academic year data reveals which devices had a higher percentage of errors than other devices. Sparklines, a function in Excel, are used to illustrate trends of problem percentages for each device. The result shows that some devices, such as device numbers 10007, 20005, 20004, and 20003, have increasing error percentages, much higher than other devices' percentages in AY15–16. The admin website reports reveal problems were not associated solely with device issues, but also with kiosk and users' authorizations.

Table 11.7
Percentage of Problem Transactions by Device and Academic Year

Device Num	AY 13-14	AY 14-15	AY 15-16	Sparklines
10007	9%	22%	38%	
20005	19%	27%	35%	
20004	7%	22%	33%	
20003	7%	15%	33%	
20001	7%	26%	28%	
10004	12%	17%	25%	
10005	11%	17%	22%	
20014	7%	22%	21%	
20012	15%	11%	20%	
10008	10%	18%	20%	
20016	7%	15%	20%	
20017	6%	-	19%	
20010	12%	17%	18%	
10012	15%	12%	18%	
10003	11%	27%	18%	
20009	9%	16%	18%	
20015	8%	15%	18%	
20013	8%	14%	16%	
20006	8%	10%	16%	
10006	7%	7%	15%	
20007	6%	16%	14%	
10002	7%	6%	13%	
20008	7%	9%	13%	
10001	13%	31%	13%	
10011	21%	12%	11%	
20011	6%	-	10%	
10009	16%	17%	10%	
20002	20%	24%	-	
20018	7%	14%	-	
10010	9%	11%	-	
Total	11%	16%	20%	

Findings

The quantitative analyses in this study revealed patterns in the usage of the self-checkout laptop kiosk. Spring term and Week 10 are identified as peak periods, as well as around 2:00 p.m. on Monday, Tuesday, and Wednesday having the highest volume lending hours and days. These lending time trends are comparable with the main library usage (figure 11.9). Transactional patterns reveal that high-use periods parallel significant milestones in academic schedules and that most of the users are undergraduate students. The analysis supports the notion that the self-service has been accessible to DUL users when they need it. During the three academic years, however, the number of checkouts in AY 15–16 has decreased 53.2 percent compared to the number in AY 13–14. One-time users are observed to be 36.5 percent, which indicates they didn't return to use the service again. Only 0.4 percent of users accounted for 11 percent of the total checkouts.

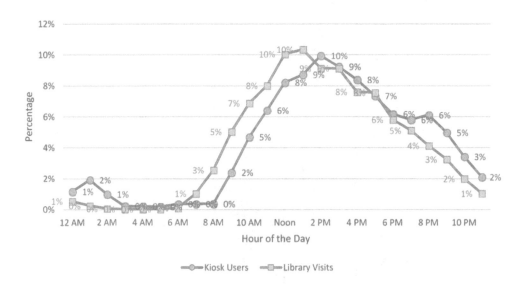

Figure 11.9
Proportions of Kiosk Users and Library Visits by Hour.

The analysis of the data identifying problems highlights that the service has a reliability issue. The proportion of problem transactions increased from 11 percent to 20 percent with a noticeable decline in the number of laptop checkouts. It might be the case that more users confronted problems negative influenced the number of checkouts. It is a serious service issue when 45% of users have faced errors (AY15-16). For ongoing management, the ratio of problems to checkouts should be examined regularly, and devices with high error issues should be repaired and replaced. It is possible to handle negative experience with the service and support troubleshooting by arranging staff availability during the peak time periods. Also, the kiosk vendor's continued support and cooperation in managing critical issues will help support improvement of the service.

Reflection

A laptop is an important tool for students to facilitate their academic success.[5] According to a mobile device survey in 2015 by Pearson, 88 percent of college students own a laptop and use it for college work more than other mobile devices.[6] Although this study's results present a decline in the use of the self-checkout laptop service, it remains a core technology lending service for students. In order to increase the number of checkouts and returning users, preferred software and e-resource access for students in the Engineering, Business, and Arts & Sciences, colleges having the most users, are possible. Also, another type of computer operating system, such as Windows, can be added as an option to these devices.

This study is valuable in providing actionable information to managers using quantitative data analysis methods and visualization options from Excel to uncover patterns and problems to improve the service, which other library managers can replicate to explore their own laptop kiosk service status. In order to improve service quality, managing problems and preventing kiosk defects are necessary. In addition, qualitative studies are required to understand the experiences of users who encounter errors or do not use the service again. These target groups can help uncover detailed experiences and identify needed improvements for providing a sustainable and satisfactory service. Qualitative studies alongside quantitative analysis will enhance data-driven decision-making. This study didn't cover cost analysis, but it remains an interesting topic for future study.

Notes

1. Weina Wang and Mandissa Arlain, "Laptops to Go: Toward a Sustainable Self-Service Lending Model," *Computers in Libraries* 34, no. 3 (April 2014): 12–16.
2. Wang and Arlain, "Laptops to Go."
3. Wendy S. Wilmoth, "Circulating Laptops in a Two-Year Academic Library: A Formative Assessment," *Georgia Library Quarterly* 52, no. 4 (2015): article 8, https://digitalcommons.kennesaw.edu/glq/vol52/iss4/8; Weina Wang, Kelly Dermody, Colleen Burgess, and Fangmin Wang, "From a Knowledge Container to a Mobile Learning Platform: What RULA Learned from the Laptop Lending Program," *Journal of Access Services* 11, no. 4 (2014): 255–81; Bernd Becker, "Circulating Laptops in Academic Libraries," *Behavioral and Social Sciences Librarian* 33, no. 2 (2014): 125–29; Terri Summey and Art Gutierrez, "Laptops to Go: A Student Assessment of a Library Laptop Lending Service," *Journal of Access Services* 9, no. 1 (2012): 28–43; Louise Feldmann, Lindsey Wess, and Tom Moothart, "An Assessment of Student Satisfaction with a Circulating Laptop Service," *Information Technology and Libraries* 27, no. 2 (2008): 20–25.
4. Joyce Chapman and David Woodbury, "Leveraging Quantitative Data to Improve a Device-Lending Program," *Library Hi Tech* 30, no. 2 (2012): 210–34.
5. Wang et al., "From a Knowledge Container."
6. Harris Poll, *Student Mobile Device Survey 2015: National Report: College Students* (London: Pearson, 2015), https://www.pearsoned.com/wp-content/uploads/2015-Pearson-Student-Mobile-Device-Survey-College.pdf.

Section 2

Bibliography

Becker, Bernd. "Circulating Laptops in Academic Libraries." *Behavioral and Social Sciences Librarian* 33, no. 2 (2014): 125–29.

Chapman, Joyce, and David Woodbury. "Leveraging Quantitative Data to Improve a Device-Lending Program." *Library Hi Tech* 30, no. 2 (2012): 210–34.

Feldmann, Louise, Lindsey Wess, and Tom Moothart. "An Assessment of Student Satisfaction with a Circulating Laptop Service." *Information Technology and Libraries* 27, no. 2 (2008): 20–25.

Harris Poll. *Student Mobile Device Survey 2015: National Report: College Students.* London: Pearson, 2015. https://www.pearsoned.com/wp-content/uploads/2015-Pearson-Student-Mobile-Device-Survey-College.pdf.

LaptopsAnytime home page. Accessed February 15, 2018. https://laptopsanytime.com/.

Summey, Terri, and Art Gutierrez. "Laptops to Go: A Student Assessment of a Library Laptop Lending Service." *Journal of Access Services* 9, no. 1 (2012): 28–43.

Wang, Weina, and Mandissa Arlain. "Laptops to Go: Toward a Sustainable Self-Service Lending Model." *Computers in Libraries* 34, no. 3 (April 2014): 12–16.

Wang, Weina, Kelly Dermody, Colleen Burgess, and Fangmin Wang. "From a Knowledge Container to a Mobile Learning Platform: What RULA Learned from the Laptop Lending Program." *Journal of Access Services* 11, no. 4 (2014): 255–81.

Wilmoth, Wendy S. "Circulating Laptops in a Two-Year Academic Library: A Formative Assessment." *Georgia Library Quarterly* 52, no. 4 (2015): article 8. https://digitalcommons.kennesaw.edu/glq/vol52/iss4/8.

Title: Triangulating an Assessment Plan

Abstract: While many resources discuss the importance of creating an assessment plan, few describe the specifics of such a process. There are many ways to create a plan; this chapter will detail one specific process and the reasoning behind it. *Triangulating* refers to the process of seeking input from multiple sources, including the library's strategic plan, the dean and leadership team, and library faculty and staff. This process of seeking input from bottom to top, mapped directly to the library's strategic plan goals, resulted in a detailed plan that is easy to follow.

Keywords: assessment plan, planning, strategic plan, strategic goals, organizational buy-in, organizational development

Project focus: organizational practices (i.e., strategic planning); assessment concepts and/or management

Results made or will make case for: more funding, improvements in services, improvements in spaces, changes in library policy, proof of library impact and value, decisions about library staffing, how money or resources may be directed

Data needed: Varied—this planning method can be used with any type of data that you prefer to collect.

Methodology: qualitative, quantitative, mixed method, ethnography, evaluation or survey

Project duration: ongoing (continuous feedback loop)

Tool(s) utilized: spreadsheet software, large printouts, Post-it Notes.

Cost estimate: < $100

Type of institution: university—public

Institution enrollment: 15,000–30,000

Highest level of education: doctoral

Section 2

Chapter 12

Triangulating an Assessment Plan

Starr Hoffman

Introduction

While many resources discuss the importance of creating an assessment plan, few agree on what such a plan is. Is an assessment plan a road map for all assessments undertaken at the library? Is it a list of only those assessments that directly relate to the current strategic plan? Is it a document detailing what indicates the success or failure of a given initiative? Is it a report on the outcome of assessments in a given period?

Even fewer resources describe the specifics of how to create such a plan. Those that exist are primarily internal documents or online guides, rather than purposeful, deliberate contributions to the library literature. There are many different processes; this chapter is not an attempt to describe them all, but rather to describe one specific process and the reasoning behind it. The term *triangulating* in this chapter title refers to the process of seeking input from multiple sources and stakeholders including the institution's strategic plan, the library's strategic plan, the dean and leadership team, and library staff (library faculty, professional staff, and classified staff). This process of seeking input both from top to bottom and from bottom to top, mapped directly to the library's strategic plan goals, resulted in a detailed plan that is easy to follow.

Context

The Institution

The University of Nevada, Las Vegas (UNLV) is a young (established in 1957) public institution in a diverse urban environment. It was designated a Minority-Serving Institution by the US Department of Education and has the second-most diverse student body in the United States.[1] UNLV's current strategic goals are focused on its Top Tier initiative to be recognized as a top public university in the areas of research, education, and impact on the local community. This Top Tier plan centers around five university-wide areas:

1. academic health center
2. community partnerships
3. infrastructure and shared governance
4. research, scholarship, and creative activity
5. student achievement

The Libraries

The UNLV University Libraries are divided into five library divisions, which are further divided into multiple departments. The libraries' strategic plan describes library goals that are nested within university-wide goals in the five areas listed above. Many of these goals involve multiple library divisions, while a few are division-specific. The libraries' strategic plan is on a two-year cycle (2015–2017) that corresponds with the biennial state legislative funding model. The top-level library goals for 2015–2017 are

1. **Academic health center:** University Libraries will develop a next-generation Health Sciences Library incorporating state-of-the-art technology while remaining high-touch among students, faculty, practitioners, and the southern Nevada community.
2. **Community partnerships:** University Libraries fosters the intellectual, cultural, and economic development of the region with collections and services that advance knowledge and scholarship about the region, support regional businesses and industries, and prepare the region's K–12 students for UNLV.
3. **Infrastructure and shared governance:** University Libraries continues to enhance its robust infrastructure to support evolving methods of research, scholarship, and creative activity across UNLV's disciplines.
4. **Research, scholarship, and creative activity:** University Libraries contributes throughout the research life cycle, from identification of opportunity to dissemination of results.
5. **Student achievement:** University Libraries collaborates broadly to ensure student achievement through direct instruction, partnering with faculty on assignment design, and development of learning experiences outside the classroom.

During the development of the UNLV Libraries' 2015–2017 Assessment Plan in late fall 2015, I was new to UNLV and was relatively inexperienced in formal assessment processes. My position (Director, Planning and Assessment) had been vacant for about a year, so despite the libraries' strong cultural value of assessment, there were gaps and inattention in many areas. Because of the university libraries' strong culture of participatory governance, transparency, and collaboration, there was a desire for broad participation in decision-making and assessment planning, particularly to increase buy-in for assessment activities.

Section 2

Defining the Assessment Plan

The term *assessment plan* means different things to different people. For me, an assessment plan is an outline of the assessment activities an organization plans to perform, contextualized within the structure of the organization's strategic goals and desired objectives. My reasons for creating such a plan include the following:

- Defining **who** is doing **what** to assess **which** goals.
- Enabling me to coordinate assessment activities across five divisions, sixteen departments, and two research centers.
- Identifying specific, measurable success metrics.
- Using as an outline for the final strategic plan report at the close of the two-year cycle, to assess and report outcomes.

Crafting the Assessment Plan

Triangulating from Multiple Levels

I started the assessment planning process with my own input. In order to clearly connect goals and their assessments, I created a spreadsheet with five tabs, one for each strategic theme and overarching goal. Each spreadsheet was divided into the following columns: subgoals, key measures of success, related survey questions, and other assessments. The subgoals and key measures were copied directly from the libraries' strategic plan (in its narrative format). Next, I read through questions from the libraries' recently completed local Ithaka S+R survey of faculty and students (fall 2015) and from the libraries' previous 2012 user survey (designed in-house). This helped me identify questions from the Ithaka survey that were directly related to library goals and thus might be good assessment choices. I also identified questions from the older user survey that might be useful for this purpose and noted that these questions should be considered for inclusion in the upcoming library user survey scheduled for fall 2016. I added these related survey questions to a new spreadsheet column, including even seemingly tangentially related questions so that we could explore all options in subsequent library-wide discussions.

I then added information about existing assessments of which I was already aware in the "other assessments" column. I also added my initial ideas about potential assessments and left blank space for notes in later meetings. For example, for the goal "Increase and enhance the online delivery of unique, regional primary sources to support scholarship worldwide about the region," its key measure as written in the original strategic plan is "More use of unique, regional content." The assessment notes that I added describe that this can be accomplished by comparing use data for Special Collections from the past few fiscal years, as well as performing a citation analysis of Special and Digital Collections content to see how often our unique resources are used in scholarly research. During this initial planning process, I received informal feedback from the dean, particularly to help fill in my lack of knowledge about specific projects in progress at my new institutional home (see figure 12.1).

Goals / Initiatives	Key Measures of Success	Related Ithaka Questions	Other Assessments
Research, Scholarship and Creative Activity			
Strengthen investment in the Libraries' diverse and multi-format collections to enable the production of high quality, widely disseminated, and influential research, scholarship and creative activities.	Faculty and students judge library collections as sufficient for their research needs.	*Ithaka Faculty MR5: Overall, how would you rate your library's... Collection of research-related materials or content? (1-7 scale)*	
Strengthen investment in the Libraries' diverse and multi-format collections to enable the production of high quality, widely disseminated, and influential research, scholarship and creative activities.	Faculty judge library collections as sufficient for curricular needs.	*Ithaka Faculty MR7: How would you rate your library's... collections of teaching-related materials or content? (1-7 scale)*	
	Library staff programs and priorities are informed by the research lifecycle.	N/A	After Research Planning Committee's lifecycle is complete, compare it to library services, etc. Connect library-offered workshops, instruction, services (other?) to specific points on the research lifecycle.
Increase and enhance the online delivery of unique, regional primary sources to support scholarship worldwide about the region.	More unique, regional content is made available online.	N/A	Special and digital collections data – new collections (compare current cycle to previous).
Increase and enhance the online delivery of unique, regional primary sources to support scholarship worldwide about the region.	More use of unique, regional content.	N/A	Special and digital collections use data (online and print retrieval; compare current cycle to previous); citation analysis of special/digital collections content; focus group or interview with special collections patrons.
	Faculty, graduates and undergraduates value the Libraries' contribution throughout their individual research process.	*Ithaka Faculty Q26: How dependent would you say you are on your college or university library for research you conduct? (1-10 scale)* *Ithaka Faculty Q27a: How important is it that... the library serves as a starting point or "gateway" for locating information for my research? (1-6 scale)*	Also User Satisfaction Survey – Fall 2016?
	More faculty, graduates and undergraduates participate in individual research consultations and group workshops.	N/A	Compare counts of consults and workshops to previous cycles.
	Faculty, graduates and undergraduates are satisfied with individual research consultations and group workshops.	*Ithaka Undergrad Q22 / Grad CA12: Indicate level of agreement... Campus librarians or library staff help me develop the research skills to find and use academic sources of information for my coursework or research projects*	Is Melissa collecting post-consultation assessments? Post-workshop assessments? If so, then we don't need to use the user satisfaction survey. ....User satisfaction survey, Fall 2016. Focus groups or interviews that follow a consult, emails from students/faculty after consults, data on repeat consults from individuals.
Enable the dissemination, preservation and discover of research through Digital Scholarship@UNLV and other platforms.	More content deposited into the institutional repository.	N/A	Compare IR # items deposited to previous cycles.
	Additional colleges and departments deposit scholarly content into the institutional repository.	N/A	Check colleges/depts. depositing into IR to determine if additional have done so (compared to previous cycle).
Journals and their impact factors to use annually for this purpose.		N/A	

ResearchScholarship | StudentAchievement | CommunityPartnerships | Infrastructure | HSL

Figure 12.1
Original spreadsheet, showing strategic goals and initial assessment ideas.

After this stage, I brought the spreadsheets to the senior leadership team (the dean's direct reports, also called "Library Leadership Team" or LLT). I subsequently brought them to Library Council, which is a group of middle managers across the libraries; these meetings are open to all libraries employees and the agendas and minutes are posted internally. After completing the exercise (described below) with both groups, I brought the resulting document back to LLT for further discussion, before finalizing it.

The Exercise: Getting Organizational Input on Assessments

This collaborative, iterative exercise worked similarly with both LLT and Library Council. I printed each spreadsheet on poster-sized paper (roughly three by four feet) and posted them on a wall in the meeting room. Each was printed in a different color to better distinguish each of the five thematic sections (health center, community partnerships, infrastructure, research, and student achievement). I provided the participants with pens and Post-it Notes in five different colors to represent the five library divisions (administration; research and education; cataloging, acquisitions, and discovery; library technologies; and special collections).

Each participant was given a pen and Post-it Notes in his or her division's color. They were asked first to study each spreadsheet and place a blank Post-it Note on any subgoal in which their division was involved. When complete, this provided a clear indication of which divisions were most invested in particular goals and where there was (or should be) collaboration between divisions. This also helped me to quickly check for gaps: any subgoals not identified as belonging to a division (which had no Post-it Notes). After this round, there was a brief discussion of gap areas, collaborations, and related thoughts.

Participants were then asked to read through the spreadsheets a second time and write specific projects (and any planned assessments) related to the subgoals on their Post-it Notes. They were also asked look at subgoals they didn't "own" and write any additional assessment ideas in the "other assessments" column. As in the previous step, in which the absence of Post-it Notes indicated a gap, in this step the absence of text was a clear flag indicating subgoals that lacked specific projects or previously identified assessments (see figure 12.2).

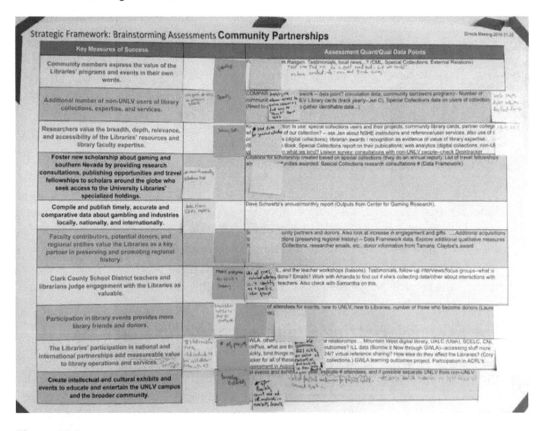

Figure 12.2
Printed spreadsheet marked up with Post-it Notes during library meeting.

In the LLT meeting, this second round was followed by a longer discussion. The senior leadership reviewed all the related survey questions that I identified and chose specific questions to use as assessments (or partial assessments) of particular subgoals. This helped us quickly identify the parts of the Ithaka S+R local survey results that were most relevant to our strategic plan and also helped me determine which questions were most important to include in our fall 2016 user survey. We also reviewed the assessment ideas that had been added to each of the five areas. Those identified as most effective were further developed through a discussion of various metrics and ideas of success for specific projects. These discussions were particularly detailed for goals that were "owned" by more than one library division or related to satisfaction outcomes.

To further illustrate how this worked, I will return to my example for the goal "Increase and enhance the online delivery of unique, regional primary sources to support scholarship worldwide about the region." As stated earlier, its key measure in the strategic plan was "More use of unique, regional content," to which I had added specific assessment notes suggesting a citation analysis of Special and Digital Collections content to see how often our unique resources are used in scholarly research. During the LLT meeting, our Director of Special Collections noted that one of the division's librarians follows up annually with patrons who regularly perform research in Special Collections and provides a bibliography of their work. This bibliography was noted in the division's annual report but hadn't been reported to assessment previously. I edited my assessment notes to refer specifically to this bibliography and made a note to follow up with the librarian about getting a copy each year.

The Library Council meeting involved less discussion of assessment details because of the number of participants. More time was spent on the initial step, identifying department involvement in various subgoals, than had been done in the LLT meeting. This was an important difference, because the council meeting helped identify department-level projects, not all of which had bubbled up to the division level in the LLT meeting. Because this meeting involved a greater number of library personnel, it also built staff familiarity both with the strategic plan and with the goals that were most closely related to specific departments. This helped solidify use of the strategic plan as an active, living document, particularly as this exercise was executed at the halfway stage of the strategic cycle.

The LLT meeting lasted about two hours, with seven participants. The Library Council meeting, which involved less group discussion, lasted about an hour and a half and involved about twenty or so participants. I compiled the notes from these two meetings into a revised version of the spreadsheet, which was discussed further in a subsequent LLT meeting. The end result was two versions of the assessment plan:

1. the final five-tabbed spreadsheet organized by the five goal areas (see figure 12.3), and
2. a second spreadsheet organized by library division (one tab per division), which was more easily actionable for each division director (see figure 12.4 and table 12.1).

Goals / Initiatives	Key Measures of Success	Assessment Quant/Qual Data Points
Community Partnerships		
Offer expert consultations and training in specialized library databases to regional businesses and industries to support economic innovation in southern Nevada.	Community members express the value of the Libraries' programs and events in their own words.	Publicity info from Raegen. Testimonials, local news...? (CML, Special Collections, External Relations)
	Additional number of non-UNLV users of library collections, expertise, and services.	COMPARE - Data Framework -- data point? (circulation data; community borrowers program)-- Number of community who hold UNLV Library cards (track yearly--Jen C). Special Collections data on users of collection. (Need to consider how to gather identifiable data...)
Provide research support, fellowships, and individual consultations to scholars across the globe interested in studying Las Vegas and southern Nevada, and to those who create new forms of scholarship or media based upon UNLV research and library collections and consultations.	Researchers value the breadth, depth, relevance, and accessibility of the Libraries' resources and library faculty expertise.	Kinds of information to use: special collections users and their projects, community library cards, partner colleges--what is their use of our collection? --ask Jen about NSHE institutions and reference/user services, also use of open online collections (digital collections); librarian awards / recognition as evidence of value of library expertise. (Business by the Book, Special Collections report on their publications; web analytics (digital collections, non-UNLV use)); ILL data on what we lend? Liaison survey: consultations with non-UNLV people--check Desktracker (LibAnalytics). GWLA and other consortial participation.
Foster new scholarship about gaming and southern Nevada by providing research consultations, publishing opportunities and travel fellowships to scholars around the globe who seek access to the University Libraries' specialized holdings.	--	Citations for scholarship created based on special collections (they do an annual report). List of travel fellowships and other opportunities awarded. Special Collections research consultations # (DF).
Compile and publish timely, accurate and comparative data about gambling and industries locally, nationally, and internationally.	--	Dave Schwartz's annual/monthly report (Outputs from Center for Gaming Research).
Collaborate with regional organizations and institutions to engage communities in discovering, discussing, studying, and preserving regional history and related issues of concern. Develop partnerships with community leaders, the gaming industry, and regional organizations to collect oral histories, archives, and other primary sources that document their impact and activities.	Faculty contributors, potential donors, and regional entities value the Libraries as a key partner in preserving and promoting regional history.	Survey of community partners and donors. Also look at increase in engagement and gifts. ....Additional acquisitions for special collections (preserving regional history) -- DF data. Explore additional qualitative measures through Special Collections, researcher emails, etc.; donor information from Tamara; Claytee's award
Continuing programming with Clark County School District teachers and librarians to assist them in preparing K-12 students for academic success at a research university.	Clark County School District teachers and librarians judge engagement with the Libraries as valuable.	Outreach, CML, and the teacher workshops (liaisons). Testimonials, follow-up interviews/focus groups--what is already being done? Emails? Work with Amanda to find out if she's collecting data/other about interactions with CLark County teachers. Also check with Samantha on this.
	Participation in library events provides more library friends and donors.	Numbers of attendees for events; new to UNLV, new to Libraries, number of those who become donors (Laurel is tracking this).
Continue to develop national and international partnerships with other research libraries and the library information industry.	The Libraries' participation in national and international partnerships add measureable value to library operations and services.	GWLA, other partnerships/consortial relationships..., Mountain West digital library, UALC (Utah), SCELC, CNI, LinkPlus, what are the measurable outcomes? ILL data (Borrow it Now through GWLA)--accessing stuff more quickly, bind things more cheaply? 24/7 virtual reference sharing? How else do they affect the Libraries? (Cory Tucker for all of these that deal with collections.) GWLA learning outcomes project. Participation in ACRL's Assessment in Action.

+ ≣ ResearchScholarship ▾ StudentAchievement ▾ CommunityPartnerships ▾ Infrastructure ▾ HSL ▾

Figure 12.3
Post-meeting version of spreadsheet, incorporating comments and edits.

Table 12.1
Spreadsheet Reorganized by Division; Example Showing Division with Fewer Assessment Projects

Library Technologies Division - Assessments for Strategic Plan		
Research & Scholarship		
NONE		
Student Achievement		
NONE		
Community Partnerships		
Additional number of non-UNLV users of library collections, expertise, and services.	Assessment: Use Data Framework to compare across years: circulation data, community borrowers program, number of community who hold UNLV Library cards (track yearly--Jen/RED). Special Collections data on users of collection. SC: counts of patron interactions. LibTech: digital collections feedback forms.	Assessment, Tech, SC, RED
Infrastructure		
Users value services from a variety of locations/mobile devices.	Website/database access details (IP addresses off- and on- campus, user-agent string for devices--desktop vs mobile, diff kinds of mobile. devices); count of e-resources available on mobile *Ithaka U-ROL16 / G-ROL16: How often do you access information or resources for your coursework or research projects online from an off-campus location (such as through a proxy server, VPN, or by logging in through your college or university account)?*	Assessment, Tech
Users value 24/7 access to collections and services.	Assessment: Data Framework -- data points on: gate counts/occupancy, room use data, computer use in Library(?). (Data provided by Admin.)	Admin, Tech, Assessment
Respond to user demands for services through assessment and refinement of existing library portals, platforms and virtual services....	WADS usability assessments. Also...Note improvements to library catalog user interface, records, databases, WEBSITE, and other services.	Tech
Library staff are satisfied with the extent of IT infrastructure needed to evolve services.	Consider IT satisfaction survey.	Tech, Assessment
Academic Health Center		
NONE		

Library Administration - Assessments for Strategic Plan		
Research & Scholarship		
Submit additional library grants.	Financial Data Framework: compare number of grants submitted to previous cycle.	Assessment / Admin
Receive more funding from library grants.	Financial Data Framework: compare amount of total grant funding received to previous cycle.	Assessment / Admin
Student Achievement		
Student retention, progression, and completion is influenced by library efforts.	RED: GWLA study data, RPC numbers, learning analytics. Admin: space revision impact on RPC?	RED; Admin
Community Partnerships		
Community members express the value of the Libraries' programs and events in their own words.	Admin: Publicity info from DirComm. (Also, testimonials, local news...?) SC: post-event surveys.	SC, Admin
Participation in library events provides more library friends and donors.	Admin: Numbers of attendees for events; new to UNLV, new to Libraries, number of those who become donors (Laurel tracks this). (To become data points in Data Framework?)	Admin, Assessment
Create intellectual and cultural exhibits and events to educate and entertain the UNLV campus and the broader community.	Admin/SC: List events and exhibits per year. Indicate # attendees, and if possible separate UNLV from non-UNLV.	SC, Admin, Assessment
Infrastructure		
Users value 24/7 access to collections and services.	Assessment (provided by Admin): Gate counts per time of day. (+ Any other ways we gather user comments on library hours.) LibTech: database/website access by time of day.	Admin, Tech, Assessment
Users heavily utilize library facilities.	Assessment: Data Framework -- data points on: gate counts/occupancy, room use data, computer use in Library(?). (Data provided by Admin.)	Assessment, Admin
-- (More financial and in-kind donations from the community.)	Compare donor pipeline development to previous years, progress of donors through pipeline over time. Management plan for major gifts developed (yes/no).	Admin
Address staff space challenges in Lied Library.	Compare staff spaces (# offices, desks/work areas, etc.) before and after renovations. Note square footage added from addition of old Honors College space.	Assessment, Admin
Increase frequency of communication with the campus and the external community to show the Libraries' value and impact.	Note #/frequency of: Between the Lines, other newsletters, press releases, campus-wide emails, other communications. Count number & dates of products. Also note social media presence from SC (work with SC on this).	Assessment, Admin
Academic Health Center		
Participate in curriculum development to embed evidence based practice into problem based learning.	Curriculum review; track library admin/faculty participation?	Admin
Hire a librarian and plan initial library services at the HSL.	Date of hire / budget line; initial service plan completed.	Admin
Develop the space and the technology infrastructure for initial library services.	Basic space/technology infrastructure created.	Admin
Plan an integrated Health Sciences Library in the first academic building of the Medical School for faculty, students, practitioners and the community at large.	Plan for library created.	Admin

+ ▤   Admin ▾   Assessment ▾   CAD ▾   RED ▾   SpecColl ▾   LibTech ▾

Figure 12.4
Spreadsheet reorganized by division, instead of by strategic theme (see tabs at bottom).

Results

These two versions of the assessment plan guided our assessments for the following year. The original full version organized by goal area is primarily for myself, the dean, and as a record for the organization and lists every assessment we perform. This helps me keep track of everything we assess across the organization. Organizing the plan by thematic goal also helps me to keep these top-level goals foremost in my mind and to focus on a holistic, library-wide view. This document also guided my organization of the dean's annual report, which is a calendar-year report on library outcomes. Since this January 2017 report was due six months before the upcoming strategic plan final report, it served as a preview of (and practice for) the final report for the strategic plan. This process helped me narrow down the assessments that are most relevant to our strategic goals, which in turn guided the creation of the second assessment plan, organized by library division.

This second version is for broader use within the library. This assessment plan by division is shorter; it is not as comprehensive, but rather highlights assessments to be used as specific checkpoints for strategic outcomes in our final report at the end of our current strategic plan cycle (summer 2017). This version has helped guide my conversations with division directors and check on progress in their areas. Its shorter length makes it a more manageable document for the organization. We are currently sharing this plan organizationally as a Google Sheet. In our upcoming cycle for 2017–2019, I plan to experiment with Tableau dashboards for the new strategic plan and assessment plans to better align with our growing and dynamic data visualization environment.

Another Cycle: Next Steps

At the time of writing, we are currently using the plan to assess our outcomes at the end of this strategic cycle. Our data will not be complete until the end of the fiscal year, at the end of June 2017, but we're able to assess our progress over the majority of the previous two years. The libraries also need to update or create new strategic and assessment plans. However, as we are currently in the midst of a search for a new Dean of Libraries (expected to start in fall 2017), we are in the process of creating an interim plan. This plan will focus on broad goals without identifying specific projects—to serve as a framework for making decisions that support the university's strategic goals. Many of the broad objectives from our previous strategic plan are transferrable, as the plan was originally designed as more of a decision-making guide than a document outlining specific projects (which are often driven by individual departments or divisions, with the guidance of LLT).

As mentioned above, I plan to experiment with a Tableau dashboard for the new plan that will link both strategic goals and assessments. Our existing data in Tableau will enable me to directly link to data and other outputs from related assessments so that the strategic and assessment plans are immediately tied to updated results. My goal is not only to encourage library faculty and staff to check in regularly on project outcomes, but also to accustom them to using the strategic framework as an active decision-making tool.

Reflection

The most rewarding part of creating the assessment plan has been seeing people across the organization take ownership of and talk about assessments they're already doing. This has made me quite proud of (and excited about) what we have already accomplished in the libraries! Another rewarding aspect of this process has been having an organized plan that has actively guided my work and those of others in the organization. Without it, I would have found it quite difficult to keep track of various assessments and the specific goals that they support. This was particularly easy to do with the plan in spreadsheet form, with everything clearly laid out, instead of buried in long narrative text.

Among the more difficult parts of the process were prompting departments and individuals about projects or assessments that may have fallen through the cracks. This was most common for projects owned by committees or other cross-functional groups. Because I had been at the institution for such a short period of time, I wasn't able to bring any of my own institutional awareness to help, and thus could only read older documents and ask lots of questions. I feel more confident about being able to keep track of projects and assessments in future cycles, when I will be involved from the beginning.

Another difficult aspect was collating (and cognitively processing) notes from the planning exercise with Library Council session. The large number of people involved resulted in a lot of information to process; this was easier with LLT, because it is a smaller group. Finally, finding out about some projects well after they were under way made it hard to determine how to best assess them. Only summative, not formative, assessment was possible for most of these projects when caught at a late stage.

Lessons Learned and Best Practices

- It would be helpful to more directly involve the frontline staff in future plan-ning cycles. Although all library faculty and staff were invited to the Library Council meeting (which is aimed at middle managers), few non-managers attended. During the next strategic planning cycle, I plan to hold an all-library staff workshop-style meeting to work on strategic initiatives and gather input.
- Create a "cheat sheet" version of the final assessment plan to use for reports and strategic planning feedback. Not all assessments can be included in an organization-wide report—at least, not if the report is to be digestible (one to three pages). It was very helpful to me to pre-identify the assessments we plan to use for the reports versus those that are more useful for individual divisions and departments to internally gauge their own success. During the next cycle, I may further pare down this version, as keeping it shorter would be more useful for reports.
- Close the loop with all departments, not just divisions, on their assessments. Even if these department-level assessments are not included in the organiza-tion-wide report, they provide useful insight for departments and should spark conversation with the Assessment Unit.
- Add "checkpoint dates" into the plan to prompt the Assessment Unit to touch base with divisions and departments on their assessments, how they are going, data they have gathered, and so on. This would help avoid a "crunch" at the end of the strategic planning cycle, ensure that surveys are designed and sent

in plenty of time, assist in creating a time line for surveys and other activities, and ensure that data is collected properly from the beginning. I plan to schedule these on an Assessment Unit calendar at the beginning of the next cycle. I am considering checking in with two to four departments a month for general assessment and planning conversations.

Broad Applicability of the Process

This assessment planning process is quite flexible and could be easily adapted to other institutions. The number of input exercise meetings could be adjusted to meet the needs of libraries with vastly different sizes and with different layers and types of organizational structure. Important aspects to keep in mind during the process include:

- What decision-making groups exist in your organization?
- What existing meetings or organizational structures may be good places to seek input?
- Is there an existing process for holding all-library activities or meetings?
  » What options exist for library-wide communication about assessment planning activities?
- If a strategic plan already exists, are the goals in a format in which assessment details can be easily added (short goals, bullet points, spreadsheet, etc.)? If not, what work needs to be done to distill the strategic point to this format? Who should be involved?

Note

1. Bianca Cseke, "UNLV Designated as Hispanic Serving Institution," *UNLV Scarlet and Gray Free Press*, February 22, 2016, http://www.unlvfreepress.com/unlv-designated-as-hispanic-serving-institution/; Keyonna Summers, "UNLV Ranked Second Most Diverse Campus in the Nation," news release, UNLV News Center, September 9, 2015, https://www.unlv.edu/news/release/unlv-ranked-second-most-diverse-campus-nation.

Bibliography

Cseke, Bianca. "UNLV Designated as Hispanic Serving Institution." *UNLV Scarlet and Gray Free Press*, February 22, 2016. http://www.unlvfreepress.com/unlv-designated-as-hispanic-serving-institution/.

Summers, Keyonna. "UNLV Ranked Second Most Diverse Campus in the Nation." News release, UNLV News Center, September 9, 2015. https://www.unlv.edu/news/release/unlv-ranked-second-most-diverse-campus-nation.

Title: Leveraging Research to Guide Fundamental Changes in Learning: A Case Study at Kreitzberg Library, Norwich University

Section 2

Abstract: Despite the arrival of the digital age, explosion of online resources, and proliferation of personal devices, the library remains a vital component of the campus experience. Invested with new and changing blends of program offerings, the library is evolving alongside teaching and learning styles and student expectations. The academic library is poised at the threshold of an uncertain future—book box, archive, student hub, campus nexus, quiet study, active collaboration, classroom, or all of the above—where does the library go from here? Leveraging our database of over seventy-five academic libraries, we guide institutions by marrying trends with their unique cultures.

Keywords: library, academic library, learning environments, classroom

Project focus: assessment methodologies, techniques, or practices; spaces; user behaviors and needs; assessment concepts and/or management; concepts/theory

Results made or will make case for: more funding, improvements in services, improvements in spaces, changes in library policy, proof of library impact and value, decisions about library staffing, how money or resources may be directed

Data needed: Readily available data is built into our database—i.e., hours of operation, undergrad and graduate student populations, volumes in the collection, etc. Site visits to academic libraries document more tailored quantitative data on seat counts, seat types, allied programs, etc.

Methodology: qualitative, quantitative

Project duration: over 5 years

Tool(s) utilized: In-person site visits documenting library programs, seat types, seat quantities, etc. It is a relatively low-tech process requiring man-hours more than anything else.

Cost estimate: $100–$500

Type of institution: college—private, college—public, university—private, university—public; varies

Institution enrollment: < 5,000; As noted, our database captures over seventy-five institutions, so enrollment varies. In terms of the specific case study of Norwich University, it is 2,200.

Highest level of education: varies; as noted, our database captures over seventy-five institutions, so highest level of education provided varies. In terms of the specific case study of Norwich University, it is a master's/professional degree.

Chapter 13

Leveraging Research to Guide Fundamental Changes in Learning

A Case Study at Kreitzberg Library, Norwich University

Richard M. Jones

Context

Questions We Hear

Despite the arrival of the digital age, explosion of online resources, and proliferation of personal devices, the library remains a vital component of the campus experience. Invested with new and changing blends of program offerings, the library is evolving alongside teaching and learning styles and student expectations. The academic library is poised at the threshold of an uncertain future—book box, archive, student hub, campus nexus, quiet study, active collaboration, classroom, or all of the above—where does the library go from here? And what framework is in place to guide these decisions? Librarians, campus planners, presidents, faculty, students, and boards of trustees regularly pose these questions as we enter into a planning and design project for their academic library.

We have learned that empirical data and comparative analysis among a peer group is very well received. Confronted with this challenge, we have gathered firsthand research on the state of the library on campus. Leveraging this research to understand past and present conventions and to speculate about the future, we guide higher education institutions by marrying trends and benchmarks with their unique cultures. No two campuses are alike, and neither are their libraries, but this tool equips us to draw comparisons, look at variation, and ask why.

Our Database

Our database of over seventy-five academic libraries tracks seat count, seat type, allied and resident partners, learning environment types, and other characteristics. The institutions surveyed are predominately New England and eastern seaboard, but we also have gathered information about college and university libraries during our travels across the United States and Canada. Including qualitative assessment alongside these quantitative characteristics lends context to the numbers. Anecdotal information gathered in the process is so critical to interpreting the numbers. For example, one school we visited had a dramatically skewed allocation of student carrels. It was only through conversation that we discovered that the mandatory senior thesis comes with being assigned a carrel in the library for the semester. It is for this reason that we gather our information firsthand.

Slightly more than half of these libraries have not seen significant renovations in over ten years. The balance represents altogether new libraries, or those that have benefited from major renovations in the last decade. We have chosen this ten-year break point as a means of comparing new and old, and the shift between the two is increasingly apparent.

Our database spans public and private institutions, ranging in size from 350 to over 40,000 undergraduate full-time equivalent (FTE) students. Despite this diversity, we find consistent characteristics cutting across our survey.

While many campuses have multiple libraries, capturing specific disciplines or areas of study, our survey is focused on the main library of a campus. We do this to maintain some consistency in our data across institutions. Although specialty libraries (e.g., law, business, art, music, etc.) contribute to the academic profile of an institution, these typically cater to a graduate student population. Our research focus is on undergraduate students as a target audience. That said, we have done targeted studies of specialty libraries to serve a particular client. For example, while working with the University of Vermont Medical School library, we took time to visit a half-dozen regional peer medical school libraries.

A Case Study

To best describe how we apply this research to a client's specific challenges, we will use a case study to demonstrate what this looks like in practice. After completing studies looking at targeted aspects of Kreitzberg Library at Norwich University, Northfield, Vermont, in 2011 and 2012, Jones Architecture was hired for the redesign of the library at large. The existing library was designed in 1991. Although the "bones" of the building—general organization, deferred maintenance, finishes, accessibility, and so on—remained strong, there were programmatic deficiencies that had developed over time as a result of the changing nature of academic libraries. Aspects of the library's operations and program were being left behind, and with each semester that passed, the gate count was declining. The goal of the project was to return the library to its status as a vital resource for students, faculty, and staff and to create a destination gathering place to build community that had been missing on campus.

Communicating Results and Impact

Sharing the Story and Evolving Our Methodology

While presenting our preliminary work to the board of trustees, we were questioned at length. How and why did we arrive at these specific programmatic recommendations? Many of the questions outlined above were asked—challenging the state of the academic library, its role on today's campus, even the relevance of the book itself! We realized that what we were using as our "research" was in fact anecdotal. It lacked rigor and documentation. It was this experience that challenged us to begin developing our database of research. We visited a handful of Norwich University's peer institutions, documented our observations, analyzed our findings, and where appropriate adapted our recommendations to reflect current trends and benchmarks. As a result of this more rigorous process, the board and building committee got fully behind the project and we were able to move forward.

Key Metrics

Seat Count

One significant deficiency that we identified early in the process was purely the seat count within the library. The number of undergraduate FTE who could find a seat in the library was significantly fewer than at peer institutions. Surveys of the campus population confirmed that this had an exponential effect in terms of gate count. There were not enough seats in the library, and as a result, students were less likely to even go to the library to try and seek out a seat. The library seat count was 218 seats, or roughly 10 percent of the undergraduate FTE population. This tracks low against our database in terms of libraries that are more than ten years old (pre-2006), which are more typically tracking at 15 percent. It is well below our database in terms of newer libraries (since 2006), which track at 21 percent. On a campus the size of Norwich University, this gap of 11 percent results in a deficit of 230 seats. Our project remedies this in part, adding 220 seats to the library allocation. This anticipates growth from the current 2,100 students to 2,400 over the next decade, reaching Norwich University's goal of 18 percent of undergraduates able to find a seat in the library. Space and budget

Section 2

constraints limited the expansion of the seating capacity in part, but larger campus goals also played into this decision. Recent renovations to the Wise Campus Center provide significant study space, and future projects with three existing academic buildings and one new academic building will fold in study spaces as part of the program. A more distributed model such as this was deemed more appropriate for Norwich University's campus, allowing them to feel comfortable with the 18 percent target rather than the benchmark 21 percent goal. See figures 13.1 and 13.2.

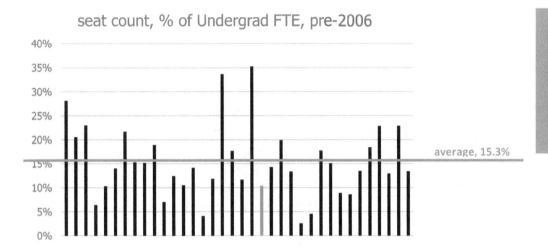

Figure 13.1
Seat count, academic libraries, pre-2006. An average of 15.3 percent of undergraduates can find a seat in the library. Norwich University, our case study, is indicated in blue.

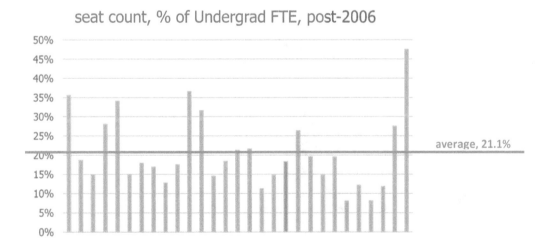

Figure 13.2
Seat count, academic libraries, post-2006. An average of 21.1 percent of undergraduates can find a seat in the library. Norwich University, our case study, is indicated in blue.

Seat Type

You can have as many seats in a library as undergraduates (although that would be a stretch!), but if the blend of seat type is misaligned with student expectations, then they will not be used. Our database tracks six types: desk/carrel, workstation, open table, group study, lounge, and instruction. Desk, carrel, workstation, and lounge are self-explanatory. Open table is the classic image of the reading room—a long table occupied by multiple people either working together on a shared project or working alongside one another on discrete projects. Group study is intended to capture rooms within the library, often with glazed doors or interior glazing allowing transparency, that are for use by groups of four, eight, twelve, or more students. These spaces are typically supported by tools and technology such as a flat screen or a marker board, and so on. Instruction spaces are rooms that are used for teaching. They may be part of a registrar's allocation yet housed within the library. Or they may be for librarians to use as a space for multiple functions: teaching people how to use new technologies, training faculty on new pedagogical approaches, teaching students how to conduct research, or hosting students for review of special collections materials.

In terms of Kreitzberg Library, the blend of seat types was heavily tilted toward the desk/carrel, indicative of libraries of that vintage. There were very few group study rooms, and no instruction spaces. A wide corridor and stacks area had been co-opted by the library staff as an ad-hoc computer classroom. Lounge seating was very limited. Dense stack space dominated multiple floors, although the staff was in the midst of a major project to deaccession materials and find floor area for more seating. Staff levels were also built around an older model that required greater support for periodicals, processing, and other functions. Attrition had left some vacant staff space that was being considered for potential seating.

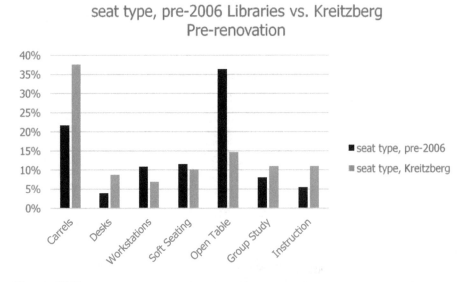

Figure 13.3
Seat Type, academic libraries, pre-2006, compared with Kreitzberg Library pre-renovation.

As figure 13.3 indicates, libraries from pre-2006 tend to be more heavily weighted toward individual study. Desks, carrels, and open table seating dominate the seat type blend, comprising a composite 63 percent of the total seats in this generation of libraries. Workstations are prevalent, as the personal device was still evolving. Group study rooms, lounge seating, and instruction spaces are not as commonplace. Kreitzberg Library was emblematic of this era; carrels and desks alone comprised 47 percent of the existing seat type blend.

When we compare this pre-2007 data with academic libraries from the past decade, we see substantial shifts in the blend of seat types. Open table seating continues as the predominant type. Desks, carrels, and workstations all take dips, reflective of trends in the classroom and pedagogy to develop curriculum around group projects. Instruction space, lounge seating, and group study rooms are all trending upward. These trends are captured in figure 13.4, where we compare current benchmarks to the Kreitzberg Library program and design solution.

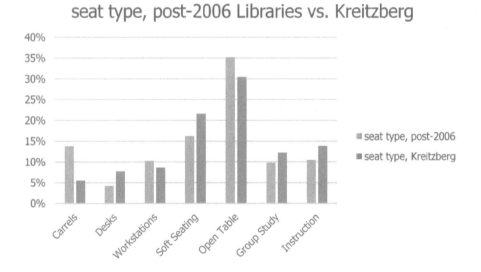

Figure 13.4
Seat type, academic libraries, post-2006, compared with Kreitzberg Library post-renovation.

You will see that we do not align our recommendations for Kreitzberg Library one-to-one with what we see as trends in the marketplace. Data is slippery and can be used to make arguments for and against any number of things. We utilize our research as markers along a spectrum. Institutions may need to augment or reduce seat quantity or one type over another, owing to the specific and unique culture of their place. It may simply be a matter of available space. In the case of Kreitzberg Library, the primary motivation was to increase the quantity of soft seating, open tables, group study rooms, and instruction space at the expense of the carrel seating. This brings Kreitzberg Library into better alignment with typical seat type blends for current academic libraries. See figure 13.5.

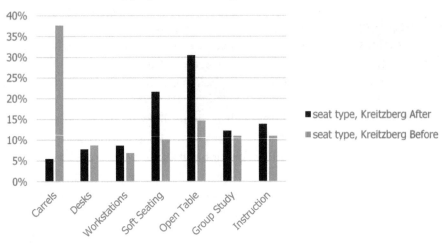

Figure 13.5
Seat type, Kreitzberg Library before and after renovation.

Allied Programs

Academic libraries have always been home to special initiatives, dedicated in-house expertise, research units, and other resident programs. There are common programs found in many libraries: special collections, archives, media (microfilm and microfiche decades ago, now much more broadly speaking), map rooms, art galleries, or multipurpose/event spaces. Many campus libraries host specific research units that are tailored to a collection owned by the library or targeting the research emphasis of an institution, for example the Schuster Institute for Investigative Journalism at Brandeis University, or the Center for Humanistic Inquiry at Amherst College. Students are now supported in myriad ways by special programs often housed within libraries, such as tutoring, writing, counseling, computer/IT help, math, and green room or practice presentation spaces. And faculty are supported by teaching and learning centers where teachers learn to be better instructors.

Kreitzberg Library houses both a counseling center and an academic achievement center. The former supports the emotional well-being of the student population and the latter supports the academic well-being. The academic achievement center is used for specialized testing, tutoring, writing, and general academic support of students regardless of performance level. It helps students to raise levels of achievement regardless of whether they arrive as a struggling student or a high-achieving student. It is also home to the special collections and archives, an important steward of Norwich University's history, and regularly used as a resource for coursework, even hosting classes in the special collections space to review sensitive material. These partner programs remained, although some were modified to better serve new program needs and continue to be instrumental to the life and vitality of the library. Additionally, the counseling and academic achievement centers are now clustered around a shared "commons" area used by students for group study and collaborative work. Testing rooms used by the academic achievement center become group study rooms after hours, making full use of the available space. See figure 13.6.

Figure 13.6
Norwich University, Kreitzberg Library, photo of commons shared by academic achievement center and counseling center. Photo © William Horne 2015.

The gap in terms of partner programs at Kreitzberg Library was primarily with resources for librarians to teach faculty and students. By filling in two floor areas, Norwich University was able to capture two distinct instruction spaces. Conceived as "sandboxes" or "test beds" for teaching and learning, these two instruction spaces had goals that were very different. On the north side of the library, a new space was developed that was intentionally low-tech (see figure 13.7). Flexible tables and chairs, moveable whiteboard easels, and a simple projector and screen allow faculty to change modes from face-forward lecture to group work on the fly. Because the space is flanked by two group study rooms that can accommodate eight students each, faculty are able to break out small teams to these rooms for group work in the course of class and keep an eye on them through interior glazing. On the south side of the library, a more high-tech active learning space was developed (see figure 13.8). With perimeter flat screens, fixed tables, and flexible chairs, this space enables faculty to share content from the main projection screen out to teams or pull team content up to the main screen.

Figure 13.7
Norwich University, Kreitzberg Library, photo of north pod flexible classroom, group study rooms beyond in background. Photo © William Horne 2015.

Figure 13.8
Norwich University, Kreitzberg Library, photo of south pod active learning classroom. Photos © William Horne 2015.

Although primarily intended for use by librarians for teaching strategies, new technologies, and new pedagogical approaches, both rooms quickly became in very high demand from the faculty at large. The library conducted an RFP process requiring faculty to articulate how they would leverage the specific characteristics of each room in their pedagogical approach. As we have seen with other projects focused on learning spaces, such as our work with Harvard University on a pilot classroom for undergraduate classes at Harvard Hall, a debate ensued among faculty about these two spaces. Older faculty trend toward the more low-tech approach. Younger faculty embrace the technology, and we hear that they are "spoiled for other rooms on campus" as a result. This may sound like a generalization, but it is something that we have heard in our post-occupancy follow-up at Harvard University, Northeastern University, and Norwich University in the past several years.

An army marches on its stomach, and so do students. The last allied program that we touch on in this section is the café. Food policy can be a contentious issue in libraries, and justifiably so, with the threat of rodents and the havoc that they can wreak on a collection. However, with libraries dating from the post-2007 era, we do see twenty-nine of the thirty libraries that we have surveyed allowing food and drink of some kind into the building, even if they required it be covered with a lid, or be limited in some other fashion. In fact, most libraries from the past decade have a café on premises to supply caffeine, light food, and other offerings to students throughout the day and late into the night. Although Norwich University's predominately military culture is driven in large part by the ritual of "mess hall" and dining at Wise Campus Center, the new café in Kreitzberg Library offers a destination to fill the gaps around routine meals (see figures 13.9 and 13.10).

Figure 13.9
Norwich University, Kreitzberg Library, photo of café and lounge seating at new entry.
Photo © William Horne 2015.

Section 2

Figure 13.10
Norwich University, Kreitzberg Library, photo of booth and lounge seating at new entry, adjacent to café. Photo © William Horne 2015.

Service Point and Administration

The existing service points at Kreitzberg Library were originally dispersed. A main circulation desk was positioned immediately adjacent to the main entry, with reference desk and other librarians dispersed around the building. The reconfiguration afforded an opportunity to consolidate library administration, which allows for more efficient operations and workflow. Moreover, administrative services are located behind a single service point, where cross-trained personnel are able to answer general questions of all types and reach out to librarians for more specialized questions (see figure 13.11). This approach is mirrored in our database of peer institutions.

Figure 13.11
Norwich University, Kreitzberg Library, photo of centralized service point. Photos © William Horne 2015.

Summary

Although our database captures other information, such as hours of operation, volumes, periodicals, vintage or renovation history, and detailed notes on partner programs, these four points (addressing quantity and blend of seat type, complementary allied programs, and service point and operations) were the most critical touchstones for our work with Norwich University and central to our planning effort and the transformation of Kreitzberg Library.

Outcomes

Gate Count

Although not the only measure, gate count is certainly one indicator of vitality and success. In the two years prior to the renovation, 2013 and 2014, Kreitzberg Library saw year-over-year declines averaging 15 percent. In the fall 2015 semester, the year-over-year gate count in September, October, and November increased by 35 percent, not including almost 7,000 people that entered from the adjoining museum (note: there was not a people tracker on the museum entrance in prior years so we are excluding it from the data set). For the month of December 2015, which of course includes exam period and is historically one of the most heavily trafficked months, the gate count against the previous year was up 83 percent.

Utilization

While the library has not conducted a formal assessment of how long each visit to the library has increased (there was little or no data on this prior to the renovation for comparison's sake), anecdotal information shows a very noticeable increase in "length of stay" for students. A study was undertaken in fall 2016 by the library of student utilization of various spaces. This ranked some twenty-five spaces into three clusters—ten heavily used, ten middle ground, and five least used areas. The most heavily used areas are without a doubt group study spaces of all kinds—rooms, clusters of lounge furniture at whiteboards, and media viewing. Open table areas, booth seating, and soft seating areas fall into the middle ground. More physically isolated quiet study spaces and bar seating in the café were least used.

Instruction Spaces

Utilization of the classroom spaces compared favorably to the university average. Utilization rate of all classrooms on campus averages 44 percent of total class time, and the Kreitzberg Library classrooms averages 55 percent. Plus, the classrooms are reserved for many hours for use by librarians for their instruction to faculty and students, which is not accounted for in the registrar allocation. Each semester since fall 2015 has seen an increase in the number of faculty submissions for use of the rooms. Moreover, these rooms are being used as "sandboxes" and exploratory spaces for faculty and administration. Providing an environment where faculty can work with the library to explore teaching methodology and approach informs other projects on campus. In the case of Kreitzberg Library, these spaces are being used to evaluate classroom design in advance of renovations to three academic buildings and one major new building on campus.

Leveraging the Findings

We continue to get post-occupancy feedback from Norwich University on the state of Kreitzberg Library: what works, what doesn't, and speculation as to why. This comes in the form of anecdotal feedback, testimonials, and actual studies of space utilization and gate count. With other work on campus at the moment, we often stop by and look in for ourselves to see things firsthand. For the purposes of our research, we see this as a feedback loop that cycles back and informs recommendations to our clients. As noted above, each institution is unique and no library should necessarily track in line with our database benchmarks one-to-one. It is the overlay of this research, with anecdotal observations, and the unique culture of the place that results in a tailored solution.

Reflection

Key Collaborations

Throughout the process, we leaned on any number of people at Norwich University. The registrar played a role in evaluating classroom typologies available on campus and where gaps existed, as well as utilization rates. The building committee and library staff had a vision of a revitalized place of research, learning, study, and socialization that could not have been realized in full without their help. The student body has been active in the process, in terms of early surveys, and participating in town hall and design meetings, as well as post-occupancy feedback. The Norwich University facilities team and administration pushed the design team to validate our recommendations through a rigorous peer assessment process in 2012, and that initially set us on a course of research that has added value to our consultancy.

Lessons Learned

- The value of surveys cannot be overestimated. To get well-rounded representation, canvass all of the populations that you are serving (faculty, student, staff, and administration). Questions should be subjected to trial runs and drafts and need to be asked in specific ways. For example, don't ask people to rate the importance of twenty-five projects. Ask them to spend $100 on twenty-five projects. This way you clearly see what rises to the top, and they are forced to create priorities.
- Build adequate time into the construction and training schedule for technology in the classroom. Allow time for installing, testing, commissioning, training, and troubleshooting—all of which needs to happen in a dust-free setting after

construction is complete. Faculty cannot expect to walk into a high-tech active learning classroom on day one and hit the ground running; they need training!

- Beyond training, faculty need to understand that teaching in an active learning setting is fundamentally different from the face-forward lectures that they created five years ago and have been tweaking and adjusting since. It is a rethink of how to deliver content to students. Class sessions are composed of recorded lecture content that students watch in advance, short face-forward lectures delivered in class, team projects (digital or analog), group discussion, and individual work. This requires faculty to create new content and build coursework for this pedagogical approach.

- A diverse blend of seat types is important. It is equally important to zone and distribute these within the building. The mezzanine should not be all a single seat type—all open tables, for example. Provide a diverse blend of seat types, distributed in a diverse manner, but clearly zoned within the building.

- The concept of "see and be seen" so often leveraged in campus centers and other student life settings has made the leap over to libraries. What we refer to as "social learning," or groups of students sitting together, with multiple devices, working on discrete projects, is dominating library space. So much of this generation is about being together while you are doing things. That is being reflected in the space, furniture, and amenities.

What's Next?

- The pendulum has swung about as far as it can (without snapping off) toward group work, collaborative study, and social learning. Most libraries have retained quiet study floors intermingled with stack space through this trend away from solitary work. Recently, we have begun to see greater reaction to this trend. Libraries have started incorporating quiet study rooms, often nested within more open floor plates composed of group work areas. North Carolina State's D. H. Hill Library renovation includes a glass-fronted *silent* room at the first floor along the main circulation spine. This allows for the visibility of the library, while insuring silence—meaning not even keyboard clatter—for those students that need it.

- Versatile spaces, easily adaptable from one mode to another while maintaining their intrinsic character, are instrumental to the future viability of the library.

- New partnerships are forming every day within academic libraries—classrooms, visualization environments, makerspaces, and digital scholarship, to name a few.

- The library should support the student in myriad ways: as a social destination, a home of teaching and learning, and a place of research. It should be a place for people with information in it, not the other way around. Today's academic library should be an active site of social engagement, discovery, and knowledge sharing and creation.

Section 2

Title: Answering the Question before It's Asked: Building a Library Impact Dashboard

Abstract: This chapter presents how DiMenna-Nyselius Library at Fairfield University successfully created an impact dashboard that demonstrates the value of the library to its institutional stakeholders, including the CFO, provost, and faculty. It focuses on the creation process and advice for replication. Questions explored are Who is our audience? What story do we want to tell? What data is available? Practical strategies on grouping pre-existing data to tell a story aligned with institutional goals are presented. Possible formats are offered, including simple static dashboards using LibGuides to more advanced real-time updating dashboards requiring programming knowledge to interface with systems.

Keywords: impact dashboard, value, data, marketing, strategic planning, academic library

Project focus: organizational practices (i.e., strategic planning); data use and technology; assessment concepts and/or management

Results made or will make case for: proof of library impact and value, how money or resources may be directed

Data needed: Data displayed by the impact dashboard includes circulation statistics, faculty surveys, information literacy statistics, and database usage statistics.

Methodology: quantitative, dashboard; Focus is less on the methodology used to generate the data and instead on the development of an impact dashboard and its importance as an information management tool that is used to display metrics and other key data points to simplify complex data sets and communicate the library's value.

Project duration: less than 3 months

Tool(s) utilized: Data source tools included digital gate counters, Google Analytics, instruction and reference analytics, MISO results, and COUNTER statistics. Technology: web authoring content management system. Also PHP, SQL, and JavaScript language were employed for advanced real-time displays.

Cost estimate: < $100

Type of institution: university—private

Institution enrollment: 5,000–15,000

Highest level of education: master's/professional degree

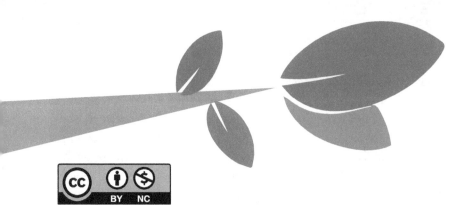

CC BY NC

Chapter 14

Answering the Question before It's Asked

Building a Library Impact Dashboard

Jacalyn Kremer and Robert Hoyt

Imagine you have a new chief financial officer or president at your college or university who upon arriving on campus wonders aloud why a library is still needed in the twenty-first century. Are you prepared to answer the question, succinctly and efficiently? This was the situation confronted by DiMenna-Nyselius Library at Fairfield University in 2015.

Context

DiMenna-Nyselius Library serves the research needs of approximately 4,000 undergraduates and 1,000 graduate students at Fairfield University, a private Jesuit university in Fairfield, Connecticut. The library currently employs twenty-one full-time staff members, thirteen of whom are professional librarians. Prior to 2014, none of the staff was formally tasked with assessment. This changed in July 2014 when the new position of Assessment Librarian was created at the DiMenna-Nyselius Library. This change was in response to the national zeitgeist in higher education where there was an increased demand for developing and sustaining a culture of assessment. This demand was fueled by rising tuition prices, staggering student debt, and shrinking state budgets, all of which contributed to calls for financial accountability. At the same time, parents, students, federal and state governments, and accreditation agencies were calling for colleges and universities to prove their efforts resulted in student learning. At our own institution, Fairfield University was undergoing a strategic planning process in 2014 that focused, in part, on developing an economically sustainable business model incorporating outcomes-based decision-making and operational efficiencies as well as on assessing student learning outcomes.[1] In response to demands for assessment and accountability on the local and national levels, the new assessment librarian was tasked with engaging in Fairfield University's strategic plan process in order to align the library's work with the university's goals and develop a library culture of assessment.

Building a Foundation

The first task of the new assessment librarian was to institute an assessment team. In selecting who would be invited to participate, special emphasis was placed on including librarians from all areas of the library. Why was it important to have a diverse team composition? The objective of the Assessment Team was not in collecting the data per se, but to *act* on the data in a systematic way to improve services, enhance collections, develop the library's human resources, and align library activities with the university's strategic plan. The diverse composition of the Assessment Team provided the broad support and buy-in necessary for coordination of disparate assessment efforts and the opportunity to combine data, analyze it holistically, and, perhaps most importantly, *act* to produce systematic changes.

Led by the assessment librarian, the group convened with the aspirational goal of operating as a community of practice—a group of people "who share a concern or a passion for something they do and learn how to do it better as they interact regularly."[2] The first several meetings of the Assessment Team focused on establishing this community of practice through discussions based on shared readings about the status of assessment in academic libraries and higher education. The Assessment Team spent three months of intensive readings and discussions[3] using the Process Learning Circle Format, wherein a meeting has four phases: ordered sharing, reflective study, commitment to action, and regrouping.[4] These discussions allowed us to establish a shared baseline of assessment knowledge and to explore together these two fundamental questions:

- Why build a culture of assessment?
- What value does the library bring to our university, and can this value be measured?

Turning Data into Story

Like most academic libraries, the DiMenna-Nyselius Library collected large amounts of data, but most of our data was neither publicly available nor easily shared. The library dean challenged the assessment team to develop a new outlook on data and requested that the assessment team create a public-facing data display to tell the DiMenna-Nyselius Library's story and demonstrate its value to its stakeholders. What might that public-facing data display look like? To find out, the assessment team surveyed the academic library landscape to see how other academic libraries were presenting data to communicate their value. The Assessment Team selected and analyzed other libraries' efforts at data displays, with open discussions guided by the following questions:

1. Who is the audience of the data display?
2. Does the data display communicate the library's value? If so, what value is highlighted?
3. Is there a central story line of the data display?
4. What key metrics do they focus on?

Through our discussions and analysis of other data displays, the Assessment Team decided the primary audience for our data display would be senior administrators and faculty. Next, we brainstormed what contributions the library made to our university community and what story these contributions tell about our library. Many on the Assessment Team were active participants in the university's strategic planning process, and they embraced the idea of aligning the library's work with the university's strategic plan and using the data display to highlight this alignment. This focus on the university's strategic plan drove the story we hoped to tell and the key metrics we selected. It also helped shape the data display format itself as we explored this question: What data display format is most effective in providing a high-level, strategic view of an organization?

In analyzing other libraries' data displays, the team made sure to explore four formats: the balanced scorecard, return on investment (ROI), value calculators where dollar values are calculated for core library services, and digital dashboard.[5] The first three approaches incorporate a financial component, quantifying in dollars the contributions of the academic library. Frank discussions occurred during team meetings on whether it was "possible to create an expression of the full worth of the academic research library based on the measurement of both tangible and intangible value."[6] Ultimately, the Assessment Team rejected the first three approaches, in part because we felt there were significant drawbacks in communicating the library's value predominantly in economic terms.[7] Instead, the Assessment Team envisioned an approach focused on the library's contribution to the university's core missions of student learning and faculty research, which does not always directly map to a dollar figure.

After eliminating the financial-related display formats, the Assessment Team decided to adopt a digital dashboard design. For our purposes, we define the term *dashboard*, using the definition of Stephen Few, an expert on dashboard design, as "a visual display of the most important information needed to achieve one or more objectives, consolidated and arranged on a single screen so the information can be monitored at a glance."[8] Dashboards can be categorized as analytical, operational or strategic.[9] An analytical dashboard allows data interaction and offers context, such as past years' data. An operational dashboard's goal is to monitor operations, and its design is usually dynamic. A strategic dashboard focuses on high-level performance indicators that, when displayed, can be easily correlated to an organization's strategic goals. Since the Assessment Team wanted to align the data display with the university strategic plan, we chose a public-facing strategic dashboard as the best approach in communicating library *impact* to senior administrators and faculty. We named our digital display the Library Impact Dashboard.

Creating the Dashboard

Prior to creating the dashboard, whenever we had to gather data for a larger purpose (e.g., the annual report), we utilized a kitchen sink approach—we provided everything we had, just because we had it. The process of creating the dashboard forced us to be discriminating with the data we selected to display. First, we reviewed the university's six goals or "essential priorities" in the new strategic plan and identified the following essential priorities that aligned most closely with the library's core services: "Student Learning," "Innovations in Operations," and "Renewing a Sense of Community."[10] We modified the titles of these three essential priorities to arrive at three categories of data to include in the Impact Dashboard: Student Learning, Organizational Responsiveness, and Research Central. We added a fourth category of Faculty Research and Teaching in order to speak to our faculty audience. The Assessment Team then began the collaborative process of looking at the large amount of data we generate and selecting the indicators that best fit in each category to prove our contributions to the larger institution, mindful that a common mistake is to include too many indicators that do not gauge strategic goals.[11] The selection process for indicators greatly benefited from the varied viewpoints offered by the diverse team members, resulting in indicators that reflect the efforts of all staff.

Through our review of other libraries' data displays, we found that the most effective displays tended to be the ones that were succinct and targeted for audiences outside of the library. This meant we had to avoid as much jargon as possible and include figures that could be easily interpreted at first glance. The Assessment Team concurred that the most effective displays reviewed were ones that attempted to directly relate library statistics to their impact on the university community. This led us away from our past practice of relying on a counting-stuff approach to one that attempts to get at what effect we have. For example, instead of showing how many books are in our collection and how many databases we have, we choose data that shows how many books were read and how many articles were downloaded. This new perspective of using data to show impact was critical in telling an effective story to senior administrators and was an important shift in perspective for the Assessment Team.

Whatever the goals of the dashboard project, the design of it had to be complementary to the content because a dashboard with no cohesive theme—a jumble of numbers and figures—cannot be persuasive. We decided to structure our Impact Dashboard into four sections, each representing one of the categories mentioned previously that were derived from the university strategic plan. Simple statements of facts acted as the building blocks of each section. Each fact was a single sentence expressing a statistic about the library, which we would date and link to the resource it was discussing (see figure 14.1). The links to the resource discussed in the statistic doubled as advertisement for our myriad services that the audience may not be aware of, thereby demonstrating our impact both through informing readers that a service exists and how much said service is utilized. This was determined to be necessary because, often, senior administrators are not fully cognizant of all the services provided by the library.

Throughout the conception of this Impact Dashboard, the currency of the information was always a concern. In reviewing other universities' displays, we found that outdated information diminished the quality of many of the statistics present, especially when dealing with rapidly changing sectors like e-book usage. This led us to include dates for each fact on the Impact Dashboard. Inclusion of the dates provided the audience with a sense of currency, but it also provided the Assessment Team with a built-in deadline because we did not want any statistics to be more than one year old. Featuring the dates concurrently with the library facts forces us to revisit the page throughout the year to ensure that this snapshot of the library does not become outdated. Additionally, it embodies the spirit of transparency that the university's strategic plan wishes to employ across the institution.

While investigating how to host the Impact Dashboard, we considered LibGuides and the university's content management system, TERMINALFOUR. We chose TERMINALFOUR because it allowed more freedom in design and layout of the content and provided the ability to add automation in the future, and we had staff proficient with HTML and CSS. This freedom allowed us to lay out our four categories on one page with supporting statistics in a grid underneath each heading (see figure 14.1) and granted us the opportunity to pull some data in real time. The grid that this formed has plenty of white space and allowed readers to quickly and easily process the information without much cognitive load. The aesthetics of the Impact Dashboard were analogous to the style of the rest of the library website so that it would be representative of the organization. We conceived the design of each of the four category sections as a large header with a background photograph and the text of the essential priority overlaid. We chose each of the photographs because they related directly to the priority they were accompanying and they were readily available. For example, a picture of a student and a reference librarian at our reference desk represented our Student Learning category section. This image was chosen because the reference desk, along with our reference instruction, are the main points of contact between students and librarians, and these points reinforce, in a concrete way, the idea of library staff impacting students. Underneath each image, we decided to place a tagline or quote that links the university priority directly to the library. For example, the Student Learning priority tagline was "Advancing Student Research Skills." The Assessment Team then mined the data collected from our information literacy classes and individual research appointments to select statistics that most clearly show this connection. The tagline acts as a bridge from the category to the statistics and helps the audience map our impact directly to the university's stated priorities (see figure 14.1).

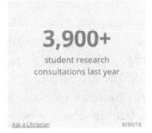

Figure 14.1
The Student Learning section of the Library Impact Dashboard.

For the first iteration of the Impact Dashboard, we used the data on hand. Prospectively, we intentionally implemented methods to collect data that we did not have readily available but wanted to include in future iterations of the Impact Dashboard. In addition to collecting information for the next version, we considered our current processes for collecting data and how we could improve said processes to facilitate a more agile dashboard. Automating the collection of statistics from our gate counter was one of the improvements that came out of this planning. Previously, we would have to manually check to see the gate counter data, tabulate, and then input the statistics into the dashboard to update it. We set up a PHP script that fetches the hourly gate counts and writes the counts to a relational database every day. In the Impact Dashboard, we were able to leverage this automation by having the dashboard display visitor counts to the library that update automatically each day. We chose to have the Impact Dashboard show the number of visitors to the library in the past year on a rolling basis. As a side benefit, since setting up the gate counter logs to be recorded regularly, we have been able to analyze them with more granularity and use them to adapt our schedule to our students' needs (see table 14.1 for data points included in the Impact Dashboard, and see figure 14.2 for another example of a category section).

Table 14.1
Impact Dashboard Categories and Data Points

Categories	Data Point 1	Data Point 2	Data Point 3
Student Learning	# of research classes with number of students in attendance in past year	# of views of our library-produced online research guides in past year	# of student research consultations in past year

Faculty Research and Teaching	# of downloads of faculty work from institutional repository in past year	% of faculty who feel working with a librarian contributes to their research	% of faculty who are satisfied with library services
Organizational Responsiveness	# of e-books checked out in past year and total # of e-books in collection	# of streaming films	# of articles downloaded from # of databases
Research Central	# of visits to the library in the past year	# of students who used 24/7 computer lab last month	# of online visitors to our library website last year

Figure 14.2
Faculty Research and Teaching section of the Library Impact Dashboard. To see full dashboard, visit https://www.fairfield.edu/library/about/assessment/dashboard/.

In the future, more of our statistics will be collected automatically and the Impact Dashboard will pull from the most recent data on demand. This will remove the onus of updating the Impact Dashboard regularly and will make the information present more timely. We set up a MySQL database in order to store data at regular intervals for statistics from various sources such as circulation, gate counts, reference desk usage, and card entry swipes. This MySQL database can be queried on demand and provide near real-time information in the future for the Impact Dashboard. In addition to easing the maintenance of the Impact Dashboard, this automation will improve our ability to assess and analyze library statistics on a more regular basis.

Communicating Results and Impact

In late March 2015, as we put the final tweaks on the Impact Dashboard, the provost told our library dean that a senior administrator, new to education, was questioning the necessity of having an academic library in the digital age. Within twenty-four hours of hearing these concerns, we were able to publish the Library Impact Dashboard on the library website and send a link to the provost for her to share with the president's office and senior administrators. The new senior administrator was impressed with the breadth of our work and the value we bring, as well as our ability to respond with relevant data so quickly. In this case, the single link to our Impact Dashboard told the new administrator more about our work and the role an academic library can play to advance the university mission than a multipage report. We were successful in designing a dashboard that communicated the library's value to its audience using a careful balance of data, text, and images that engage and inform.

The library homepage highlights and links to the Library Impact Dashboard, making it available to all who are interested. One by-product of creating the Impact Dashboard is that it gives library staff one place to see all of the important work of the library showcased; it tells the story of the whole library, reflecting the efforts of all staff. It is the "elevator speech" in dashboard form. It is a unifying document all library staff can point to and know their efforts contributed to the results.

The Assessment Team revisits the Impact Dashboard at annual report time each year and reviews it at regularly scheduled meetings. We look to see if there are any changes—positive or negative—in our major indicators. We close the assessment loop by asking if the data requires us to take actions for improvement. The Assessment Team continues to have a diverse makeup of committed library staff who have the agency to take action.

The Assessment Team annually considers whether it should add new indicators to the dashboard and whether old ones are no longer relevant. This annual process allows us to recraft the story as needed each year based on new scans of the university environment. As our own university's priorities change, we modify the Impact Dashboard to align with those priorities, as well as with national higher education challenges. It is vital that the dashboard be flexible and easily changeable in order to continue to be tied into the university's evolving strategic plan.

We are able to leverage the work we did in selecting the indicators to other areas. We reuse the indicators created for the dashboard by inserting them into communications with senior administrators and faculty. For example, we repackage the data displayed on the Impact Dashboard as an infographic for the annual report, and we feature the Impact Dashboard on our digital signage in the library lobby.

Reflection

The Library Impact Dashboard was born from the Assessment Team, and our team approach was crucial in its creation. The diverse composition of the team allowed for various viewpoints, albeit with competing priorities at times. The competing priorities were actually a boon to the development of the library story because it aided in the establishment of a more complete narrative that touched on all aspects of the library, not just the ones most visible to patrons and administrators. The process itself of creating an impact dashboard can be positive, as the team members create and work towards a shared strategic goal bringing together disparate sections of the library that may not often interact.

It is critical to decide early in the process of creating a dashboard who the audience will be. If the audience is senior administrators outside the academic library, linking the library dashboard to the university's strategic plan or goals is especially important. Language selection that mirrors the language used by the university administration becomes essential. A benefit of DiMenna-Nyselius Library aligning our Impact Dashboard with the university's strategic plan is that it positions the library as a team player and one willing to engage with senior administrators on strategic direction initiatives.

In our daily work, it can be easy to not see the forest for the trees and be bogged down with massive data sets. Isolating, publishing, and reviewing major indicators helps us to stay focused on our primary initiatives that have the most impact on our community.

Notes

1. Fairfield University, *Fairfield 2020*, strategic plan (Fairfield, CT: Fairfield University, 2015), 15, https://www.fairfield.edu/hostedfiles/documents/Fairfield2020_TheWayForward.pdf.
2. Etienne Wenger-Trayner and Beverly Wenger-Trayner, "Introduction to Communities of Practice," Wenger-Trayner.com, 2015, http://wenger-trayner.com/introduction-to-communities-of-practice/.
3. Important readings include the following: Association of College and Research Libraries, *The Value of Academic Libraries,* researched by Megan Oakleaf (Chicago: Association of College and Research Libraries, 2010), http://www.ala.org/acrl/sites/ala.org.acrl/files/content/issues/value/val_report.pdf; Association of College and Research Libraries *Connect, Collaborate, and Communicate*, prepared by Karen Brown and Kara J. Malenfant (Chicago: Association of College and Research Libraries, 2012), http://www.ala.org/acrl/sites/ala.org.acrl/files/content/issues/value/val_summit.pdf; and, Meredith Gorran Farkas, "Building and Sustaining a Culture of Assessment: Best Practices for Change Leadership," *Reference Services Review* 41, no. 1 (2013): 13–31, https://doi.org/10.1108/00907321311300857.
4. Geoffrey Caine and Renate Nummela Caine, *Strengthening and Enriching Your Professional Learning Communit* (Alexandria, VA: ASCD, 2010), 37–38.
5. For an example of the balanced scorecard approach, see Case Western Reserve University, "Balanced Score Card," Kelvin Smith Library, accessed February 9, 2018, http://library.case.edu/ksl/aboutus/assessment/bsc/. To learn more about return on investment (ROI) approach, see Bruce Kingma and Kathleen McClure, "Lib-Value: Values, Outcomes, and Return on Investment of Academic Libraries, Phase III: ROI of the Syracuse University Library," *College and Research Libraries* 76, no. 1 (January 2015): 63–80, https://journals.acrl.org/index.php/crl/article/view/16402. To see an example of a value calculatorsee "Library Value Calculation Experiment 2009," Cornell University Library, Assessment and Communication, accessed February 15, 2018, https://ac.library.cornell.edu/value.
6. Stephen J. Town and Martha Kyrillidou, "Developing a Values Scorecard," *Performance Measurement and Metrics* 14, no. 1 (2013): 11.
7. Association of College and Research Libraries, *Value of Academic Libraries*, 6–7.

Section 2

8. Stephen Few, "Dashboard Design: Taking a Metaphor Too Far," *DM Review* 15, no. 3 (2005): 18, Academic OneFile.
9. Stephen Few, *Information Dashboard Design* (Sebastopol, CA: O'Reilly Media, 2006), 40–42.
10. Fairfield University, *Fairfield 2020*, 1.
11. Michael K. Allio, "Strategic Dashboards: Designing and Deploying Them to Improve Implementation," *Strategy and Leadership* 40, no. 5 (2012): 26, https://doi.org/10.1108/10878571211257159.

Bibliography

Allio, Michael K. "Strategic Dashboards: Designing and Deploying Them to Improve Implementation." *Strategy and Leadership* 40, no. 5 (2012): 24–31. https://doi.org/10.1108/10878571211257159.

Association of College and Research Libraries. *Connect, Collaborate, and Communicate: A Report from the Value of Academic Libraries Summits.* Prepared by Karen Brown and Kara J. Malenfant. Chicago: Association of College and Research Libraries, 2012. http://www.ala.org/acrl/sites/ala.org.acrl/files/content/issues/value/val_summit.pdf.

———. *The Value of Academic Libraries: A Comprehensive Research Review and Report.* Researched by Megan Oakleaf. Chicago: Association of College and Research Libraries, 2010. http://www.ala.org/acrl/sites/ala.org.acrl/files/content/issues/value/val_report.pdf.

Caine, Geoffrey, and Renate Nummela Caine. *Strengthening and Enriching Your Professional Learning Community: The Art of Learning Together.* Alexandria, VA: ASCD, 2010.

Case Western Reserve University. "Balanced Score Card." Kelvin Smith Library. Accessed Feburary 8, 2018. http://library.case.edu/ksl/aboutus/assessment/bsc/.

Fairfield University. *Fairfield 2020: The Way Forward.* Strategic plan. Fairfield, CT: Fairfield University, 2015. https://www.fairfield.edu/hostedfiles/documents/Fairfield2020_TheWayForward.pdf.

Farkas, Meredith Gorran. "Building and Sustaining a Culture of Assessment: Best Practices for Change Leadership." *Reference Services Review* 41, no. 1 (2013): 13–31. https://doi.org/10.1108/00907321311300857.

Few, Stephen. "Dashboard Design: Taking a Metaphor Too Far." *DM Review* 15, no. 3 (2005): 18, 67. Gage Academic OneFile.

———. *Information Dashboard Design.* Sebastopol, CA: O'Reilly Media, 2006.

Kingma, Bruce, and Kathleen McClure. "Lib-Value: Values, Outcomes, and Return on Investment of Academic Libraries, Phase III: ROI of the Syracuse University Library." *College and Research Libraries* 76, no. 1 (January 2015): 63–80. https://journals.acrl.org/index.php/crl/article/view/16402.

Town, Stephen J., and Martha Kyrillidou. "Developing a Values Scorecard." *Performance Measurement and Metrics* 14, no. 1 (2013): 7–16.

Wenger-Trayner, Etienne, and Beverly Wenger-Trayner. "Introduction to Communities of Practice." Wenger-Trayner.com, 2015. http://wenger-trayner.com/introduction-to-communities-of-practice/.

Section 2

Title: Closing the Gap: The Library in Academic Program Review

Abstract: Academic program review drives changes in the curriculum and the budget. By becoming involved in these reviews, libraries can integrate better with the curriculum process, justify budget requests related to identified deficiencies, and plan for programmatic and regional accreditation reviews. Because administrators closely examine these documents, the impact of participation can be particularly significant, providing the library with a unique opportunity to demonstrate value with relatively little effort. Academic program review can also provide an important opportunity for libraries to "close the gap" in assessment, making improvements to services and collections based on internal self-study and external peer review.

Keywords: academic program review, collection development, accreditation, report templates, assessment planning, institutional effectiveness, small library assessment, library services assessment, data management, core collection, collection analysis

Project focus: organizational practices (i.e., strategic planning); collections; spaces; services (i.e., customer service at reference desk); data use and technology; assessment concepts and/or management

Results made or will make case for: more funding, improvements in services, improvements in spaces, improvements in collections, changes in library policy, proof of library impact and value, a strategic plan or process, decisions about library staffing, how money or resources may be directed

Data needed: collection, service, and usage statistics by program or subject

Methodology: quantitative, evaluation or survey

Project duration: less than 3 months

Tool(s) utilized: LibInsight, Excel, LibQual, Bowker Book Analysis System, ACRL*Metrics*

Cost estimate: $100–$500

Type of institution: university—public

Institution enrollment: < 5,000

Highest level of education: master's/professional degree

Chapter 15

Closing the Gap
The Library in Academic Program Review

Bridgit McCafferty and Dawn Harris

Context

Texas A&M University-Central Texas (A&M-Central Texas) is one of the smaller universities in the Texas A&M system. We have been in existence for seven years and are newly accredited. Over this time, we have had the unique opportunity to create new processes for established academic practices, including academic program review. Program review is the method institutions use to complete internal and external assessment of their degree programs. This ensures that they are aligned with best practices across the academic field, spurring changes that ultimately advance the achievement of identified student learning outcomes. Though many libraries participate in cocurricular review of their collections and services, most are not involved in program review for academic departments. If they are, it is often through a simple collection analysis.

This lack of involvement is reflected in the library literature. Not much is written about the topic, though there are a few contributions that are important: the case study, "Undergraduate Program Review Processes," by Costella and colleagues in particular.[1] These authors advocate for a holistic approach to academic program review that includes all aspects of library services. Schwartz, in "The University Library and the Problem of Knowledge," argues that library involvement in academic program review is an effective way to show that collections contribute to the strategic goals of the research university.[2] Other authors—for instance, Pancheshnikov, in "Course-Centered Approach to

Evaluating University Library Collections for Instructional Program Reviews," and Loo and Dupuis, in "Organizational Learning for Library Enhancements"—provide insight into the way that libraries can assess support for individual programs through collection analysis and other data.[3] Taken together, these articles provide a compelling case for the importance of library involvement in academic program review using holistic assessment measures that look at all aspects of library support.

At A&M-Central Texas, we started thinking about this topic when, in 2012, the university designed the process now used for academic program review. The new method aligned with the work of Bresciani in *Outcomes-Based Academic and Co-curricular Program Review.*[4] At the same time, the university was also pursuing initial Southern Association of Colleges and Schools Commission on Colleges (SACSCOC) accreditation. Part of the accreditation standards required institutions to show that they sufficiently support each academic program with services, learning resources, and collections. Going through these evaluations simultaneously led the library to a major, ongoing library assessment project to satisfy both requirements.

Communicating Results and Impact

To satisfy the requirements of both accreditors and the program review process, we determined the need to create a template report for the library. We use it to evaluate collections, services, and library personnel in support of each academic program. We complete this report for each program during its program review, which occurs every five years for our undergraduate programs and every seven years for our graduate programs. This template satisfies the need to show the capabilities of our library during program review, documents our support of student and faculty in individual departments for accreditation reaffirmation, and, most importantly, provides us with an ongoing process for continuous improvement based on the needs of individual programs.

Creating the Template

The Office of Institutional Effectiveness at our university initially asked us to create this template. At the start, it was our primary audience, though we eventually grew to understand the impact these reports could have on upper administration and program faculty. Academic program review is a wide-ranging activity at most universities, and it gets appraised and approved at many levels. This meant that our reports were ultimately considered by a variety of stakeholders.

To appeal to these stakeholders, we developed a narrative with selective charts. In our other assessment reports, we tend to rely on graphical representations of data, so this was a departure from our standard approach. We chose this so that we could curate the data, rather than having faculty search for information. The narrative allowed us to tell our story. We also decided to take an all-encompassing approach when developing this template by discussing our services, facilities, learning resources, and personnel, as

Section 2

well as the library collections for that academic program. Including each aspect of the library was important, because most faculty have a good idea of our collections in their subject, but not our learning resources, services, and facilities. This was also useful for accreditation, because we are required to show that our services and learning resources, in addition to our collections, are adequate to support every academic program.

The template we developed has several main categories: library collections, collection access, collection budget, library services, and library staff. We chose these categories to mirror our regional and subject accreditation requirements with the idea that we would be able to use these reports to demonstrate improvement longitudinally, as well as to establish adequacy. For each category, we include many avenues of assessment. For instance, under "library collections," we evaluate collections by size, subject area, publication year, and quality. We also report statistics related to periodicals, circulation, and database use. While some of these statistics are common in more traditional collection evaluations, we tried to find unexpected ways to cross-reference data; for instance, we compare the use of subject guides with that of databases to paint a more complete picture of electronic usage overall.

Below are excerpts from the template that we use to illustrate the depth and breadth of a particular subject going through program review. In addition to tables of figures, the report includes narratives to give details concerning material usage, collection accessibility, collection plans, material budget creation, reference services, library layout, library technology, and library staffing.

Library Summary Report: *<Subject>*

The following report outlines Library collections and services in support of the *<subject>* Program at Texas A&M University-Central Texas. The goal is to demonstrate the Library's sufficiency for students and faculty researching *<subject(s)>*.

Library Collections

The University Library provides access to high quality information resources that support undergraduate, graduate, and faculty research. Our resources include books, periodicals, VHS, DVD, microfilms, textbooks, children's resources, young adult items, and the University Archives. The size of each collection is as follows:

Items	Size
List various library collections	

Each of these collections has content related to *<subject(s)>*. The total sizes for collections related to these areas are as follows:

Items	Size
List collections to support subject	

In addition to books, the Library offers many periodicals related to *<subject(s)>*. Most are available electronically through multiple Library databases. Databases that benefit <subject(s)> students and faculty include subject specific resources, such as:

List databases applicable to subject

Our database subscriptions can be further evaluated by looking at the subject breakdown of periodicals available electronically in areas related to *<subject(s)>*:

Subject	Size (Percentage)
List subjects	

Subject	Percentage Owned in October 20XX	Percentage Owned in September 20XX	Percentage Owned in September 20XX	Percentage Owned in September 20XX	Percentage Owned in September 20XX

These basic title categories can be analyzed more granularly using the Bowker Book Analysis System. The following is a summary of the subjects available related to <subjects(s)>

Subject	Size (Percentage Owned)
List subject from Bowker	

These categories can be further broken down as follows:

Subject	Size (Percentage Owned)
List subject sub-categories from Bowker	

Section 2

We also thought about what information would be valuable to faculty as they write their assessment for the external reviewer, particularly related to the program curriculum. Not every program review includes the entire library report for the external reviewer, though many include it as an appendix. Faculty ultimately determine what is relevant. By being provided with the right data from the library, the faculty can choose the information they need to integrate into their program review. This includes specific information about how our library supports the curriculum for that department, since this is one major focus of program review. As an example, we note if the program heavily uses e-reserves, class guides, or one-on-one library consultations. Many external reviewers look for evidence that students receive instruction related to the breadth of research in their academic field, especially at the graduate level, so this information is vital for faculty who are working on their review. Wherever possible, we shaped the template to mirror the larger requirements of program review as we understood them.

Finally, we considered the criteria for good practices in outcomes-based academic program review, defined by Bresciani.[5] Though not all of these criteria were relevant to the library's project, we did find value in several of the recommendations, including having a clear goal, fostering collaboration, using the data to create change, and provisioning resources to support improvement. The ultimate goal was to enhance our collections, learning resources, and services based on a collaborative evaluation of our support for individual programs. We wanted this report to be the beginning of a long-term partnership between program faculty and our subject liaisons. To reach this end, we chose data that would be actionable for both parties; for example, instructional assessments for a program compared to the full student population, which help indicate where changes needed to occur.

Making Time for Program Review

Once our template was finished, we completed the program review reports for 2012. Though these were well-received by faculty, they took a few months to finish, and we realized that this was not sustainable. We are a small library with a small staff. There was no way to do this project every year without a major efficiency improvement. To solve this problem, we decided to work smarter rather than harder. Each year the library collects data for the IPEDS Academic Libraries Survey, the ACRL Library Trends Survey, our annual report, our collection evaluation, and the university's continuous improvement process, in addition to scheduled program reviews. To ensure adequate staff time to complete these reports, we went through a process of aligning the categories for each evaluation, changing how we collect the data overall.

To do this, we chose a yearly census date for library data that aligns with the dates for IPEDS Academic Libraries Survey and the ACRL Library Trends Survey. We then looked at each category of statistics that the library needs in a given year, including administration, acquisitions, circulation, reference, instruction, technical services, and collections. We mapped the requirements of each report to these categories. Our goal was to collect data once annually to satisfy as many of these needs as possible. To this end, we planned strategically and considered issues like granularity of data, collection procedures, and data storage. We also considered all of our assessment needs, which were quite broad.

Through a regularized method for collecting statistics once annually, we have been able to cut down drastically on the amount of effort required to complete assessment tasks. This way, when we write our program review reports, we can focus our efforts on curating the data and using it to improve what we offer to support each program, rather than collecting new data, which would take a prohibitive amount of time. Following the formula of our annual data collection process, the time it takes to complete the program review reports has been reduced from several months to one week.

Gauging the Impact

Our participation in the program review process has impacted our relationship with the rest of the university substantially. The reports that we generate are shared with program faculty, who then incorporate our data into documents for external reviewers and university administrators. Most of these constituents have some knowledge of what the library offers but are not fully aware of our services in support of specific academic programs. These reports are, therefore, an important way to advertise the library. We view them as a "deep dive" into a cross-section of library data curated to promote everything the library offers to a well-defined group of students and faculty.

For faculty, this deep dive can have a positive impact. Though we have not formally studied this impact, we have observed it for several years now. We find that faculty who are involved with program review tell their colleagues about the services we report, often because they have learned so much, conveying some version of "I had no idea the library did this." They also make collection requests based on our findings and work with us to improve learning resources and services, which we can usually tailor to their program. Most importantly, when faculty know what we offer, they are more likely to advocate for us, viewing librarians as key partners in educating their students. This is significant, because this advocacy occurs when faculty convince students that library resources are crucial to student success. Faculty advocacy can also improve the way our deans view the library.

Similarly, administrators—who are generally required to sign off on program review—become more willing advocates of the library when they see us as central to the university's core teaching mission, which this report promotes. By aligning the library with the program curriculum, faculty, and facilities, we make the vital role we play more evident. This report is also a good way to draw the attention of administrators to important services we offer that may benefit one particular program in a way that is not immediately intuitive. For instance, our film studies program heavily relies on a combination of e-reserves and video streaming through the library. We are lucky to be able to offer these services, despite the fact that there is a cost associated. Through the program review, we can highlight their significance and justify the cost to our administrators, who might otherwise consider it a secondary amenity without a defined value. There are so many examples of niche services the library offers, and these reports allow us to highlight them for administrators.

Section 2

The library liaisons are also impacted. They are able to make data-driven improvements to their subject areas on a routine basis, based on input from program faculty, administrators, and external reviewers. The opportunity to get such pertinent feedback is meaningful for our librarians. Having an objective third party look at what you are doing is always valuable. Further, by taking part in this process, the liaisons are also often aware of major changes in curriculum before they happen, since program review leads to such alterations. This allows our liaisons to be proactive in shifting our collections before new curriculum takes effect.

Ultimately, the students are the greatest beneficiaries. They get faculty who are much better prepared to guide them to use the library. When they arrive, they get assistance that is better tailored to their needs and collections that are of higher quality. If they rely on niche services due to their major, they are less likely to lose these services because our administrators understand their importance.

Leveraging the Findings

We leverage these reports by dedicating funds to improve our collections and services in response to the findings. To this end, since 2015, we have spent several thousand dollars annually on this project. This funding follows from the criteria for good practices outlined by Bresciani.[6] Providing the data is not enough. Resource support, even if only a small amount, must buttress the project if you expect real change. In FY2016, for instance, we were able to improve our history, education, criminal justice, and psychology collections based on our program review reports. As we are a new university, this is an effective, data-driven method to make a big impact on the quality of our collections and services. Having funding also allows a more substantial collaboration between faculty and the library. The program review report is not a discrete event, but rather, the beginning of a long-term partnership to enhance, mutually, the library and the academic program.

In addition to funding, we plan to find more opportunities to engage in institutional effectiveness activities with departments from across campus to leverage the success we have had. We have a long-term plan to map the library services and resources to programmatic learning outcomes for incorporation into our program review reports. This will mean some major planning and new points of data collection for the library, which may take several years. We feel that this effort is worth it because we can use it to show the library's value related to student learning outcomes in a more concrete way.

In the next two years, the library also plans to examine the impact our reports have on faculty so that we can tailor them for maximum effect. If we can identify the most useful information, the information that encourages faculty to be more engaged with us, we will better reach them. When we originally created the template, we did not consider this, but now want to revise it to ensure we are maximizing the impact. We will do this through focus groups with faculty where they can discuss with us what is most useful about our reports. One question that we plan to ask during these focus groups relates to database and journal usage. This is data that we know is significant to our faculty, and we will use their input to determine a more robust way of showing usage, which we feel is underreported in the current iteration of our template.

Finally, by looking at each program individually, our librarians now think about our services in a more customized way. Each report shows how personalized the needs of our students are in a given program. In response to this realization, we are approaching our services from a new angle to leverage this viewpoint. Currently, we are creating a menu with varying options that can be adapted to the needs of a program or course in order to engage with faculty, allowing them a greater degree of flexibility.

Reflection

The engagement this project promotes between librarians, administrators, and faculty is a crucial consequence. These reports tell the library's story. In a time where libraries must show university administration that we are valuable, demonstrating our commitment to educational quality is essential. Our contributions to student learning and success are sometimes difficult to articulate, but partnering in academic program review puts us on the front lines of institutional accountability. To this end, the greater guidance in the development of our collections and services is highly rewarding. Libraries are often institutions where there is never enough money, where wish lists outpace budgets, and this process gives us an opportunity to make real change based on hard data.

The excessive amount of time it took to complete program reviews the first year was a barrier to our success, but instead of giving up on the project, we turned a setback into an opportunity for better efficiency. By aligning our assessment data across reports and collecting it once annually, we can focus on creating positive change based on our evaluations, which is the ultimate goal. Though this alignment was the most challenging and time-consuming part of the process, it saved us work in subsequent years. There is one secondary ongoing barrier, related to our funded improvements. Because program review usually occurs late in the spring, we must rush to spend the funds after the external reviews are received, but before the end of the fiscal year. During the FY2016, for instance, we purchased 487 books in the time span of three-and-a-half weeks. This is problematic, and we are considering dedicating funds in the year after the program review, rather than in the same year.

The collaboration between the library and our institutional effectiveness office was pivotal to our success. We were lucky, as a new institution, that there were no preconceived notions about the role the library would play in program review. This allowed our library to be more involved than the libraries at many other schools. This also aided us because we did not add to the faculty workload; we simply enhanced what they were already doing.

By planning assessment appropriately, and aligning the work so that we do not rerun data each time someone requests information, we save a lot of time. This allows us to tackle seemingly big projects because the information is already there. We have used this lesson in other ways. For instance, we participate in many community grant programs, and we are now aligning our annual reporting so that the common data we use for these grant applications is routinely collected in a predictable way. By collecting data using patterns that satisfy different requirements, we do more to share results with the administration, which leads, in turn, to greater institutional support for the library. This helps to overcome the biggest challenge we face, which is our small staff. The data we collect also helps us to justify better staffing, such as the recent move of a part-time faculty librarian to full-time in support of our College of Education.

Academic program review can be an exceptional vehicle for gaining faculty and administrative buy-in. Because our reports concentrate on a specific academic program, they provide an opportunity to showcase the library's value in context. So much of the focus at universities is on the quality of individual programs, student success in attaining degrees, and student achievement of individual learning outcomes. By curating our existing library data to create a narrative about how we support a specific group of students, we make a much better case for the library as an instructional partner. This has a big impact.

Finally, academic program review works better when it is holistic, encompassing everything the library offers in support of an academic program. Simply evaluating collections would not have the same impact. Many of our faculty are fairly familiar with the collections we have in their area, but not with the support services we offer to assist their students. We find that faculty who are involved in program review tend to learn about services they later use. In this way, our involvement in program review helps the library overcome a routine problem: how to get faculty aware of, and invested in, library services and learning resources. A holistic approach also supports accreditation reaffirmation. For these reasons, this approach is a best practice.

We recommend involvement in academic program review for all libraries. By becoming involved in this process, we have discovered that it reaches many constituencies at once. As demonstrated by our project to align our data collection, even the smallest library can do this, with the appropriate planning.

Notes

1. John Costella, Tom Adam, Fran Gray, Nicole Nolan, and Catherine Wilkins, "Undergraduate Program Review Processes: A Case Study in Opportunity for Academic Libraries," *Journal of Academic Librarianship* 39, no. 2 (2013): 169–74, https://doi.org/10.1016/j.acalib.2012.09.016.
2. Charles A. Schwartz, "The University Library and the Problem of Knowledge," *College and Research Libraries* 68, no. 3 (2007): 238–44, http://crl.acrl.org/index.php/crl/article/viewFile/15866/17312.
3. Yelena Pancheshnikov, "Course-Centered Approach to Evaluating University Library Collections for Instructional Program Reviews," *Collection Building* 22, no. 4 (2003): 177–85, EBSCOhost; Jeffery L. Loo and Elizabeth A. Dupuis, "Organizational Learning for Library Enhancements: A Collaborative, Research-Driven Analysis of Academic Department Needs," *College and Research Libraries* 76, no. 5 (2015): 671–89, https://doi.org/10.5860/crl.76.5.671.
4. Marilee J. Bresciani, *Outcomes-Based Academic and Co-curricular Program Review* (Sterling, VA: Stylus, 2006), EBSCOhost.
5. Bresciani, *Outcomes-Based*, 63–97.
6. Bresciani, *Outcomes-Based*, 87–94.

Bibliography

Bresciani, Marilee. *Outcomes-Based Academic and Co-curricular Program Review: A Compilation of Institutional Good Practices*. Sterling, VA: Stylus Publishing, 2006. EBSCOhost.

Costella, John, Tom Adam, Fran Gray, Nicole Nolan, and Catherine Wilkins. "Undergraduate Program Review Processes: A Case Study in Opportunity for Academic Libraries." *Journal of Academic Librarianship* 39, no. 2 (2013): 169–74. https://doi.org/10.1016/j.acalib.2012.09.016.

Loo, Jeffrey L., and Elizabeth DupuisA. "Organizational Learning for Library Enhancements: A Collaborative, Research-Driven Analysis of Academic Department Needs." *College and Research Libraries* 76, no. 5 (2015): 671–89. https://doi.org/10.5860/crl.76.5.671.

Pancheshnikov, Yelena. "Course-Centered Approach to Evaluating University Library Collections for Instructional Program Reviews." *Collection Building* 22, no. 4 (2003): 177–85. EBSCOhost.

Schwartz, Charles. "The University Library and the Problem of Knowledge." *College and Research Libraries* 68, no. 3 (2007): 238–44. http://crl.acrl.org/index.php/crl/article/viewFile/15866/17312.

Section 2

Title: An Ounce of Performance Is Worth Pounds of Promises: The Impact of Web-Scale Discovery on Full-Text Consumption

Abstract: A recent industry white paper presents three points relevant to ROI of web-scale discovery services: (1) time saved searching via single-search box versus time spent searching multiple databases; (2) increased usage of licensed content; and (3) savings in document delivery costs. This article addresses point 2 and presents an effective method of demonstrating the value of web-scale discovery services by analyzing the amount of full text consumed via discovery interface relative to the amount consumed overall and via native interfaces. This simple assessment can be used with great effect to demonstrate significant ROI on web-scale discovery.

Keywords: web-scale discovery, usage, metrics, assessment

Project focus: assessment methodologies, techniques, or practices; collections; data use and technology

Results made or will make case for: improvements in services, proof of library impact and value, a strategic plan or process, how money or resources may be directed

Data needed: database usage statistics

Methodology: quantitative

Project duration: ongoing (continuous feedback loop)

Tool(s) utilized: EBSCO Admin, Excel

Cost estimate: < $100

Type of institution: college—public

Institution enrollment: 5,000–15,000

Highest level of education: master's/professional degree

CC BY

Chapter 16

An Ounce of Performance Is Worth Pounds of Promises

The Impact of Web-Scale Discovery on Full-Text Consumption

Anthony J. McMullen

Section 2

Introduction

"What a great idea! I never would have thought to do that." This was the reaction of a friend when I suggested he consult Amazon.com product reviews and use the Google shopping application to comparison-price prior to making a new laptop computer purchase. Despite my friend's surprise, I did not really believe this was any kind of great idea; I just assumed this was what people did. Where else can consumers go to gain access to thousands of product reviews and price points from dozens of retailers? As it turns out, my assumption is based in reality. A recent CNBC report indicates 55 percent of all consumers report beginning their online shopping on Amazon's website.[1] A 2017 article from Business Insider reports a strikingly similar environment, with 52 percent overall beginning their shopping on Amazon, and a full 62 percent of the 18-29-year-old demographic preferring the retail giant as a starting point.[2] What's the attraction? As reported in the CNBC article, ease of use is the most frequently cited answer to this question.

Ease of use—for me, this was the hook, the common denominator between user preferences in the consumption of products and in the consumption of information. Anybody who reads the library science literature can most assuredly say they have seen this phrase in titles, abstracts, and bodies of text. In fact, a quick search of 2007–2017 content in the *Journal of Academic Librarianship* reveals 125+ occurrences of "ease of use." The idea is nothing new. In 1931, S. R. Ranganathan thought it important enough that he included it in his fundamental and enduring theory, the five laws of library science. The fourth law, save the time of the reader, is in spirit the same thing as ease of use. This basic principle of removing barriers to information and saving the time of the user is the driving force behind the creation of federated searching and web-scale discovery (WSD) tools.

Time saved is one of the benefits identified in a recent industry white paper discussing the return on investment (ROI) of WSD services.[3] A second benefit is increased usage of licensed content. This white paper, along with the information on ease of use as it relates to online shopping starting points, is the catalyst for the assessment methods discussed in this chapter. In evaluating the efficacy of my library's WSD instance, EBSCO Discovery Service (EDS), I went beyond simple counts of searches, sessions, and numbers of full-text articles retrieved. My search for information led me to ask not only "How much?" but "From where?" I was specifically interested in the quantity of full-text accessed via EDS versus quantity accessed via the native search interfaces. The data I have uncovered has solidified my presumptions that WSD provides a significant ROI.

Context

In February of 2015, as part of a university-wide shift to an institutional portal, my library's design team implemented a new website featuring an embedded EDS single-search box. While we had had EDS since 2013, prior to the implementation of the institutional portal we provided access via a Discovery Search hyperlink on the library's homepage. Our goal with the redesign was to remove barriers to information and create efficiencies in the information-seeking process. We knew from our webpage analytics that the Find Articles and A–Z List were the two most clicked links on our site. We also knew that once users arrived at either of those pages, they had difficulties navigating through the lengthy alphabetical lists of resources that had grown to more than seventy-five and one hundred entries respectively. By providing single-search box access to virtually all of the content included in the various resources on the A–Z list, we expected to see increases in the number of full-text accesses from our various databases.

Like most academic libraries, by 2015 we had greatly increased the percentage of our budget dedicated to electronic resources. The number of printed journal subscriptions had been reduced from more than 1,000 titles to slightly more than 200. Meanwhile, the number of online journals available to our users had increased exponentially to more than 70,000 unique titles, all linked to our abstract and indexing (A&I) databases with our link resolver. Along with this shift to subscription-based full-text and A&I databases, we also acquired our first pay-per-article service. With this model, we deposit funds into an account, thereby granting our users instant access to thousands of scientific and technical journals we could not afford otherwise. The content is searchable on our EDS platform, and every time a user downloads an article our account is debited accordingly.

Our collection of monographs was on a similar track by 2015. We had reduced the size of our print collection by more than 50,000 volumes while simultaneously expanding the number of titles we purchased electronically. We had also begun to provide access to very large collections of e-book titles with demand-driven acquisition (DDA) and evidence-based acquisition (EBA) models of collection development. As is the case with the pay-per-article service, library users access the DDA and EBA titles on our EDS platform. The fact that these DDA/EBA and pay-per-article collections are any different from traditional library collections is entirely invisible to the user. All the user sees is the familiar PDF icon or Get Full Text link (see figure 16.1).

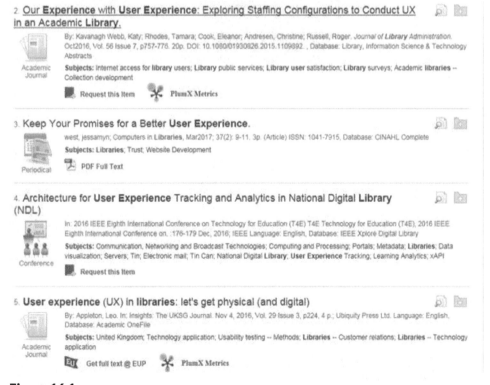

Figure 16.1
EDS search results illustrating access to full text with "Get full text @ EUP" and "PDF Full Text" links. ILL requests are submitted with "Request this Item" links.

In addition to expanding our offerings of online journals and e-books, we transformed our interlibrary loan (ILL) service by offering greatly expedited loan fulfillments via consortium memberships. Most ILL requests for books are now filled within two to three days. And most requests for journal articles are now filled electronically and within twelve hours. Gone are the days of waiting for the mail carrier, then trying to read a third-generation photocopy reduced to 75 percent in an effort to save paper. The method of placing and receiving ILL requests has also evolved. Library users rarely submit paper request forms or fill out our blank online request form— most ILL requests are generated via EDS and the A&I databases with Request This Item hyperlinks (See figure 16.1).

This is the current state of affairs at the Baron-Forness Library of Edinboro University of Pennsylvania. Nothing we have done is cutting edge or outside of the parameters of contemporary academic library practices. It is merely a reflection of the wants and needs of today's library users. Just as consumers of goods value ease of use and one-stop shopping, library users value the same. An abundance of evidence in the library literature supports this position. In their 2011 paper, Connaway, Dickey, and Radford identified convenience as a primary consideration in the information-seeking process.[4] This echoes the findings of a 2007 focus group study, which found that students and faculty alike prioritize convenience and immediacy in locating information.[5] Both studies support the findings of Griffiths and Brophy, who concluded in 2005 that students will sacrifice quality of information for effort and time spent and that search engines had altered students' perceptions and expectations.[6]

Demonstrating the value of EDS would require only a very basic statistical analysis, as usage data would certainly show increases in the number of full-text downloads. This will be easy, or so we thought.

Communicating Results and Impact

Edinboro University of Pennsylvania is accredited by the Middle States Commission on Higher Education (MSCHE). As part of the 2013–14 MSCHE reaccreditation efforts, all academic departments developed goals and objectives with specific and measurable outcomes. The library's Assessment Committee, charged with developing the objectives and outcomes, assigned measurement of the outcomes to one of the library's subcommittees, or "teams," as we call them. The Technology Team, a group I facilitate, was responsible for measuring the following outcome: "Library users will locate content from disparate library collections via a single search."

I had been using EBSCOhost's reporting features for years to gather data on number of searches, sessions, and full-text downloads in the library's suite of databases. I was familiar with the capabilities and limitations. As a result, measuring this outcome appeared to be a very straightforward task. We could simply compare the number of search sessions and full-text downloads initiated via EDS to those same data points initiated at the native database interface. Our suspicions were that a substantial number of library users would migrate from the unwieldy A–Z list to the easy-to-use and prominently placed EDS search box. The compelling evidence, as we thought, would be an appreciable increase in full-text downloads. Our hypotheses were supported by current reports from the field. In his 2010 publication, Doug Way concluded that the increase in full-text downloads at Grand Valley State University was directly linked to the implementation of WSD.[7] A 2014 paper presented at a UKSG conference found that all four of the WSD services examined significantly increased usage of content.[8] And at Western Carolina University, Kristin Calvert found that the implementation of WSD resulted in increases in the usage of the library's licensed electronic content.[9]

What we found, however, when we began to examine basic usage data of our EBSCOhost licensed content, is that our suspicions were not necessarily confirmed (see table 16.1).

Table 16.1

Full-Text Downloads of EBSCO-Licensed Content and Linkage from EBSCO to Outside Services, 2012–2017

Year	Full-Text Downloads	Links to Outside Services
2012	159,890	6,831
2013	140,195	13,291
2014	133,333	19,287
2015[a]	141,975	27,601
2016	108,200	23,223
2017[b]	57,410	14,948
a. EDS single-search box implemented in February. b. Includes data for January–May only.		

In 2015, the year in which we implemented the revised webpage with the embedded EDS search box, we do see a modest increase of 6.5 percent in the number of full-text downloads of EBSCO licensed content. We also see a substantial increase of 43 percent in the number of links to outside services, such as content linked via our link resolver and items requested via ILL. This is the sort of trend we expected to see. However, in 2016 there is a precipitous drop-off of 23.8 percent in full-text downloads along with a more modest decline of 15.8 percent in links to non-EBSCO resources. Some of this decline in usage could be attributed to declining enrollments, increasing reliance on freely available web-based resources, and changes to subscription databases, but it was still counter to our expectations.

As we examined the data more deeply, we noticed additional and unanticipated details. Of the 159,890 full-text downloads in 2012, EBSCOhost's widely adopted multidisciplinary database Academic Search Complete (ASC) was the source of 82,802 of them. That equals 51.8 percent of all downloads of EBSCO-licensed content. Similarly, the 2013 and 2014 percentages were 53.4 percent and 51.1 percent respectively. When we examined the data from 2015, the year we implemented the EDS single-search box, we noted the ASC downloads had dropped to 58,022, or 40.9 percent of all EBSCO downloads. In 2016, the ASC downloads had fallen to 39,238, or 36.3 percent. And from January to May in 2017, the number of ASC full-text downloads stands at 20,654, or 36.0 percent.

We knew from anecdotal evidence that library users were heavily reliant on ASC. For instance, we were accustomed to students saying, "I searched the library site," when really what they meant was, "I searched Academic Search Complete." But the realization that ASC was the source of more than half of the downloads of our EBSCO content was an alarming one. After all, we subscribed to more than eighty additional EBSCOhost databases, many of them with full-text content. It would stand to reason that as overall usage of EBSCOhost's multidisciplinary ASC had decreased as a percentage of all EBSCOhost downloads, usage of at least some of the discipline-specific EBSCOhost full-text databases would have increased. This led us to question what percentage of full-text downloads are triggered via EDS as compared to those triggered from the native, stand-alone databases. This was worth a closer look, and as it turns out, offered meaningful measurement to the outcome stated in paragraph one of this section: "Library users will locate content from disparate library collections via a single search."

One of the useful features of EBSCOhost's administrative back end, aptly named EBSCOadmin, is the ability to determine which search boxes and search interfaces library patrons are using to locate and download articles. In our case, and in order to measure our outcome, we needed to know how much of the overall EBSCOhost database usage could be traced back to EDS. Isolating this data in EBSCOadmin is very straightforward. With minimal effort we determined roughly 30 percent of all full-text downloads of EBSCO content were triggered via activity in EDS in 2015 and 2016, the first two years following the implementation of the single-search box. And so far in 2017, nearly 40 percent of the full-text downloads are triggered from EDS. On top of this, we determined that links from EDS to non-EBSCO content (other platforms, link resolver, ILL requests) eclipsed 40 percent of all EBSCO link activity in 2015 and 2016 and is greater than 53 percent thus far into 2017 (see table 16.2).

Table 16.2
EDS Full-Text Downloads and Links to Non-EBSCO Content

Year	EDS Downloads / % of All EBSCO Content Downloads	EDS Links to Non-EBSCO Content/ % of All EBSCO Links to Non-EBSCO Content
2015	43,452 / 30.6	12,307 / 44.6
2016	32,277 / 29.8	10,011 / 43.1
2017	22,190 / 38.7	8,026 / 53.7

The evidence was clear. EDS was working as it was designed to work—as a unifying service that brings together full-text content from disparate platforms and enables library users to easily request materials not available in full text. The Technology Team reported our findings to the library Assessment Committee for inclusion in the annual assessment report and to aid in the strategic planning process as the library continues to transform. Our findings are a beginning rather than an end and are a single component of the larger and ongoing assessment process. We must continue to examine library use patterns holistically as user behaviors and expectations continue to evolve. In the short term, a usability study of the library's webpages and the EDS interface could help to expose some design elements in need of attention. More strategically, we must decide if the benefits of EDS are worth the effort and financial resources required to maintain it as a separate platform, or if a next-generation library system with integrated resource management, link resolving, and WSD provides a greater ROI.

Leveraging the Findings

While the Technology Team will continue to gather basic data on EDS, it is imperative that we refine our reporting techniques so that we can more accurately and thoroughly illustrate the ROI of EDS. This is particularly important in an environment of shrinking budgets, one in which we need hard evidence to justify expenses. Accordingly, we have begun the process of examining our usage data at the database level. For instance, thus far in 2017, we know that 75 percent of all full-text downloads of EBSCOhost e-books are triggered via EDS as opposed to those triggered by users searching the EBSCOhost e-book database directly. This is a substantial ROI. It is particularly compelling in an environment where the rate of growth of our e-book collection continues to outpace print. We can further illustrate ROI by examining the other EBSCOhost full-text databases through the same lens (see table 16.3).

Table 16.3
EBSCOhost Database Full-Text Downloads: Percentage of Downloads Triggered via EDS Interface, January–May 2017

Database Name	EBSCOhost Database Full-Text Downloads: % Triggered via EDS
Academic Search Complete	18.5
America History & Life	43.4
Applied Science & Technology Source	47.4
Art & Architecture Source	48.3
Business Source Complete	60.8
CINAHL Complete	64.2
Communication Source	14.1
Computers & Applied Sciences Complete	45.2
Current Biography Illustrated	54.5
Education Source	44.5
Health Reference Center: Consumer Edition	33.3
Health Reference Center: Academic Edition	8.3

Historical Abstracts	39.9
Humanities Source	69.5
Legal Collection	79.9
MAS Ultra: School Edition	79.6
MEDLINE Complete	55.8
Middle Search Plus	95.4
Military & Government Collection	17.7
Newspaper Source	7.5
Nursing Reference Center	11.1
Primary Search	25.4
PsycARTICLES	34.5
Psychology & Behavioral Sciences Collection	43.0
Regional Business News	62.3
Religion & Philosophy collection	84.3
SocINDEX	42.6
Sociological Collection	65.8
SPORTDiscus	51.9

Armed with this data, illustrating the ROI of EDS is an uncomplicated matter. For instance, if we assume the cost of the Business Source Complete database is $5,000 annually, and we know that EDS is responsible for almost 61 percent of the activity in the database, we can confidently illustrate that EDS has returned $3,050 from the subscription cost. As we perform identical operations on the other full-text databases, it does not take long to underscore the dividends EDS pays.

The next logical step in this process is to perform similar calculations for the EBSCOhost A&I databases, using counts of link-outs to non-EBSCO content in the place of full-text downloads. It is also vital that we develop processes to measure the impact of EDS on non-EBSCO resources such as JSTOR, Project MUSE, and LexisNexis as our electronic collections continue to grow.

Reflection

Gaining buy-in for WSD and a library website featuring an embedded EDS search box was in many ways an uphill battle at my library. As a result, it is rewarding for me to see the positive impact EDS has made thus far. It is particularly gratifying to see the impact on the discipline-specific "niche" resources such as MEDLINE and SocINDEX—resources that many are unaware of and ones that are often buried in A–Z database lists. I look at the data and recall a quote from the department secretary at the library school I attended. Her name was Barb. When a student asked about how much storage space she had on her new computer, Barb replied, "I don't want to know *how* it works, I just need it to work." Similarly, students are not concerned with the names of the databases they use to find their articles, they just want to write their papers.

Collaboration with the Technology Team was vital in implementing the single-search box design, and later in collecting, interpreting, and sharing the data. Presenting our design, justifying our design choices, and outlining the expected impacts with a unified voice was crucial to the success of the project. Transparency, openness, and empathy were also keys to success—they help us to accept the notion that just because we do not "like" something does not mean it is not a good plan. The very idea of EDS was a controversial one at Baron-Forness Library. Without the vote of confidence from the entire library faculty and staff, we would not be discussing the impact of EDS because it would have failed from the outset.

Given an opportunity to redo the project, I would do a much more thorough job of gathering together pre-EDS and pre-single-search-box data in order to more meaningfully demonstrate the impact. I also believe organizing the data based on academic year instead of calendar year likely presents a more normalized view of the numbers from year to year. Another thing I would do differently is to incorporate reference desk transactions into the data. We have ample anecdotal evidence indicating a sizable decrease in the number of "How do I find articles?" questions, but no way of correlating "hard" data with pre- and post-EDS implementation.

The best advice I have for those interested in assessing the impact of WSD is twofold: (1) Have some fun. If you have a passion for design, the research process, and user experience, you will enjoy seeing things begin to play out in the data; (2) Do not be disappointed if the data is not exactly what you expected it to be. This is part of the process. Assessment is ongoing. It gives us opportunities and motivation to try again, to do things differently. Instead of giving up, make some changes and observe the results.

Notes

1. Krystina Gustafson, "More Shoppers Are Starting Their Online Search on Amazon," CNBC, September 26, 2016, http://www.cnbc.com/2016/09/27/amazon-is-the-first-place-most-online-shoppers-visit.html.
2. Eugene Kim, "New Data Shows Amazon Is Eating into Google's Territory—and It's Only Going to Get Worse," *Business Insider*, January 6, 2017, http://www.businessinsider.com/amazon-gains-share-in-ecommerce-searches-2017-1.
3. EBSCO Information Services, "Measuring the Benefit of EBSCO Discovery Service in Corporations—White Paper," EBSCO Help, July 6, 2016, https://help.ebsco.com/interfaces/EBSCO_Discovery_Service/EDS_FAQs/Measuring_Benefit_of_EDS_Corporations.
4. Lynn Silipigni Connaway, Timothy J. Dickey, and Marie L. Radford, "If It Is Too Inconvenient, I'm Not Going after It: Convenience as a Critical Factor in Information-Seeking Behaviors," *Library and Information Science Research*, 33 (2011): 179–90.
5. Chandra Prabha, Lynn Silipigni Connaway, Lawrence Olszewski, and Lillie R. Jenkins, "What Is Enough? Satisficing Information Needs," *Journal of Documentation*, 63, no. 1 (2007): 74–89.
6. Jillian R. Griffiths and Peter Brophy, "Student Searching Behavior and the Web: Use of Academic Resources and Google," *Library Trends*, 53, no. 4 (2005): 539–54.
7. Doug Way, "The Impact of Web-Scale Discovery on the Use of a Library Collection," *Serials Review*, 36, no. 4 (2010): 214–20.

Section 2

8. Michael Levine-Clark, "The Effect of Discovery Systems on Online Journal Usage: A Longitudinal Study," *Insights* 27, no. 3 (2014): 249–56.
9. Kristin Calvert, "Maximizing Academic Library Collections: Measuring Changes in Use Patterns Owing to EBSCO Discovery Service," *College and Research Libraries* 76, no. 1 (2015): 81–99.

Bibliography

Calvert, Kristin. "Maximizing Academic Library Collections: Measuring Changes in Use Patterns Owing to EBSCO Discovery Service." *College and Research Libraries* 76, no. 1 (2015): 81–99.

Connaway, Lynn Silipigni, Timothy J. Dickey, and Marie L. Radford. "If It Is Too Inconvenient, I'm Not Going after It: Convenience as a Critical Factor in Information-Seeking Behaviors." *Library and Information Science Research* 33 (2011): 179–90.

EBSCO Information Services, "Measuring the Benefit of EBSCO Discovery Service in Corporations—White Paper." EBSCO Help. July 6, 2016. https://help.ebsco.com/interfaces/EBSCO_Discovery_Service/EDS_FAQs/Measuring_Benefit_of_EDS_Corporations.

Griffiths, Jillian R., and Peter Brophy. "Student Searching Behavior and the Web: Use of Academic Resources and Google." *Library Trends* 53, no. 4 (2005): 539–54.

Gustafson, Krystina. "More Shoppers Are Starting Their Online Search on Amazon." CNBC. September 26, 2016. http://www.cnbc.com/2016/09/27/amazon-is-the-first-place-most-online-shoppers-visit.html.

Kim, Eugene. "New Data Shows Amazon Is Eating into Google's Territory—and It's only Going to Get Worse." *Business Insider*, January 6, 2017. http://www.businessinsider.com/amazon-gains-share-in-ecommerce-searches-2017-1.

Levine-Clark, Michael. "The Effect of Discovery Systems on Online Journal Usage: A Longitudinal Study." *Insights* 27, no. 3 (2014): 249–56.

Prabha, Chandra, Lynn Silipigni Connaway, Lawrence Olszewski, and Lillie R. Jenkins. "What Is Enough? Satisficing Information Needs." *Journal of Documentation* 63, no. 1 (2007): 74–89.

Way, Doug. "The Impact of Web-Scale Discovery on the Use of a Library Collection." *Serials Review* 36, no. 4 (2010): 214–20.

Title: Show Them the (Data-Driven) Goods: A Transparent Collection Assessment Tool for Libraries

Abstract: Libraries are steeped in data! We have metrics on usage, acquisitions, trial resources, and our patron-driven models. For subject experts, those public-facing librarians charged with reference, instruction, and outreach, the data deluge can be overwhelming and unhelpful in terms of actionable next steps in their work. This chapter will introduce the "Content Gains and Losses" report, a sortable and highly usable curated monthly report distributed library-wide. This chapter will detail six ways in which librarians have used this report and the included data to advance assessment in their own subject areas, networking with faculty, and collection development.

Keywords: collections, data analysis, value, capacity building, return on investment, data-driven assessment

Project focus: assessment methodologies, techniques, or practices; organizational practices (i.e., strategic planning); collections

Results made or will make case for: more funding, improvements in collections, proof of library impact and value, a strategic plan or process, how money or resources may be directed

Data needed: monthly acquisitions for all resources including streaming platforms and DDA; ILL monthly activity data; special collections monthly acquisitions; ProQuest (or other major vendor represented in your collection) monthly gains and losses report

Methodology: quantitative

Project duration: ongoing (continuous feedback loop)

Tool(s) utilized: Tableau (for data visualization)

Cost estimate: $2,000–$5,000

Type of institution: university—private

Institution enrollment: 30,000+

Highest level of education: doctoral

Section 2

Chapter 17

Show Them the (Data-Driven) Goods

A Transparent Collection Assessment Tool for Libraries

Caroline Muglia

Recently, I took my first trip to San Antonio, Texas. Under the guise of conference attendance, my real goal was to gaze at the Alamo, the eighteenth-century mission compound
that had been home to religious organizations and revolutionary battles; had been burned,
readapted, and somehow, amidst a growing modern city, still loomed. My imagination of
this historic landmark eclipsed its reality so much that when I finally stood before the
Alamo and its missions, disappointment was the only lasting emotion I could muster.
Instead of a multi-acre, sparsely populated, pristinely beautified UNESCO site, the Alamo
was located down the street from a Ripley's Believe-It-or-Not theater and a DoubleTree
chain hotel. All the photos I recalled creatively kept the concentrated urbanization out of
frame. I replicated this fantasy when I took my own photos and tightly focused into the
buildings and its grounds. When I showed the photos to friends, I decided to explain both
the perspective of the building that disappointed me (zoomed out) and the one I captured
in photo (zoomed in). Somehow the juxtaposition of images reconciled my imagination
with a newfound love for a historic marker standing among its twenty-first-century coun-
terparts. One year later, when I decided to curate and internally distribute a monthly report, the Content Gains and Losses report, that offered a glimpse into usable data points
for my fellow librarians at University of Southern California (USC) Libraries, I employed

the same tactics I used with my Alamo photos. I offered specific data points (zoomed in) as well as their (sometimes messy) context (zoomed out).

Based in Los Angeles, USC Libraries serves 42,000 student FTE (graduate students slightly outnumber undergraduates) and twenty-four libraries and information centers. USC's Collections Division budget, which is responsible for nearly all acquisitions of library resources, is around $14 million.[1] For these resources, we have metrics on e-usage, circulation, acquisitions, trial resources, and our patron-driven acquisitions models. We have statistics related to instruction and reference, click rates for our digital library, head counts, gate counts, and search functionality metrics, to name a few. This means that USC Libraries is steeped in so much data! USC is not alone in experiencing the data deluge that has become commonplace in academic libraries. Every resource, no matter how niche, produces data points, which we *could* use to inform our work. In an increasingly metrics-driven environment, librarians feel pressure to utilize all relevant data points to shape collections, show value, and interact with vendors on the financial decision-making of our resources. Of course, with this "collect 'em all" effort, academic librarians collect more than they actually need or can reasonably use to impact decisions. Data had become part of the narrative even for those of us who don't deal in data! Of course, data always existed in libraries, but not to the scale that we see today.[2] When I meet with a vendor's representative to discuss its offerings, I am usually greeted with a pitch covering the features of new resources and a few massive spreadsheets containing data that reveals what my users demand. Normally, I lightly sift through the material during the conversation and then temporarily discard the printed spreadsheets to a pile on my desk until I have time to pore over the details, most of which are dizzying and sometimes contradictory to my own internal findings.

The data analytics and reports produced by vendors (and so many others) provide useful information. But when I attempted to translate this information to engage my colleagues, I experienced a disconnection. My colleagues did not have consistent information about our current collection and usage, so they could not participate in conversations of collection reshaping. When I presented statistics provided by vendors, most of my colleagues posed questions regarding our recent acquisitions (What do we have in this subject area? Did we ever buy that resource?) and not the potential for future ones. They had some, but certainly not a cohesive orientation of the collection for the simple reason that it had never been available to them.

This report was born from a need to close the gap between the focus of my work as a Collection Assessment Librarian and what my colleagues who were not steeped in that level of data needed to know to effectively contribute to the collection development strategy. Before this reporting tool was developed, librarians had very little information about new acquisitions in the collection and no information on withdrawals from the collection. Data analytics is a cornerstone of my work as a Collection Assessment Librarian in a large library system. For academic librarians in the subfield of collection assessment, strategy, and evaluation, the goal is to use the data to illustrate the value of the library system on campus and to shape the collection in its content and format to bolster the research and scholarly mission of the university.[3] The goal is to show a fruitful return on investment of expensive resources in support of the larger academic enterprise of which we are a part. Being steeped in this volume of data is not everyone's job, although there is a strong argument in favor of integrating assessment into every librarian's job to create a more sustainable collections program and culture of assessment.[4]

Libraries are at the center of usable, but fast-moving data generated from various sources, including vendors, e-resource platforms, and ILS and DDA programs. With trends that suggest increasing data production and consumption, libraries need to do more than curate data. We need to break it down into actionable bites for our peers with the intent of employing data for decision-making. In the case of USC Libraries, a new ILS and acquisitions increasingly focused on e-resources, including DDA, contributed to the growth in data availability. Whose job is it to gather the data and tell everyone not only *that* it is usable, but to *illustrate* ways in which to use it? I realized that I could share all my information.

For subject selectors, those public-facing librarians charged with reference and instruction, the data points urging them to *add this* and *cancel that* can be overwhelming and unhelpful in terms of actionable next steps in their work. I introduced the Content Gains and Losses report, a sortable and highly usable curated monthly report distributed library-wide. I assemble the report from a high-level perspective, but offer the details of the report in a tailored view that empowers rather than intimidates the intended audience of the report and users of the data.

The Content Gains and Losses report shares the new monthly resources available to users. The report tabs include
- Monograph titles in print and electronic
- Databases
- Serials in print and electronic
- Other formats including music and audiovisuals
- Demand-driven acquisition (DDA) triggered titles and other activity
- Interlibrary loan and document delivery: borrowing, lending, document delivery
- Acquisitions of special collections (including ONE Library and Cinema Archives)
- E-resources from USC Norris Medical Library, our counterpart on the medical campus, that was, up until recently, operated through a separate ILS
- Additions and withdrawals from our ProQuest comprehensive plan

USC librarians have applauded the report's utility in interacting with teaching faculty and in determining how ILL and the DDA program can be used to strengthen their subject areas. Administrators find this information useful in guiding the budget. And staff, some of whom are responsible for gathering statistics for branch libraries, used this report to fill in the blanks of analytics tools that are either cumbersome to use or time-consuming to maintain.

This chapter will detail the ways in which librarians and staff have used this report and the included data to advance assessment in their own subject areas, network with faculty, and perform collection development. This report represents the first iterative and consistent document in our libraries that uses collections data to inform and communicate with reference and instruction librarians, administrators, and other stakeholders. The goal of the Content Gains and Losses report is to inform librarians about the collection growth overall, and not just in their area of expertise. In this way, the Collections division is attempting to illustrate a comprehensive view of the changes in the collection over time.

While not the most glamorous assessment tool, the Content Gains and Losses report provides an opportunity to learn the evolution of our changing collection overall, develop outreach plans based on new resources, intentionally develop a collection based on gaps found through ILL data, and support budgetary decisions related to return on investment. Each of these factors contributes to the Collection Assessment Program at USC Libraries and effectively launched an educational campaign focused on assessment for all librarians.

The culture of collection assessment and its accompanying tools for outreach are well established in library literature.[5] As a result of declining budgets, a premium on physical space, the increased acquisitions of e-resources, and even complex license and sharing agreements, libraries experience increasing pressure to demonstrate their value and impact to the communities they support. Assessment provides a framework, statistics, and tools to both make the value case and justify budgetary decisions. In an academic environment, libraries are specifically urged to demonstrate their support of current research and scholarship as well as forecast their support of research in burgeoning disciplines. This is no small task, but one that separates a thriving library system from a failing one.

Collection assessment is "an organized process for systematically analyzing and describing a library's collection."[6] The field of collection assessment has evolved in the last ten years to encompass the abundance of data available from vendors, platforms, e-books, and more. Collection assessment tools and methods fall, generally, into two categories: collection-centered and use- or user-centered. The former analyzes the content of a collection for quantity and quality, makes comparisons to peer institutions, focuses on the collection's physical condition, and measures against core subject titles. The latter focuses on how materials are being used and by whom.[7] This approach helps the library gain insight into the perceived needs of a library user, or perceived demand. Today, it is most common to take a hybrid approach of collection and use- or user-centered assessment. Both methods of assessment are integral to shaping a strong and relevant collection, and both raised important guiding questions in the development of an assessment tool that reflected the new acquisitions and recent withdrawals from an expansive set of resources at USC Libraries.

Because I had neither a predecessor in the Collection Assessment position nor a reporting tool to modify, the development of the Content Gains and Losses report was shaped by immediate user need—what did my colleagues need to know about the changes in our collection each month? Homegrown collection assessment tools are usually intended for internal use by staff of the library. Some libraries publicly display New Books lists on their website for promotional purposes. Other libraries display assessment (if not collection assessment) tools and projects. University of Washington has a famously strong assessment program not specifically focused on collection assessment. its website offers the details of various projects dating back to 2014.[8] Duke University's Assessment and User Experience department also publicizes its assessment projects focused on usability, observation and way-finding, and surveys.[9] Even OCLC, a vendor, offers GreenGlass, a collection assessment tool for large-scale projects and data collected from resource sharing initiatives.[10]

Certainly, other libraries have developed internally focused tools of data collection and dissemination of library resources. However, they are not often discussed at conferences or detailed in literature. The Content Gains and Losses report was born from a pressing need and serves utility not as a public-facing tool, but rather as a workhorse of granular information about the shape of the collection at our libraries. Indeed, the report succeeds in offering a simple method of accessing a comprehensive list of new resources each month. With greater focus on visualization, the data contained in the Content Gains and Losses report can be more easily cross-referenced and compared. Moreover, visualization of the raw data is also more appealing to share with teaching faculty, administration, and other stakeholders. The tool also has its limitations. The report doesn't provide overviews—either monthly, quarterly, or yearly. An aerial view of the data and its change over time, and not just an overview of ways to employ the report, would be helpful to all users.

Communicating Results and Impact

The Content Gains and Losses report is an exercise in "form meets content." The report itself is the communication to my users—fellow librarians and staff making decisions about the shape of our collection. Because the report is iterative, part of the communication to users is the modification of report's content based on their comments and suggestions.

The report is designed with access points for any user. The Report Summary tab from the inaugural report in October 2015 (figure 17.1), as well as the same Report Summary tab from May 2017 (figure 17.2), aids the diverse user base on the basic structure and the ways in which users can view and download the report. (The report started on Google Sheets and moved to the libraries' intranet site, SharePoint, as a result of the university's subscription to the platform.) Because of my iterative approach, the first Report Summary details different information than later reports.

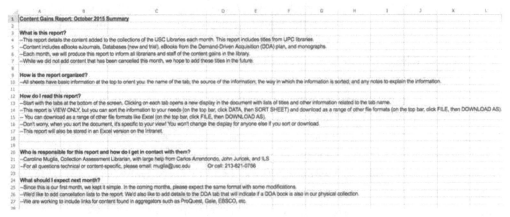

Figure 17.1
Report Summary tab from the inaugural Content Gains and Losses report in October 2015.

May Content Gains Report: Summary

May report, what's changed?
Nothing new here!

What should I expect in the next month or so?
Fund codes to be added to titles.

What is this report?
This report details the content added to the collections of the USC Libraries each month.
Content includes monographs, eBooks, serials, Databases (new and trial), eBooks from the Demand-Driven Acquisition (DDA) plan, and other formats.
This report does NOT include materials on Reserve, materials with a No-Loan/Reference status, Shadowed resources, or audio-visual materials in the Cinema Library (monographs are included).

How is the report organized?
All sheets have basic information at the top to orient you: the name of the tab; the source of the information; the way in which the information is sorted; and any notes to explain the information.

How do I read this report?
Start with the tabs at the bottom of the screen. Clicking on each tab opens a new display in the document with lists of titles and other information related to the tab name.
This report is VIEW ONLY, but you can sort the information to your needs (on the top bar, click DATA, then SORT SHEET) and download as a range of other file formats (on the top bar, click FILE, then DOWNLOAD AS).
You can download as a range of other file formats like Excel (on the top bar, click FILE, then DOWNLOAD AS).
Won't worry, when you sort the document, it's specific to your view! You won't change the display for anyone else if you sort or download.
This report will be stored in an Excel version on the Intranet.

Who is responsible for this report and how do I get in contact with them?
Caroline Muglia, Head, Resource Sharing & Collection Assessment Librarian, Co-Associate Dean for Collections, and Katherine Bartolomea, Collections Librarian
With great help from ILS, ILL, and Special Collections

Figure 17.2
Report Summary tab from the Content Gains and Losses report in May 2017.

The Report Summary contains the following sections posed as questions to emulate what the user may ask:

- What's changed?
- What should I expect in the following month (or so)?
- What is this report?
- How is this report organized?
- How do I read this report?
- Who is responsible for this report and how do I contact them?

In its most recent iteration, the report contains ten tabs that display unique monthly data points—including a statement that reminds users how to read the contents of the tab and how the tab is sorted—and a varying number of columns that provide metadata on the topic of the tab (see appendix 17.1 for sample pages of the report). The report adds statistics provided by ProQuest because, as it is a major provider of a range of resources available to USC users, its own gains and losses represent valuable information for librarians, teaching faculty, and students. ProQuest statistics also include Impact Factor and SJR Ranking, two actionable data points especially important to teaching faculty.

The source of the data that populates the Content Gains and Losses report means that in order to provide a comprehensive report, numerous databases must be accessed and the data normalized for comparison to other data points sourced from different systems. The report draws from eleven platforms, including foremost USC Libraries' integrated library system (ILS), Ex Libris's Alma. As a result of mismatched data points from one system to another, this report does not contain every possibly relevant data point. Instead, we focused on an iterative process wherein data points are continually added and refined. Collection assessment data points including EZproxy outputs and vendor and in-house usage data are excluded from the report for two reasons: first, this data was time-consuming to collect manually and was fraught with inconsistencies; second, for those users of the report interested in further usage details, it was provided on a case-by-case basis.

Table 17.1 displays the report tab name as well as the names of any subtabs associated with the main tab. For example, ILL contains borrowing, lending, and document delivery data. Each of these data points reflects different types of patron need and output from the ILL service on campus. The third column lists the sources of data, and the final column provides the language used on each tab to ensure user orientation on each tab of the report.

Table 17.1
Names and Details of Content Gains and Losses Report Tabs

Tab Content	Subtab Content	Source of Data	How to Read Contents Statement
Special Collections Acquisitions	None	ArchiveSpace	The Special Collections report shows newly cataloged materials and newly discoverable material. "Accession" is the legal, intellectual, and physical ownership of materials.
ILL	Borrowing, Lending, Document Delivery	ILLiad, RAPID, OCLC	(Specific to Borrowing) Multiple entries of the same title indicate different requests.
New Print Monographs	None	ILS (Ex Libris)	
New E-books	None	ILS (Ex Libris)	E-book titles will overlap with DDA titles.
DDA Activity	None	EBook Central (ProQuest) and EBSCO	This list contains e-books that have been added through the demand-driven acquisition plan.
New Other Formats[a]	None	ILS (Ex Libris)	
New Serials	None	ILS (Ex Libris)	
New Databases	Trial Databases	Springshare	
E-resource (Medical Library)	None	ILS (Ex Libris)	
ProQuest Gains and Losses	Gains and Losses (from comprehensive package)	Vendor provided	

a. Other formats include scores, audiovisual, federal and government documents, maps, and video games.

Since the report is an iterative one, its growth is based on user feedback and suggestions. The initial report subscribed to the product development technique of releasing a minimally viable product (MVP). This development method presents a sufficient product for users with the expectation of multiple rounds of improvement based on user feedback.[11] In this case, the Content Gains and Losses report began as a curated ILS-generated list of new acquisitions. After I conducted a survey of colleagues in the libraries, it became clear that among the most pressing issues in librarians getting more intentionally involved in collection development was transparency of the monthly acquisitions. The report started at that point of need. From there, the report grew to include ILL statistics, then DDA activities that could be useful in conjunction with the new acquisitions report.

The most successful method for user feedback consisted of email exchanges and targeted in-person conversations with power users and those who did not use the report at all. Because the report provided new information to subject selectors in a new format, I aimed to gather perspectives on the following questions:

- Are you using the report?
- If so, in what ways is it helpful to your work in collection development?
- What are your suggestions for improvement of format, layout, and content?
- If not, then why is preventing you from accessing the report?
- What could be done in terms of training, orientation, or skill sharing that would increase the likelihood that you would access the report?

Since the report followed principles of a minimally viable product, it was imperative that its contents and format evolve to meet user needs. Overwhelmingly, the users and potential users of the report wanted to become aware of the ways in which their colleagues used the report. Initially, I explained that the report *could* aid in collection development decisions or in outreach and engagement. However, the users and potential users of the report wanted what I referred to as "on the ground" examples. So did I! It was the only way I could modify the report to meet shifting or emerging user demands.

The success of the report as a mechanism for further transparency in collection development practices can be seen in four major ways, all taken directly from conversations with users of the report: ILL and DDA activities, empowering subject selectors, providing a rich engagement and outreach tool to teaching faculty, and consistently sharing value to administrators and other stakeholders.

Transparency in Interlibrary Loan and Demand-Driven Acquisitions Programs

Since the report includes activities generated from the Interlibrary Loan and Document Delivery department (IDD), subject selectors and collection development librarians could plainly compare popular borrowed titles that could reflect a gap in the home collection. In this case, the subject selector could order the title for the home collection or add it to the demand-driven acquisitions (DDA) pool with strong evidence that it would be used. Even if no action was taken, the information remains readily available and accessible to those who could amend the collection to represent the needs of its users.

In a related way, librarians are made aware of the demand-driven acquisitions programs that fuel strategic collection development at the libraries. While most librarians had familiarity with the DDA programs available to USC users, they did not have a deep knowledge of its impact on collection growth in their subject areas or the cost of titles in their area. The report remedied this void. Each month, subject selectors can view the titles accessed from the DDA pool that correspond to their subject area, if the title was used as a loan or triggered for a purchase, and the amount of money spent per title per usage. Subject selectors focused even more on the details of this tab when the fund code structure changed at the libraries and the cost of DDA was assigned to the subject fund code rather than a generic DDA fund code, where those expenses had been accounted for in previous fiscal year cycles. Since DDA activity impacted a subject selector's annual budget distribution, the cost per title increased in level of importance.

Empowering Subject Selectors

At USC Libraries, the Content Gains and Losses report was the subject selectors' first glimpse into the overall acquisitions each month, as well as a detailed account of the acquisitions and new resources in their subject areas that had been part of an approval plan or DDA program. With the knowledge of new acquisitions, subject selectors became familiar with the volume of resources owned, leased, or subscribed to through the libraries, which in turn led to a greater appreciation for the collection overall.

The report also provided evidence of gaps in subject areas that allowed the subject selector to consider targeted acquisitions to close the gap. In several instances, the subject selectors regularly cross-referenced both the gaps in their subject area and new acquisitions with the ILL statistics to glean more. One subject selector learned that much of the usage of books in an LC subclass he maintained was attributed to ILL's lending to other schools. Conversely, another subject selector took notice of the overlap between new print book acquisitions and DDA activity of the same titles. This indicated to the subject selector that while the titles may have been needed, users preferred the electronic format of those particular titles offered through the DDA program.

Finally, many subject selectors used the report to confirm discoverability of the resources they acquired earlier. At USC, subject selectors may buy a resource, but often they are not the ones receiving the resource. Instead, the resource cycles through Technical Services before it's added to a crate and sent to the appropriate branch library, where it is added to the collection and made available for loan or usage. While subject selectors remained aware of the process, many did not express confidence in the time lapse between acquisition and availability. The report offered a method of tracking their acquisitions to confirm that users could access the resource.

Outreach and Engagement

Teaching faculty play an instrumental role in collection development. That is, if you can get a moment of time to discuss library resources! At USC, subject selectors use multiple tactics to engage teaching faculty on library-centric topics: scheduling instruction sessions, participating in reference interviews, sitting on committees, and so much more. The Content Gains and Losses report provided a new method of engagement with teaching faculty. Many subject selectors sorted the report to isolate the LC class or subclass that corresponded to the subject area of the teaching faculty members before sending the modified report to them. This promoted an exchange with the faculty members regarding new acquisitions or confirming the acquisitions they may have recommended the month before. The report also provided an opportunity for the subject selectors to lead a conversation about the importance of the faculty member's role in collection development.

Several librarians used the modified report as the basis of a departmental newsletter or short presentation for the department with which they liaised as part of their job. An example of utilizing the data from this report can be found in Carolyn Caffrey Gardner's monthly newsletter to the sociology department that she developed as part of her liaison responsibilities (see appendix 17.2). Gardner combined general news featuring the libraries with detailed information on new and available resources. She highlighted new and trial databases, journals, and books all in the area of sociology. She derived these details from the Content Gains and Losses report, including the links allowing a reader to click directly into the resource.

Another liaison in Japanese studies appreciated the column that featured the original script of non-Roman language resources. She shared the report with faculty in the Japanese department who were interested in viewing new titles in their purview that contained the original, rather than the Romanized, script of those resources. The Japanese department faculty requested incorporating the column that contained the original script into the report. Once we did, the librarian became a power user of the report on behalf of the faculty who found the information useful in their research and teaching practice.

Interacting with Stakeholders

Indeed, teaching faculty members are not the only audience for which the report could inspire engagement with the libraries. The report is also used as part of interactions with various stakeholders in the libraries and through the university. Most often, the statistics compiled in the report provides a macro-level perspective of growth over time. For grant applications, Association of Research Libraries (ARL) reporting, and university-wide assessments, the monthly reports can be aggregated for annual metrics that can be presented in various forms: libraries acquisitions in comparison to growth and interest in research and scholarship on campus; evidence of the annual allocated Collections budget expenditures; and support of new programs, disciplines, or even teaching faculty with related resources. The report has also enabled the libraries to contribute data points to the Office of Institutional Research's growing data sets used to learn more about the behaviors and needs of students on campus. Since the report is a tool of the Collection Assessment Program, its utility is best to show value of my job to my colleagues, the dean of the libraries, and peers in other libraries attempting to promote the culture of collection assessment in libraries.

Leveraging the Findings

The utilization of the report illustrates its impact as a straightforward tool for assessment and evaluation of the libraries' resources and selected services. Still, there is more work

Section 2

to be done toward a comprehensive report with increased functionality and flexibility within the libraries and to benefit the university. In the next phase of development of the report, it will grow to include relevant usage metrics generated from the activity in the Digital Library. Instruction and reference, areas that produce a high volume of data points, may also be included to compare new acquisitions to engagement of teaching faculty in the collection development process, or even reference queries about resources and the usage of those resources in subsequent months. In order to achieve additional development, new stakeholders will need to be engaged and new data sources investigated. In later phases, I hope to draw in search statistics from the libraries' website and even head counts of branch libraries.

While not the highest priority of the report features, visualization remains an important tool in facilitating a conversation using data. Currently, we are preparing the report for visualization in Tableau, software that produces interactive data visualization products marketed to academic institutions. We chose the Tableau platform because of its ubiquity in the library community and on USC's campus. The goals of visualizing the report are simple: make the numbers more exciting to view and more actionable in terms of cross-referencing within the report and sharing with stakeholders. While the spreadsheets are still widely accessed, the goal is to shift to an entirely visual display and a permanent location on the libraries' website where any visitor to the site will have a chance to view and interact with the data from the report.

Reflection

The Content Gains and Losses report is a highly collaborative product that requires monthly maintenance to retrieve current data points. The collaborative partners will likely increase as the report's functionality shifts to include a broader snapshot of the libraries and is positioned to engage with university-level questions about value. The report is highly replicable in any institution irrespective of its size, collections scope, budget, or personnel to contribute to the report. Three points aided my development of the initial report and its many iterations.

Keep It Simple, Relevant, and Interesting

Any employee of the libraries could have created a report from the ILS to determine some of the findings illustrated in the Content Gains and Losses report. But none did. Still, many of those same people had questions related to collections details that would become the basis of the report. This indicated to me that a report that subject selectors wanted to use must be simple to view, relevant in its content, and interesting enough to return the next month. I kept the design uncluttered, simple, and consistent, a departure from the raw data that populated the report. Each month, the pages remained in the same order (always beginning with a Report Summary tab), and changes to the content of the report were clearly noted. The report was released around the same time each month (second week of the month to reflect the resources from the month prior) and stored in a shared folder accessible to all employees of the libraries. The monthly content was timely and could answer collection development questions and could be used for engagement with teaching faculty. Because I received feedback from report users, the subject selectors remained interested in the level of detail in each tab and the order of the report.

Show and Tell (and Repeat)

It is not enough to provide access to data. It is not enough to curate the data. In order for most people to take actionable steps informed by the data, you need to show them. Perhaps *showing* is starting small with a few usable data points solicited by fellow librarians. Perhaps *showing* is offering different questions that can be answered using the data. Learn the method that works for your colleagues and cultivate them! Then, do it all over again. The intended audience did not get involved in reading the report in its first months. The user base slowly increased as I employed suggestions of early adopters and began iterating the content, layout, and format of the report. At each juncture, I explained the function of the report and stewarded subject selectors through various ways of engaging with the report.

Tell People What You're Up To

I released the inaugural Content Gains and Losses report in October 2015, five months after starting my position as Collection Assessment Librarian. In my search for collaborators, I spoke with every subject selector and staff member affiliated with collection development or data management. Telling colleagues my goals for this project, even in its infancy, facilitated fruitful conversations about the needs of the libraries in the area of assessment. I brainstormed so many ideas, some of which manifested in the report and some that did not. Still, the ability to speak about an idea, especially one that addresses a long-term need of the libraries, strengthened the end result and the path moving forward to future phases.

Appendix 17.1

Sample Pages from the Content Gains and Losses Report

Section 2

	A	B	C	D	E	F
1	**Name of report: eBook additions**					
2	Sorted: By Call #					
3	Source: ILS					
4	Notes: eBook titles will overlap with DDA titles.					
5						
6	**Title**	**Author**	**Language**	**Original Script**	**Call #**	**Catalog Date**	**URL to HOME**
7	The role of fossil fuels in the U.S. food system and the American diet	Canning, Patrick N., author	eng		A 93.73:224	2017-05-09	https://library.usc.e
8	The influence of income and prices on global dietary patterns by country, age, and gender	Muhammed, Andrew, author	eng		A 93.73:225	2017-05-09	https://library.usc.e
9	Farm household income volatility : an analysis using panel data from a national survey	Key, Nigel David, author	eng		A 93.73:226	2017-05-09	https://library.usc.e
10	The potential effects of increased demand for U.S. agricultural exports on metro and nonmetro employment	Zahniser, Steven, author	eng		A 93.73:227	2017-05-09	https://library.usc.e
11	National Park Service Centennial Act	United States, enacting jurisdiction	eng		AE 2.110:114-289	2017-05-09	https://library.usc.e
12	An Act to Amend the Inspector General Act of 1978 to Strengthen the Independence of the Inspectors General, and for Other Purposes	United States, enacting jurisdiction	eng		AE 2.110:114-317	2017-05-09	https://library.usc.e
13	Federal Property Management Reform Act of 2016	United States, enacting jurisdiction	eng		AE 2.110:114-318	2017-05-09	https://library.usc.e
14	The language of museum communication : a diachronic perspective	Lazzeretti, Cecilia	eng		AM125 .L39 2016	2017-05-15	https://library.usc.e
15	The digital scholar : how technology is transforming scholarly practice	Weller, Martin	eng		AZ195 .W45 2011	2017-05-05	https://library.usc.e
16	On reference	Bianchi, Andrea	eng		B105.R25 O52 2015	2017-05-15	https://library.usc.e
17	Drafts for the Essay concerning human understanding, and other philosophical writings	Locke, John, 1632-1704	eng		B1253 1990	2017-05-15	https://library.usc.e
18	The emotions in early Chinese philosophy	Virág, Curie, 1970-	eng		B127.E46 V57 2017	2017-05-15	https://library.usc.e
19	Confucius beyond the analects	Hunter, Michael, Ph.D	eng		B128.C8 H883 2017	2017-05-15	https://library.usc.e
20	The Correspondence of John Locke: Vol. 8. Letters 3287-3648	Locke, John 1632-1704 Author	eng		B1296	2017-05-15	https://library.usc.e
21	The correspondence of John Locke	Locke, John, 1632-1704	eng		B1296 .A4 2010	2017-05-15	https://library.usc.e

	A	B	C	D	E
1	**Name of report: DDA activity**				
2	Sorted: LC Class				
3	Source: GOBI, EBL, sibrary				
4	Notes: This list contains eBooks that have been added through the demand-driven acquisition plan. "Trigger" and "Usage" refer to				
5					
6	**LC Class**	**Title**	**Date triggered**	**Subject**	**In Print in USC Collection?**
7	BF199 .H364 2012eb	Handbook of Research Methods for Studying Daily Life	2017-05-19	Psychology	X
8	BF341 .N377 2011eb	Nature and Nurture in Early Child Development	2017-05-31	Psychology	X
9	BF575.A3 S86 2010eb	Microaggressions in Everyday Life : Race, Gender, and Sexual Orientation	2017-05-18	Psychology, Social Science	X
10	BF724 .A253 2011eb	Adolescence and Beyond : Family Processes and Development	2017-05-11	Psychology	X
11	BF76.7 .B447 2012eb	APA Style Simplified : Writing in Psychology, Education, Nursing, and Sociology	2017-05-10	Literature, Psychology	X
12	BH301.S7 .B733 2013eb	The Sublime in Modern Philosophy : Aesthetics, Ethics, and Nature	2017-05-18	Philosophy	X
13	BQ5775.J3 K4413 2013eb	Record of Miraculous Events in Japan : The Nihon ryōiki	2017-05-10	Religion, Fiction	X
14	BV3427.M6 D35 2013eb	Robert Morrison and the Protestant Plan for China	2017-05-04	Religion	X
15	C8245 .M495 2011	The Darker Side of Western Modernity : Global Futures, Decolonial Options	2017-05-17	History, Geography/Travel	X
16	DE71 .A25 2011eb	Great Sea : A Human History of the Mediterranean	2017-05-05	History, Geography/Travel	X
17	DS318.6 .A26 2015eb	The Coup : 1953, The CIA, and The Roots of Modern U.S.-Iranian Relations	2017-05-10	History	X
18	DS63.1 .A375 2011	Critical Turning Points in the Middle East : 1915 - 2015	2017-05-03	Geography/Travel, History	X
19	DS732 .S57 2013eb	Sinophone Studies : A Critical Reader	2017-05-19	History, Social Science	X
20	DS918 .M56 2013eb	Understanding the Korean War : The Participants, the Tactics, and the Course of Conflict	2017-05-10	History	X
21	E184.A1 .F739 2015eb	Diversity Explosion : How New Racial Demographics are Remaking America	2017-05-05	Social Science, History	X
22	E185.625 .O55 2013eb	Therapeutic Antiracism : Afro-Asian Solidarity in 20th-Century Black America, Japan, and Okinawa	2017-05-19	History, Social Science	X
23	E76.85 .L66 2012eb	Decolonizing Museums : Representing Native America in National and Tribal Museums	2017-05-28	History	X
24	E839.5 .W44 2013eb	Celebrity Politics	2017-05-08	History, Social Science	X
25	E840.2 .C86 2012eb	The Decline and Fall of the United States Information Agency : American Public Diplomacy, 1989-2001	2017-05-08	Political Science, History	X
26	E97.6.B3 N48 2013eb	Indian Play : Indigenous Identities at Bacone College	2017-05-07	Education, History	X
27	F869.L89 N3194 2010eb	Black Los Angeles : American Dreams and Racial Realities	2017-05-03	Geography/Travel, History, Social Science	X
28	HA31.2 .S873 2009	Survey Methodology	2017-05-29	General Works/Reference, Social Science	X
29	HD30.3 .C37155 2013eb	Case Studies in Organizational Communication : Ethical Perspectives and Practices	2017-05-13	Business/Management, Social Science	
30	HD31.B6135 2013eb	Reframing Organizations : Artistry, Choice, and Leadership	2017-05-24	Business/Management	
31	HD62.6 .J67 2016	The Jossey-Bass Handbook of Nonprofit Leadership and Management	2017-05-08	Business/Management	
32	HD6509.C48 G37 2012eb	From the Jaws of Victory : The Triumph and Tragedy of Cesar Chavez and the Farm Worker Movement	2017-05-10	Business/Management, Economics	X
33	HD66.L456 2002	The Five Dysfunctions of a Team : A Leadership Fable	2017-05-23	Business/Management	
34	HD69.B7 B256 2012eb	Authentic™ : The Politics of Ambivalence in a Brand Culture	2017-05-17	Business/Management, Social Science	X
35	HD69.B7 H345 2011eb	Brand Failures : The Truth About the 100 Biggest Branding Mistakes of All Time	2017-05-30	Business/Management	
36	HF5415.32 .O547 2012eb	Online Consumer Behavior : Theory and Research in Social Media, Advertising and E-tail	2017-05-04	Business/Management	X

Appendix 17.2

Carolyn Caffrey Gardner's Newsletter to the Sociology Department

Dear Sociology:

We're almost to the end of the semester! Please feel free to contact me about purchasing materials, research help, or library instruction. Any suggested items for purchase will be ordered at the start of the new fiscal year, July 1st. You can find more information on Sociology Library Resources at http://libguides.usc.edu/soci.

-Carolyn Caffrey Gardner
Librarian for Sociology & Gender Studies
(213) 821-2299
ccgardne@usc.edu

New Database: Scopus

Scopus is a robust citation index similar to Web of Science. It contains altmetric impact data for the journal articles, conference papers, and books for all subject areas. Create author alerts and track citation analytics t department, university, or author.

Trial Database

SAGE Research Methods Datasets Trial access to this database will expire 6/5/2015. Please provide feedback on its content before then to assist in purchasing decisions.

New Journal

Newly added to our collection:

- Girlhood Studies (All issues from 2008 to present)

Summer Reading

Looking for a great beach read this summer? Taking a break for sociology texts? Leavey Library has a popular reading collection that rotates

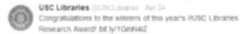

USC Libraries @USCLibraries · Apr 24
Congratulations to the winners of this year's #USC Libraries Research Award! bit.ly/1GmR462

Section 2

The USC Libraries third annual Research Award recognizes excellence and creativity in the use of Libraries' research collections. Undergraduate and graduate students are invited to submit papers or projects they have completed at USC in a class during the spring, summer, or fall semesters of 2015 that use library resources. First place graduate students can win $500 and undergraduates up to $300. For more information see:

http://libguides.usc.edu/researchaward

to include all the latest bestsellers. Find out more, including the current title list, at http://libguides.usc.edu/popular

Selected New Books

- Playing fans: negotiating fandom and media in the digital age
- Non-representational methodologies: re-envisioning research
- Systems theory and the sociology of health and illness: observing healthcare
- Ethnography for the internet: embedded, embodied, everyday
- Some men: feminist allies in the movement to end violence against women
- Building financial management capacity for NGOs and community organizations
- The power of the past: understanding cross-class marriages
- Globalization: the paradox of organizational behavior

You are receiving this email because you have signed up on the Sociology Research Guide or have received it through a listserv.

unsubscribe from this list   update subscription preferences

Notes

1. *ARL Statistics* webpage, Association of Research Libraries, accessed June 1, 2017, http://www.arl.org/publications-resources/arlstatistics.
2. Peter Hernon and Robert E. Dugan and Joseph R. Matthews, *Managing with Data* (Chicago: American Library Association, 2015), 12-20.
3. Jim Agee, "Collection Evaluation: A Foundation for Collection Development," *Collection Building* 4, no. 3 (2004): 93.
4. Amos Lakos and Shelley E. Phipps, "Creating a Culture of Assessment: A Catalyst for Organizational Change," *portal: Libraries and the Academy* 4, no. 3 (2004): 345–61; Steve Hiller, Martha Kyrillidou, and Jim Self, "When the Evidence Is Not Enough: Organizational Factors That Influence Effective and Successful Library Assessment," *Performance Measurement and Metrics* 9, no. 3 (2008): 223–30; Lizabeth A. Wilson, "Building the User-Centered Library," *RQ* 34, no. 3 (1995): 297–303.
5. Jane Schmidt. "Musings on Collection Analysis and Its Utility in Modern Collection Development," *Evidence Based Library and Information Practice* 5, no. 3 (2010): 62–67; M. P. Ciszek and

C. L. Young, "Diversity Collection Assessment in Large Academic Libraries," *Collection Building* 29, no. 4 (2010): 154–61; Russell F. Dennison, "Quality Assessment of Collection Development through Tiered Checklists: Can You Prove You Are a Good Collection Developer?" *Collection Building* 19, no. 1 (2000): 24–27; Elizabeth Henry, Rachel Longstaff, and Doris Van Kampen, "Collection Analysis Outcomes in an Academic Library," *Collection Building* 27, no. 3 (2008): 113–17; James Cory Tucker and Matt Torrence, "Collection Development for New Librarians: Advice from the Trenches," *Library Collections, Acquisitions, and Technical Services* 28, no. 4 (2004): 397–409.

6. Peggy Johnson, *Fundamentals of Collection Development and Management* (Chicago: American Library Association, 2004), 269.
7. Agee, "Collection Evaluation," 93.
8. "Assessment Projects," University of Washington Libraries, accessed August 20, 2017, http://www.lib.washington.edu/assessment/projects.
9. "Assessment and User Experience," Duke University Libraries, accessed August 20, 2017, https://library.duke.edu/about/depts/assessment-user-experience.
10. "SCS and GreenGlass," OCLC, last updated September 22, 2017, https://help.oclc.org/Library_Management/SCS_and_GreenGlass.
11. "The Lean Startup Methodology," The Lean Startup, accessed June 1, 2017, http://theleanstartup.com/principles; Steve Blank. "Why the Lean Start-up Changes Everything," *Harvard Business Review* 91, no. 5 (2013): 63–72.

Bibliography

Agee, Jim. "Collection Evaluation: A Foundation for Collection Development." *Collection Building* 4, no. 3 (2004): 92–95.

Association of Research Libraries. *ARL Statistics* webpage. Association of Research Libraries, accessed June 1, 2017. http://www.arl.org/publications-resources/arlstatistics.

Blank, Steve. "Why the Lean Start-up Changes Everything." *Harvard Business Review* 91, no. 5 (2013): 63–72.

Ciszek, M. P., and C. L. Young. "Diversity Collection Assessment in Large Academic Libraries." *Collection Building* 29, no. 4 (2010): 154–61.

Dennison, Russell F. "Quality Assessment of Collection Development through Tiered Checklists: Can You Prove You Are a Good Collection Developer?" *Collection Building* 19, no. 1 (2000): 24–27.

Duke University Libraries. "Assessment and User Experience." Accessed August 20, 2017. https://library.duke.edu/about/depts/assessment-user-experience.

Henry, Elizabeth, Rachel Longstaff, and Doris Van Kampen. "Collection Analysis Outcomes in an Academic Library." *Collection Building* 27, no. 3 (2008): 113–17.

Hernon, Peter, Robert E. Dugan, and Joseph R. Matthews. *Managing with Data: Using ACRLMetrics and PLAmetrics.* Chicago: American Library Association, 2015.

Hiller, Steve, Martha Kyrillidou, and Jim Self. "When the Evidence Is Not Enough: Organizational Factors That Influence Effective and Successful Library Assessment." *Performance Measurement and Metrics* 9, no. 3 (2008): 223–30.

Johnson, Peggy. *Fundamentals of Collection Development and Management.* Chicago: American Library Association, 2004.

Lakos, Amos, and Shelley E. Phipps. "Creating a Culture of Assessment: A Catalyst for Organizational Change." *portal: Libraries and the Academy* 4, no. 3 (2004): 345–61.

Lean Startup. "The Lean Startup Methodology." The Lean Startup, accessed June 1, 2017. http://theleanstartup.com/principles.

OCLC. "SCS and GreenGlass." OCLC. Last updated September 22, 2017. https://help.oclc.org/Library_Management/SCS_and_GreenGlass.

Schmidt, Jane. "Musings on Collection Analysis and Its Utility in Modern Collection Development." *Evidence Based Library and Information Practice* 5, no. 3 (2010): 62–67.

Tucker, James Cory, and Matt Torrence. "Collection Development for New Librarians: Advice from the Trenches." *Library Collections, Acquisitions, and Technical Services* 28, no. 4 (2004): 397–409.

University of Washington Libraries. "Assessment Projects." Accessed August 20, 2017. http://www.lib.washington.edu/assessment/projects.

Wilson, Lizabeth A. "Building the User-Centered Library." *RQ* 34, no. 3 (1995): 297–303.

Title: Q-methodology: A Versatile, Quick, and Adaptable Indirect Assessment Method

Abstract: Q-methodology is a mixed-method approach used to identify opinions shared among populations on issues they consider important. The focus is on the nature of the opinion segments and the extent to which they are similar or dissimilar, so a large sample is not necessary. Q studies can be easily and quickly implemented in a variety of library-related contexts where understanding viewpoints (and subjectivity of those viewpoints) is important.

Keywords: subjectivity, mixed methods, methodology

Project focus: assessment methodologies, techniques, or practices

Results made or will make case for: improvements in services, improvements in collections, how money or resources may be directed

Data needed: Varies depending on what is being examined. Basic information such as department/major and status (year for student; title for faculty) is needed for most studies.

Methodology: mixed method

Project duration: less than 3 months

Tool(s) utilized: 2–3 staff members to plan and facilitate sessions using the methodology, statistical package (Excel or SPSS) for analysis

Cost estimate: < $100

Type of institution: university—public

Institution enrollment: 15,000–30,000

Highest level of education: doctoral

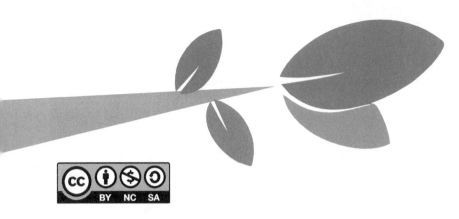

CC BY NC SA

Chapter 18

Q-methodology

A Versatile, Quick, and Adaptable Indirect Assessment Method

Eric Resnis and Aaron Shrimplin

Context

User opinions and attitudes play a key role in library service development, implementation, and assessment. Gathering and analyzing these opinions in a structured manner can provide challenges of their own, including garnering wide and meaningful participation. Furthermore, user values and beliefs can vary between institutions, so relying solely on the literature to understand user opinion often discounts their personal and institutional experiences.

One way to assist with these challenges is to utilize Q-methodology. Strengths of Q-methodology include reasonably quick implementation, lower sample sizes, and straightforward analysis. Q-methodology is a fully developed method for the systematic investigation of human subjectivity.[1] In this context, subjectivity simply means the communication of one's opinion or point of view on a certain topic. Q is an intensive method and involves a small sample size. Because of that, results are not statistically representative of a larger population. The purpose of the method is to present an overall view of the types of thinking that exist in relation to a specific subject or topic. It does not tell how much of the population subscribes to a certain way of thinking. To answer that question, follow-up with a large sample survey would be needed.[2] The methodology is well suited to quick explorations of user attitudes and beliefs regarding the library in general or any specific library service or resource.

Q-methodology was first introduced in 1935 by British physicist and psychologist William Stevenson.[3] Q-methodology has wide use in the communication, health science, and political science domains and has found some use in the field of academic librarianship. Dick and Edelman used the methodology to prioritize journal titles as candidates for possible cancellation.[4] Hurst and colleagues and Brinkman and Krivickas examined opinions on e-book usage,[5] while Waller, Revelle, and Shrimplin looked at faculty opinions regarding scholarly communication issues.[6] More recently, Kelly and Young examined the library priorities of undergraduates using Q,[7] while Lumley investigated librarian attitudes regarding social justice.[8]

Method and Implementation

A Q-study involves three basic procedures.[9] First, a set of opinion statements about some topic is collected. Second, study subjects read the statements and order them along a continuum of preference, usually from agree to disagree. This is known as a Q-sort. Third, data is analyzed using a statistical technique called factor analysis. The factors that emerge from the analysis indicate segments of subjectivity (opinion) on the specific topic.

Step 1: Opinion Statements

The first step of a Q-study, after establishing the topic of interest, is to collect statements that represent conversation on the topic. The conversation surrounding a specific topic is known as a concourse. There are numerous ways to capture a concourse. Interviews are a common procedure for this step, where a small number of subjects (five to ten) are presented with open-ended questions on the specific topic. Interviews typically last twenty to thirty minutes. A concourse can also be captured from literature on the topic of interest. Note that in this context, literature can refer to scholarly publications, but also to comments or opinions published in traditional and electronic media and other nonacademic outlets. Interviews and literature statements are often combined to ensure that a wide range of opinion is represented. Opinion statements gathered anecdotally could be considered for inclusion, but research should not focus solely on statements collected in this manner. In a Q-study investigating librarian attitudes toward online reference, the concourse for the study was captured using essays, online discussion groups, blogs, and conference presentations where people expressed opinions about online reference.[10]

This process often results in a considerably large number of opinion statements (in the hundreds), so it is necessary to reduce the statements to a manageable number for the next step of the process. Statements may be chosen using unstructured sampling, a basic technique in which statements presumed to be relevant to the topic are chosen in such a way that all possible issues are represented in the sample.[11] The final number of statements represent the diversity of opinions on the topic without favoring some to the exclusion of others. In a study completed at Miami University looking at students and the library as place, a concourse was obtained by asking students to participate in a free-text exercise. Students were asked to spend a few minutes writing about their opinions about the library and its services. The free-text exercise resulted in 140 statements, of which 42 were chosen using an unstructured sample that expressed an array of opinions on library as place. The researchers were confident that the final statement sample was comprehensive in scope and balanced in content.[12]

Another technique for choosing statements is to apply the design principles of factorial experimentation. With this approach, Q-sample statements are assigned to conditions designated and defined by the researcher. In another study done at Miami University on attitudes toward e-books, investigators conducted seventeen in-person interviews with faculty and students, at both the graduate and undergraduate level.[13] Interviews were transcribed, and over 200 opinion statements were extracted. To reduce the opinion statements to a manageable number yet ensure that those selected were representative of the overall collection, a simple factorial design was used to guide the final assignment and selection of statements. When reading through the concourse, it was noted that statements were about issues (readability, access, or task) and about direction (pro, mixed, or con). As a result of this insight, 45 statements were chosen according to the design framework presented in table 18.1.

Table 18.1
Example Table of Design Framework for Q-Sample Composition

	Main Effects	**Levels**		
A.	Issues	(a) Readability	(b) Access	(c) Task
B.	Direction	(d) Pro	(e) Mixed	(f) Con
Note: Each of the nine cells in the A x B (3 x 3) factorial framework is fitted with five statements for a total Q-sample of n = 45.				

Step 2: The Q-sort

Once opinion statements have been finalized, the next step is termed the Q-sort. The Q-sort requires thirty to forty-five minutes to complete, and participants can be recruited through open calls. During the Q-sort, participants are provided with a set of the selected statements from step 1, a step-by-step guide on how to sort the statements (see appendix 18.1) and a worksheet to order the set of statements (see table 18.2). The worksheet contains a distribution grid that resembles a normal bell-shaped curve, and the total number of boxes in the grid is determined by the final number of statements selected during step 1.

Table 18.2

Q-sort Worksheet (for 36 Statements)

Most Strongly Disagree				Neutral/Not Sure			Most Strongly Agree			
−5	−4	−3	−2	−1	0	1	2	3	4	5

To complete the worksheet, participants first familiarize themselves with the broad array of opinions, and then separate the statements (note that each statement is numbered) into two piles: agree and disagree (see figure 18.1). Then, participants work through each pile to prioritize statements from those that they most agree with (and most disagree with) to those that are more neutral. Once order of preference has been determined, participants enter the number of each statement on the grid (see figure 18.2). Demographic information may be collected at this stage, and participants are asked if they are willing to be interviewed at a later date. Follow-up interviews may be used to confirm the findings from step 3 but are not required for the protocol. Typically, in a follow-up interview, an investigator will describe how a person associated with a particular factor type thinks about a topic. This description is often in the form of a narrative. The individual participating in the follow-up interview will then have a chance to comment on the narrative and provide feedback on how well it describes him- or herself.

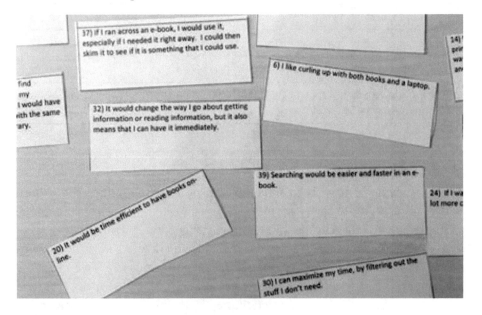

Figure 18.1

Image of laminated Q-statements that would be used in a Q-sort.

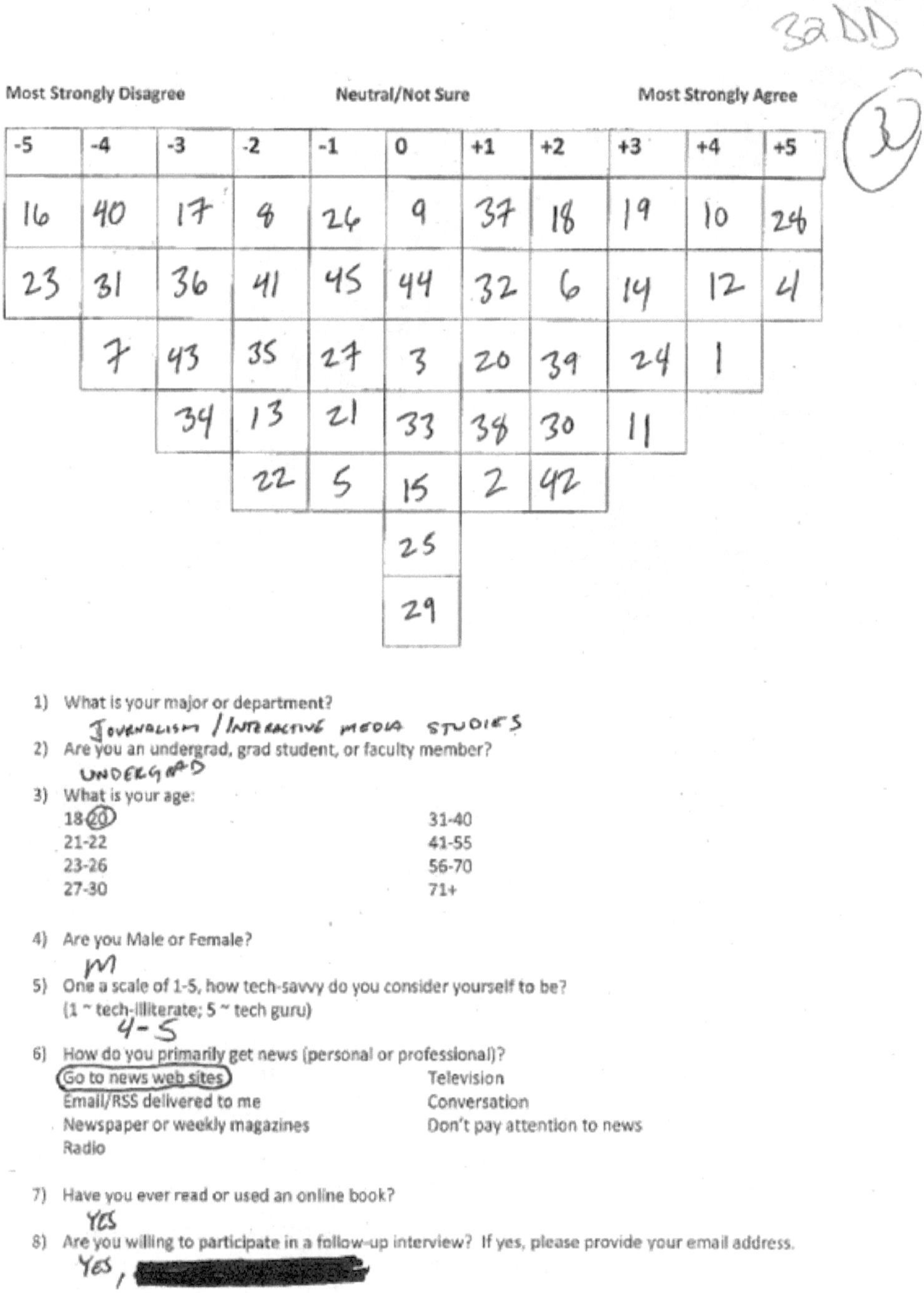

[handwritten: 32 DD, 3]

Most Strongly Disagree					Neutral/Not Sure				Most Strongly Agree	
-5	-4	-3	-2	-1	0	+1	+2	+3	+4	+5
16	40	17	8	26	9	37	18	19	10	24
23	31	36	41	45	44	32	6	14	12	4
	7	43	35	27	3	20	39	24	1	
		34	13	21	33	38	30	11		
			22	5	15	2	42			
					25					
					29					

1) What is your major or department?
   JOURNALISM / INTERACTIVE MEDIA STUDIES
2) Are you an undergrad, grad student, or faculty member?
   UNDERGRAD
3) What is your age:
   18-20 *(circled)*   31-40
   21-22   41-55
   23-26   56-70
   27-30   71+

4) Are you Male or Female?
   M
5) One a scale of 1-5, how tech-savvy do you consider yourself to be?
   (1 ~ tech-illiterate; 5 ~ tech guru)
   4-5
6) How do you primarily get news (personal or professional)?
   Go to news web sites *(circled)*   Television
   Email/RSS delivered to me   Conversation
   Newspaper or weekly magazines   Don't pay attention to news
   Radio

7) Have you ever read or used an online book?
   YES
8) Are you willing to participate in a follow-up interview? If yes, please provide your email address.
   YES, ▓▓▓▓▓▓▓▓▓

Figure 18.2
A completed Q-sort worksheet from an e-book study, along with several demographic questions and the option to opt in for a follow-up interview.

Step 3: Data Analysis

Analysis of Q-sorts is conducted using a statistical package, such as PQMethod, which is tailored to the requirements of Q-studies (see figure 18.3).[14]

[side tab: Section 2]

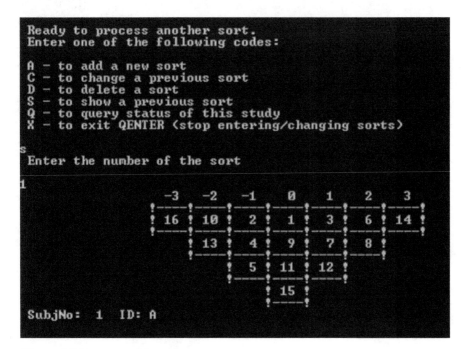

Figure 18.3
Screenshot from PQMethod showing the results of a Q-sort.

Each Q-sort is intercorrelated with the others, and the resulting correlation matrix is factor analyzed using the Principal Component Method.[15] A factor analysis is completed to reveal which attitudinal typologies are the most typical, where a factor indicates a group of participants that think similarly on the topic. Analysis focuses on factor loadings, which measure how saturated a participant is on a given factor. An example of a factor analysis is included in table 18.3.

Table 18.3
Example Table of Factor Loading Scores[a]

Factor Loading Scores					Major	Status	Gender
Subject #	Factor 1	Factor 2	Factor 3	Factor 4			
29	33	21	(52)	12	Psychology	Undergrad	Male
30	−25	(79)	02	−19	Journalism	Undergrad	Male
31	(62)	−01	27	22	Psychology	Undergrad	Female
32	(60)	13	27	26	Family Studies	Undergrad	Female
33	(74)	−21	30	05	Zoology	Undergrad	Female
34	25	23	−06	(64)	Psychology	Undergrad	Female

Note: A higher positive score indicates a more positive association (agreement) with that factor. A higher negative score indicates a more negative association with that factor. () indicates that the loading was statistically significant ($p < .01$).

a. Example from results of Susan Hurst, Kevin R. Messner, Andrew Revelle, and Aaron Shrimplin, "Conflict and Consensus: Clusters of Opinions on E-books," conference papers, ACRL 14th National Conference, March 12–15, 2009, Seattle, WA, http://www.ala.org/acrl/sites/ala.org.acrl/files/content/conferences/confsandpreconfs/national/seattle/papers/226.pdf (used with permission).

In this example from an e-book study at Miami University, subject 29, a male psychology undergraduate, loaded significantly on factor 3. Individuals that loaded on this factor think similarly about e-books. The study's investigators described factor 3 individuals as pragmatists. Subject number 30 loaded on factor 2, referred to as technophiles. Subjects 31, 32, and 33 all helped define factor 1 and were characterized as book lovers. Subject 64, a female undergraduate in psychology, loaded on factor 4 and is described as a printer. Further characteristics of each factor type are available in the study.

Note that the factors determined during the analysis step do *not* represent all possible points of view; they represent distinctive ways of thinking that exist in the given population. As Q has confidence in its individual observations, it is expected that small groups of subjects will reflect the structures existing in some larger population of subjects. As the unit of analysis is a topic and not an individual, adding more individuals to the study will at some point not yield any new information, unless the new participants truly express a different point of view. As mentioned before, Q provides information on the points of view that exist on a certain topic; it does *not* indicate how much of the population subscribes to a certain point of view. A more traditional method could be utilized to gain that information following the Q-study.[16]

In addition to the factor analysis, an idealized sort can also be completed for all opinion statements (example provided in table 18.4). An idealized Q-sort is used in the interpretative process to help compare and describe the distinctive ways of thinking. Furthermore, it assists in realizing how opinion statements are distinguished from or related to each other across the factors. In short, an idealized Q-sort represents how a hypothetical individual loading 100 percent on a factor would order the Q-statements used in the study. Investigators will often create idealized Q-sorts to study and interpret their meaning. Subjects that have a high positive factor score on only one factor think very similarly to the hypothetical Q-sort. As a result, these subjects are good candidates for follow-up interviews. To validate the narrative describing a factor type, investigators will often read the descriptive narrative to a follow-up candidate and look for confirmation—a response equivalent to "Yes, that is how I think about this topic."

Table 18.4

Example Table of Factor Loading Scores[a]

Statement	Factor Arrays			
	1	**2**	**3**	**4**
I like curling up with both books and a laptop.	−1	0	+3	0
If I can get an electronic copy (of an item), then I would be more likely to use it.	−3	+2	+3	−1
I do not really see a downside to e-books.	−5	+1	−4	−3
There are times when it is beneficial to have paper, so I can write on it, or view it anywhere.	+3	0	+5	+2
I personally think having e-books would defeat the purpose of having a physical library.	−3	−5	−1	−4

Note: Positive scores indicate level of agreement with statement, while negative scores indicate level of disagreement. A 0 indicates no strong opinion.

a. Example from results of Susan Hurst, Kevin R. Messner, Andrew Revelle, and Aaron Shrimplin, "Conflict and Consensus: Clusters of Opinions on E-books," conference papers, ACRL 14th National Conference, March 12–15, 2009, Seattle, WA, http://www.ala.org/acrl/sites/ala.org.acrl/files/content/conferences/confsandpreconfs/national/seattle/papers/226.pdf (used with permission).

The last piece of analysis involves transforming the quantitative data into narrative profiles for each individual factor. In this context, *profile* simply means a description of opinions and behaviors that are typical of someone who subscribes to a certain point of view or factor. In interpreting the factors, the examination is not done simply by looking at individual statements or examining only extreme scores for each factor. Rather, how statements are placed in relation to one another in each factor, and the comparative placement of statements in different factors, must be examined quite closely. Some opinions will not make sense when looking simply at individual statements, but should make sense when examined holistically. In this step, it is necessary to use the data to tell a story using a qualitative process.

Communicating Results and Impact

When communicating the results of a Q-study, it is extremely important to note that the results indicate identified points of view on a certain topic and that one cannot assume how much of a given population subscribe to any given point of view. This should be indicated clearly in any communication and likely reiterated throughout the process.

The profile, or narrative summary, of a given factor is powerful in helping others understand the distinct points of view on the topic that was researched. Factor loading data might be interesting for some, but focusing on the quantitative data may cause unnecessary confusion and distraction in understanding the results of the study. Finally, when communicating the results of a Q-study, it is essential to indicate and describe how the study answers the inquiry question at hand and how the Q-study will be utilized with existing research or next steps to follow up on the research.

Q-studies can be very powerful in two areas. First of all, they provide a straightforward mechanism for determining distinctive points of view on any given library service or resource. This can help to confirm or supplement points of view that are heard anecdotally or through direct contact with library users. It can be easy to assume that a few complaints on a certain service are representative of the population. Q can assist in determining the other points of view that exist on the same topic and add scientific rigor in confirming ranges of opinion that are observed on a day-to-day basis. It can also unearth points of view that are not voiced loudly, yet held deeply by those at the institution.

Furthermore, the results of a Q-study indicate points of view that are unique to one's institutional context. While the literature can provide information on how certain populations view a topic, the same opinions may not be held by those at one's institution. Factors such as personal development, socioeconomic status, and institutional values and mission all play into how individuals shape their own thinking and frames of reference. Q-studies provide a mechanism for better understanding those opinions.

Leveraging the Findings

On its own, a Q-study is quite powerful in describing how members of a given population think about library resources or services. Depending on the scope of the research

Section 2

question, a Q-study may need to be completed in conjunction with other research methods, either as a follow-up or as an introductory inquiry method. For instance, a large-scale survey might indicate high satisfaction with group study rooms, but not provide much information on how those rooms are used by individuals or whether faculty opinions are determined by personal use or by what is heard from students. In this context, a Q-study could be utilized to determine what opinion structures are held by both faculty and students with regard to group study rooms.

There are other instances where a Q-study will not provide enough information to fully answer the inquiry question, and supplemental methods will be required. For instance, a Q-study will provide distinct points of view on open access, but it will not indicate how many faculty subscribe to a certain point of view or what could be done to assist in changing opinion. It can be tempting to parse and microanalyze statements from a certain point of view, but this is not a valid use of the research method. To get at this information, it would be necessary to follow up with a large-scale survey or similar method.

Reflection

A Q-study can be a very useful tool in understanding user opinion, but there are many facets that need to be understood before completing a study, including what information will be garnered from the study and what will not. This is especially crucial when communicating results to others who will not have a strong understanding of the method and what can be determined from using it.

In conducting a Q-study, several things were learned throughout the process. The first involves recruitment of participants. As a Q-study is looking for a diversity of opinions, it is important to recruit participants with that in mind. *To achieve this, it is important to ensure that the early scan of literature and opinions is thorough. It is also important to utilize sampling (stratified or random) to help ensure that a wide range of participants have the opportunity to participate. Studies that rely on librarian connections and library student employees can provide helpful information, but likely do not include a diversity of opinions on the topic.*

A Q-sort takes a decent amount of time to complete, and fitting that time into an undergraduate's life can be challenging. Trying to capture students at a campus gathering spot such as a student center will garner interest and participation, but it may not result in quality data. Asking a student to complete a twenty- to thirty-minute Q-sort when he or she has barely allocated that much time for lunch will result in a Q-sort that is hurried and likely not completely thought through. The same can be said for having faculty complete a sort in their office where distractions are often the norm.

Two considerations can assist in ensuring quality data. The first is a clear time and location for completing the Q-sort. A reserved study room in the library may assist, or a central room at the student center. Participants have an appointment time to complete the sort, and distractions are kept at a minimum during this time. The second is incentives for introductory interviews or Q-sort completion. With incentives and appropriate advertising, it should not be difficult to garner the participation required to complete the research. Note that incentives should be appropriate to your institution.

Finally, properly planning and structuring interviews is crucial in obtaining valuable information and opinion statements that can be utilized in the second stage of a Q-study. This usually is not difficult with most faculty, as a simple conversation will easily uncover opinions and ways of thinking on a multitude of subjects. However, a similar question regarding library preferences posed to undergraduates will likely result in a short conversation. Starting the conversation with a free-write prompt can help undergraduates to articulate their thoughts about the library more effectively. The interview is then focused on better understanding what was written during the free-write, while still using interview prompts as a guide for the conversation.

Appendix 18.1

Sorting Instructions

Note that these instructions mesh with the grid that is designed for 36 opinion statements. Certain numbers may vary depending on the number of opinion statements that are used.

The objective here is to sort the statements along the continuum from the ones that you most disagree with to the ones that you most agree with.

1. Look at all the opinion statements to familiarize yourself with the range of issues.

2. Sort the issues into 2 piles. One should contain the statements that you *agree* with—for any reason. The other pile contains those statements that you do *not agree* with—for any reason. The piles do not have to contain equal numbers of statements.

3. From the pile of statements that you agree with, select the one item (only one) that you *Most Agree* with. Place this item at the extreme right of your workspace.

4. From the remaining *Agree* pile, select two statements that are now more agreeable to you than the others in the pile. Place these statements in column just to the left of the statement already selected in Step 3.

5. Next, select from the remaining *Agree* pile the three statements that you now *Agree* with the most. Place these three statements in another column just to the left of the two statements selected in Step 4.

6. Next, select from the remaining *Agree* pile the four statements that you now *Agree* with the most. Place these four statements in another column just to the left of the three statements selected in Step 5.

7. Next, select from the remaining *Agree* pile the five statements that you now *Agree* with the most. Place these five statements in another column just to the left of the four statements selected in Step 6.

8. Select from the remainder of the *Agree* pile the six statements that you *Agree* with the most. Place these six statements in another column just to the left of the statements from Step 7. If you have run out of statement in the *Agree* pile and cannot finish this step, proceed immediately to the next step. If you have extra unsorted statements at the end of this step, combine the extras with the *Not Agree* pile and go on to the next step.

9. Now, work with the pile of statements that you do *Not Agree* with. From the pile of statements that you do not agree with, select the one item (only one) that you find *Most Disagreeable.* Place this item at the extreme left of your workspace.

10. From the remaining *Not Agree* pile, select two statements that are now *Most Disagreeable* to you than the others in the pile. Place these statements in a column just to the right of the statement already selected in Step 9.

11. From the remaining *Not Agree* pile, select three statements that are now *Most Disagreeable* to you than the others in the pile. Place these statements in a column just to the right of the statements already selected in Step 10.

12. From the remaining *Not Agree* pile, select four statements that are now *Most Disagreeable* to you than the others in the pile. Place these statements in a column just to the right of the statements already selected in Step 11.

13. From the remaining *Not Agree* pile, select five statements that are now *Most Disagreeable* to you than the others in the pile. Place these statements in a column just to the right of the statements already selected in Step 12.

14. Place any remaining statements in the middle of your grid.

15. Now, look at your arrangement. Feel free to move issues around to make sure that your opinion is reflected correctly.

16. When everything is sorted as you want, write the statement numbers in the blank boxes in the grid on your answer sheet.

Notes

1. Steven R. Brown, "A Primer on Q Methodology," *Operant Subjectivity* 16 (1993): 91.
2. Bruce F. McKeown and Dan B. Thomas, *Q Methodology* (Newbury Park, CA: Sage, 2013).
3. William Stevenson, "Technique of Factor Analysis," *Nature* 135 (1935): 297.
4. Margaret Jorgensen Dick and Marla Edelman, "Consequences of the Budget Crunch: Using Q Methodology to Prioritize Subscription Cancellations," *Journal of Nursing Education* 32 (1993): 181–82.
5. Susan Hurst, Kevin R. Messner, Andrew Revelle, and Aaron Shrimplin, "Conflict and Consensus: Clusters of Opinions on E-books," Conference Papers, ACRL 14th National Conference, March 12–15, 2009, Seattle, WA, http://www.ala.org/acrl/sites/ala.org.acrl/files/content/conferences/confsandpreconfs/national/seattle/papers/226.pdf; Stacy Brinkman and Jennifer Krivickas, "Attitudes toward E-books among Visual Arts Faculty and Students," *Art Documentation: Journal of the Art Libraries Society of North America* 34, no. 1 (Spring 2015): 71–88.
6. Jen Waller, Andrew Revelle, and Aaron K. Shrimplin, "Keep the Change: Clusters of Faculty Opinion on Open Access," in *Imagine, Innovate, Inspire: The Proceedings of the ACRL 2013 Conference*, ed. Dawn M. Mueller (Chicago: Association of College and Research Libraries, 2014), 360–72, http://www.ala.org/acrl/sites/ala.org.acrl/files/content/conferences/confsandpreconfs/2013/papers/WallerRevelleShrimplin_Keep.pdf.
7. Savannah Kelly and Brian Young, "Examining Undergraduates' Library Priorities through Q Methodology," *Journal of Academic Librarianship* 43, no. 3 (May 2017): 170–77.
8. Risa Lumley, "The Academic Library and Social Justice: A Q-Study of Librarian Attitudes" (doctoral dissertation, California State University at Santa Barbara, 2016), http://scholarworks.lib.csusb.edu/etd/418.
9. For additional information on Q Methodology and its application in libraries, see slides from Jen Waller, Stacy Brinkman, Kevin Messner, and Aaron Shrimplin, "Minding Your Ps and Qs: A Q-Methodology Workshop," PowerPoint slides and partial speaker notes (presentation at ACRL 2015 Conference, Portland, OR, March 25–28, 2015), http://hdl.handle.net/2374.MIA/5203.
10. Aaron Shrimplin and Susan Hurst, "A Virtual Standoff: Using Q Methodology to Analyze Virtual Reference," *Evidence Based Library and Information Practice* 2, no. 4 (December 2007): 3–21.
11. McKeown and Thomas, *Q Methodology*, 28.
12. Aaron Shrimplin and Matthew Magnuson, "Net Generation Students and the Library as Place," in *Proceedings of the Library Assessment Conference: Building Effective, Sustainable, Practical Assessment, September 25–27, 2006, Charlottesville, Virginia*, ed. Francine DeFranco, Steve Hiller, Lisa Janicke Hinchliffe, Kristina Justh, Martha Kyrillidou, Jim Self, and Joan Stein (Washington, DC:

Association of Research Libraries, 2007), 285–92

13. Aaron Shrimplin, Andy Revelle, Susan Hurst, and Kevin Messner, "Contradictions and Consensus: Clusters of Opinions on E-books," *College and Research Libraries* 72, no. 2 (March 2011): 181–90.

14. Peter Schmolck, The QMethod Page, accessed May 26, 2017, http://schmolck.userweb.mwn.de/qmethod/.

15. Schmolck, QMethod Page.

16. For an example of a follow-up that utilized a large-*n* survey, see Andy Revelle, Kevin Messner, Aaron Shrimplin, and Susan Hurst, "Book Lovers, Technophiles, Pragmatists, and Printers: The Social and Demographic Structure of User Attitudes toward E-books," *College and Research Libraries* 73, no. 5 (2012): 420–29

Bibliography

Brinkman, Stacy, and Jennifer Krivickas. "Attitudes toward E-books among Visual Arts Faculty and Students." *Art Documentation: Journal of the Art Libraries Society of North America* 34, no. 1 (Spring 2015): 71–88.

Brown, Steven R. "A Primer on Q Methodology." *Operant Subjectivity* 16 (1993): 91–138.

Dick, Margaret Jorgensen, and Marla Edelman. "Consequences of the Budget Crunch: Using Q Methodology to Prioritize Subscription Cancellations," *Journal of Nursing Education* 32 (1993): 181–82.

Hurst, Susan, Kevin R. Messner, Andrew Revelle, and Aaron Shrimplin. "Conflict and Consensus: Clusters of Opinions on E-books." Conference Papers, ACRL 14th National Conference, March 12–15, 2009, Seattle, WA. http://www.ala.org/acrl/sites/ala.org.acrl/files/content/conferences/confsandpreconfs/national/seattle/papers/226.pdf.

Kelly, Savannah, and Brian Young, "Examining Undergraduates' Library Priorities through Q Methodology," *Journal of Academic Librarianship* 43, no. 3 (May 2017): 170–77.

Lumley, Risa. "The Academic Library and Social Justice: A Q-Study of Librarian Attitudes." Doctoral dissertation, California State University at Santa Barbara, 2016. http://scholarworks.lib.csusb.edu/etd/418.

McKeown, Bruce F., and Dan B. Thomas. *Q Methodology*. Newbury Park, CA: Sage, 2013.

Revelle, Andy, Kevin Messner, Aaron Shrimplin, and Susan Hurst. "Book Lovers, Technophiles, Pragmatists, and Printers: The Social and Demographic Structure of User Attitudes toward E-books." *College and Research Libraries* 73, no. 5 (2012): 420–29

Schmolck, Peter. The QMethod Page. Accessed May 26, 2017. http://schmolck.userweb.mwn.de/qmethod/.

Shrimplin, Aaron, and Susan Hurst. "A Virtual Standoff: Using Q Methodology to Analyze Virtual Reference." *Evidence Based Library and Information Practice* 2, no. 4 (December 2007): 3–21.

Shrimplin, Aaron, and Matthew Magnuson. "Net Generation Students and the Library as Place." In *Proceedings of the Library Assessment Conference: Building Effective, Sustainable, Practical Assessment, September 25–27, 2006, Charlottesville, Virginia*. Edited by Francine DeFranco, Steve Hiller, Lisa Janicke Hinchliffe, Kristina Justh, Martha Kyrillidou, Jim Self, and Joan Stein, 285–92. Washington, DC: Association of Research Libraries, 2007.

Shrimplin, Aaron, Andy Revelle, Susan Hurst, and Kevin Messner. "Contradictions and Consensus: Clusters of Opinions on E-books." *College and Research Libraries* 72, no. 2 (March 2011): 181–90.

Stevenson, William. "Technique of Factor Analysis." *Nature* 135 (1935): 297.

Waller, Jen, Stacy Brinkman, Kevin Messner, and Aaron Shrimplin. "Minding Your Ps and Qs: A Q-Methodology Workshop." PowerPoint slides and partial speaker notes. Presentation at ACRL 2015 Conference, Portland, OR, March 25–28, 2015. http://hdl.handle.net/2374.MIA/5203.

Waller, Jen, Andrew Revelle, and Aaron K. Shrimplin. "Keep the Change: Clusters of Faculty Opinion on Open Access." In *Imagine, Innovate, Inspire: The Proceedings of the ACRL 2013 Conference*. Edited by Dawn M. Mueller, 360–72. Chicago: Association of College and Research Libraries, 2014. http://www.ala.org/acrl/sites/ala.org.acrl/files/content/conferences/confsandpreconfs/2013/papers/WallerRevelleShrimplin_Keep.pdf.

Section 2

Title: Assessing Discovery: How First-Year Students Use the Primo Discovery Tool

Abstract: In recent years, library discovery tools have both gained wide implementation and produced much discussion regarding how helpful and intuitive they are to students. In this chapter, an instruction librarian and a cataloger describe how they joined forces to gain better understanding of student use of the Primo discovery tool to improve teaching and to enhance a discovery tool interface. To achieve this goal, we implemented a series of short exercises and a survey in English 1101 and 1102 classes, which provided students with hands-on experience and increased librarians' understanding of how first-year undergraduate students use the discovery interface.

Keywords: teaching and learning, user experience, library discovery tool

Project focus: information literacy assessment; user behaviors and needs

Results made or will make case for: improvements in services, discovery tool interface enhancements

Data needed: survey results

Methodology: mixed method

Project duration: less than 6 months

Tool(s) utilized: Qualtrics, staffing—two librarians

Cost estimate: < $100

Type of institution: university—public

Institution enrollment: 15,000–30,000

Highest level of education: doctoral

Chapter 19

Assessing Discovery
How First-Year Students Use the Primo Discovery Tool

Karen Viars and Sofia Slutskaya

Introduction

In recent years, library discovery tools have gained wide implementation in academic libraries.[1] Information literacy instruction has been a long-term goal for academic libraries, and as discovery tools become more widely used, addressing how discovery and instruction interact is becoming increasingly important. The Georgia Institute of Technology (Georgia Tech) Library, in the midst of a five-year library renewal process, has also implemented Ex Libris Alma and Primo discovery. Learning how first-year students interact with this complex tool is a valuable exercise both for the students, who need research skills for academic success, and for librarians, who can learn how to improve both library instruction and the discovery interface. For this project, the Humanities Librarian, who teaches the English 1101 and 1102 classes, and the Metadata Strategist, who works directly with the Alma and Primo interface implementation, joined forces to develop an assessment for first-year students' experiences with the discovery tool. Our goal was to learn both how they use the tools available to them, which are a rich array of resources beyond the traditional OPAC, and how we can help them by simplifying the experience and providing supportive guidance as they learn.

As mentioned above, the Georgia Tech Library uses Primo as both a discovery tool and as a library catalog interface. Georgia Tech patrons can start their research on the library homepage using the "one-box" search box that defaults to the Everything search scope that, in Georgia Tech's implementation, includes the library catalog, articles+ search, the Georgia Tech-Emory shared collection, and theses and dissertations. The other option is to click on the library catalog link on the library homepage to access the search box that defaults to the library catalog. From this page, patrons can select various scopes, including the Everything scope. Due to a major renovation initiative taking place at the same time as Alma and Primo adoption, the Georgia Tech interface was implemented with minimal initial customization. This makes collecting user feedback and making improvements that are the most critical to patrons vital early in the implementation.

Context

Literature Review

The literature on use and implementation of discovery tools in academic libraries is vast. The literature on technical services addresses various aspects of discovery interface selection and implementation, while public services librarians are concerned with how helpful and intuitive cloud-based discovery services are to patrons.[2] Librarians must also consider whether discovery tools should be taught as a primary means of finding library materials. All concerned agree that a close look at user experience with discovery systems is essential for gaining a better understanding of users' searching behavior, expectations, and needs.

The literature on discovery tool use in information literacy instruction is multiplying. There are a number of case studies published in recent years addressing discovery tool usability testing in different institutions and also individual librarians' approaches to teaching a discovery tool.[3] There are also a number of attempts to look at the broader picture of incorporating discovery tools into information literacy instruction by surveying administrators or instruction librarians of academic libraries about their institutions' practices.[4] Case studies and broader surveys note the same contradiction: the wide adoption of discovery tools in academic libraries, including their acceptance by faculty and students, and the instruction librarians' reluctance to accept and teach discovery tools. The concerns expressed about the discovery tools are also universal: the large number of search results is overwhelming and confusing, students do not learn to search individual databases, and resources that are not indexed in the discovery tool can be overlooked and forgotten. On the other end of the spectrum, however, is the realization that discovery tools are important in teaching critical-thinking and evaluation skills and providing opportunities for implementing the new ACRL information literacy framework.[5] There is general agreement that despite discovery tools' similarities, implementation and adoption are a unique experience that depend on each institution's customizations, instruction program organization, and patrons' needs.

Changes at the Georgia Tech Library

Our Alma and Primo implementation in January 2016 coincided with many other organization changes in the Georgia Tech Library, including moving the majority of the physical collection to a state-of-the-art off-site Library Service Center (LSC) shared with Emory University and embarking on a multiyear multimillion-dollar library building renovation project. Members of the Georgia Tech community can request items from the LSC for same-day delivery to the library and to faculty members' offices. In addition to new physical spaces, the library is planning new services; pilot programs for many of these are currently in place. Some representative examples include charging lockers for library patrons' use, a self-service laptop kiosk, roving reference on all floors of the library, and a data visualization lab. Renewal of both library buildings is planned to be completed by 2020.

One of the Georgia Tech Library's strongest partnerships is with the faculty in the Writing and Communication Program, who teach English 1101 and 1102. The instructors of these classes are selected for the Marion L. Brittain Fellowship, a postdoctoral position that offers up to three years of innovative teaching experience. New fellows are hired yearly. The curriculum is multimodal, using the acronym WOVEN to represent written, oral, visual, electronic, and nonverbal modes of communication. In addition to the writing skills typically taught in freshman English classes, students may also design works of art; produce podcasts; or design games, posters, infographics, or another physical or digital form using multiple means of communication. These classes share instructional outcomes and provide their instructors the opportunity to focus on a wide variety of possible topics to achieve them. Some recent class topics have included the works of Harper Lee, robots, the role of fantastic literature in the modern world, letter writing, and animals and technology.

In 2016, a large majority—86 percent—of Georgia Tech freshmen were engineering majors.[6] Science, technology, and mathematics are also frequent choices for majors. Students may also major in literature, media and communication, history, sociology, or business. Working with these students and faculty has created an instruction program with a strong focus on information literacy skills applicable to a wide range of research.

Using the Discovery Tool for Classroom Instruction and Information Literacy

When using a discovery tool in a library instruction session, it becomes necessary to evaluate the tool's effectiveness at guiding students to greater levels of information literacy. As Primo is a new tool to the Georgia Tech campus, students, faculty, and staff, assessing its usefulness becomes increasingly important. Thus, we decided to approach the assessment of Primo in its application as a teaching tool in library instruction classes for English 1101 and 1102 classes. We selected these classes for several reasons.

First, the literature demonstrates that there is often a gap between students' grasp of college-level research and tools and the level of expertise required of them to research successfully for their classes.[7] Learning to use the discovery tool effectively could make a difference for these students in their current classes and for the rest of their college careers. Additionally, these students would be approaching the research experience as tabula rasa; most students taking English 1101 or 1102 are new to Georgia Tech. They

Section 2

would then be evaluating the discovery tool on its own merits, without the influence of experience with the library catalog's previous interface. Students of all majors are required to take these classes, ensuring that our respondents have a variety of goals and interests in how they use library resources, including the discovery tool. And lastly, as noted above, the library has a strong instructional partnership with the Writing and Communication Program, which teaches English 1101 and 1102.

Methods

We designed the research methods to evaluate both the students' use of the discovery tool interface and their opinions of the experience. Using the Qualtrics survey software, we asked students to complete tasks using the Primo discovery tool; while the goals remained the same from class to class, we were able to customize questions to fit the class's topic. Hereafter, we refer to these as the "exercises." For example, one exercise was to locate a book by its title. One of the classes, which focused on dystopias in young adult literature, was asked to locate *For the Win* by Cory Doctorow. In a different class, focusing on Southern literature, we used *Now Is the Time to Open Your Heart* by Alice Walker for the same question. Our goal was to provide students the experience of using the discovery tool in a way that is similar to the research they would be doing for their classes, as well as to demonstrate to them that the library has relevant resources.

We wanted to gain a comprehensive view of students' use and comfort level with the Primo interface, so we asked them to complete six exercises:

- Search for a book by title.
- Search for works by a specific author.
- Search for a journal by name.
- Find a newspaper article on a specific topic.
- Search for works on a specific topic.
- Search for a DVD by title.

We also asked students to complete survey questions (hereinafter called "the survey") on the following topics:

- how often they use the catalog and for what purposes
- their overall impressions of the interface
- what they like best about the interface
- suggestions for changes
- how comprehensible the language on the interface was to them
- whether they have request items from the library service center
- ratings for
  - ease of searching
  - organization of search results
  - relevance of search results
  - aesthetic appearance of the website
  - an open response field for any additional comments

Both the exercises and the survey questions were distributed to students in a single

Qualtrics document. Students could choose to stop participating in the research at any time, so no questions were mandatory for a student to continue through the assessment instrument.

Participants

The survey was conducted in the spring semester of 2017. When approached with the idea of their classes participating in this research, faculty were positive and supportive of providing students the opportunity. One faculty member noted with approval that the survey questions were tailored to her class's topics. The assessment was disseminated in three different English 1102 classes. No demographic or personal information was collected to make participants more willing to complete the exercises. From the available pool of participants, 104 students present in class on the day library instruction was offered, 84 chose to complete the exercises. Responses to the survey questions ranged from 70 to 81 participants. None of the questions were mandatory, so the total number of responses for each question was used when analyzing the results.

Results

Exercises Results

Primo exercises were graded according to the grading rubric we developed to evaluate users' responses. For multipart questions, each part was graded separately—for example, each part of these questions was graded separately: Does the GT Library have the book xxx (title)? Where is it located? What is the call number? (see table 19.1). Overall, students succeeded in answering questions about finding physical items; the success rate was the highest for questions that dealt with locating books and DVDs. This is not surprising, as library catalogs have always been the most suited for discovering physical materials. Widespread use of tools like Amazon ensured that most users are very comfortable with faceted navigation and can easily limit their search results by format, decreasing the number of available choices and making the selection of the correct item much simpler.

Table 19.1
Primo Exercises Success Rates

Question	Success Rate
Does GT Library have the book xxx (title)?	95.24%
Does GT Library have books by xxx (author)?	98.81%
Does GT Library have the DVD xxx (title)?	94.05%

The results in table 19.1 also show that students were successful in determining a type of physical item even when multiple options were present. Grading the exercises showed that the biggest areas of confusion in terms of interface design are Primo search scopes and understanding electronic journals availability and coverage. These problems can be addressed both in teaching Primo and by making small interface adjustments.

Our question about finding newspaper articles on a specific topic was the only question with an error rate (61%) higher than the success rate (39%). The errors can be divided into two groups: (1) students found an article, but it was not on topic; or (2) students did not find an article at all or claimed that newspapers were not part of the resource. The first error is typical, as students often evaluate relevance by the presence of one or more keywords in the titles in the search result list.[8] It is also consistent with issues students experienced in finding a book on a specific topic. The second error, however, is related to students' inability to distinguish between Primo's multiple search scopes. A likely scenario is that participants who limited their searches to the library catalog for the physical items searches did not realize that they had to switch back to the Everything scope to find newspaper articles.

The other challenging task, with a failure rate of almost 30 percent, was determining electronic journal availability. While the majority of respondents found the journal in question, many struggled with interpreting coverage dates. The coverage of one journal was described in Primo as: "Available from 2006 volume: 1 issue: 1." Some students interpreted this description as the library providing access only to issue 1 of the journal, or only to issues from 2006. Additional usability testing to determine the best language to describe coverage or content-specific help may be necessary to ensure that undergraduate students can interpret electronic journal coverage correctly.

Survey Results

Many students reported not using the library catalog often. Less than 5 percent of respondents use Primo more than a few times a month; a majority use the catalog either less than once a year (37%), less than once a semester (22%), or once a semester (23%). Answering the question "What are some of the things you have used GT library catalog for in the past?" 46 percent said that participating in this exercise was their first experience in using the Georgia Tech discovery system. Twenty percent of respondents indicated their surprise at the number of resources that were available for students to use in their research. As to reasons to use the library catalog, 44 percent of participants listed completing projects and assignments. Only 10 percent mentioned searching for books and films for entertainment.

Overall, the undergraduate students' impression of the site was very positive. We organized responses to the question "What is your overall impression of the site?" into three categories: positive, negative, and neutral. Examples of positive responses were

- Very clean and easy to search
- Very impressive
- Super helpful i wish i knew about it earlier

Examples of negative responses include

- it's very bland and sometimes does not give me what I want
- Cramped
- A little complicated to use

Responses like "average" or "so-so" were coded as neutral. Of the seventy recorded responses, 65 percent were positive, 12.3 percent were negative, and 10 percent were neutral.

Additional analysis of responses to this and other questions allowed us to identify a number of recurring themes. Many undergraduates pointed to the rich content and how many resources were available to them. The abundance of content was mentioned as a response to both "What is your overall impression of the site?" and "What do you like most about the site?" Students also appreciated the online resources, noting that they could do their research efficiently by using resources that were immediately available to them rather than searching the stacks or waiting for a print copy to be delivered from the Library Service Center or via interlibrary loan. Another theme was the ease of use; twenty-three respondents use the word "easy" when describing what they like about the current implementation. Five additional students, in the same vein, used the term "simplicity" or a variation on the word. Students found the interface straightforward to navigate and generally well organized. The ability to refine search results was the third major theme. Respondents liked being able to use facets to narrow their results and increase relevance. They also liked the advanced search option and the ability to use different scopes in the Primo interface to access the specific resources they need.

Themes also emerged from negative responses. Students had trouble identifying the difference between scopes, and so some asked for resources that they were unable to find, such as newspapers. Another theme was aesthetic; some students would like a different appearance for the interface. These responses fell into two subcategories; some responses provided general ideas of what they would like to see, using terms like "modern," "visually appealing," "interesting," and "fun." Others offered valuable specific requests, like changing the size of the search box, making the search button appear in the same place on all pages, and changing the font size. Another theme centered around searching and refining results. Respondents asked for changes to make faceted searching possible from the basic search box. They also asked about more clarity among the scopes, being able to search within a results set, and searching within a specific format (e.g., audiovisual) from the basic search. The need for training on how to use the system, and the possibility of providing video tutorials or content-specific help were also mentioned in responding to both "What is your overall impression of the site?" and "If you could change something about the site, what would it be?"

Comparing the Two Results Sets

While students generally had a positive view of the discovery tool interface, as we found in the survey questions results, this enthusiasm did not directly translate to effective searching. Other researchers' experiences, as well as anecdotal reports, support our findings. For example, Hossain Shoeb found that students self-reported high levels of competence regarding information literacy skills, though only 25 percent of them correctly answered questions that required information literacy.[9] Confronting the limits of their skills does not always lead students to conclude that they need help with information literacy skills.[10] While, in this case, there are changes that the library can make to bolster the user experience with the discovery tool, students' misplaced overconfidence is likely also playing a role in their experiences with searching.

The authors' hope is that this information literacy intervention, early in these students' college careers, will begin integrating information literacy into their cognition, a process that happens over time.[11] Knowing that information literacy instruction helps students to consider information literacy a valuable skill also motivates our current and future instruction goals.[12]

Communicating Results and Impact

Within the library, the authors shared the results of our research with the library's Content Discovery Group, which is responsible for library content discoverability and making adjustments to the discovery tool interface to ensure a positive user experience. At one of the group's regular meetings, we provided information about the tasks that students were able to complete successfully and those with which they struggled. We also provided feedback from the survey about the students' thoughts about the user experience. Doing this research provided us with the opportunity to give greater insight to the group tasked with making the library's resources readily available.

We also communicated the results of our research to the Head of the Campus Engagement and Scholarly Outreach Department (CESO) and the Associate Dean of Learning and Research Services via email. Researching how students use the discovery tool and what they think of the experience furthers the library's mission, in regard to both discovery and information literacy. We also communicated the results and the intended changes to the faculty members who so generously allowed us time in their classes to complete this research, as well as to the Director of the Writing and Communication Program (WCP) and the Chair of the School of Literature, Media and Communication, in which the WCP is housed. Sharing this research and our plan to address the challenges it illuminated helps to strengthen our relationship with the program and school by demonstrating our commitment to listening to student feedback and making appropriate changes.

Leveraging the Findings

The Content Discovery Group, which includes the Assistant Dean for Content Strategy, will incorporate the research findings to assist with their decisions about altering the existing interface to address the concerns and recommendations or migrating to a new one. The benefit to the students (and, we believe, faculty, staff, and community users) will be an improved and more intuitive user experience, which will help and support their research.

Beginning in fall semester 2017, English 1101 and 1102 classes will be taught by a group of five librarians from the CESO department, including the Humanities Librarian. Sharing this research benefits these librarians in their preparation to teach by alerting them to the types of tasks students find easy or challenging, as well as sharing students' overall impressions and attitudes toward the discovery tool.

Reflections

There were several exciting and rewarding parts of this research process. One of the most positive outcomes of this project was increasing undergraduate students' awareness of the Georgia Tech Library discovery search tool and, more generally, of library resources. Having to complete the survey right after completing the exercises made participants more conscious of the tool's strengths and shortcomings. We hope that the fact that the exercises were related to their class topic made the entire process of evaluation more practical and relevant. The opportunity to strengthen our existing partnership with the WCP was rewarding. This research was also a valuable exercise for instruction. We learned more about which aspects of the discovery tool are the most confusing and require additional training and extra explanations—and possibly, more class time. This makes our instruction more effective and relevant to the student. We recommend doing this kind of assessment with a group or department where a strong relationship already exists, as it does require faculty cooperation and support. Making the assessment instrument relevant to class topics increased instructors' buy-in and students' acceptance of the discovery tool, so a willingness to customize the assessment to each class is also worthwhile, but does take additional time. One of the key collaborations and most rewarding elements was the opportunity for the authors to work together to better understand each others' needs and ways of using the discovery tool; we recommend reaching out to colleagues who work in other groups or departments to develop projects that benefit the library as a whole.

Despite the abundance of Primo usability studies results, we strongly recommend regularly and formally collecting user feedback as important for each institution implementing and promoting a discovery tool. Each institution's implementation is unique, and many researchers agree that "in order for each institution to take full advantage of the customizations available in their discovery tool and to make informed decisions on how to present their discovery tool to their users, libraries should conduct their own assessment on a regular basis."[13] The other important lesson is that patron assessment of using a discovery tool should impact not just the information literacy instruction, but also the tool customization and improvement. There needs to be ongoing communication between librarians teaching information literacy instructions and staff responsible for the discovery interface maintenance. The user feedback does not just help determine necessary changes, but also what changes are the most critical.

We have two additional recommendations: Allow time to complete institutional review board paperwork; we did not have any additional required paperwork, but that may also be a consideration at a different institution. We were able to complete our institutional review board application within the time frame we had planned, but it would have been easier with more time. We also recommend allowing abundant time to evaluate the assessment instrument in a pilot program before deploying it in classes. While our instrument worked well, we could have discovered significant problems with it while already in the midst of the research.

This research is highly replicable at many institutions, as the requirements are librarian cooperation, expertise, and time; a means of deploying the survey instrument; and faculty and student cooperation and support. Providing a clear rationale for using an assessment instrument to evaluate students' experiences is a vital aspect of securing faculty cooperation, as is explaining the goal of the assessment to students, especially in cases like ours, where students' only incentive to participate is an interest in assisting us to understand them and the catalog better. In cases of low participation, we suggest examining the presentation of the project to faculty and students, exploring other incentives permitted by IRB and institution guidelines, and revising the assessment materials if responses indicate they discourage participation.

Notes

1. Marshall Breeding, "Library Systems Report 2017," *American Libraries* 48, no. 5 (May 2017): 30–31, https://americanlibrariesmagazine.org/2017/05/01/library-systems-report-2017.
2. Kelsey Brett, Ashley Lierman, and Cherie Turner, "Lessons Learned: A Primo Usability Study," *Information Technology and Libraries* 35, no. 1 (March 2016): 7-25, https://ejournals.bc.edu/ojs/index.php/ital/article/view/8965/pdf; Richard Guajardo, Kelsey Brett, and Frederick Young, "The Evolution of Discovery Systems in Academic Libraries: A Case Study at the University of Houston Libraries," *Journal of Electronic Resources Librarianship* 29, no. 1 (2017): 16–23; Aaron F. Nichols, Emily Crist, Graham Sherriff, and Megan Allison, "What Does It Take to Make Discovery a Success? A Survey of Discovery Tool Adoption, Instruction, and Evaluation among Academic Libraries," *Journal of Web Librarianship* 11, no. 2 (2017): 85–104.
3. Karen Joc, Peta J. Hopkins, Jessie Donaghey, and Wendy Abbot, "Two Roads, One Destination: A Journey of Discovery," in *VALA 2016: Libraries, Technology and the Future Proceedings*, (Melbourne: VALA, 2016), http://www.vala.org.au/vala2016-proceedings/vala2016-session-15-joc; Barbara Valentine and Beth West, "Improving Primo Usability and Teachability with Help from the Users," *Journal of Web Librarianship* 10, no. 3 (2016): 176–96; Elena Azadbakht, "Information Literacy Instruction with Primo," *Reference and User Services Quarterly* 54, no. 3 (2015): 23–26.
4. Nancy Fawley and Nikki Krysak, "Learning to Love Your Discovery Tool: Strategies for Integrating a Discovery Tool in Face-to-Face, Synchronous, and Asynchronous Instruction," *Public Services Quarterly* 10, no. 4 (2014): 283–301; Nichols et al., "What Does It Take to Make Discovery a Success?"
5. Kevin Patrick Seeber, Joan Petit, and Sara Thompson, "Teaching 'Format as a Process' in an Era of Web-Scale Discovery," *Reference Services Review* 43, no. 1 (2015): 19–30; Valentine and West, "Improving Primo Usability and Teachability."
6. Georgia Institute of Technology, *2016 Mini Fact Book* (Atlanta: Georgia Institute of Technology, 2017), https://www.irp.gatech.edu/mini-fact-book.
7. Sung Un Kim and David Shumaker, "Student, Librarian, and Instructor Perceptions of Information Literacy Instruction and Skills in a First Year Experience Program: A Case Study," *Journal of Academic Librarianship* 41, no. 4 (2015): 449–56.
8. Fawley and Krysak, "Learning to Love Your Discovery Tool," 286–87.
9. Zahid Hossain Shoeb, "Information Literacy Competency of Freshman Business Students of a Private University in Bangladesh," *Library Review* 60, no. 9 (2011): 762–72.
10. Don Latham and Melissa Gross, "Instructional Preferences of First-Year College Students with Below-Proficient Information Literacy Skills: A Focus Group Study," College and Research Libraries 74, no. 5 (2013): 430–49.
11. Geoff Walton and Mark Hepworth, "A Longitudinal Study of Changes in Learners' Cognitive States during and Following an Information Literacy Teaching Intervention," *Journal of Documentation* 67, no. 3 (2011): 449–79.
12. Kim and Shumaker, "Student, Librarian, and Instructor Perceptions of Information Literacy Instruction."
13. Nichols et al., "What Does It Take to Make Discovery a Success?" 13.

Bibliography

Azadbakht, Elena. "Information Literacy Instruction with Primo." *Reference and User Services Quarterly* 54, no. 3 (2015): 23–26.

Breeding, Marshall. "Library Systems Report 2017." *American Libraries* 48, no. 5 (May 2017): 22–38. https://americanlibrariesmagazine.org/2017/05/01/library-systems-report-2017.

Brett, Kelsey, Ashley Lierman, and Cherie Turner. "Lessons Learned: A Primo Usability Study." *Information Technology and Libraries* 35, no. 1 (March 2016): 7–25. https://ejournals.bc.edu/ojs/index.php/ital/article/view/8965/pdf.

Fawley, Nancy, and Nikki Krysak. "Learning to Love Your Discovery Tool: Strategies for Integrating a Discovery Tool in Face-to-Face, Synchronous, and Asynchronous Instruction." *Public Services Quarterly* 10, no. 4 (2014): 283–301.

Georgia Institute of Technology. *2016 Mini Fact Book*. Atlanta: Georgia Institute of Technology, 2017.

Guajardo, Richard, Kelsey Brett, and Frederick Young. "The Evolution of Discovery Systems in Academic Libraries: A Case Study at the University of Houston Libraries." *Journal of Electronic Resources Librarianship* 29, no. 1 (2017): 16–23.

Hossain Shoeb, Zahid. "Information Literacy Competency of Freshman Business Students of a Private University in Bangladesh." *Library Review* 60, no. 9 (2011): 762–72.

Joc, Karen, Peta J. Hopkins, Jessie Donaghey, and Wendy Abbott. "Two Roads, One Destination: A Journey of Discovery." In *VALA 2016: Libraries, Technology and the Future Proceedings*. Melbourne: VALA, 2016, http://www.vala.org.au/vala2016-proceedings/vala2016-session-15-joc.

Kim, Sung Un, and David Shumaker. "Student, Librarian, and Instructor Perceptions of Information Literacy Instruction and Skills in a First Year Experience Program: A Case Study." *Journal of Academic Librarianship* 41, no. 4 (2015): 449–56.

Latham, Don, and Melissa Gross. "Instructional Preferences of First-Year College Students with Below-Proficient Information Literacy Skills: A Focus Group Study." *College and Research Libraries* 74, no. 5 (2013): 430–49.

Nichols, Aaron F., Emily Crist, Graham Sherriff, and Megan Allison. "What Does It Take to Make Discovery a Success? A Survey of Discovery Tool Adoption, Instruction, and Evaluation among Academic Libraries." *Journal of Web Librarianship* 11, no. 2 (2017): 85–104.

Seeber, Kevin Patrick, Joan Petit, and Sara Thompson. "Teaching 'Format as a Process' in an Era of Web-Scale Discovery." *Reference Services Review* 43, no. 1 (2015): 19–30.

Valentine, Barbara, and Beth West. "Improving Primo Usability and Teachability with Help from the Users." *Journal of Web Librarianship* 10, no. 3 (2016): 176–96.

Walton, Geoff, and Mark Hepworth. "A Longitudinal Study of Changes in Learners' Cognitive States during and Following an Information Literacy Teaching Intervention." *Journal of Documentation* 67, no. 3 (2011): 449–79.

Section 2

Author Bios

Marwin Britto is the Business, Economics, Education and Public Policy Librarian at the University of Saskatchewan. His online, face-to-face and blended teaching experiences span K-12, ESL in Canada and Japan, community college, and university undergraduate and graduate levels. His leadership experiences in higher education include positions as Director of the Educational Technology Center, Executive Director of Online Learning, Director of Instructional Technology, Chief Information Officer, Associate Dean of the University Library, and University Librarian. Marwin has delivered more than 140 refereed conference presentations and authored 60+ refereed papers in academic journals and conference proceedings in the areas of distance education/online learning, teaching and learning, teacher education, instructional technology, library science and change management. He holds four graduate degrees including a Masters in Education (specializing in Educational Technology), a Masters in Business Administration, an ALA-accredited Masters in Library and Information Science, and a Ph.D. in Instructional Technology. For further information, visit https://ca.linkedin.com/in/marwinbritto and www.marwinbritto.info.

Kirsten Kinsley is an Assessment Librarian at the Florida State University Libraries and a liaison with the College of Criminology and Criminal Justice, and a co-liaison for the Department of Psychology and the College of Social Work. Kirsten completed her Master of Science in Library and Information Studies in 1999 and received a Master of Science and Specialist in Education degrees in Counseling and Human Systems in 1995 from the Florida State University. In 1989, she graduated with a Bachelor of Science in Psychology with Honors. Ms. Kinsley previously worked for the FSU Career Center Library and Law Research Center and has been working in libraries on campus in various capacities since 1991. Kirsten seeks to foster and measure how the library through campus collaborations can contribute to student and faculty success.

Kyle Ainsworth received a bachelor's degree in history from the College of William and Mary (2006), and has master's degrees in history and library science from the University of Southern Mississippi (2010). He is the special collections librarian at Stephen F. Austin State University as well as project manager for the Texas Runaway Project.

Jackie Belanger is the Director of Assessment and Planning at the University of Washington Libraries. She leads the Libraries assessment program by developing quantitative and qualitative assessments designed to improve Libraries services and resources and to communicate the value of the Libraries to stakeholders. Recent major projects undertaken in collaboration with colleagues and institutional partners include: the 2016 Libraries Triennial Survey; a design thinking project to understand the needs of transfer students; and an analysis of Libraries chat reference transcripts to improve research support for faculty and students. As co-chair of the Libraries Strategic Planning Working Group, she is responsible for the Libraries strategic planning process and works to align Libraries' data gathering efforts with strategic initiatives. Recent publications include work on assessing student learning outcomes and using assessment management systems.

Dr. Susan Breakenridge has 25 years of academic library experience including administration, technical services and public services. She is currently the Director of Technical Services, Facilities and Business Administration at Rowan University Libraries in Glassboro, New Jersey. Her education background includes a Masters of Business Administration and a Doctorate of Education in Educational Leadership. Dr. Breakenridge has taught business courses for 20 years. Her research interest include library usage, academic library safety and security, disruptive innovations, legal and ethical issues in teaching with electronic resources, and innovative teaching techniques.

Chelsea Dinsmore serves as the Director of Digital Production Services for the University of Florida George A. Smathers Libraries and is the Technical Director for the Digital Library of the Caribbean (dLOC). Since 2009, she has organized and managed digital projects within the government documents community, including the creation of regional federal depository Centers of Excellence (COE) for the Panama Canal and the National Recovery Administration collections. She is currently involved in research to improve the accessibility of digital collections by rehabilitating legacy metadata. Ms. Dinsmore holds an MLIS from the University of Texas at Austin and an MS in History from the University of Florida.

Rachael Elrod is the Head of the Education Library at the University of Florida. Her research interests include the assessment of library services, the information seeking behavior of students, and the use of 3D printing for educational purposes. She is currently a researcher on a 3-year IMLS grant titled Researching Students Information Choices: Determining Identity and Judging Credibility in Digital Spaces. She has an MSLS from the University of Kentucky, an M.Ed. in Counseling Psychology from the University of Louisville, and a B.S. in Psychology and Sociology from Campbellsville University. She is currently working on an Ed.D. in Higher Education Administration at the University of Florida.

Maggie Faber is the Data Visualization and Analysis Librarian at the University of Washington Libraries. She helps analyze and communicate assessment results and libraries-related data by developing interactive dashboards and visualizations. Recent projects include creating a suite of dashboards to communicate the qualitative and quantitative results of the 2016 Libraries Triennial Survey and working with University of Washington's Foster Business Library on the results of their space assessment project. She also provides data visualization support for students, faculty, and libraries staff through office hours, workshops, and consultations. Recent presentations include visualizing the results from space assessment projects and taking action on survey results.

Amanda L. Folk is currently the Head of Teaching & Learning at The Ohio State University Libraries. Prior to assuming that position, she was the Coordinator of Regional University Library System Libraries at the University of Pittsburgh and the Director of the Millstein Library at the Pitt-Greensburg campus. Amanda is currently a PhD candidate in social and comparative analysis in education at the University of Pittsburgh's School of Education, and she received her MLIS from the University of Pittsburgh's School of Information Science in 2006. Her current research examines first-generation college students' experiences with research assignments in service of understanding how librarians can productively address social-class and racial achievement gaps.

Diane Fulkerson is the Director of Library Services for the University of South Florida Sarasota-Manatee campus. She received an MA in history from the State University of New York College at Brockport, and her MLS degree from the University at Buffalo-SUNY. As an active member of the Association of College and Research Libraries, she is past chair of the Women and Gender Studies Section and was a member of the task force that developed the Framework for Information Literacy in Higher Education. She has presented several times on the using the Framework for library instruction. Her current research focuses on the impact of library instruction and services on student success.

Dawn Harris has been the Acquisitions and Cataloging Librarian at Texas A&M University—Central Texas in Killeen Texas since April 2016. Prior to that, she spent thirty-one years in public libraries before retiring as Assistant Director of Library Services at Killeen City Library System. She holds a Master of Science in Information Studies from the School of Information at the University of Texas at Austin.

Sarah Hartman-Caverly, MS(LIS), MSIS, is an assistant librarian at Penn State Berks, where she liaises with the Engineering, Business and Computing division. From 2013-17, she was an assistant professor and reference librarian at Delaware County Community College. Her research agenda examines the compatibility of human and machine autonomy from the perspective of the library profession's commitment to intellectual freedom and expertise in data management technologies, data governance, and fair information practices. Prior to her work in public services, Hartman-Caverly spent five years in e-resource management and systems librarianship at baccalaureate- and associate-degree granting institutions. She can be reached at smh767@psu.edu.

Jonathan Helmke received bachelor's degrees in political science and business from Wartburg College (1996), and has a master's degree in library science from Indiana University (1997). He is currently the Associate Director for Library Information Services at Stephen F. Austin State University and is leading the implementation of the strategic plan for the library. He served as the University Archivist (2011-2016) and Assistant Director for Technical Services and Library Systems at the University of Dubuque (2006-2016) and at Butler University in various capacities including the library's efforts concerning the integration of technology and information literacy into the College of Business curriculum. His research interests include how the library contributes to the University's recruitment and retention efforts and the role of high-impact practices in library services.

Starr Hoffman is Director of Planning and Assessment at the University of Nevada, Las Vegas Libraries, where she leads the assessment program and strategic planning. She has presented internationally on creating data inventories and aligning assessment plans with library strategic plans and parent institution plans. She edited the book *Dynamic Research Support for Academic Libraries* (2015) which describes varied examples of research support services in libraries. Her work draws on her expertise in data analysis, higher education administration, and research support accumulated during her career and education. She holds a PhD in Higher Education (2012), a Master's in Library Science (2006), and a MA in Art History (2004). Her dissertation studied the leadership and educational attainment of academic library deans. You may reach Starr at starr.hoffman@unlv.edu or view her portfolio at: https://geekyartistlibrarian.wordpress.com/.

Robert Hoyt is Web & User Experience Librarian, DiMenna-Nyselius Library, Fairfield University. Robert has been a librarian since 2012 and has been at Fairfield University since 2014. Tasked with running and maintaining all online patron interfaces, Robert aims to enhance user experience, adopt functional new technology, and effectively aid in the usage of library resources. In addition to his work at Fairfield University, Robert is the co-founder of Reftab, a cloud-based asset management system and helped design an English language learning platform in Japan, Eigooo.

Richard M. Jones (rick@jonesarch.com), AIA, LEED AP BD+C, Director/Founder. Rick has worked in higher education design and planning for over two decades. In the spring of 2011, following 15 years of practice with various firms in Boston, Rick founded Jones Architecture, a higher education focused, service-oriented practice. With a particular research focus on learning environments and academic libraries, the practice now serves the New England region. Dating back to 2003, Rick has been a regular speaker at conferences and Universities on topics of education and sustainable design, including: AIA National, Build Boston, EnvironDesign, ERAPPA, Learning Environments, Massachusetts Institute of Technology, Northeastern University, Norwich University, SCUP Regional and International, the Society of Teaching and Learning in

Higher Education, the University of Maine, and Wentworth Institute of Technology. Rick received a Master of Architecture from Harvard University's Graduate School of Design and a Bachelor of Architecture from the University of Kentucky.

Hae Min Kim (hk433@drexel.edu) is a data analyst at Drexel University Libraries. She earned PhD in information science at the College of Computing and Informatics at Drexel University in Philadelphia, PA., in 2015. Her research interests lie in the areas of library assessment, information services, user perceptions, and service quality. She is particularly interested in understanding how people utilize information through applications and library services and perceive the quality of services. Her research has so far focused on understanding external applications such as social media uses in libraries, including the dissemination of library contents on Twitter, information flows among active users of library Twitter services, and service quality evaluation of library social media services. She has published articles in Proceedings of the American Society for Information Science and Technology and the JCDL, and presented at the Library Assessment Conference and the Evidence Based Library and Information Practice conference.

Jacalyn Kremer, Head of Library Academic Partnerships and Assessment, DiMenna-Nyselius Library, Fairfield University. As head of assessment at her library, Jacalyn strives to collaboratively explore, identify, adopt, and apply effective assessment processes for library operations and services. With the goal of communicating the value of the library in student learning and with a focus on campus partnerships, Jacalyn manages multiple assessment projects with colleagues across her university. In addition to her assessment work, Jacalyn has given numerous presentations on the role of libraries in promoting academic integrity and is the author of the chapter "Honor Bound: Assessing Library Interventions into the Complex Problem of Academic Integrity" in the book *Putting Assessment into Action.*

Bridgit McCafferty has served as the Director of the University Library at A&M-Central Texas in Killeen, Texas for five years. She worked in library instruction, outreach, and collection development prior to becoming the director. She has a Master of Library Science degree from Indiana University in Bloomington, Indiana, in addition to a Master of Arts in Literature from Texas A&M University in College Station, Texas. She co-authored *Literary Research and British Postmodernism: Strategies and Sources*, published in 2015 by Rowman and Littlefield.

Anthony J. McMullen (amcmullen@edinboro.edu) is Systems Librarian at the Baron-Forness Library, Edinboro University of Pennsylvania, one of the 14 universities comprising the Pennsylvania State System of Higher Education. Anthony joined the Edinboro faculty in August, 2007. Prior to coming to Edinboro, he served as Systems Librarian at Seton Hill University in Greensburg, Pennsylvania, Reference Librarian at the John F. Kennedy School of Government, Harvard University in Cambridge, Massachusetts, and Reference Librarian at the Erie County Library System in Erie, Pennsylvania.

He has been active in the profession for 20+ years. Anthony's areas of interest include graphical interface design, user experience, website heuristics, ethnography, and emerging technologies and their impact information search and retrieval. He earned his MSLS from Clarion University of Pennsylvania and MSEd from Capella University where he completed the Instructional Design for Online Learning program in December, 2008.

Caroline Muglia has served as the Co-Associate Dean for Collections, Head, Resource Sharing, and Collection Assessment Librarian at the University of Southern California (USC) where she has worked since 2015. Prior to her role at USC, Caroline worked as a Manuscript and Digital Archivist at the Library of Congress, and later, as a Data Librarian for an educational technology firm in Washington, DC. She serves as an adjunct professor in the USC Marshall Business School's Masters in Management in Library and Information Science (MMLIS) program where she teaches a course in collection development and management. Caroline was recently selected as a cohort member of the 2018-2019 ARL Leaders Fellowship. She received her MLIS from the University of North Carolina, Chapel Hill. She can be reached at muglia@usc.edu.

Talia Nadir is a research & Instruction librarian and an Information Literacy specialist at the University of St. Thomas, St. Paul, Minnesota. She is a subject liaison to English, Communication & Journalism, American Culture & Difference, Justice & Peace Studies, Studies, Film Studies, and Women Studies. Talia has been embedded in a variety of courses and has given numerous presentations on her collaboration with faculty. Her work focuses on promoting critical library instruction practices and information literacy in higher education.

Megan Oakleaf is an Associate Professor in the iSchool at Syracuse University where she teaches "Reference and Information Literacy Services" and "Planning, Marketing, and Assessing Library Services." Her research interests include outcomes assessment, evidence-based decision making, information literacy instruction, information services, and digital librarianship. She is the author of the Value of Academic Libraries Comprehensive Review and Report and Academic Library Value: The Impact Starter Kit. She also served on the faculty of the ACRL Immersion Program. Previously, Megan served as Librarian for Instruction and Undergraduate Research at North Carolina State University. In this role, she provided and assessed information literacy instruction; she also trained fellow reference librarians in instructional theory and methods. Megan earned her PhD in library and information science at UNC-Chapel Hill and her MLS at Kent State University. Prior to a career in librarianship, she taught advanced composition in Ohio public secondary schools.

Nazimah Ram Nath is an Assistant Director and Librarian for Collections, Content Discovery and Copyright in SMU Libraries, Singapore Management University. Her interests include content development and discovery, outcomes assessment, evidence-based decision making and copyright education. Nazimah holds an MSc in Information Studies from Nanyang Technological University of Singapore and a BA (Hons) in English from the National University of Singapore. Prior to her current position, Nazimah served in the National Library Board of Singapore where she managed library operations at the National Library. Alongside a career in librarianship, Nazimah had also taught Bibliographic Organization in Nanyang Technological University. She welcomes discussions with industry colleagues and can be contacted at nazimah@smu.edu.sg.

Eric Resnis serves as Organizational Effectiveness Coordinator for the Miami University Libraries in Oxford, Ohio, where he oversees assessment, effectiveness initiatives, and professional development. He is presenter coordinator for ACRL's Assessment in Action Road Show, and is President (2018-2019) of the Academic Library Association of Ohio, the Ohio chapter of ACRL. He regularly publishes and presents on the value of assessment in meeting information literacy outcomes, strengthening liaison roles, and demonstrating library impact towards institutional outcomes.

Linda Reynolds has been at Stephen F. Austin State University since 1998 and has been Director of the East Texas Research Center since 2007. She received her master's degree in library science from University of North Texas (2001) and became a Certified Archivist in 2007.

Erika Scheurer is Associate Professor of English and Director of Writing Across the Curriculum at the University of St. Thomas, St. Paul, Minnesota. She teaches writing and literature at all levels, from underprepared first-year students to graduate students. Her current research focuses on how faculty across the disciplines use writing as means of covering course content.

Trey Shelton is the Chair of the Acquisitions & Collections Services Department in the George A. Smathers Libraries at the University of Florida. Trey previously served as the Electronic Resource & Acquisition for the Libraries. His work focuses on collaborating with librarians, administrators, consortial partners, vendors, and publishers to coordinate the acquisition, discovery, and assessment of collections for the Libraries. His scholarly interests focuses on assessment of collections and acquisitions practices and methods, including the collection development methods, use of metrics to benchmark and analyzing ROI, and technical processes and workflows aimed at improving user access and discoverability. Trey received his M.A. in Library and Information Science from the University of South Florida.

Aaron Shrimplin is the Associate Dean of Libraries at Miami University in Oxford, Ohio where he is responsible for administrative services, including budgeting, strategic planning, facilities, assessment, communications, and technology. He is a senior member of the libraries' leadership team and enjoys developing talent throughout the libraries. He is an avid gardener and enjoys investing, DIY home-improvement-projects, and spending time with his family (married with two boys, 11 and 14 years old).

Sofia Slutskaya is a Metadata Strategist at the Georgia Institute of Technology Library. Over the years, she has held a variety of positions in both public and technical services. Her professional interests include cataloging print and electronic materials, e-resource management, and e-book acquisitions. Sofia's role at Georgia Tech Library is to provide strategic and technical guidance on cataloging and metadata practices for the library's physical and digital collections.

Laura I. Spears, PhD. (laura.spears@ufl.edu), is the Associate Assessment Librarian with the University of Florida Libraries. Her job responsibilities include examining a variety of library data that demonstrates library impact on the life of the library user, both students and faculty. Her research examines library value in public library funding advocacy and values assessment in academic libraries. Recent publications focused on overnight library use perceptions, academic library funding and academic librarian ethics training and development.

Jessica Szempruch, MLIS, is a librarian at the University of South Florida, Sarasota-Manatee. She received her Master's in Library and Information Science from the University of South Florida. Jessica was a member of the 2017 ALA Emerging Leaders cohort, and participates actively in the Florida Library Association. Her research interests stem from her passionate belief in the essential roles academic librarians can play in fostering student success, enhancing student engagement, and supporting retention efforts.

Karen Viars is the Humanities and Science Fiction Librarian at the Georgia Institute of Technology Library, and the liaison to the School of Literature, Media and Communication. Prior to graduate studies in information science, she was an instructional designer and incorporates this work into her practice as an academic librarian. Her research interests include educational psychology, information literacy, and fan studies.

Holt Zaugg (holt_zaugg@byu.edu) is the Assessment Librarian at the Harold B. Lee Library at Brigham Young University. He holds bachelor's degrees in Psychology and Education, Masters' degrees in educational design and library science and a doctorate degree in Educational Inquiry, Measurement, and Evaluation. He has over 20 years experience working in the K-12 school system, including 11 years as an instructor for teacher professional development. His current focus is on assessment of academic library services and spaces. Some examples of this assessment program includes development of library personas, communication network analysis, interactions between employees and patrons, website analysis, and student study spaces. He seeks to further understand trends and patterns in academic libraries to provide safe and caring spaces for students to study, collaborate, and learn.